MESSAGES

The Washington Post Media Companion

* *

The Washington Post Writer's Group

Allyn and Bacon

Boston London Toronto Sydney Tokyo Singapore

Series Editor: Stephen Hull
Series Editorial Assistant: Amy Capute
Cover Administrator: Linda K. Dickinson
Cover Designer: Suzanne Harbison
Manufacturing Buyer: Louise Richardson
Production Service: Lauri Wilson

ISBN 0-205-13037-2
Printed in the United States of America

10 9 8 7 6 5 4 3 2 1   96 95 94 93 92 91 90

 This textbook is printed on
recycled, acid-free paper.

Contents

Chapter Eight • The Image Makers—Public Relations Today   210

Chapter Nine • Advertising   234

Chapter Ten • Media and Society   262

Chapter Eleven: Media and Politics   286

Publisher's Foreword

The book you hold in your hand is unusual in mass communication education. Most compilations of articles on media are on the scholarly side, and while very useful, are somewhat removed from our daily experience of media. They are glances from afar. We set out to publish something closer to the action.

The mass media today have unprecedented impact on our daily lives. We are bombarded by messages of every sort: informative, entertaining, and most of all, persuasive. We are daily persuaded to buy something, vote for someone, or think a certain way about a company or an institution or a government. In the face of this saturation it is easy to become desensitized, to stop thinking clearly or critically about the messages we are asked to process. That is a mistake, particularly for the student of communication, who like all of us is a user of media, but who one day may also be one of its creators.

But if the media are the source of so many messages, they also provide the vehicles for understanding them. In this book you will find 91 articles on the media from the pages of *The Washington Post*, itself one of the most prominent voices of one of the oldest, most prominent mass media. Individually these pieces range from straightforward news stories on media industries and issues, to profiles of media creators, to thoughtful overviews of trends in media today. And that is exactly their value; their focus on the media today. Together, these articles are a cross-sectional look at the mass media and their place in our society over the last few years. They are not scholarly. They are day-to-day dispatches from the front lines.

In organization, *Messages: The Washington Post Media Companion* closely parallels the structure of the usual beginning course in mass communication. It is intended to be used as a supplement to a regular textbook, or to an instructor's notes, both of which will provide depth, rigor, and a grounding in history and research. It is our hope that what *Messages* will provide is good writing from one of the great newspapers of the day. Enjoy.

Preface

John Campbell launched the first successful American newspaper—the *Boston News-Letter*—in 1704. For fifteen years he enjoyed a monopoly in the colonies. Then, James Franklin, the more celebrated Benjamin's older brother, began publishing the New-England Courant and became America's first "media critic." Campbell's newspaper, he said in the first issue of the Courant, suffered from an excess of "dullness." Campbell responded with a denial and demanded chapter and verse. Franklin had the last word:

"[The critic] need not tell you where you're flat and dull; "Your Works declare, 'tis in your skull."

In the subsequent history of the American media, criticism has had uneven traditions. Newspapers criticized one another vigorously and frequently in the 19th Century. The *New York Courier and Inquirer* announced in 1836 that "we are compelled, for the first time, to soil our columns with an allusion to a beggarly outcast [James Gordon Bennett] who daily sends forth a dirty sheet in this city under the title of *The Herald*." Bennett could hold his own in that company. He said of Horace Greeley's *Tribune*: "The *Tribune* establishment, from top to bottom, has been recently converted into a socialistic phalanx...that has produced on public affairs and the public mind a more deleterious, anti-Christian, and infidel effect...than all the publications that have hitherto appeared from the time of Voltaire."

This critical tradition—or polemic, as the case may be—is a relic of the past insofar as newspapers are concerned. The ownership of the American press is now concentrated in a relative handful of large communications conglomerates. Local monopolies have arisen in virtually all of our cities. So there are few competitors left to criticize. Self-criticism is a rarity and where it exists is rarely aggressive. Some of the slack has been taken up by the "alternative press," by both local and national magazines and by various authors and academicians. But the audience for these forms of criticism is limited and, so far as we can tell, so is the impact.

The critical tradition has never existed within the broadcasting industry and has not taken hold despite the ever-growing competitiveness within the broadcasting marketplace. The evening news programs have very sizable local and national audiences that undoubtedly would be receptive to press criticism, for example, or to criticism of local and network news practices. A thorough investigation of the techniques of "60 Minutes" by its competitor, "20-20" would be made into fascinating television. But broadcasters, out of a sense of vulnerability or for other commercial reasons, do not nurture programming of that nature.

So the burden of broadcasting criticism falls primarily on newspapers and magazines. That is true with respect to literature, films, the recording industry, and other expressions of the popular culture. Much of what is done along these lines may not qualify as true "criticism," which is often defined as systematic analysis within a framework of certain aesthetic and philosophical principles and standards; academic work, in a word. The book, film or record review, by way of contrast is designed, essentially, to introduce an audience to a new work or production. In that sense its critical value may be of less significance than its commercial value as a form of publicity.

In any case, it is newspaper and magazine writers who produce the reviews, the criticism and the commentary on our popular culture and its various media of communication and art. As you will find in these essays, writers approach these critical tasks not only from abstract aesthetic positions but from political, sociological, ethical, and historical perspectives as well. They take sides in the various wars and skirmishes that are constantly occurring within the media and within the larger culture as well. They promote some value systems and seek to discredit others; they can be preachy on subject such as ethics, social justice, highbrows, and lowbrows. They may disagree on definitions of obscenity and pornography and the political implications involved.

But in demographic terms, the essayists represented in this volume have much in common in addition to a common employer, *The Washington Post*. We are, without exception and by government definition, members of the upper middle class. Racially, we are overwhelmingly (but not entirely) white. Few of us have had special training or instruction in the arts and crafts of "criticism." We tend to come out of universities and colleges with degrees in the liberal arts, with interest in politics and popular culture, with general experience as newspaper reporters and with present assignments that are to one degree or another the result of happenstance rather than design. There is, thus, an accidental and amateurish quality to much of what we do. But it is a quality that can lend freshness, authenticity and variety to the work.

Editors at *The Post* have for many years encouraged the development of popular and relevant forms of criticism and created in various sections—Style, Book World, and Outlook, among others—forums in which it all fits and from which most of these pieces were taken.

Richard Harwood
Ombudsman
The Washington Post

CHAPTER ONE

Books and Publishing

Pantheon Publisher Departs

Eleanor Randolph, March 1990

At first, the publisher's abrupt departure at Pantheon Books seemed like one of those strange little whirlwinds that ruffle the shirttails of only a few effete New Yorkers.

But the real issue at Pantheon is whether there is room in the book-publishing business for good books that don't make big bucks. Pantheon has always been a small, serious house that publishs authors concerned about world issues. Jean-Paul Sartre, Gunter Grass, Boris Pasternak, R.D. Laing—there have not been many joke books. Jacqueline Susann would have trouble getting her phone calls returned.

Pantheon, until recently, was known as a publisher that rocked along, earning more respect in most years than profit. Last year, however, it lost $2 million to $3 million, according to some accounts. The reasons for this loss are not simple. Some say it's because the corporate owners wanted Pantheon to look like a loser for business reasons. Some, like conservative George F. Will, suggest the house lost money because it published liberals.

Others said the publisher of Pantheon guessed wrong when be thought Americans yearned to read an autobiography by Dr. Spock, the man who raised about two generations of Americans. Deemed by some booksellers as too serious, Spock hit the market like a wet diaper.

1

At Random House, which is worth about $800 million and which owns Pantheon, a $3 million mistake would barely give an editor heartburn. But for $20 million Pantheon, it's big money.

Pantheon's troubles broke into the news this month when Andre Schiffrin, its managing director, resigned after 28 years. Schiffrin, who undoubtedly has some kind of agreement that the sanctity of his retirement fund depends on silence, has issued only a very general statement.

"I cannot describe in detail the conversations I had with Random House management over the past weeks relating to my departure from Pantheon," he said at one point. "I think it must be clear to everyone, however, that I would not walk away from my life's work if there had not been very profound differences in the approaches to Pantheon's future."

Schiffrin's departure stunned the publishing community. Six of Pantheon's top editors resigned in protest. Writers protested outside Random House. Publishers Weekly called it "a sad day" and added that it "cannot help but appall anyone who believes in book publishing as ultimately something more than a plain act of commerce."

Of course, publishing is commerce, after all, and as another publisher of worthy books told the New York Times recently: "At the end of the day, there has to be enough left to publish again tomorrow." Moreover, the new head of Pantheon has promised to continue to publish worthy books. "It is my intent not to change the editorial orientation of Pantheon," said new publisher Fred Jordan.

But editors in New York say that they hear the sound of profit—Tartars coming over the hill. And they believe that in the constant war between money and excellence, the men with the calculators are winning.

Last year's best-sellers make it clear why Pantheon's owners might want the company to shed its earth shoes and start showing a little leg. The top ten non-fiction best-sellers in 1989, according to Publishers Weekly, told readers how to get rich, how to cook an instant gourmet meal or what it was like to be Jackie Kennedy or Nancy Reagan. Number one was a book called "All I Really Need to Know I Learned in Kindergarten" by Robert Fulghum, which may also tell all you really need to know about what sells books. It sold 902,000 copies.

Pantheon had not one single book in the top ten. Nor in the top 20. Its titles for 1989 explain why. They included Barbara Ehrenreich's "Fear of Falling; the Inner Life of the Middle Class." Ian Gibson's biography of Federico Garcia Lorca earned ecstatic reviews. "It earned respect, but not much profit," said one Pantheon person. "I guess that's what we're famous for."

The New York Times Book Review section for March 25 reinforced that fame. The book with the coveted top billing on the front page of the section is a first novel by an unknown writer named Jessica Hagedorn. It is called "Dogeaters," and it is being published by Pantheon this spring.

The reviewer calls it "a rich small feast of a book"—a feast that might have been considered inedible by other publishing houses in Manhattan's crazy publishing world.

Years ago when Pantheon was established, the owners named it after the Roman temple designed to worship all the gods. Readers deserve to wonder if it will be renamed to commemorate the one god who reigns with increasing vigor in the publishing world. Goodbye Pantheon Books. Hello Bottom-Line Publishing.

At War over the Cheever Legacy

David Streitfeld, September 1988

John Cheever was a diffident man, raised to believe the acceptance of any tribute was improper. As a child, he once claimed, he used to wake in the night crying: "No thank you, oh no thank you." He didn't keep copies of his books in the house, avoided interviews during most of his life and argued against publication of his bestselling and award-winning selected stories in 1978 because "Who's going to buy a book just to read them again?"

Late in his career, Cheever was asked if his work would eventually become dated. "Oh, I don't anticipate that my work will be read," he replied. "...I might be forgotten tomorrow; it wouldn't disconcert me in the least."

It didn't happen like that. Six years after his death, there's a growing consensus that Cheever's tales of suburban love, angst and redemption are among the finest postwar American fiction. But his modesty is taking its toll.

Cheever barely made a will—he was so sick when he signed the document he could only scratch an X—much less dealt with the disposition of his literary estate. As a result, an acrimonious, expensive battle is being fought over an omnibus collection of 68 Cheever stories. Most of these the author seems to have considered too weak to republish, but then he initially said that about his best work, too.

Academy Chicago, an independent, medium-sized publisher, says it has a valid contract to issue "The Uncollected Stories of John Cheever." Until a judge issued an injunction against it last month, Academy had planned to unleash 100,000 hard-cover copies right about now. It was to be the firm's biggest and most prestigious publication ever; this was a chance to be put on the literary map.

John Cheever's widow Mary, his daughter Susan and his eldest son Benjamin say, however, that Academy has broken both the spirit and the letter of the contract, and they have claimed copyright violation in federal district court in White Plains, N.Y. The book, the Cheevers argue, contains stories that aren't good enough to be republished and that they didn't intend to let Academy have. A New York judge stopped the book at least temporarily, pending the outcome of an earlier suit filed by Academy in Chicago. Today, a judge there will begin hearing the case.

"To stop the book that they wanted to publish, I think we'd go to any length," says Ben Cheever.

"God knows we've been harassed and beleaguered, but the last thing we're going to do is give up," says Jordan Miller, who owns Academy with his wife Anita.

So far, the only winners are the lawyers. The Cheevers' court costs are well into six figures and may top $300,000; Academy Chicago says it will escape, at best, with a $200,000 bill. "I'm going to be badly in debt," says Mary Cheever, who spent one morning last week taking stocks over to the bank as collateral for a loan. Jordan Miller says the case "is going to make it a hell of a lot harder for us to function." On both sides, much of the money that would be earned on a successful book is now gone.

The publisher and the family each say that doesn't really matter. "To me, the whole thing from the beginning is a matter of honor," says Susan Cheever. "All a writer leaves is his words. My father left a tiny bit of money and his copyright. For someone to come along and use those copyrights without my mother's permission, and furthermore to use them in a way that my father would not have approved of, seemed to me to be just unacceptable."

Jordan Miller responds that "We've behaved in a perfectly legal, moral way...They had an opportunity to sign our contract or not sign it. They knew what we were, they knew what we had in mind, they knew what 'The Uncollected Stories of John Cheever' means. In knowing all this, they had the option to proceed or not. They chose to proceed. We simply want that action validated by the court."

A source who knows both parties says the concentration on honor and morality—or lack thereof—is largely a smoke screen. "Hidden behind the moralistic stances on both sides is a financial issue," he says. "John would have probably found it very saddening, and at the same time highly amusing."

It began as the simple desire of a fan. Franklin Dennis, an independent New York publicist for several small and medium-sized literary publishers, lives near the Cheever family home in the Hudson Valley town of Ossining. Dennis met John Cheever several times in the late '70s, asked him to sign a couple of books, told him how much he admired his work.

Like any fan, Dennis quite naturally wanted more. He ran across some uncollected stories in anthologies, searched unsuccessfully for the author's never-reprinted first book, "The Way Some People Live," and sought out fine-press versions that had been done of individual stories.

"It looked like there was a body of work worth exploring," Dennis recalls. A couple of years ago, a mutual friend suggested he write Ben Cheever about a volume of uncollected fiction. "Ben called me on the telephone and said, 'Sounds like a great idea.'"

One of Dennis' clients is Academy Chicago. Founded in 1976 by the Millers, the 12-employee house publishes about 25 books a year on a wide range of topics. Dennis broached the idea of a Cheever collection, and the Millers were understandably enthusiastic. After all, the previous omnibus of his work, "The Stories of John Cheever," has gone through nine printings and 120,000 hard-cover copies; it won the National Book Critics Circle Award and a Pulitzer Prize and, in paperback, the American Book Award; and it was considered, as the reviewer for The New York Times wrote, "a grand occasion in English literature."

A contract was soon drawn up by Academy for a book titled "The Uncollected Stories of John Cheever." It provided for the author's royalties to be split equally between two parties: Mary Cheever and the man who had the idea and was now the book's editor, Franklin Dennis. While the advance was minuscule—a total of $1,500, half on signing the contract and half on publication—Dennis could have eventually earned a hefty sum of money.

If all 100,000 copies of the first printing were sold, Dennis' share would have been about $175,000. From the paperback reprint sale to Dell Publishing, he would have garnered an additional $56,375. When the book club and foreign rights sales were added in, Dennis could have made much more than a quarter-million dollars for less than a year of part-time work, basically consisting of securing copies of the stories, writing a brief "editor's note," and shepherding the project into print.

"I thought it was a very generous offer that Jordan Miller made me," Dennis says. "I thought if the Cheevers or their agent finds this unacceptable, they'll change the contract and I'll abide by it."

As for whether it was an equitable percentage, he notes dryly that "Sometimes editors come up with ideas. I came up with this idea. Apparently it was a good idea. Everyone's very excited about it."(Once the fireworks began, Dennis offered to cut his share of the take to 20 percent.)

The Cheevers didn't change the contract, which was approved with inconsequential modifications in August 1987 by one of the country's largest and most powerful literary agencies, International Creative Management.

"I depend on my literary agent to protect me," says Mary Cheever. "In my innocence, I thought she was qualified to go over a contract and tell me to sign it, but it turns out I was mistaken."

That woman "retired last fall," ICM says. Wayne Kabak, general counsel of ICM's parent company, Josephson International, commented this week that "the position [Mary Cheever's] been taking in court is that the contract adequately protects her interests but the publisher is failing to honor it. That seems to be inconsistent with what she is saying to you about ICM."

In a letter to Mary Cheever last Oct. 6, Jordan Miller wrote "how delighted we are to be publishing the uncollected stories. Apparently there are more than 60 of them and we're looking for others..." In late December, Franklin Dennis met Mary Cheever for the first time. He gave her two packets of photocopied stories.

Here's where accounts start to diverge sharply. Mary Cheever told the New York judge that she thought it was up to her to choose among these pieces to compile the completed book: "I thought I should wait until (Academy) asked me what I thought about them. They never did"—no doubt because Academy was planning to put all the stories in the book.

Around this time, Ben Cheever—who says he had thought, as did his mother, that Academy Chicago was some sort of university press—claims he began to get a better idea of the size and scope of the book. He was helped along by Andrew Wylie, his new literary agent. Wylie is an often-controversial figure who is known for being very aggressive in his pursuit of the best deal possible for his clients.

"Andrew said he didn't think the arrangement was felicitous at all," says Ben. "We sent a lawyer's letter asking (Academy) to forget the contract, saying the contract was no good." The real intent, he claims, was considerably milder: to open up negotiations about the format of the book, its publication date, the choice of stories.

Jordan Miller responds that he didn't see it that way then and doesn't believe it now. As soon as Wylie entered the picture, he says, the Cheevers simply wanted out. "They never once said we object to this story, or that story, or that story. They never once asked us, in writing or otherwise, to eliminate a story or body of stories. That contradicts everything they say about wanting a smaller book."

He adds that "they wanted to break the agreement so they could take this book to a large publisher. They want to do that because they'll get a $750,000 advance, which Wylie will engineer." (The advance that Academy gave Mary Cheever works out to $11.03 per story. It says it didn't have the cash flow to offer more.)

In response to the letter from the Cheevers' lawyer, Academy filed suit in early March to validate its contract. "It was a self-protective measure," says Jordan Miller. The battle was joined.

When the lawyers became involved, things got bitter. At the American Booksellers Association convention in May, Academy Chicago gave away a promotional booklet containing three of the stories. The Cheever lawyers demanded a sticker be placed on each saying: "This sampler is not authorized by the family of John Cheever." (Because of the controversy the case is engendering, those booklets are now hot items on the rare book market, with asking prices between $25 and $45.)

Charges and countercharges are flying. Mary Cheever says Academy demanded $2.5 million to drop the book. Jordan Miller says this was merely a "riposte" and not a serious ultimatum.

Franklin Dennis, meanwhile, says Ben Cheever and Andrew Wylie offered him 25 percent of a future deal if he would walk away from Academy. Ben's response: "Absurd."

Mary Cheever adds that "I sometimes think that any amount of money, like the million in all we got for the [rights to her husband's unpublished] journals, I think that people smell it. Know what I mean? I think they smell it and say, 'There's money in Cheever stuff.'"

And she doesn't want anyone to get the wrong idea about that million dollars: "Divided into four parts"—for her and the three children— "and paid out over five years, it doesn't make anybody very rich."

John Cheever's first short story, "Expelled," appeared in The New Republic on Oct. 1, 1930, when he was barely 18. Asked decades later how it felt to have a piece in a prestigious national periodical while still a teen, Cheever replied: "Eighty-seven dollars, that's what it felt like."

Money was always on his mind, possibly because he almost never had a satisfactory amount of it. Not until his fourth novel, "Falconer," came out in 1977 was he financially secure. The Cheever family argues that many of the works in the Academy volume—50 of which were published before 1947, the date of the earliest piece in the selected "Stories"—were done simply to put food on the table. To reprint 100,000 copies of them, they say, is something John Cheever never would have permitted.

Scott Donaldson, Cheever's biographer and the author of an introduction to the "Uncollected Stories," agrees that "Many of them are not up to his usual standard," but adds, "all are very interesting, and have some things in them that are Cheeverian. It'd be useful."

Academy Chicago is fond of pointing out that three of the stories in their volume won O. Henry Awards, one was included in "Best American Short Stories of 1939," and others have been anthologized.

But would John Cheever have republished them and, if not, should his wishes be respected? What makes the question additionally pertinent is the accompanying issue of whether he would have wanted his letters published (about 40,000 copies, edited by Ben, are coming from Simon and Schuster in late November) or his journals (edited by Susan and Ben, these will show up from Knopf in a couple of years condensed into a single volume, with a multivolume set following at the end of the century).

Material in both of these deals explicitly with Cheever's lifelong struggle with bisexuality—a matter about which he was relatively circumspect. Not until Susan published her memoir "Home Before Dark" in 1984 was the general public enlightened on this topic.

The letters combine high-level intrigue ("The Updikes were there and I did everything short of kicking him in the trousers"), writing struggles ("I made so many bargains with the devil about the completion of a book that when I put down the last word, I took a bath, put on clean underwear, and went to the doctor to see if anything was missing"), off-the-cuff lit crit ("Edmund Wilson has printed a collection of questionable short stories and in one there is a long description of carnal copulation which would have done carnal copulation irreparable damage if it hadn't been quite as deeply rooted") and low-level intrigue ("When I was twenty-one Walker Evans invited me to spend the night at his apartment").

It's often quite lively stuff, but did their author want his public to know that he never had less than the highest esteem for his buddy Updike? The same will be even more true of the journals, in which he speaks frankly and frequently about his sexual appetites. Susan Cheever, asked to comment on this, says only that "if I had any doubts, I wouldn't be publishing the journals."

No matter who wins the court battle, it's likely that a volume of stories will sooner or later be issued. The family concedes they may have to do a smaller, "completely different" collection to recover their legal expenses.

Perhaps that's for the best. In his final years, Cheever's attitude toward his fans shifted. He readily signed books, began doing interviews. "Writing is very much like a kiss," he said. "It's something you can't do alone." If he had lived, one could argue that held eventually have come around to the publication of some sort of "Uncollected Stories."

Franklin Dennis, the originator of this misbegotten project, wants a copy. "Even if I had to pay for it, I'd buy it," he says. "John Cheever was my favorite writer, and he remains my favorite writer."

Russell Baker, the Modest Scribe

Jim Naughton

A howling ambulance shatters the peace in Mimi Baker's garden.

"One of the reasons that I settled here is that the hospital is right up the street," her husband, Russell, says. "One block from that is the nursing home and around the corner is the cemetery. I don't have to drive anywhere to end my life here."

Just a few minutes later, another ambulance screeches past.

"There's probably somebody dying in there," Baker says. "The drivers are volunteers and the only way you can get them is to let them play with the siren."

Dressed in a cinnamon-colored button-down (that he doesn't) and a pair of dirty white corduroys, Baker, 63, has divided the morning between working in the garden and answering his mail. He answers every letter, he says, because people shouldn't be made to feel that journalists are inaccessible.

Baker and Mimi live in an early-19th-century home that sits on one of the busier streets in this semi-charming Loudoun County town. There is an auto body shop on the opposite corner. Traffic drones slowly by. Despite this, the garden manages to feel like an oasis. The back porch is framed and shaded by a twisting, leafy vine. The long aisle of lawn is punctuated with a goldfish pond and bordered by short, lush trees. None of this makes it siren-proof.

"There has to have been a major air accident nearby," Baker says as yet another roaring emergency makes itself known.

Talking to Baker is enough like reading the twice-weekly column that has enlivened the op-ed page of the New York Times for 27 years for one not to notice the differences between man and author. But there are differences. In person, the humor is similar—quick, dry and accessibly cerebral—but darker. The sarcasm has a sharper edge. He seems at once to be burnishing and undercutting his image as a wry wise man.

In writing a column, you create a personality," he says. "And you become very quickly a prisoner of that person who is the column."

Baker felt his imprisonment most keenly in 1982 when the folks who condense books for Reader's Digest rejected "Growing Up," Baker's memoir coming of age in the Depression. "A couple of them said, 'The readers will be disappointed. This is not funny at all,'" he recalls. 'It is even rather a *grim* book.'"

The whole incident put him in mind of a man named Douglas McKay, who once had been secretary of the interior.

"They thought they could get him elected to the Senate from Oregon," Baker says. "So they wrote a lot of speeches for him and he went around reading them. One day, having read his speech, he laid it down and said, 'Now I would like to say a few words of my own.'

"And in a way, when I did 'Growing Up,' that's what I was saying. The memoir is a way of breaking out. It's seeking freedom."

In his search for freedom, Baker has found fortune and acclaim. "Growing Up" won the Pulitzer Prize and sold more than a million copies. Its sequel, "The Good Times," a self-mocking evocation of his early newspaper days, has been among the 10 best-selling books in the country since its publication seven weeks ago.

"I've just had the good luck to escape the meaner reviewers," he says, "people like me. I wouldn't have let me get away with this."

One of Baker's trademarks is an excessive, even annoying modesty. Friends say there is nothing manipulative in his self-deprecation. "It is not an act," says James Reston, the former Washington bureau chief who brought Baker to the Times. "It is genuine with him. He's always been that way, long before anybody even knew him."

Perhaps so, but in "The Good Times," his humility weakens the book. Baker paints himself as so ineffectual a figure that the reader is at a loss to understand how he rose from police reporter to London correspondent at the Baltimore Sun and from the Times's Washington bureau to a spot as a regular columnist. There is the sense of a tale not told, the unsettling feeling that the narrator is deliberately concealing himself. One is still engaged, charmed, even, and the book feels authentic, except as regards its author's character.

"There are people in this world, thank God, who don't go around shouting to everyone how good they are," says former Times reporter Harrison Salisbury, a Baker contemporary who has written a history of the paper. But as if to clear up any confusion, Salisbury adds, "Any idea that Russ wasn't a top-notch, absolutely brilliant reporter is just nonsense."

His considerable talent notwithstanding, Baker's relationship with his work has often been an uneasy one.

The hardest thing to get at in journalism is motive, and the novelist always knows that," he says. "But in journalism you don't know. What really motivated Jim Wright? Newt Gingrich you can make a pretty good guess about. He's kind of a two-dimensional, paper cutout kind of character. But the interesting politicians have motives you can't even get at."

Lyndon Johnson, for instance. "Of all the politicians I ever covered, he was the only one who was really interesting to me," Baker says. "Shakespeare would have loved Johnson, wouldn't he? What would Shakespeare have done with this great towering figure? Was he King Lear? Or Macbeth? Or Falstaff? He had a little bit of all of them."

But it was (and is) well nigh impossible to get those sorts of musings into a newspaper, and Baker, who had covered the White House, the State Department and the Senate, became increasingly dispirited. The pivotal moment in "The Good Times" occurs to the veteran reporter as he sits outside the room where the Senate Armed Services Committee has convened:

"Here I am, thirty-six years old. When my father was thirty-six he had been dead three years. Still he managed to build something, to leave something behind that can still be seen, touched, used. Given three years more than my father had, how have I used the time? I have built nothing worth leaving and don't even know how. Instead I spend my life sitting on marble floors, waiting for somebody to come out and lie to me."

From that moment on, Baker writes, he was prepared to end his reporting days.

"I'd lost faith in the ability of the work to do what I one time thought it could do, which was at least to help spread the good cause of enlightenment," he says from a seat on the back porch. There is a quick, ironic smile before he adds, "Most often you were spreading confusion and misinformation."

Baker never had to resolve this difficulty, thanks to Charles "Buck" Dorsey, then managing editor of the Sun. With timing that, Baker writes, reminded him of "those climactic interventions in my high-school 'Aeneid' when Juno or Minerva or Venus...came down themselves from Olympus to save one of their favorites from destruction," Dorsey offered him a column. The Times, at Reston's behest, matched the Sun's offer. Quite a shock, Baker says, "suddenly to discover I was an asset." Suddenly, too, to find himself free of the fetters of conventional reporting.

(Not to mention conventional editing. The Times then was working under the dictum that if it was well written it must be dishonest, he says.)

Baker and Art Buchwald were the preeminent humor columnists of the '60s and '70s. They often lunched together and, Salisbury says, one could occasionally hear them working out the next day's columns, each in his distinctive style.

"Buchwald always had a gag," Salisbury says. "With Russ, he just wrote what was on his mind. That dry satirical style, that was him."

Another of Baker's hallmarks, Reston says, is that "though his criticism is sometimes sharp, it is never personal. He never wounds."

This is not something a self-respecting humorist would want repeated in public. In Baker's case, it seems not quite true. His appraisal of how politics has changed in the past 30 years is tart, and not particularly merciful.

"I don't know why anybody goes into it as a career anymore," he says. "It can't be much fun."

The chief culprit, he says, is television.

"The press hasn't figured out a way to combat television's ability to deceive," he says. This has made for bitter reporters—"you can see it in the phony aggressiveness with which they address candidates sometimes. "Trying to pull something over on me, aren't you?' There's that kind of approach"—and fraudulent candidates, the 1988 campaign being a case in point.

"If the George Bush of the campaign had sprung fully formed from the head of Zeus, you would have said this guy is a monster," he says. "The minute the campaign was over, I think within six hours of the network pronouncement, there he was, old preppy Bush back again. What happened to the monster of the campaign? If you hadn't known that Bush was there before the campaign, you would have felt you'd been defrauded."

Dan Quayle, he adds, is another example of a television candidate. "He looks so good you've got to elect him to something," Baker says. "There was a senator from Maryland like that. John Marshall Butler. He looked so much like a senator he didn't have to open his mouth, and it was to the party's despair that he occasionally did." Despite these changes, Baker says, Washington remains, in many ways, the place it was when he left it 15 years ago.

"It is a town where the greatest virtue of character you can have is good judgment. It's not creative ability. It's not a town that's interested in creative things, but 'he has good judgment'—that's more highly esteemed than an ability to build something or have an idea.

"That kind of town," he says, "is apt to be a little dull. Good judgment, after a while, is depressing. You yearn in Washington for somebody to do something outrageous."

Looking for outrageousness, he moved to New York in 1974 and found it "a liberating experience."

"You stepped out in the street and there was an electricity there. Suddenly you were moving twice as fast. There was excitement about the place. I never felt that in Washington. Suddenly I was seeing the world in an entirely refreshing perspective.

"One of the things I realized was in Washington, we always sat around and talked about 'what's going on out in the country? And in New York I suddenly said, 'I'm out in the country!' I'm out in the country and nobody gives a rat's ass what's going on in Washington!'"

He left New York six years ago but still spends three or four days a month there "to keep in touch with man's inhumanity to man, and because I have a New York audience."

That audience broadened considerably in 1982 when Baker wrote his first memoir.

"Letters came from places that had never heard of the New York Times. Never heard of my work as a columnist. Small towns in Texas. Whitefish Bay, Wisconsin," he says, "It's astonishing how many people lived the same life at a given time and the experiences they had in common."

Baker was "flabbergasted" by the success of "Growing Up."

"I was writing about a world that seemed to have existed 200 years ago," he says of his Depression childhood. "I had one foot back there in this primitive country life where women did the laundry running their knuckles on scrub boards and heated irons on coal stoves. That was an America that was completely dead."

Finishing the book left him somewhat depressed, Baker says. "I had a great sense of being old when I finished," he says. Still, he was eager to continue the story.

"The real satisfaction of doing it," he says, "is the fact that you are giving your life some coherence. What is a life? It's a mess. It's a mess of details. It's like the Congressional Record. And who wants to read all that?"

"The Good Times" is breezier, more upbeat. The structure is loose, picaresque, allowing Baker to rove through his memories imparting the often giddy, gritty flavor of postwar journalism. He had originally conceived the book as "a man searching for his father. But that's such a banal commonplace." Still, Baker's relationship with a succession of journalistic fathers—from Buck Dorsey to James Reston—infuses the book with some of the warmth that made "Growing Up" so appealing.

"I knew everybody was going to say 'Well, what about famous men? You met famous men," Baker says. "But that was precisely the book I didn't want to write. Everybody's done that."

Instead he presents some of the leading politicians and journalists of the day "the same way as I did in 'Growing Up' with the uncles. I had those weird uncles. Well, here was a weird guy who turns out to be Lyndon Johnson."

His ulterior motive, Baker says, was to present "a kind of apology to all those people out there who are down on journalists, think they are a bunch of over-educated, arrogant tyrants who have lost all contact with common humanity.

"I wanted to show we come out of the same place they do," he says. "I'm just an ordinary guy who came out of an ordinary background and learned this business from the ground up. There was no plot. There is no establishment that anointed me and sent me underground to subvert the country."

But the true rewards of having written these two memoirs are more personal. "Something that's funny that happens after you have done these books," he says, "they seem to become what really happened. When you think of the past after you have done this, you think in terms of the books that you've written. It closes a door on a part of your life. So maybe in a way it is cathartic.

"It takes on the weight of truth to you. I think I can now forget everything I didn't put in books. And maybe that helps. Maybe that's healthy."

The Man Who Deserted Minnesota

David Streitfeld, August 1989

"It's clear to me that when people read my books they like me a little less at the end than at the beginning. My fourth book, 'Company A, Chaaaaaaarge!,' is evidently the worst. Nobody bought it at all."

So says western author Dusty Pages, also known for "Wagons Westward!!! Hiiiii-YAW!" and "Pa! Look Out! It's—Aiiiiieee!" At book signings, Dusty keeps waiting for readers to come up and declare, "Your book saved my life, Mister," but instead only gets asked: "You wouldn't know where the little boys' room is, wouldja?"

Dusty is a character in a sketch by Garrison Keillor, and it wouldn't be unfair to see a trace of his creator in him. Four years ago, Keillor was a genuine folk hero, one who had risen to prominence not through media machinations or by purveying trash but with the slenderest reed possible: his voice and the simple, seemingly artless tales he told with it. People held "Prairie Home Companion" parties; when the show was on, they turned their phones off. Almost single-handedly, he made Minnesota chic.

"Lake Wobegon Days" became one of the biggest bestsellers of the decade, and Keillor was on the cover of Time magazine. Even then, his status might have survived, but the wrong things happened. He left his longtime companion and producer, to whom he had lovingly dedicated "Lake Wobegon Days," for the Danish woman who had been a foreign exchange student in his high school graduating class 25 years before. He gave up the show to move to Denmark, where he seemed to stay only long enough to change planes. Resettled in New York, he quickly announced a series of farewell tours. He published two more books in quick succession. Now he's going back on the radio on a regular basis this fall with a new series, "Garrison Keillor's American Radio Company of the Air."

Hardly anyone thinks of him as a folk hero anymore. Now he's just a writer, and it's fashionable not to be crazy about him. Even Minnesota has dropped off the nation's "in" lists. And while Keillor still has a comparatively large audience—his latest book, "We Are Still Married," spent 13 weeks on the bestseller list—he knows his popularity peak is past.

"I will never have a book again that sells a third as many copies as 'Lake Wobegon,' and how could one possibly be dismayed by that?"

17

Keillor asks, sitting in a grungily upscale breakfast joint near his Manhattan home. "To have your success behind you is the most calming, most peaceful feeling. Why should one ever want to repeat something so tumultuous—this catastrophe of good fortune?

"You don't believe me, huh?"

Keillor, who looks as if he just woke up, is nothing if not believable. Eating a bagel about the size of a life preserver, he explains the love he feels for his adopted city and talks obliquely about fame.

In Denmark, he felt a tremendous frustration from being in the middle of a great tale he could not tell—the story of his rise and the intrusions of fame. "I still think it's such an interesting story," he says earnestly. "But I wouldn't, I couldn't trust myself to tell it. I had ulterior motives of punishing the wicked and lifting up the righteous, and no writer with any sense would go and do a story with his armor on. Stories can only be written naked."

Still, from the cheeky title on down, "We Are Still Married" seems filled with little riffs of Keillor writing about what happened to Keillor. You don't have to know the inside story to get the joke, but it adds to the entertainment.

Take his well-known distaste for what he sees as invasions of his privacy—especially pesky questions from reporters and everyone else about his personal life. "I don't appreciate a book that's packed full of people grumbling at me," he writes in the story "My Life in Prison." There was a real book that did exactly this, "The Man From Lake Wobegon," by Michael Fedo but Keillor gives it the pseudonym "Geek: An Unauthorized Biography of You Know Who (The Big Jerk)." He quotes a sample passage:

"'He was awful darn hard to work with,' recalls Chuck Frick, who parked cars behind the World Theater. 'He'd come in here before the show and hardly speak to us, maybe say, "Hi, how ya doin'"— what kinda recognition is that for guys that bust their butts parking cars so he can have an audience? Once I gave him a tape of my songs and didn't hear back about it for three weeks, and then he didn't offer any constructive criticism or anything, just said, "Sorry, it isn't quite right for us"—what kind of thing is that to say? I worked on those songs for six years and he dismisses them with six words.'"

In "Your Book Saved My Life, Mister," there's this:

"I know what it's like to be disappointed by a hero. You think I don't know? Believe me, I know. I met my idol, Smokey W. Kaiser, when I was twelve...I had waited outside the YMCA in Des Moines for three hours while he regaled the Rotary with humorous anecdotes, and when he emerged at the side door, a fat man in tight green pants tucked into silver-studded boots, he looked down and growled, 'I don't sign pieces of paper, kid. I sign books. No paper. You want my autograph, you can buy a book. That's a rule of mine. Don't waste my time and I won't waste yours.'

"Smokey's problem," the narrator concludes, "was that he was a jerk."

And then there's the list of forthcoming Keillor books opposite the title page, including "Shawn of the New Yorker" and "What Will Our World Be Like in the Year 1990?" None of these books will appear, of course, at least not from him. But in the year 1990, he expects his life to be much the same: living in his cherished New York and writing.

"New York," Keillor says in a voice that no one would quite describe as sweet-sounding but which has had all the rough edges, all the Midwestern tang, worn away by years of broadcasting, "is the only place in this land of ours for a writer to live and feel normal about being a writer."

Now, you may be thinking that only a very successful writer would say this about New York—someone with a BMW, and standing reservations at fancy restaurants, and a multi-room apartment with a maid and a view of the river—but even if Keillor could have all this and much more, his feelings for the city go further.

He's almost anonymous here. In a metropolis where even Jackie Onassis goes mostly unhasseled, Keillor escapes notice. He looks like a car mechanic who is amiable but a little slow, and even as he takes time out to correct some galley proofs of a forthcoming New Yorker story, the diners in the surrounding booths ignore him. Snatches of their conversations—"If he's stupid enough to get himself in trouble . . . "Well, you were staring at the ambulance..."—drift over, but these tales of woe go unheeded. Finally, satisfied, Keillor looks up.

"By George, it's a good piece of work," he proclaims. "Now I've got to go convince him I've been struggling with this for hours." He moves off slowly to look for a phone.

Keillor does good pieces of work. If "We Are Still Married" had come from a newcomer, its humor and cleverness would be marveled over. "Lake Wobegon Days" isn't talked about much anymore, but the book seems likely to become a classic, read long into the 21st century. And moving has recharged his literary batteries. The city has reignited old passions—for baseball, newspapers (as long as they're not writing about him), trains. At times, in fact, Keillor's New York boosterism threatens to resemble Ed Koch's famous criticism of rural life—an attack that helped derail his candidacy for governor.

"If you live your quiet noble life in Vermont," Keillor declares, "I hope you like trees a lot. I hope you enjoy putting your arms around them, and talking to them."

As opposed to Koch, Keillor says this so gently even a Vermonter couldn't take offense. So the only response is to mention the usual litany of New York ills: the drugs, the crime, the panhandlers, the homeless, the expense...

"All I can talk about is what I see. People who talk about the fear on the streets and the drug problem and so on are talking about things that undoubtedly are true, but most of them are talking about things that are not their own experience. They're talking about stories that they've read in the paper. Part of the purpose of the press in all of its history has been to scare us, to our delight."

He is holding a copy of "Lake Wobegon Days," lost in thought. On its back, the jacket displays a large photograph of him. This is noticed by the man in the next booth, whose shirt is completely unbuttoned, displaying vast expanses of chest. It is not a hot morning.

Breakfast is over. Keillor stands up, heads toward the exit.

"Garson!" the man shouts. "How are you?"

"Not so bad then," Keillor says, not slowing down but not quite speeding up, either. "And yourself?"

"Not so bad then," the man repeats, and gives a kind a wild laugh. "I saw the picture...You're him!"

"Everybody's got to be somebody," says Keillor over his shoulder. He makes it out to the street unscathed.

Closing the Book on Old-Style Publishing

Jonathan Yardley, November 1989

In the "book room," where review copies are stored by the staff of The Washington Post Book World, the shelves are crammed floor-to-ceiling with glossy, expensive items for the Christmas trade: As happens whenever the calendar rounds into December, the publishers are counting on big seasonal sales to blacken the bottom line at year's end. But this year, according to a spate of recent reports, they're not likely to be rescued by gift books or anything else; this year, according to those in the know, the book business is in big trouble.

No matter where you read about it—Publisher's Weekly, the Wall Street Journal, the American Scholar, the Economist, the New York Times—what you're told is that book publishing's trouble isn't merely one of those cyclical declines that every industry suffers from time to time, but a fundamental problem that will mandate basic changes in the way the industry conducts its business. As the Journal's Meg Cox put it in a comprehensive overview published last week:

"The outlines of a restructured industry are already beginning to emerge. Advances have crashed. More jobs will be lost. All over town, publishers are trying to rid themselves of blockbuster fever and, in some cases, to integrate more intelligently the imprints and subsidiaries they gobbled up quickly. There are predictions of imminent change in the way the book business is conducted—fewer titles, shrewder marketing, less money for authors. Another possible result: more mergers and acquisitions of publishing houses."

For some people this means bad news, and many of them don't deserve it: Robert Bernstein, for example, who resigned in haste as chairman of Random House after nearly a quarter-century of well-regarded service, or the 20 employees of E.P. Dutton who were high-handedly dismissed by the firm's current owner, Penguin USA. But for publishing as a whole, possibly even for writers and readers of books, the prospect of a restructured industry could well turn out to be good news; if ever an industry has been in need of fundamental change, publishing is it.

That is because book publishing as it now exists is a bizarre, wholly inefficient blend of its otherworldly past and its uncertain future. It's a business that pretends to be up-to-date even as it

21

stubbornly clings to outmoded practices that require an excess of labor and overhead; at the same time, oddly enough, it's a business that, in its clumsy rush toward modernization, has managed to abandon traditional practices that served it well in the past.

The solutions to its internal problems will involve restructuring as basic as the problems themselves and will, by all accounts, entail forcing the industry to accept leadership at least as well versed in business as in books. How books are distributed, ordered, warehoused, marketed—all of these and many others will be, or at least should be, reexamined as the industry struggles to come to terms with the 20th century. But there are other aspects of publishing that will not demand changes so basic as these, merely that it make sense out of practices that are now wholly nonsensical.

Chief among these are two that get right to the essence of publishing: the responsibilities of editors and the processing of manuscripts. In the past couple of decades there has been a radical change in the role of editors, and it has had radical effects. Whereas previously editors' principal tasks were the selection and editing of manuscripts for publication, now their chief responsibility is the mere acquisition of "properties." This is why authors complain that "Maxwell Perkins is dead"—editors no longer have time to give writers and their manuscripts the intimate attention for which Perkins was celebrated—but there is more to it than that.

Because acquisition is now editors' principal job, because they are judged for pay and promotions on how many books they bring in and how much those books earn, the entire emphasis within what might be called the editorial culture is on volume rather than quality and character. Each editor seems to assume that the more manuscripts he or she brings in, the greater are the chances that one or more of them will succeed. So editors spend vast amounts of time on the phone with agents, or in meetings with other editors in which proposed contracts are voted up or down, and surprisingly little time with authors.

The result is unhappy authors, of course—authors are always unhappy—but, more important, the publication of too many ill-considered and unnecessary books. Far more are now being published than the market can absorb, which means that more and more books are losing rather than making money. So far the industry's response has been to pay ever higher advances in the competition for that ever-more-elusive best seller, but that is expected to change; more realistic advances will be mere window-dressing, though, unless the problem of acquisition is addressed and the duties of editors reconsidered.

Among those duties is ostensibly the editing of manuscripts, and it is here that a second publishing practice demands reconsideration. Astonishing though it may be to anyone out there in the real world, the editorial departments of most trade publishing houses have stoutly, stubbornly resisted the switch to word processors that has already occurred in virtually every other form of publishing. While newspapers and magazines are now written, edited and typeset through electronic means, book publishing still insists on paper manuscripts and all the outmoded, inefficient, costly procedures they entail.

Thus it was that a year and a half ago, having completed the manuscript of a book, I offered to deliver it to my publisher on floppy disks, ready for editing on the ubiquitous Word Perfect software. The offer was rejected out of hand. "We don't do that," I was told. "We want paper." Thus began an editorial process that may have been sensible in the 1950s but is preposterous in the 1980s, when electronics offer vast improvements in efficiency, quality control and—you'd think publishers would care about this—economy. At university presses and other publishers who long ago went electronic, production costs have been reduced by as much as 30 percent; but in good old trade publishing, where in this respect if no other Maxwell Perkins and his era are very much alive, quill and foolscap are still the preferred instruments of production.

There's nothing unusual about my story, believe me; in recent years, as more and more authors have turned to word processors, I've heard more tales than I can remember of authors eager to help publishers facilitate the editing and typesetting process, and publishers turning them down without a moment's careful consideration. These same publishers fancy themselves to be "players" in the world of international communications, but they haven't even figured out, in the age of computers, how to work on word processors. Until they do—until they learn to compete in the modern world on its terms instead of their own—no amount of restructuring or managerial change will do them a scintilla of good.

It Was a Good Hear

Gail Forman, January 1988

Living in "double time," call it. I get twice as much out of my day as I did before I discovered the pleasures of listening to books recorded on tape—and I feel a lot happier and calmer, too. It is no exaggeration to say that discovering audio books has changed my life.

Before I started listening three years ago, I felt frustrated about how few books I had time to read. I'd fume as I sat stuck in my car during rush hour. I'd rage as I wasted precious moments doing dishes or laundry. As an English teacher with an abiding love for literature, I often felt as I imagine a drug addict does without a "fix." I craved what kept me going but just couldn't get enough. The days were too short and I had too much work to do to find the time to sit down and read a novel "just for fun."

When I did read for relaxation, the piles of newspapers, magazines and journals took precedence over novels, plays or poetry. I felt keenly the truth of Wordsworth's immortal words, "The world is too much with us; late and soon,/ Getting and spending, we lay waste our powers."

Nostalgic memories of my youth kept popping up, a time when I thought nothing of whiling away a Sunday afternoon deep in Madame Bovary or Middlemarch, when I would stay up late into the night reading the Magic Mountain, when a leisurely bath meant an opportunity to loll in the tub with the Karamazov brothers. For years, though, my Sundays have been devoted to correcting student essays, while the only reading I do late at night is preparation for the next day's classes. And it's pretty hard to read a book during a quick shower.

When a friend suggested that I try renting taped books, I demurred. I like to read books, not hear stories. I don't approve of "painless learning." I like classics, I don't read "trash" and I abhor condensed anything. Nor am I good at taking in information aurally, I protested. I don't think I could pay attention. Besides, it wouldn't be as satisfying as reading, I objected.

But out of desperation, I decided to give it a try. I called Books on Tape, a California outfit with an inventory of more than 2,000 unabridged recorded books, a mixture of classics and contemporary, fiction and nonfiction. I ordered Out of Africa, one of the masterpieces I had always wanted to read but never got around to starting although it

24

has been sitting on my shelf for years. Since this was pre-Meryl Streep/Robert Redford, I hadn't been able to substitute seeing the movie for reading the book.

Springing for first class postage, I received my "book" in two days. A compact box of nine 1 1/2-hour tapes arrived, preaddressed and post paid for the return trip. When I was finished, all I needed to do was seal the box and drop it in the nearest mailbox.

With trepidation and curiosity, I turned on the first tape. "I had a farm in Africa at the foot of the Ngong hills," the mellifluous voice of reader Wanda McCaddon began, and my life has not been the same since. Now I'm never without a taped book, and I live what I call the "expanded day" aspect of life.

With my Walkman on my belt and my earphones plugged in, I listen as I race around doing housework—washing laundry, preparing salads, cleaning up the dinner table, even vacuuming no longer seem onerous chores. Whereas I always used to be in a snit when I performed these necessary but unrewarding jobs—and pity the person who got in my way while I did them—now I almost look forward to them as an excuse to continue hearing an especially interesting section of a taped book.

I listen in my car and don't mind the commute to work. I purchased a tiny tabletop speaker to be able to listen to my Walkman without earphones, too. I listen while I ride my exercise cycle and find the tapes actually an incentive to do so. I haven't figured out a way to listen while I use my hair dryer, but I do listen as I apply my makeup and no longer wish it could be tattooed on my face to save time.

Though I would never just sit down to listen to a book, not when I could be reading, listening, it turns out, can be as pleasurable as reading—different but with its own rewards. As it would be if I were reading a great novel, another world is available to me through a recorded book, with the difference that I do not have to suspend daily tasks to get to it. No matter how fragmented my day, no matter how many conflicts, I know that when I get in my car to drive home, I can turn on the book and there is continuity. Chaotic thoughts give way to calmness, and I'm glad for the escape.

At other times, in contrast, the sound of silence is important, so when I find my mind drifting, I know that I need to pay attention to what's going on in my own head. That's when I turn off the machine and give reign to my own thoughts.

To people who worry about the "dangers" of having a tape going while driving or doing other risky tasks, I reply that it's no different from listening to the news on the radio. I hear the book but I also pay attention to the road, and when something requires my full awareness, I unconsciously tune out the audio. The nice part is the ease with which I can rewind the tape if I've lost the thread, though I find that if it's a good book I've chosen, I'm a better listener than I expected to be.

Thanks to recorded books, I have experienced a new relationship with the human voice, and I love the sound of the different readers' accents and intonations. Mostly the people who read unabridged books are professionals, though not usually famous actors and not the authors themselves. Sometimes I practice imitating their sounds or trying out different ways of emphasizing certain passages, for every reading is an interpretation.

And I feel an unmatched intimacy with a book whose words enter my head through my earphones. After all, language is primarily sound, and when a well-written book is read aloud, each word counts, as it should. If the reader is fine, the language of the work—poetry or prose—shines. An example is Dem Cheng's Life and Death in Shanghai, which I heard a few weeks ago. This harrowing tale of one victim's heroism during the Cultural Revolution in China, a best-seller, is beautifully described by the author's tough but lyrical prose. The reading by Penelope Dellaporta perfectly corresponds to my imagined idea of the way Cheng, now a Washington resident, must sound in Chinese.

Since 1985 I have heard more than 70 books on tape. Some are old friends I'd never gotten around to rereading—all of Jane Austen's novels, for example, also Jane Eyre, Hard Times, Jude the Obscure and Cry, the Beloved Country. Others are new works that had passed me by when they first came out. That's how I discovered the genius of John Gardner—and went through October Light, The Sunlight Dialogues, Grendel and others—and Larry McMurtry, especially Lonesome Dove. Because I sometimes exchange tapes with friends to keep the cost down (rented tapes average around $15, about the price of a new hardcover novel), I've enjoyed books I never would have ordered on my own: The Manticore, The Left Hand of Darkness. Biographies such as Nabokov's Speak Memory and history books have taken on new interest to me, as have travel accounts such as From Heaven Lake.

Now I am a books on tape evangelist. I go around preaching the importance of making the most of our time on earth. I search out my subjects with keen insight because the type of person who likes to listen to audio books is hard to define. According to the president of the Maryland-based Recorded Books company, Henry Trentman, "the common denominator is an active mind—manic people who like to keep their minds occupied." So if you see me waxing eloquent at a party, it's a safe bet that I'm extolling the virtues of audio books. And I modestly admit that I've made my share of converts.

Last year when I visited my sister in Chicago, I told her about my passion and tried to persuade her to try it, but she put up all the same arguments against it that I had mustered before I converted. I could see by the expression on her face that she thought I had fallen over the edge, and I could also see that she had no intention of taking my good advice despite my repeated efforts to bring her into the fold.

A month later my sister called to say she had just finished her first taped book. "You have given me the best gift I have ever received," she said. "You've shown me how to make my day seem longer, how to enjoy the literature I love but haven't had time for and, most of all, how to calm myself when I am angry. Now I don't yell at my family when I'm doing mindless tasks, and I hardly mind doing the dishes. My rage level is much lower. Thank you."

Washingtonian Flo Gibson, reader extraordinaire who started her own company (Audio Book Contractors) a few years ago—after many years as a reader for other commercial companies and for the Library of Congress "Talking Books" program—considers audio books perfect for times "when hands and eyes are occupied but the mind isn't." They give book lovers a marvelous opportunity to reread classics, catch up on more recent titles and discover new authors.

CHAPTER TWO

Magazines

Folding Frenzy

Charles Trueheart, July 1990

Magazines are dropping like flies. The fatalities of the season include Psychology Today, 7 Days and, most recently, and shockingly, Manhattan inc., which only a few years ago was being celebrated and imitated for its path-making feature journalism.

Like the miner's canary, this funeral procession from the newsstand portends more general economic trouble, or at least reflects a pervasive fear of it. In uncertain times, who will make uncertain financial commitments, whether it be a $20 check for a year's subscription or a $2 million contract for a year's worth of advertising space? The magazine publisher can be forgiven for spending only half his time trying to rescue his magazine from perdition in the marketplace; he must spend the other half putting the property in the right order to unload.

With these folded magazines are extinguished whole editorial sensibilities and publishing stratagems, even journalistic histories that included the headiest of days. And of course readers too are abandoned when a magazine ceases publication. They found something to like no matter their numbers.

Gone but Not Forgotten

Psychology Today gasped its last in February. Once the darling of the magazine industry and the most-mentioned reading of the bourgeoisie, PT had changed a few too many hands, undergone too many remakes, appeared on too many sticky stamps in too many clearinghouse mailings. The magazine is in what Hollywood calls "turnaround"—a revival is promised in a few months.

A similar reinvention is in the works for Ms., which effectively folded its glossy, mass-market self a few months ago, having lost its original soul years ago. Ms. ultimately became the victim of its success. Service articles and feminist journalism that used to be unique to Ms. are now staples of all the Seven Sisters magazines, not to mention a host of working-woman-type second-generation magazines.

Perhaps the most anguished closing thus far was that of 7 Days, a sophisticated Manhattan weekly beloved by its flock. Its end had a summary quality: Even as its owner found the bottom of his deep pockets, 7 Days was on its way to winning the National Magazine Award.

In an industry that could sustain smallness, or even encourage it as a noble undertaking, things might have been different. But even modesty is no guarantee of success. Just last week, the president of Yale University pulled the plug on the Yale Review, a journal with a distinguished tradition and a history of university subsidies Yale was forced to abandon.

Critical Condition

There have been other wakes this spring. For Long Island Monthly, which certainly seemed like a good idea when it started. For Southpoint, formerly the promising start-up Southern, which Time Warner's eager-to-please new subsidiary, Southern Progress Inc., had bought and tried to spit-shine. And then, two weeks ago, for Manhattan. inc. ne plus ultra of '80s magazines, responsible for a marvelous brand of faux-critical (and ultimately glorifying) profiles, and launcher of many writing and editing careers.

Manhattan, inc. technically will not die. It will be swallowed whole by a men's magazine called M, and the package re-christened with a name about as awkward as it is possible to imagine—M, inc. The editor of M, inc. will be M's editor, Jane F. Lane, not Manhattan, inc.'s well-known Clay Felker, who'll be the new magazine's editor at large—suggesting which magazine's editorial styles will wear the pants in the marriage. M is designed for today's on-the-go, briefcase-carrying young male airport-newsstand visitor. Contents: Cars. Clothes. Sports. Gadgets. Stars. Babes.

Another lip-smacking swallow: Conde Nast last week bought Cook's, the sophisticate's cooking magazine, and fed it (or at least its subscriber list) to Conde Nast's own cooking magazine, Gourmet. Mother Earth News and Smart, the old natural-living gazette and the mannered young monthly owned by entrepreneur Owen J. Lipstein, are both teetering.

Mere survival does not ensure good news. The New Yorker's editorial revival under Robert Gottlieb has not been echoed by the confidence advertisers show with their buys. The three weekly news magazines, No. 1 Time, No. 2 Newsweek and No. 3 U.S. News & World Report, must pay dearly for the continued allegiance of their increasingly distracted readers. Spy, another '80s success, has been looking for investors for an embarassing number of months. The Forbes family's stab at downtown hip, Egg, limps. Entertainment Weekly, the expensive spring launch by Time Warner, staggers, while sibling Life, now publishing monthly, ponders a rosier future as the weekly it once was. Even TV Guide is struggling.

The Masculine Mystique

Withal, would-be editors don't stop huddling with confederates and patrons to create new magazines. New ones appear all the time, gushing promise and ignoring the ubiquity of doom.

Los Angeles, for instance, has been pronounced underserved by magazines, and within the next year or so will be treated to an urbane new monthly called Buzz and an as-yet-unnamed weekly from Knapp Communications, publisher of L.A.-based Architectural Digest. Meanwhile, another entrepreneur is taking steps toward launching California Republic, a fortnightly journal covering California politics.

The greatest industry enthusiasm in this skittish season seems to be magazines for guys. In addition to the forthcoming M, inc., men (and women) soon may be able to choose among Men, a new launch from the former publisher of Cook's; Men's Life, forthcoming from Murdoch Magazines; another men's title from Straight Arrow (the Rolling Stone people); and Details, done over with the man in mind. Men's Health has been around a while to improve the male body, and GQ even longer to improve its appearance and behavior. Forbes and Business Week are also concocting new magazines clearly aimed at men and their fancies.

All this attention could make a fella blush. But will he then subscribe?

Grace Mirabella & the Vagaries of Vogue

Martha Sherrill Dailey, July 1988

On the 13th floor of the Conde Nast building, outside the office of Grace Mirabella, life at Vogue seems to glide by as expected. A hungry young illustrator pleads with anyone passing through to have a look at his portfolio. Two young women discuss the definition of "chin-length" hair and whether theirs is too short for a ponytail. The slightly exasperated dowager receptionist answers calls to vacationing staff that are being forwarded to her phone line. A woman photographer dressed in black waits to take a picture of Mirabella, who is finishing up the October issue, her last.

"I'm trying to be attractive about this," says Mirabella, who pouts and shrugs a little and whispers something about "politesse."

She's trying to be attractive when she talks about the way she was fired after 36 years at Vogue—after 17 years as editor-in-chief. Although she was assured all year by the management at Conde Nast Publications that she shouldn't worry about the rumors in print that she was being replaced, Mirabella ultimately learned the truth from the television. Or at least her husband did.

"He got home ahead of me," she remembers of June 28, "and somebody called and said, 'Listen, have you heard Liz Smith?'"

The gossipy "Live at Five" broadcast announced that Anna Wintour, the former editor of British Vogue who arrived in New York less than a year ago to revamp House and Garden, would be taking over Mirabella's post, the most illustrious in the realm of fashion, Aug. 1.

Thinking at first it was simply another rumor—Seventh Avenue and the city papers had been utterly fascinated with the upheavals taking place at Conde Nast—Mirabella, 50, called chairman S.I. Newhouse at home that night and was shocked to be told the story was true.

In Newhouse's office the next morning she went over the details of her "resignation." And she will return there today, to pick up her settlement papers after spending her last hours at the magazine.

While waiting out the month of July, Wintour, 38, has made her presence felt. Last week in her HG office, just eight floors below Mirabella's, she sat wearing sunglasses—as she often does indoors— and interviewed Vogue staff individually at half-hour intervals. And it was Wintour, not Mirabella, who took the front row seat as Vogue editor at the couture shows in Paris yesterday.

"I think you can't fault a company for wanting a change. That's natural," says Mirabella, 50, in her tirelessly polite way. "But how it was done—for a stylish company—is kind of tacky."

Inside the Sand Dune

To understand Grace Mirabella it's important to comprehend the color beige—her favorite. The shade of stone and sidewalks, cement and canvas, it's a steady tempo behind a frivolous melody. It's common sense amid disorder. It's not fancy or flamboyant. And there's nothing delirious about it. While gray or white can be trendy, beige remains above reproach. It's beyond fashion. Beige doesn't try to be anything but beige.

"Everybody is looking around for whatever follows the Hula-Hoop," says Mirabella. "That's not my style. I have a great interest in fashion, the way you'd expect I would. I don't have an interest in fashion no matter what it is."

Sitting in her Vogue office, she is submerged in beigeness. The walls. The carpet. The desk. The half-closed blinds. It's like walking inside a sand dune. Slides and manila folders—are scattered on a side table. It's 2:30 in the afternoon and she's already removed her earrings. On the horn with the art department, she's a tad unhappy with a story for October. "There's no glory in it," she says into the phone, adding intermittent "Mmmms" in that way smart English women have of meaning "Yes, I agree. Go on..." While her voice isn't extravagant or full of old money, it seems to have been around some of that. Her manner and looks suggest—a melding of Jeane Kirkpatrick and Dinah Shore. There's a keenness and intellectual detachment to her, and the sunny beige chin-length hair and soft edge of a woman's woman.

"There is nothing in Grace's emotional setup that would incline her toward anything chi-chi," says Alexander Liberman, Conde Nast's legendary editorial director—the man who can kibosh a Vogue cover. Liberman has worked with Mirabella and been a close friend for more than 20 years. "Her whole concept of life has deeper roots," he says.

While Newhouse planned Wintour's takeover, it's been suggested that Liberman—also a Wintour admirer—knew about it and never told Mirabella.

"These rumors and discussions had been going on a long, long time," says Liberman, who sounds like English actor John Houseman at his most sympathetic. "There were discussions about it before Anna left (New York magazine" for British Vogue. It was certainly nothing new."

But did he ever mention it to Mirabella?

"No, never. How can you discuss something like that?"

Mirabella is also too kind to explore the matter. "I'm not being evasive," she says, talking about what Liberman knew and when. "I just don't know. And I have no desire to find out."

Peacocks in the Hall

This pragmatic lady, with her subdued and sensible ways, must have felt a little bland at Vogue when she began. Raised in suburban Maplewood, N.J., she was the only child of Anthony Mirabella, a wine importer, and his wife Florence, who was born in Italy. Always good in school, she was the editor of the paper at Skidmore College, where she graduated with an economics degree.

Nothing about her upbringing, she says, prepared her for Vogue. "It was a very different place," Mirabella says of the Vogue where she got a job checking store credits for captions when she was 22. "Oh very. It was very grand. And with wonderful-looking editors who strolled like peacocks through the halls. There were wonderful characters. Deeeevine. I mean, you saw them coming. You were very aware of their presence. I can't tell you, to this day, whether you ever could have had a real conversation with any of them. I really don't know."

By 1962, when Diana Vreeland became editor, Mirabella had worked her way up to "my greatest moment in fashion" as the sportswear editor, and later as Vreeland's assistant.

Vreeland, known for issuing her first orders of the day from her morning bath, never came into work until after noon. Once there, she burned Rigaud candles and incense in her scarlet-red office, used an inner tube as a chair cushion and seemed to float behind a black lacquer desk, surrounded by leopard skin rugs and upholstery. She didn't have an ounce of beige in her.

According to Vogue lore, being Vreeland's assistant was not always easy. She used them as run-through models—making them try on gloves, sweaters, whatever—and rarely asked their opinion. For the photographers, there were endless reshoots.

"I was a terror then—just a terror," Vreeland says in her colorful, rambling memoirs, "DV." Apparently she isn't exaggerating, as she's sometimes known to do.

"It was very difficult to work for her," Mirabella concedes. "But you can get along with someone who is difficult if you admire them. And I admired Diana Vreeland—for all of her style and know-how, which she was about. Also, she had the most extraordinary sense of humor. And that could turn impossible moments around."

As fashion editor of Harper's Bazaar for 25 years before coming to Vogue, Vreeland set the stereotype of the fashion magazine editor as an eccentric sprung from the elite. And it was Kay Thompson's pale version of Vreeland in the 1957 movie "Funny Face" that moved the stereotype into the ridiculous. Hit with a revelation at her desk one morning, Thompson lifts her gloved hands and breaks into song:

Banish the black,
Burn the blue,
Bury the beige,
Think Pink!

Small wonder Mirabella never dreamed of becoming editor. She wasn't flamboyant or bohemian. She was social only when forced. "I never thought of myself as being the person—if you are typecasting—in the style of the movies. I mean, not at all."

Inheriting Vreeland's Vogue

The Vogue that Mirabella would eventually inherit was entirely Vreeland's. It was avant-garde, exotic, psychedelic and very social— European aristocrats and upper-class Americans posed with nonchalance on the pages. Celebrities—Goldie Hawn, Liz Taylor, Cher—got to be cover girls. And Vreeland's fascinating models— Marisa Berenson, Veruschka, Penelope Tree—were often pulled from society and money.

Vreeland, who has never hidden her love of artifice, went all out in the '60s. It was rich-hippie extravagance. Veruschka dressed in a bikini of gold chains. Roman sandals tied up to the knee and backdrops that always seemed to be Moorish. Tree, with her phantom face, in a bushy yak fur coat and white eyeshadow.

But the magazine, still a bimonthly, was so cutting-edge that it was failing. Some of the more outrageous clothes couldn't be found in stores, much less worn on the street. And Vogue's reputation among fashion designers had become antagonistic—Vreeland hadn't courted the Seventh Avenue advertisers with obligatory editorial layouts.

Witnesses to Vreeland's firing in 1971 have conveniently dim memories of how it was handled. But by all accounts it was sudden and brutally insensitive. "They were not very good at letting people go," Vreeland says in "DV," describing her own firing and that of longtime Vogue editor Margaret Case, who was found one morning on the pavement below her apartment. "She threw herself out a window," says Vreeland, "because she was eighty, she was out of work, she had no money—and she'd been dismissed in the most terrible way."

Mirabella was on a shoot in California when told she would be the next editor. While "it was a delight to be in," she says, she had never expressed interest in the job and doesn't know who picked her. "It's that kind of place," Mirabella says of the cryptic Conde Nast touch. "They are in the communications business but they don't know how to communicate." She also guesses she found out about it before Vreeland did.

There are still unanswered questions as to why Conde Nast fired Vreeland, the most talented and famous fashion editor in history. But the theories aren't in short supply. One thing was certain: Vreeland didn't care about business, she cared about style.

"In the '60s, women turned their backs on women's magazines," says Mirabella. "Women thought, 'That doesn't have anything to do with me, forget it'...And the newsstand sales just plummeted—not dropping, plummeted."

Andy Warhol had a theory, too. "She was fired from Vogue in 1971," he once said of his friend Vreeland, "because Vogue wanted to go middle class."

Mirabella's Magazine

It's hard to know where the '70s leave off and Mirabella begins— they seem so interchangeable.

Together she and Liberman gave Vogue a new attitude, which she calls "easygoing"—without a doubt, still one of her favorite adjectives. She wanted to drop the image of Vogue as a "ladies' magazine," to interest a new kind of reader, an intelligent and serious woman who worked for a living—a woman very much like Mirabella. Within her first year as editor, the Vreelandness of Vogue diminished and it began to take on the sense of Grace Mirabella.

"The voice of the magazine," says Liberman, "was really Grace's voice."

Covers that once boldly announced "The Beautiful People...and where to Find Them, now proclaimed articles about "The Modern Woman." The word "modern" became Mirabella's mantra. In 1973 the magazine went from bimonthly to monthly. And in 1977 it shrank to standard magazine size, roughly 8 by 11 inches.

The lounging aristocrats and jet set tribes started to vanish from Vogue's pages. Working women—journalists, writers, actresses, artists, playwrights—took their place. The effort was "to make it less grand. Less pompous. Pompous is really the word," she says.

And in a short period of time the amazon exotics were gone. Anjelica Huston modeled a bit and Cher stayed, but by '72, ultra-WASP

Karen Graham (later the Estee Lauder woman), with the tiniest, boniest nose, was on the cover. And Lauren Hutton, without the wigs and fake eyelashes she wore under Vreeland, became a star.

The Vogue models of the '70s—Lisa Taylor, Patti Hansen, Roseanne Vela and Hutton—had an unadorned wholesomeness. It was a sort of inarguable prettiness that had a broader appeal. Describing the look, Mirabella says: "She gives off this little bit more easygoing, healthier, approachable look. It's a certain kind of good looks, it's not overpolished. You don't polish up these women."

Artifice overall was downplayed, at first because Mirabella had never felt comfortable with it, and later because "the natural look" took hold. Hair became less contrived and the models wore less makeup. "Artificiality. I think there's a place for it in fashion—that's part of its charm and fantasy," she says. "But I don't think that's the whole package."

With all else neutralized, the clothes were bound to be selected with a different sensibility. While Vreeland had delved into the gypsy looks of Giorgio Di Sant'Angelo, Mirabella fell for the spareness and simplicity of Halston and Geoffrey Beene.

"Her concepts of clothing and the needs of modern women are very much like my own," says Beene. "She has a very pragmatic approach."

Mirabella, who wears a black and white Beene suit for the interview, denies she ever played favorites in the magazine. "I don't think I did. I think that at certain moments, people rise and you are hard put to ignore them," she says. "Also when a certain designer stands for that point that you are trying to make, trying to make, trying to make—then you tend to lean on them, work with them, the way you do with somebody you think is speaking your language."

In 1974 Mirabella married William Cahan, a well-known cancer surgeon at Memorial Sloan Kettering. When asked why she had never married before, she says, "I wasn't interested. I think I was really very focused. I loved my work—the whole ease of it. And I hadn't met Bill Cahan."

Cahan, Mirabella admits, influenced her work tremendously. She became more interested in covering health and fitness. "I don't think you can keep throwing hemlines at women without giving them something about their health, something about their sense of well-being," she says. And when she talks about the things at Vogue she wishes she could have done, it's always in this area. "In some ways, my sense of less artifice is really incompatible with the magazine."

Her sensible Vogue has blossomed at the magazine racks. During Mirabella's reign circulation tripled from 400,000 to 1.3 million. "Grace is a businesswoman, really," says close friend Dawn Mello, president of Bergdorf Goodman. "She's not ethereal. She always has the reader in mind."

While Vreeland's motto had always been "Give Them What They Never Knew They Wanted," Mirabella's seemed to say "Give Them What They Never Knew They Needed."

Bracing for Wintour

As much as the magazine was transfigured as it passed from Vreeland's hands to Mirabella's, it will surely change again once Anna Wintour moves in.

And not everyone is staying around for the mag-quake. Creative director Jade Hobson Charnin has announced she will be leaving soon. Associate editor Kathleen Madden is going to Self. And one of the fashion editors, Paul Sinclaire, has resigned to do some work for HG in Europe. Several other longtime Vogue staff are rumored to be leaving.

The speculation about Wintour's Vogue has been great. Sources at Conde Nast are saying that Richard Avedon won't be doing the covers, that Arthur Elgort will be shooting action covers outdoors. And stories have been printed that Wintour wants Liberman's post once he retires.

There is a feeling on Seventh Avenue that an ancient regime is dying. But the hiring and firing of a Vogue editor never happens quietly.

Life After Vogue

Back in the uncluttered beige dune, Grace Mirabella is on the phone again. Although she had asked the two secretaries outside her door to hold her calls, there's a sense that it was an impossible request.

She holds up a finger to her audience as if to say, "No, stay. Just a bit more, sorry." She seems totally engaged in what she's doing. It's hard to imagine her leaving, or the office redecorated in something like mahogany and chintz.

She puts down the phone. "I think fashion is in doldrums at the moment," she says, picking up the conversation just where it was. "And I think hemlines up and down is in lieu of any ideas...We are in a plateau, maybe. And I think that a big chunk of women have not been catered to well enough, with a certain style and with an understanding of lives."

She's getting straight-faced again. Her Jeane Kirkpatrick side is taking over, as though she has an unconquerable, unfashionable impulse to go deeper into things. "I find I have trouble with fashion as a subject," she says finally. "I get bothered. And I take it all very seriously. I don't take it in whimsical ways. Which is probably wrong."

She wants to explain herself. "I've always had a dream—and I don't know how to do this, by the way—that there should be some moment in fashion where the conversation can be as interesting as a conversation about baseball, and not peppered with isn't that deeevine..."

Although she says it's the staff at Vogue that she'll miss most, she doesn't want a goodbye party. Although two weeks ago she was given a yellow Labrador puppy by her friends—maybe as a distraction—she hasn't named it yet. (Is the dog really beige? "Yes, very.") And although two Vogue editors before her—Edna Woolman Chase and Vreeland—wrote successful memoirs, she says, "Frankly, I don't know why anybody would be interested in reading mine."

What she'd really like is another job.

"I'm talking to people, people are talking to me," she says. "Maybe by the end of August I'll have an idea." By the end of August she'll have played a lot of tennis with her husband at their country house in Westchester County. She might start horseback riding. She might have picked out fabric for new curtains. She'll have spent a week or two at the Golden Door spa in California.

And by the end of August she might get her wish—the perfect, sensible, new job. "I'm not talking about something boring," she says. "I am never talking about boring. I am always talking about style, but I think on a different level. That's what I think I might still like to do.

Keeping an Eye on the Rich and Powerful

Eleanor Randolph, February 1988

Spy magazine exists, on some level, to provide a little solace for those of us who are not rich or famous.

The purpose of this year-old publication is to take the hot air out of Manhattan's stuffed shirts, to tweak the powerful in Washington, to bleat a raspberry at the established everywhere. The magazine is sophomoric. It is underhanded. It is unfair. And when it lands in my mailbox, it is the first thing I read.

Reading Spy is like having your boss criticize you for lack of foresight as he walks into a parking meter. You laugh and then you think, how terrible of me to laugh at someone's adversity, and so you tone it down to a snicker which you try to hide as a sneeze. If the victim were a bag lady, you wouldn't laugh. But unlike some publications, Spy doesn't go after the weak and infirm. It goes after the powerful.

As co-editor Kurt Andersen explained it recently: "We don't pick on little guys and nobodies. We go for the overdog."

Thus, to read Spy is to wonder why one of their large and powerful subjects hasn't sued the short pants off these boys. (Andersen is 33; co-editor E. Graydon Carter is 38. They bring the average age of the staff up, way up to, oh, the mid-twenties.)

Suppose, for example, that you are the chairman of Revlon and you marry a very prominent newspaper gossip columnist who likes lucious red lip gloss. Okay, maybe this merits a few snickers at the Harvard Club. But Spy does a whole article called "Roy Cohn called them the Perfect Couple."

The article is introduced this way: "A marriage like that of Revlon chairman Ron Perelman and gossipeuse Claudia Cohen is a boon to everyone concerned. It is convenient. It helps two parvenues up the greasy social pole. And it takes two unpleasant people out of circulation. But come to think of it, that's probably the wrong way to introduce this story, because what it's really about is how Ron and Claudia—two very special, very caring people—overcame the obstacles of wealth, power and ego to fall in love."

Or suppose you are Lawrence Tisch, owner of CBS Inc., and until you owned the network, you were mostly addressed in the hushed, reverential tones people normally reserve for the rich and powerful.

Spy routinely refers to Tisch as a "budget-crazed dwarf billionaire." After the first reference, Tisch's public-relations man called to say that he wasn't technically a dwarf.

Height is a big deal to Spy's staff. In June, they featured a chart showing seven very rich but somewhat short men whose height was adjusted for net worth. H. Ross Perot, for example, was 5'6" really, but with assets of $2.5 billion his height is adjusted to 7'7". Tisch went from 5'5" to 6'3"; publisher and developer Mortimer Zuckerman, whose worth was listed as $250 million, rose from 5'6" to 5'8 1-2".

To be tall doesn't mean that one is off-limits. Last April they offered a piece entitled: "After searching three continents, Lawrence O'Donnell, Jr., found Six Smart Models (including the only person on earth named Cricket whose favorite book is The Brothers Karamazov)."

Andersen says the article that has generated the most mail so far was their feature last May called "Colleges of the Dumb Rich." They heard from a lot of alumni.

Nevertheless, they have not been sued for libel. The main reason, of course, is that these people are public figures who have almost no chance of winning such a case these days. More to the point, the plaintiff has to prove that the story is untrue.

So we have the courtroom scene, with the judge, jury and two rows of bored, gum-chewing journalists looking for a reason to stay awake. The aggrieved's lawyer explains to the court: "Your honor, my client is here to protest that she is not a 'bosomy dirty-book writer.'" How many seconds would it take before every phone in the courthouse is instantly attached to a reporter?

Spy, which was patterned on the British publication Private Eye, has borrowed some of the Eye's features. For example, they have pictures of people who were "separated at birth," like Teddy Kennedy and Sarah Ferguson or George Shultz and the Cowardly Lion.

But they also lack some of the substance that made Private Eye more than a joke magazine.

Still, it's only one-year-old and not making money. So, it seems a little early to complain. The only people doing that are the subjects— i.e., targets—of Spy's voyeurism, and even then only in a whisper.

What happens if developer Donald Trump protests publicly? The answer is that the news moves out of Spy, leaps onto the AP newswire and settles into the People columns of every newspaper in America.

As it is now, only the 65,000 subscribers to Spy magazine also know the very rich and increasingly famous Mr. Trump as the "ugly cuff link buff" or more recently, the "short-fingered Bulgarian."

The Uncertain State of the New Yorker

Charles Trueheart, January 1988

For most of the past 12 months, since the tempest of William Shawn's unceremonious removal as editor of The New Yorker after 35 years and his protested succession by Robert Gottlieb, this deeply eccentric publication has been facing a familiar and difficult predicament.

Governments, businesses, religions and families all ask themselves the same questions: Can an institution whose strength seems to flow from the person of its leader survive his inevitable passing? And if so, at what cost?

The New Yorker's welcome of Gottlieb, only its third editor in 62 years, was famously inauspicious. Before his first day on the job, Gottlieb was handed a letter signed by 154 members of the staff, many of them esteemed names in American arts and letters, asking him to stay away. He showed up anyway, as the letter writers no doubt expected.

Since then, The New Yorker's writers and editors and artists—and, more indirectly and importantly, its nearly 600,000 paying readers—have been orienting themselves to the new editor's catholic tastes (for ballet, for the arcana of popular commercial culture) and pronounced distastes (for formality, for the received wisdom). Gottlieb, a man of overweening confidence and instinctive command, is at 56 still very much in his prime.

The upheaval of the magazine's editorial transition comes—not coincidentally—at an uncertain time in its corporate life. Less than three years ago, The New Yorker, long the private preserve of the Fleischmann family, was acquired by the magazine division of Samuel I. Newhouse's family communications company. Under the roof of this corporate powerhouse are book publishing's redoubtable Random House and its imprint Alfred A. Knopf, which Gottlieb ran for 19 years, and the profitable Conde Nast magazine group, with its successful revival of another relic, Vanity Fair, by editor Tina Brown. Newhouse is a man with a high tolerance for quality so long as it makes money for his company.

Most who have been at the magazine for a while date the beginning of Shawn's decline to the magazine's sale and the "distractions" that followed the installation of an aggressive new publisher (now chairman) named Steven Florio, 35 years old at the time.

Florio introduced The New Yorker to contemporary marketing practices and circulation targets considered essential to polish the magazine's dowdy image on Madison Avenue. Too many of its readers, by conventional demographic standards, were old and getting older. Old people don't buy what the advertisers sell. Dead people don't read magazines at all.

Such earthly considerations had seldom concerned the 79-year-old editor who circulated a short and emotional "Dear colleagues, dear friends, note of farewell last Feb. 12. Shawn's sorrowful departure was at the still center of a public hurricane, as magazine staff members decried Newhouse's treatment of Shawn and declared Gottlieb's appointment unacceptable.

Today, with calm restored and privacy reclaimed, people at The New Yorker are a tad bashful about their passionate display of loyalty to Mr. Shawn, as he was always known. "We thought it was preposterous to think an outsider could tend the garden in which this delicate flower bloomed," remarks E.J. Kahn, who has written for the magazine for more than 50 years. Mark Singer, a staff writer since 1974, says it more plainly: "We looked like spoiled children. We were sort of temporarily dislocated and didn't quite grasp what we were doing. It was a family tragedy."

The new chairman, for his part, talks like a man with the worst behind him: "Now they know that Florio and Gottlieb are not going to destroy the place." But it may be even more true that the place was more resilient than anyone imagined. The magazine keeps coming out, and it probably looks to most readers and to the naked eye little different from The New Yorker Shawn was publishing in his last years there.

After the unpleasantness of the transition, when the ugly family feud became for a time the talk of the town, many at The New Yorker are wary of the press. In the magazine's utilitarian offices, most conversations slalom on and off the record. Gottlieb himself favors the editor's chestnut that the magazine he puts out every week is more articulate than he could ever be: He talked to a reporter—for 90 minutes—on the condition that nothing he said be used in the article. Pen and notebook, he insisted, must remain untouched throughout.

The First 52 Issues

When Robert Gottlieb was preparing to move the 10 blocks from the Knopf editorial rooms on East 50th Street to The New Yorker's on West 43rd, he was reported to have read a year's worth of the magazine to familiarize himself with his new charge. Gottlieb had never worked at a magazine before.

Next month, when the magazine's top-hatted mascot, Eustace Tilley, appears for the 64th time on the cover of The New Yorker, Gottlieb will have overseen a full year of issues. What's different about them? Where is his imprint?

Kremlinologists would be impressed by the enthusiasm of The New Yorker's numerous armchair analysts, but not always by their memories. Contrary to much instant analysis, for example, both photographs and four-letter words did appear—several times—in William Shawn's New Yorker.

A former editor at the magazine comments wryly on the number of times he has been approached by one of its devotees in a sputter that "The New Yorker would never have done something like that under Shawn!"—usually, this alumnus goes on, "about exactly the kind of piece that Shawn would have said 'yes' to without a moment's hesitation."

But facts are facts. Gottlieb, to begin with, published a dispatch from Afghanistan by one of his Knopf authors, novelist Doris Lessing—a piece that Shawn, not two months before, had turned down. It was only the first of a series of editorial decisions that seemed designed to be provocative, and that served as declarations of the new order and interments of the old.

In late spring, Gottlieb began publishing the work of some new "Talk of the Town" writers, the core of the anonymous "we" who generate the editorial posture and cultural attitude of the magazine. The newcomers shared these unsigned columns with such formidable returning alumni as John McPhee and John Updike.

The names of new, younger critics—Mimi Kramer on theater, Terrence Rafferty on fiction—began last spring to mingle with the august bylines in the back pages of the magazine—among them Arlene Croce (dance), Whitney Balliett (jazz), Andrew Porter (music), Pauline Kael (film). Since the first of the year, The Atlantic's Holly Brubach has begun to write about fashion and free-lancer Mark Moses about popular music.

In August, eyebrows were detonated by an unsigned and exceptionally long "Notes and Comment" denunciation of Judge Robert

Bork's appointment to the Supreme Court, staking out the magazine's position weeks and months ahead of the journalistic pack on that issue.

The piece was written by Renata Adler, known for her controversial pieces in The New Yorker on the Westmoreland and Sharon libel trials, and among the journalists most likely to excite passionate reactions these days. Excite them it did, especially as Gottlieb followed up with Washington writer Lincoln Caplan's unsparing critique of the U.S. solicitor general's office under the Reagan administration.

Even as the new editor was delivering this serious judicial one-two, he was acting out his wackiest inclinations. In one of his first moves as editor, he had assigned a story to Jane and Michael Stern, popular culture mavens and former Gottlieb authors ("Elvisworld"). As "Our Far-Flung Correspondents," in September the Sterns reported from Indiana on a convention of "Wee Scots," as collectors of Scottish terrier memorabilia call themselves. When you ask New Yorker people to describe a classic Gottlieb piece, they say, with a roll of the eyes, "Wee Scots."

More startling—though still, by the standards of any other magazine, piddling—have been the visual changes. Covers are no longer, in the words of the alumnus, "the basket of flowers on your front porch."'They have become, like your laundry, bolder, brighter and cleaner. often a joke or a plot or some action is implied. Recognizable words appear. Lee Lorenz, the magazine's art director for 15 years, says Gottlieb wants "idea covers" and "visual excitement."

Cartoons, a signature of the magazine, are more numerous under Gottlieb, and Lorenz says he is being urged to go out and find new artists. "The field doesn't offer enough," he says, with a worried shake of the head. One of his editors says the Gottlieb trademark is more "pure silliness" and fewer "jokes with guys in suits."

What generated the greatest internal—and external—shock and indignation was Gottlieb's surprise publication of three black-and-white photographs in the last issue of 1987. The objections to these photos, accompanying a piece about "Bug Art" by Sue Hubbell, had less to do with broken precedents than with bad execution—the pictures were badly sized, poorly reproduced, captionless and unedifying.

Photographs have been rare because at The New Yorker, the writing was supposed to be "so clear that it made people see things," in the words of Deputy Editor Charles McGrath. "If you needed a photographer the writer had failed." All hands now agree that photography, in limited and constructive doses, may be an appropriate innovation in the magazine's pages.

But the bug incident makes people worry. Gottlieb kept his plans a secret until the last minute, seeking no one's advice or approval. A staff writer of some duration says, "I think he's tweaking somebody, but I don't know who he's tweaking and to what effect." Lorenz says he wasn't consulted, and that Gottlieb's decision was a "mistake." One of his colleagues tactfully calls the editor "a man who doesn't want to have taboos."

Upstairs, Downstairs

The three editorial floors of The New Yorker at 25 W. 43rd St. are connected vertically by haphazard stairwells, but descending to the floors below, where the magazine's salaries and bills are paid, is a more complicated matter. The visitor must leave one secure zone, travel one floor in the building's public elevator, and be buzzed into another—far plusher—zone.

The wall between church and state, as the editorial and business sides are sometimes known in journalism, is an old custom at The New Yorker. Thanks to the wall, Shawn was able to insulate his writers and editors from the fortunes of the magazine in its marketplace. (It didn't hurt, of course, that for a long time those fortunes were excellent.)

Michael Arlen, a staff writer for 30 years, thinks Shawn privately regarded The New Yorker as "a secret book club, a place to write books, that seemed to all intents and purposes like a magazine...You could always get more space, more time. The apparatus of the magazine would take a back seat to what you were trying to do."

If any apprehension preoccupies the members of the upstairs club, it is fear that the apparatus will end up in the front seat—that the new owner's bean counters will begin to encroach on their way of life. Already in The New Yorker's pages, charges one young old-timer, can be seen "a far more serious invasion of the style of the magazine than any of the changes the art department has made."

He means the palpable evidence of Florio's handiwork: Bound-in subscription and customer-service cards. Horizontal display of ads. Irregular paper stock. The musical computer chip in the Christmas vodka centerfold. And most notorious, the so-called "advertorial" sections—in effect, advertising meant to look like editorial matter.

These sections, set off from the regular pages of the magazine but bearing its imprimatur, are a necessary evil in the eyes of most editors now. But, perhaps needless to say, they had never appeared in The New Yorker until Florio decided he needed them to "jump-start the magazine."

The advertorials outraged many inside and out who found especially offensive the pseudo-New Yorker style of the "text" describing the wonders of, say, European travel or formal wear. Florio today says they have served their purpose and will cease by year's end.

Florio's efforts have also begun to yield financial results. The industry's favored measure of success—number of advertising pages—had shown the magazine in a slow decline for five years; for 1987, Florio says, it will show a slight increase (less than 1 percent) to 2,704 pages. "It's attention-getting and a morale booster," says Randall Warner, vice president of Harper's, a smaller magazine in the same market niche. But Warner points out that The New Yorker is still more than 900 pages under its 1983 level.

With some bargain offers and direct-mail solicitations—a "minimum effort," Florio says—circulation was driven up by nearly 100,000. The magazine hadn't had a major direct mail campaign since 1971, he remarks. "People saw it in dentists' offices or on an airplane, but no one ever asked them to subscribe." Just as important—to Florio, to advertisers—the median age of New Yorker readers is drifting down toward that of young families and conspicuous consumers.

The test of these numbers will come later, when subscribers are asked to renew their subscriptions. The New Yorker's renewal rate is exceptionally high among the competition—70 percent or better. But one magazine publishing veteran thinks Florio may be diluting the quality of his audience to produce short-term, and evanescent, results.

No one would call Florio's methods or his manner low-key, which may contribute to the deep suspicions he and his masters breed on the upper floors. If a story needs to be trimmed, for instance, it is hypothesized that Florio wants to squeeze in an ad for another Conde Nast magazine.

Florio is evidently so sensitized to editorial opinion that when he called the new fashion critic, Brubach, to check her traveling schedule to the European fashion shows against his own, he blurted a promise before she could even say hello: "I will never compromise you."

One New Yorker editor takes a more conciliatory line on the church/state split. "We overdid the separation," he says. "You can have a wall but you don't need barbed wire and gun emplacements. You preserve it by getting along."

Here and Now At The New Yorker

Gottlieb arrived famous. He is the man who discovered Joseph Heller and forever changed the English language when he changed the name of Heller's "Catch-18" to "Catch-22" to avoid clashing with a then-new Leon Uris novel, "Mila Eighteen." He went on to edit prodigious numbers of books, working with Naipaul, Cheever, Updike, Tuchman, Drabble, Kazin, le Carre and so on.

A man known for his discriminating tastes and his profitable publishing, Gottlieb was also thought to have unusual personal magnetism. He would cast his wise and baleful eyes upon you and speak humbly words intended to make you believe in him, confiding or seeming to confide, making a gift of his insight. A former acolyte of Gottlieb, long since estranged, says, "I feel like I've been deprogrammed from a cult."

If such charisma is analogous to the very different hold that William Shawn exerted on his writers and editors—and it is—it manifests itself differently. As has been widely noted, Gottlieb wears sport shirts open at the neck, khakis and athletic shoes to the office. In contrast to his wan and reclusive predecessor, Gottlieb is ubiquitous, bustling about the corridors, popping a question, cracking a joke.

An editor says that he's heard complaints from staffers that "Gottlieb is always in my face," but his accessibility is noted by almost everyone who remembers making an appointment days ahead of time to consult Mr. Shawn. Early on, Gottlieb took down the maze of partitions that separated Shawn's corner sanctum from the rest of the magazine, and no secretary bars his open door.

Many at The New Yorker were surprised—and some, dismayed— that Gottlieb didn't clean the house of its dead weight. His best calculation, by most accounts, was to put significant confidence and responsibility in Deputy Editor McGrath, who had been pointed toward the editor's chair when Gottlieb skated in. The transition was "happier than I could have imagined," says McGrath, who has become a kind of internal ombudsman in the new regime. "It turns out he was telling the truth when he said he had no agenda."

Together, Gottlieb and McGrath have been recruiting new talent. "Shawn made it hard to penetrate this place," says Singer. But free-lancer Susan Orlean, 32, says she wrote McGrath on the strength of a rumor last spring and now, to her persistent amazement, is a Talk of the Town regular. "In the past I was afraid even to knock, and then I knocked once and the door flew open," Orlean says.

Up on the 20th floor, in what were accounting department offices a few months ago, is a nest of mostly newcomers called (ironically, of course) "Critic's Corner." Rafferty, 36, sits in his newly painted and totally bare office, worrying over his next book review. He is, he says, "awed."

For Gottlieb's new wave of young writers, presumably the future mainstays of the magazine, Shawn is a historical figure no more palpable than the Bachrach portrait of founding editor Harold Ross that hangs at the head of a staircase. They are discovering the place and its customs for themselves.

"They don't eat lunch! They don't eat lunch!" exclaims Orlean disbelievingly. "There isn't even a candy machine." There is, however, a station for coffee and distilled water on every floor, one of the glasnost-like innovations of the Gottlieb era. Journalism with a human face.

With all these newcomers around, E.J. Kahn complains, he doesn't recognize half the people whose names are scribbled next to their unsigned Talk pieces on the hallway bulletin board. (It was ever thus. Kahn also recalls that he first met his 18th-floor next-door neighbor, George W.S. Trow, at a party. "It's high time we met each other after five years," Kahn recalls saying, to which Trow crisply replied, "Twenty.")

Gottlieb has purged from the magazine's bank of articles as many as three dozen articles completed and paid for long ago. Kahn says that for the first time in decades he and some of his contemporaries are finding their pieces returned for tightening and rewriting, and professes an unexpected satisfaction about it. "Maybe we got lazy under Shawn, I don't know," he says.

However that may be, Gottlieb is still regarded warily. His directness with writers, a refreshing change from Shawn's painful indirection, has left some with bruised feelings. One writer found Gottlieb's glib reaction to a piece "humiliating." Gottlieb, observes Singer, "takes the view that writers are children who are not be indulged; Shawn thought they were children who ought to be indulged."

Another staffer notes this distinction between editors: Shawn "had a stable of staff writers he stuck with through thick and thin," while Gottlieb is "going after pieces rather than going after writers. He picks up the brightest object he can find."

As for Gottlieb's magazine, there are persistent questions about his editorial intentions. Two key writers of "Notes and Comment" under Shawn—Jonathan Schell and Bill McKibben—have left the magazine (there were few other defections), and their absence is noted in the uneven tone and gravity of those columns.

Schell was the magazine's principal voice against U.S. involvement in the Vietnam war and author of the nuclear-age lament "The Fate of the Earth." He was, in Singer's view, "the conscience of the magazine," whereas today, "I don't see much evidence of its conscience in its pages." A senior editor, conceding as much, notes that it has been "a constant struggle" to find "Comment" writers.

More broadly, New Yorker fact writers (as the reporters are sometimes called) worry about Gottlieb's attitude toward their craft. "Here is a magazine whose central strength since World War II has been journalism," says one vet of fact, "being edited by a man who doesn't care about journalism."

This sounds overly harsh. Though Gottlieb himself often speaks disparagingly of journalists as a species, he has published some exceptional reporters in The New Yorker for the first time—David Rieff on Miami, Jonathan Kozol on the homeless, William Finnegan on South Africa, William Greider on the Federal Reserve, Raymond Bonner on Peru. And the reporters he inherited hardly have been shut out: Caplan on the solicitor general; James Lardner on the Betamax case; Robert Shaplen on the Philippines; Susan Sheehan on New Guinea; and Elizabeth Drew, several times, on politics and government.

(Gottlieb has confounded the expectations of many that he would quickly replace Drew, whose deadpan chronicles inspire fierce allegiance and deep loathing and little in between. It seems unlikely he will make a change in the near future.)

Still, now that the Gottlieb shtick has become more familiar to those around the office, even the things that once were welcomed—his directness, his informality—are analyzed and not fully trusted.

In the bare offices along the yellow corridors of The New Yorker, he is compared to Pinocchio and Svengali and called a "narcissist," a "megalomaniac" and "the guy who can't not talk in the elevator." One writer finds listening to Gottlieb's monologues "like swimming in chocolate pudding."

Some at The New Yorker were startled to find Gottlieb sharing with them his unvarnished views of their colleagues, and of Shawn, suggesting to them at worst a habit of indiscretion and at best an undeserved level of intimacy. But as one who has done business with him remarks, "For Gottlieb, taking you into his confidence is like saying "How are you?""

Such talk, as Gottlieb must understand, comes with the territory he inherited. To pass the time, they used to put Shawn on the couch, too. The old man's eccentricities were at least as pronounced. They were just very different ones, symbolic of an age and sensibility no less than Gottlieb's are today.

"Rather than God being traded for the Devil," goes one knowing line about the transition, "they've traded one set of psychoses for another."

The Years With Gottlieb

But really now. Does any magazine warrant such reverent scrutiny, such fussy devotion, such gnashing of teeth?

After all, magazines come and go. "I remember the old Saturday Evening Post, Collier's, Look, the old Life," says Kahn, nursing a vodka martini across the street at the Harvard Club after work. "I don't know that we're imperishable."

Yet for reasons not quite knowable, The New Yorker's readers feel a special relationship to the magazine, a mixture of habit, of membership, of kinship, even of personal obligation. And what they say is telling.

Upstairs in her cubicle at The New Yorker, Mimi Kramer fishes a letter from a filing cabinet. In it, after attacking her review of Joseph Papp's production of "Henry IV, Part 1" for its "rudeness" and "mean-spirited trashing of the production," a reader urges The New Yorker to treat the "fragile institution" of the city's theater "with solicitude and respect, especially when it errs."

Stapled to the letter is Gottlieb's reply. It defends the review on its merits, and then takes the offense: "Do you really believe that the role of the critic is to be polite?...What's inexcusable isn't rudeness but lack of caring, blandness and empty urbanity...The theater is fragile; what's going to help it is the truth, not respectful solicitude."

Downstairs, Gottlieb himself strides into the hall with something to show off, the poignant burden of his office. It's a short note from a subscriber, written in a shaky hand: a halting note of regret.

She has taken The New Yorker for 56 years. It was "the first Valentine my husband gave me," she writes. "I'm 85 and blind. It grieves me to give it up. I had my nurse read it. I'm so sorry. I'll miss it so."

To keep such readers and such standards in a world that beckons compromise, and to celebrate its 75th anniversary at the turn of the century, who knows what Faustian bargains The New Yorker may have to strike?

Whittle in the Waiting Room

Eleanor Randolph, March 1988

You have to go to the doctor, and you're trying to find a bright side. Oh, sure, it could hurt, it could be serious and you can be certain it will cost a lot of money. But there are always the magazines.

Any doctor's office has a treasury of well-worn and well-read publications—a vintage New Yorker, an old People that features Elizabeth Taylor before she was young, a Reader's Digest dated the year you graduated from high school. How many conversations started when somebody says, "You know, I was reading last year's U.S. News & World Report in the doctor's office last week and..."

If Whittle Communications, Inc., has its way, you can put this waiting-room scene in a time capsule. Whittle is proposing that, instead of the homey disarray of familiar magazines in doctors' offices, there should be a nice wooden rack and neat display of six new magazines called Special Reports on "Health," "Family," "Sports," "Personalities," "Fiction" and "Living."

More important to Whittle is that with the innovative "Whittle Family System," the physician must agree to subscribe to only two additional magazines from other companies.

The reason is that Christopher Whittle is trying to sell "exclusivity" to advertisers for his target of 15,000 doctors' offices in 125 major markets. One toothpaste ad, one food company, one furrier— you get the picture, an advertiser's dream.

"It sounds like we're compelling the doctor not to take any other magazines," said company chairman Whittle in a recent telephone interview. "We can't do that. We're offering a new type of waiting-room system instead of the one he has.

"It's not a lot different than Pepsi saying to Burger King, if you want us to come in, we'll be the soft drink here," Whittle said.

Advertisers would pay $1.2 million for a page in each of the quarterly issues or 24 ad pages a year. Doctors, who already spend several hundred dollars a year on magazine subscriptions, would pay Whittle anything from zero to $200, presumably depending on what kind of deal a doctor could cut with the Whittle representative.

Whittle was chairman of Esquire magazine from 1979 to 1986 and has run an empire specializing in what he calls "wall magazines"—the rack of health literature already in some doctors' offices. For his new project, Whittle says he has commitments for "an unprecedented" $37 million in advertising next year but refuses to say how many doctors have signed up.

The rest of the magazine industry has almost had a coronary over the Whittle plan. Some magazine publishers are considering taking Whittle to court. Some are going to doctors, who help keep a lot of magazines financially healthy, and promising new and better deals for their own publications.

Others, such as Rodale Press, are writing advertisers and doctors asking for mercy. Rodale, which was in the process of launching a new children's magazine, said in a letter that Whipple's incursion is an "alarming" situation and warned advertisers that they risk "injury with the public, your advertising agencies, the publishing community and physicians, alike, as a battle brews in waiting rooms nationwide."

Responding to all the fuss from Newsweek and others considering legal action, Whittle says, "They'll get nowhere, and they know it.

"We surveyed doctors' offices, and it's a mess out there. It's difficult for doctors to keep up with the magazines. They're lost. People take them home."

So his company devised a system that has been test-marketed in 1,000 physicians' offices, he said. It plans to introduce the new magazine package in September at selected offices—those of pediatricians, obstetrician-gynecologists and family practitioners. The reason: These are the three kinds of doctors' waiting rooms where Mom spends a lot of time. That is the same Mom who spends most of the family money.

What the magazine people should be protesting is not whether Whittle has a right to do this but whether the reader in the waiting room has a right to something better. Whittle's new magazines sound like instant jello, hospital food for the mind.

Instead of publications created through the tension of writers and editors agonizing over facts and trends and ideas, these Whittle substitutes are marketing tools. They are Whittle's mannequins, over which advertisers will slip their expensive sandwich boards.

Think about the magazines you receive from your insurance company, the one from the real-estate people, the specialized airline magazine that is really a company brochure. Writers for those magazines sit at their computers and spin out just enough verbal filigree to cover the ads.

Spare us more of this mind-pap. Going to the doctor is tough enough already.

Phillip Morris Tells All

Eleanor Randolph, July 1988

Quick. Name the three magazines with the largest circulations in America.

TV Guide is first, of course, with 17.2 million.

Second, with 15.9 million, is Modern Maturity, which comes with membership in the American Association of Retired Persons.

And third, with 11.2 million, is Philip Morris Magazine.

Philip Morris? Haven't seen it on the newsstands, you may say. Didn't get a notice about it from Ed McMahon.

No, Philip Morris Magaziner or PMM, is a specialty magazine that goes free to people who like Philip Morris products such as Merit, Virginia Slims, Marlboro, Benson & Hedges, Players and English Ovals, to name a few.

At PMM, there is no snooty editor who refuses to show glamorous people smoking cigarettes on their sailboat without inserting a small photo of an iron lung on the bow. Not only does this magazine take cigarette advertising, most of it is cigarette advertising.

To borrow from A.J. Liebling, Philip Morris executives wanted to enjoy America's oft-proclaimed freedom of the press, so they went out and bought one.

Philip Morris took its consumer data base, including addresses collected from' people who had written in for belt buckles and T-shirts and cigarette lighters, and bought other lists provided by merchants who hold raffles and don't know what to do with the names of the 5,000 people who didn't win a new Bronco, for example. Then they commissioned a company in New York to produce an advertising magazine, or "admag," just for them.

The smokers' admag has been in the news recently because its readers filled out a survey about their life-styles, including how many cars they own and how often eat at restaurants.

The results of this survey—which the Roper Organization processed but also acknowledged is a little short on science, even for a poll—are the basis for a new Philip Morris advertising campaign. The thrust of the $5 million effort is that smokers are not always scrounging around to find change for a dollar. They also have folding money—a lot of it.

"$1 trillion is too much financial power to ignore," the ad says. Or, as Philip Morris Magazine Publisher Guy L. Smith put it, "The smoker is both a political and economic force who has largely gone unrecognized by politicians and industry leaders."

After the Los Angeles Times wrote an article about this financial force, one person complained in a letter to the editor that the story failed to mention "a few other areas where smokers are contributing to the economy: doctor bills, hospital expenses, chemotherapy, radiation, cemetery plots, undertakers and other funeral expenses."

The magazine itself is the best that Philip Morris could buy; it is slick and bright and upbeat, as cool as menthol cigarettes would be if you could filter out the tobacco. The spring issue provides help for smokers stumped by such rude questions as: "How can you be a vegetarian and also smoke?"

The offered response: "I don't know of any animals that died to make these things."

In a recent issue, there is an exclusive interview with former President Gerald R. Ford. It includes such startling revelations as the fact that, "The first thing you notice about Gerald Ford up close is how much he looks like his pictures." Also, he has "no regrets" about his time in the White House. He and his wife enjoy just staying home and watching "Cosby" or "Golden Girls." But they don't get to do that very often because they are very busy.

Just one hot scoop after another, and it doesn't make sense until you realize that, tucked in the copy, is the entire reason for running the article—a picture of Ford "during a break in the East Room of the White House," where he is smoking a pipe.

A little bit of Charles Kuralt's work appears in virtually every issue of this quarterly. Kuralt, a smoker, has told associates at CBS that be is bewildered by his popularity at the editorial offices of PMM. He authorized PMM's use of one or two articles some time ago; suddenly, he's a regular contributor.

The summer issue, which also has a piece by Kuralt, features jogging and canoeing and depicts lean, healthy-looking people who probably feel about cigarettes the way Phyllis Schlafly feels about crack. There is a personality profile that ponders how a 101-year-old woman managed to last so long. She "took the occasional drink and smoked for many years," the story says. Her favorite brand of tobacco was Bull Durham roll-your-own, produced for over a century by the American Tobacco Co.

In this country, Philip Morris is free to print and distribute its views just like the rest of us. Its public-relations problem, however, is hidden in the fine print at the bottom of PMM's masthead. It says the magazine's "material is provided for the reader's information and enjoyment only. Philip Morris USA does not endorse or assume liability for its contents."

Nice try, folks.

CHAPTER THREE

NEWSPAPERS

The Daily Creation

Richard Harwood, January 1989

A metropolitan newspaper is a large, complex and (except for a gaggle of newsroom celebrities) a relatively invisible industrial enterprise. At The Washington Post, roughly 11,000 people are involved in the production and distribution of the newspaper each day, enough bodies to fill all the billets in an Army light infantry division. Their anonymity as a labor force is assured; most of them work while the rest of us sleep.

During the hours of darkness in 1988, they printed and delivered to the homes of subscribers more than 230 million newspapers and delivered other millions to newsstands, drug stores, hotels, supermarkets, convenience stores and 5,000 coin-operated racks at street corners, metro stops, train and bus stations, diners and fast food eateries.

Writers and editors see themselves at the center of the newspaper universe, knowing that on any given day an erroneous or disagreeable headline, story or editorial may ruffle a few feathers, including imperial feathers from time to time. But that is a triviality compared to the consequences of a mass distribution failure; that would cause a consumer earthquake.

There was no such catastrophe in 1988 but still The Post received in the normal course of business more than a half-million complaints about delivery service, billing disputes, vacation stops and starts and so on. That's a big number, but given the several hundred million transactions between distributors and readers each year, it indicates a reasonable level of consumer satisfaction.

After 40 years in this business, the daily creation of the newspaper still amazes me because the potential for news, editorial, production and distribution breakdowns and errors is so great. At 10:30 p.m. each night buttons in three separate factories (two in the District and one in Virginia) are pushed, bells ring and 13 huge presses, each of them from 50 to 60 feet long and four stories in height, begin rolling. They are fed by 1,800 pound reels of newsprint that must be "webbed" or threaded though 10 to 30 rollers and "angle bars".

At top speed a press can average up to 20,000 papers an hour, consuming on a typical weekday night nearly 75 tons of newsprint. But there is constant danger of a "web break" requiring a rethreading of the roll through the press. A simple break shuts down a press for 15 to 20 minutes; a bad break, called a "home run", will shut it down for up to an hour and a half. This could mean late deliveries for thousands of customers.

The paper's first edition is called the "cap" or "capitol." It's a small run (completed in about 30 minutes) of 75,000 to 100,000 papers which are destined for the most distant towns and rural routes in The Post's 16,000 square mile distribution zone. Some papers are trucked up to 270 miles; 35 go to Chicago, 5,000 to Manhattan. They must be off the loading docks not much later than 11 p.m.

The crews take a 30-minute dinner break after the fast "cap" run. The presses are replated with the latest news and start up again at 12:30 p.m. to produce the "late city" edition. Over the next three to three and one-half hours, more than 700,000 newspapers will come off the presses, including about 250,000 for the "final" edition. With luck the job is done by 3:30 a.m. and with luck 800,000 daily papers and more than 1 million on Sunday get to the right places in time for home delivery by 6:30 a.m. through rain, snow and dark of night.

Equipment breakdowns and bad weather can throw off the schedules. There are always problems with a carrier force of 7,000 youngsters and adults; on any given day carriers are missing on 700 to 800 routes which must then be covered by the agents who hire them. Sixty per cent of the routes are serviced by boys and girls—our "little merchants". But they deliver only about 40 per cent of the papers and have become difficult to recruit; it takes character to roll out of bed at 4:30 or 5 a.m. to haul around 7-pound Sunday newspapers in a snow storm.

All things considered, the home-delivered American newspaper at 20 cents a weekday copy is, almost literally, a giveaway. Without advertising, a Sunday copy of The Post would cost you about $7.25. But if you're unhappy with the price or the service, don't call, write or mailgram me. I do windows. I don't do circulation—ever.

The Newspaper Industry Gets a Taste of Bad News

Paul Farhi, August 1988

When they traveled to Atlanta last month to cover the Democratic National Convention, reporters and editors from The Los Angeles Times flew first class. They went home in the coach section.

In between, word had come down from publisher Tom Johnson that the brakes were being applied to the Times' gravy train. First-class travel, among the perks at journalism's cushiest operation, was out unless there was a good reason for it. Not only that, but the paper was instituting a hiring freeze, shrinking the space it devotes to news, and lopping 20 percent from expense account budgets.

While the cutbacks hardly amount to an austerity program, they do say much about the mood of the Times, and about times in the newspaper business in general.

Johnson says his paper, which carries more advertising than any in the country, has suffered a "serious decline" in profits since last year. Other newspapers aren't exactly crowing, either. After years of reaping big gains in revenue and earnings, newspapers—historically among the nation's most profitable businesses—have hit a plateau. The amount of advertising in newspapers, their primary source of revenue, is down or flat throughout the industry. Costs, especially for newsprint, are up significantly. Hiring freezes and budget squeezes appear to be the norm.

To some observers, the industry's blahs raise larger questions about the overall health of the nation's economy. Businesses, after all, pile on the advertising when their customers are in a mood to spend, and cut back in tough times. By this reasoning, it follows that if newspapers are slowing down, a recession might not be far behind.

"Newspapers have a sub-par year every year before the economy turns down," said John Morton, a Washington newspaper industry analyst. "Everyone is telling us the economy is going along favorably, but some segments (of newspaper advertising) and consumer spending are very soft. This suggests to me the economy is not as ebullient as suggested."

Most experts had expected 1988 to be a good year for newspapers, given the economy's unrelenting expansion and the prospect of a pick-me-up from olympics and election-year promotions.

Instead, Bob Coen, who forecasts media expenditures for the McCann Erickson ad agency in New York, said he has cut his newspaper advertising projections from a 1 to 2 percent increase to a decline of 1 to 2 percent. Similarly, the Newspaper Advertising Bureau last week scaled back on its advertising projections. A spokesman said the general economy wasn't sufficiently strong to sustain the original prediction.

Others, however, say softness in the general economy is less to blame than a series of isolated factors.

For example, the consolidation among retailers—usually the single largest advertisers in newspapers—seems to have had a harmful impact. In the past two years, May Department Stores, Campeau Corp. and Macy's have each made multibillion-dollar acquisitions of other department store chains, and two of the largest supermarket companies—Safeway Stores Inc. and Lucky Stores—were involved in buyouts.

The debt taken on by these retailers to complete the buyouts has made big advertisers more cost-conscious than ever, newspaper executives say. And in some markets, like Los Angeles, the mergers have placed former competitors under the same corporate umbrella, thus reducing their need to advertise. In fact, department store advertising was off 13 percent in the first quarter, according to the Newspaper Advertising Bureau.

The Oct. 19 stock market crash, meanwhile, has meant a different set of worries for publishers. A pullback by mutual fund companies and investment houses has cut into financial-services advertising, which typically accounts for about 3 percent of the advertising in a local paper.

The Wall Street slump has been most painful to the three national newspapers. Advertising is off 10.2 percent in The Wall Street Journal and down 3.6 percent at The New York Times, which reported an 11 percent decline in profit for the first-half of the year. Through June, USA Today has lost 4 percent of its total ad pages, and the paper is losing money again after a brief brush with profitability in the fourth quarter of 1987.

"I don't know whether we can come back in the range we'd like in the second half," said John Curley, chief executive of Rosslyn, Va.-based Gannett Co., which publishes USA Today and 90 other newspapers around the country. "It's like betting on horses, which I don't do."

Then there is the miniskirt theory. The fashion industry bet heavily on the mini; when it proved to be a so-so seller, retailers saw no reason to continue hyping it, said James Dunaway, a vice president at the NAB.

Similarly, he said, there wasn't another hot new consumer electronics product such as VCRs or CD players to stimulate advertising. The general merchandise and apparel advertising categories are off 16 percent this year.

The slowdown has caused at least a little concern in newsrooms around the country. While the damage is limited now, some editors naturally worry that the next round of cuts will directly affect their ability to cover the news in a year of such major stories as the election and the Olympics.

By one measure, those fears seem unjustified so far: The press contingent at the Democratic National Convention in Atlanta last month included about 1,000 more people than did the 1984 convention held in San Francisco, even though the broadcast networks cut back substantially since then.

But cost-consciousness is evident in the news pages in more subtle ways. The Chicago Tribune had budgeted an increase in the amount of space it devotes to news and photographs at the beginning of the year. But when the industry was hit with its second newsprint price hike in a year last January, "we had to eat the page increase," said the Tribune's editor, James D. Squires. Meanwhile, papers like the New York Daily News and others are using lighter newsprint, which allows them to conserve paper.

Newsprint is no trifling expense: at big-city dailies it can account for as much as 40 percent of all expenses. And since last year industry newsprint costs are up about 15 percent, according to Morton.

The industry's doldrums have not escaped the attention of Wall Street, where newspaper stocks have been among the best performers for years.

Almost all of the newspaper-dominated stocks crashed along with the rest of the market on Oct. 19. But recovery has been slow. Several of the major companies—Gannett, Knight-Ridder, The Washington Post Co., and Tribune Co.—have barely kept up with the 23 percent rise in the Dow Jones industrial average since the clash.

Investors don't seem to be impressed with the companies' earnings, which in many cases have been boosted not by increases in operating profitability but by lower corporate tax rates under the tax reform act of 1986.

Even so, J. Kendrick Noble, Paine Webber's media-stock analyst, said he is bullish on the near term. He contends that another newsprint price hike this year is not likely, and that ad volume should pick up slightly as personal consumption turns up.

Noble is among those who see no ominous signals about the broader economy in the newspaper industry's recent doldrums. The economy looks stronger than newspapers themselves, he said, because much of the growth in gross national product this year has been driven by a boom in American exports—a sector that is meaningless to the health of newspapers since it doesn't boost local advertising.

Of more importance to the industry—and perhaps a gauge of the economy's immediate future—is that the amount of classified advertising remains strong, up about 4.5 percent over last year, Noble said.

In essence, rising classified ad volumes indicate a growing economy because it shows that companies are competing for a shrinking number of workers by advertising for them in the help-wanted section. When unemployment is high, however, companies don't need to solicit workers in the classifieds.

"Historically," said Noble, "classified advertising has never gone down except when the economy is entering a recession. I think it's going to remain strong for the foreseeable future because of the declining number of young people" and the shortage of entry-level labor.

If only publishers like the Los Angeles Times' Johnson were so bullish. Johnson hedges on his predictions as he looks forward to the second half of the year. "I'm hopeful things will turn around here, but I'm not confident."

For the moment at least, newspapers have become part of the bad news they report.

Journalism's 'Underclass'

Richard Harwood, May 1989

Allen H. Neuharth last year was paid $1,500,000 in "cash compensation" as chairman of the Gannett newspaper company. His heir and second in command, John J. Curley, was paid $1,225,000.

The emoluments of their counterparts in the business were somewhat more modest—$937,228 to Arthur Ochs Sulzberger at The New York Times, $653,414 to Katharine Graham at The Washington Post, $921,597 to Stanton Cook at the Chicago Tribune Co., $866,200 to Alvah Chapman and $743,333 to James K. Batten at Knight-Ridder, $1,200,000 to Robert Eburu and $760,000 to David Laventhol at the Times-Mirror Co., $740,000 to Warren Phillips and $560,000 to Ray Shaw at Dow Jones, publisher of The Wall Street Journal.

The "cash compensation" of these executives is an inadequate measure of the wealth and rewards offered by newspaper corporations in this "era of greed," if I may borrow a phrase from the editorial pages. When Mr. Neuharth retired in March at the age of 65, he was recorded as the beneficial owner of 480,405 shares of Gannett stock currently valued at about $20,650,000. His annual pension of $700,000 or so will be supplemented for the rest of his life by deferred salary payments of $199,992 annually. In addition he has a lifetime employment contract with Gannett that will pay him $200,000 annually for the first five years and $100,000 annually thereafter, and will provide him "with benefits, facilities, services and perquisites appropriate to the services and activities he is performing for Gannett." In sum, his income from Gannett (exclusive of stock dividends) will be $1 million a year as long as he lives.

Although the numbers may differ from company to company, these economic rewards are not untypical of the news industry we have come to know and love in the past quarter century. Of nine leading publishing companies among the Fortune 500, profits in 1988 as a percent of equity (assets minus liabilities) ranged from 11 percent at E. W. Scripps to 31 percent at The Washington Post.

To some extent, the wealth has spread beyond the executive suites. The stars of television news and leading newspaper columnists, for example, have blossomed as cottage industries and great generators of wealth; no publisher or corporate CEO has yet to match Dan Rather's 10-year contract for $36 million. Those laboring in the vineyards of our metropolitan papers must often struggle to make ends meet in a world marked by inflation and their own rising expectations. But even there, the news prosperity of the '80s has had an impact. A neophyte reporter at The New York Times gets $1,000 a week after only two years' experience.

For all its affluence in this decade, the news business, like society at large, maintains within its ranks a sizable underclass. The median beginning salary of an American newspaper reporter in 1988 was $16,704; the entry-level salary for a secretary is $17,600. Some reporters, because of a surplus of applicants, are taking jobs for as little as $4 an hour. Experienced reporters in 1988 enjoyed a median wage of $20,545. Two and a half years ago, a major study of the comparative pay of men and women in journalism found that the median salary of the chief editors of America's newspapers was $29,000; for chief editors who are women, the median was $20,800.

Roughly 85 percent of the 1,645 newspapers in the United States have circulations of less than 50,000, and it is on these smaller newspapers that the journalistic "underclass," as I have termed it, is commonly found. They pay low wages, one might assume, because they are relatively impoverished enterprises. The assumption is wrong. All but a handful of these smaller newspapers are owned by "groups" or chains that commonly seek and achieve profits of 30 to 35 cents on every dollar of revenue. One chain owner, Ralph Ingersoll Jr., has claimed that he can raise his profit margins to 38 cents on the dollar. These bloated margins, to a large extent, come out of the hides and labor of the "underclass" of small-town journalism and at the expense of millions of American readers who are poorly served by shoestring news budgets. It is small wonder that barely 10 percent of American journalism school graduates choose newspaper work as a career; it's quite nice at the top, and it is often the pits at the bottom.

Extra! Extra! Who Cares?

Eleanor Randolph, April 1990

Item: The first fax newspaper war began this February in Minnesota. The St. Paul Pioneer Press started sending out a daily news digest called NewsFAX. Across the river in Minneapolis, the Star Tribune started a similar digest called Executive FAX. "We've got to experiment with other ways of delivering information than dropping dead trees on peoples' porches," explains Larry Werner, business editor of the Star-Tribune.

Item: Executives of Hearst newspapers called a meeting in Houston recently to talk about why reasonably intelligent people weren't reading the paper. At one session, an advertising director confessed that she doesn't read the paper she works for and mostly doesn't miss it. "People were stunned; it was a very telling, incredible moment," said Lawrence S. Kramer, executive editor of the San Francisco Examiner.

Item: Virtually every newspaper company has someone assigned to find out where the readers are going. The newspaper industry as a whole has sponsored at least six major groups to study their future and come up with new ideas. New Directions for News, a think-tank at the University of Missouri, has held a series of brainstorming sessions in the last two years which have produced suggestions ranging from a news-digest that wraps around the paper to a newspaper that smells like baked bread.

As more than 600 editors and educators arrive in Washington this week for the American Society of Newspaper Editors convention, one topic that has absorbed many news executives increasingly in recent years is barely on the agenda. The issue: Do newspapers have a future? And if they do, will they be a mass medium that does more than serve a wealthy segment of the public? Will future editors use their time and space to educate? Will they cover the unpopular issues? Will the hometown paper be the community watchdog? Research on who reads newspapers—and who doesn't—is widely referred to now in the journalism trade as "the gloom and doom" numbers. These data show that newspaper circulation has declined since World War II in relation to the number of households that could subscribe. Population is up; newspaper circulation is flat.

"More and more, people don't need newspapers. Intelligent individuals can lead productive lives and be informed and never read a newspaper," laments Robert Cochnar, editor of the Alameda Newspaper Group in Hayward, Calif. "And it gags me to say that."

For newspapers, many of which have reaped huge profits over the last decade, the death of newspapering is not tomorrow's headlines. Many newspapers have also continued to increase their circulation and enjoyed healthy profits.

"I don't see any point in shutting down now and saying it's too hard. It's still a wonderful way to impart information and to get information," said Benjamin Bradlee, executive editor of The Washington Post. "If we could lick the ink problem, we could do very well," he added, referring to the common complaint by readers that newspapers leave their fingers grimy.

Newspapers still get the biggest slice of the nation's advertising budget, according to data from McCann Erickson, with 26.4 percent going to newspapers, 21.8 to television, 17.9 for advertising mailed directly to the home or business, 6.6 to radio and 5.1 to magazines. The remainder goes to weeklies, yellow pages and other media.

But the news industry as a whole seems to have decided that the warning bell has tolled, and it's time to react before it's too late.

"We aren't dying, but I think we have to change," said Susan Miller, director of editorial development for the Scripps Howard newspaper chain. Miller said she recently told executives that for the year 2000, "we have to stop worrying about whether it will be a fax newspaper or computers. If we get the topics right...then we'll survive. If we get the topics wrong, nobody's going to want us in any form."

Daily newspaper circulation has stayed about the same in the last 20 years: 62,108,000 in 1970 and 62,695,000 in 1988. Between 1970 and 1988, the number of daily papers sold grew by less than 1 percent, while the number of Sunday papers sold increased 25 percent. In the same period, the number of adults in the United States grew by 36 percent and the number of households went up by 44 percent, according to the Newspaper Advertising Bureau, which provides data for newspaper advertisers. For many editors, it is the younger non-readers who create the most concern in this industry. As Albert Gollin, vice president of the Newspaper Advertising Bureau, put it recently: "With each generation, the habit of regular readership has weakened." In 1970, surveys showed that 73 percent of the 18-to-24 set read a newspaper on an average weekday. In 1989, that figure was down to 57 percent.

A visit to John F. Kennedy High School in Wheaton gives clues about what is happening to teenagers. When 17-year-old Goret Smith was asked whether she reads a newspaper even occasionally, she shook her head and explained her reason: "It's boring."

Some news executives have suggested that the increase in illiteracy in this country may explain some of the problem facing newspapers. Some estimates suggest that by the end of the decade there will be 90 million adults who either can't read English or read it so poorly they cannot function in our society.

But teenagers interviewed recently can and do read. They simply don't always choose to read newspapers. "I don't really have time," says Delilah Szegedi, age 15, who looks at the paper when it's required for school. "If I read anything it'll be a magazine." Most recently she read Seventeen magazine, she explained, "to find a prom dress."

"I look at the sports pages and glance at the front page," says Craig Simmons, a 17-year-old senior who reads Sports Illustrated and Car & Driver.

The data from newspapers show that these students are not unusual. Young people have not stopped reading entirely, and those whose parents are avid newspaper readers will probably pick up the habit. But fewer are starting out reading even the comics. Newspapers used to take comfort in the thought that young people would get interested once they really grew up—the old cliche that newspapers would go out of business if nobody turned 30. Today, even the 30-year-olds aren't as addicted as they once were.

"I think we have to work at it and have to stop putting out newspapers for 54-year-old editors like myself," said Gregory Fauve, executive editor of the Sacramento Bee. "I remember an old guy told me once, "Keep a foot in both generations and you'll make it in this business." Those editors who don't do that aren't going to succeed."

Fauve said that after news industry research showed young people were falling away from newspapers, the Bee created a new entertainment section called "Ticket" for young people and another called "Scene" for young people with families.

"Ticket" features such items as a list of places where you can eat out for less than $10. The reviewer includes an item on the restaurant with the best video games.

"Scene" analyzes Dr. Seuss or gives advice on how to keep the kids calm when they're visiting relatives: "Their favorite TV shows can help calm them down," one headline suggests.

"This doesn't mean that you diminish the investigative reporting or political reporting," Fauve added. "You have to care about trying to create readers among our young people and be willing to do things that are different. I'm not talking about turning into USA Today...or Rupert Murdoch kind of journalism either."

The Syracuse (N.Y.) Herald-Journal has begun pursuing the young even more avidly. Its youth pages include articles and cartoons that address kids as: "Hey, you. Yea, you." or "You knuckleheads" or even "Yo, buttheads."

"Our thinking right now is that fewer teenagers are reading newspapers, which means when they are 30-35 they won't be reading newspapers and our circulation will simply go down," said Herald-Journal youth editor Larry Richardson. "We decided we would give them things that they wanted to read, not only things we think they should read."

Richardson's youth page and "hj" section have piqued the curiosity of other newspaper editors. The section, which focuses on news about young people, is scheduled to become a regular weekly feature this Thursday. Richardson said that to date he has been asked to send examples of their efforts to over 100 other newspapers. Like other industries in the last decade of the 20th century, newspapers now face customers whose lives have changed drastically. They watch television. Many of them have computers. They listen to the radio during longer and longer commutes to work.

One of the most important changes for newspapers, however, has been in the lives of young women—the people who most often do the shopping in a household. Decades ago, the mother of two stayed home, had plenty of time to read the newspaper, clipped the ads and went to the store. She was an easy and direct target for advertisers.

"We are fascinated by the decline in readership among women. It is far more pronounced than among men," said Lou Heldman, who is studying the "baby boomers" aged 25 to 46 for the Knight-Ridder newspaper chain. "The number of baby-boomer women now in the workforce is between 70 and 80 percent. Sometime in the '90s it's supposed to reach 80 percent."

In readership surveys, these young people, especially the working parents, almost always talk about the lack of time available to read the newspaper. Other surveys also show these same people want some stories—like movie reviews or trend articles—in depth. The trick will be for editors to figure out how to provide both depth and a quick read.

"People today treat time like a commodity, an investment," pollster Anthony Casale said in the "Survival Guide to the Year 2000" put out by the Associated Press Managing Editors Association. "When they walk away from a newspaper, this means they aren't getting enough return on their investment."

The same survival guide noted that on big breaking stories, more people are beginning to be satisfied with the information they get from television news. In 1982, 30 percent of those surveyed got enough details on a big story from television. In 1987, that figure leapt to 42 percent.

Neil Postman, a professor of communications at New York University, told the managing editors that in the future "we're not going to go to the newspaper to get reports of events. Other media handle that. We go to the newspaper for meaning, for a narrative."

Also, he says, for a sense of community. Already one key newsman agrees. James K. Batten, chief executive-officer of Knight-Ridder, Inc., said recently that Knight-Ridder did "the most ambitious readership study in the history of our company" last fall and found that people with a real sense of connection to their community "are almost twice as likely to be regular readers of our newspapers."

Talking about newspapers that are "disconnected" with their communities, Batten described "newsrooms (that) often are over-stocked with journalistic transients...Their eyes are on the next and bigger town, the next rung up the ladder...There is always the temptation to make their byline files a little more glittering at the expense of people and institutions they will never see again."

"Out of our manic concern about being compromised, we sometimes piously keep the community at arm's length, determined not to be in anybody's pocket," Batten said. "So we come off as distant, unfeeling, better at criticizing than celebrating, better at attacking than healing."

Such talk makes other newsmen and women nervous, especially when it sounds like asking readers what they want for news. For these journalists, newspapers designed by readership polls are on a par with politicians who fabricate their persona and policies on the basis of voter polls.

"I think the notion of giving people what they want in order to have an ever-expanding market of consumers in order to capitalize your profit—well, I don't believe that's the reason the press is protected in the Constitution," said Bill Kovach, curator of the Nieman Foundation at Harvard University. "At some point managers of the press have to remember that there is a responsibility attached to the protection we have. Constantly thinking in commercial terms is ignoring that responsibility."

Kovach said that most people don't have a distinct idea of what news is available to them as choices. And he now believes that the stagnant circulation can be attributed "to the fact that news organizations are trying harder to match each other in catering to the same taste. As a result they're becoming irrelevant...The more they devote to entertainment, the easier it is to pass the newspaper up."

With such bleak talk, the question for many newspapers becomes not whether to change, but how. A recent report from the Newspaper Advertising Bureau in New York City noted that newspapers have been around for 200 years and that every product has a beginning, middle and end phase. "The newspaper enjoyed a long, rich life cycle. How long can it continue?"

Neuharth Lays off the Big Boys

Eleanor Randolph, June 1988

Al Neuharth is the creative egomaniac who founded USA Today and oversees the largest newspaper chain (Gannett) in the country. He is famous. He is rich. And about once a month, after some new stunt, many journalists can be heard exclaiming that Al Neuharth ought to be ashamed of himself.

Last week, it became clear that Al Neuharth is not ashamed of himself. In fact, it became clear that he is shameless.

When Neuharth started USA Today 5 1-2 years ago, most people in the news business snickered at a newspaper that is a headline news service, a smart-looking weather map, a good sports section and a design that looked as if it came out of a third-grade art project.

When Neuharth took a bus around the country last year to interview everyone from governors to waitresses, then called it the "BusCapade," and promoted it in his paper like a major national news story, many journalists hooted at articles that read like letters from camp.

When BusCapade became JetCapade—a junket reminiscent of Col. Robert R. McCormick's global tours decades ago as owner of the Chicago Tribune—the journalism establishment tittered. He called his staff of two dozen companions, including bodyguard, doctor, researchers and writers, the JetCateers. In print, yet.

Yuk, yuk, what a huckster, we said. Tee, hee, this guy is to newspapers what P.T. Barnum was to traveling road shows.

After last week, the news community isn't laughing anymore.

At a speech before the National Press Club here June 2, Neuharth criticized the U.S. media for being too tough on some of the world's toughest leaders. These guys at the top of repressive governments in Chile, Cuba, South Africa, for example, weren't getting a fair shake, he said. They complained, Neuharth said, that the new Ugly American is the "arrogant Nikon-carrying reporter from a big U.S. newspaper."

It's time to end the "journalism of despair," he said, and turn instead to "the journalism of hope." It's time to be "informational instead of confrontational."

On the surface, it sounds terrific. Let these guys have a say. Let these guys tell their stories. Seems fair, doesn't it?

Take another look.

First, when Neuharth was asked about the cost of his JetCateering, he said it was "substantial" but worthwhile because his global tour had two purposes. Not only was he meeting with world leaders as a journalist, he said, but he was also marketing USA Today worldwide. Nobody suspects that even Neuharth would do anything as crude as writing nice stories about people who have control over distribution of his newspaper.

But in Singapore, Prime Minister Lee Kuan Yew has been limiting or banning publications that don't suit his view of the world—the Asian Wall Street Journal and Time magazine, to name two. Neuharth, who interviewed Lee about the U.S. media, gave the leader a good run in USA Today. Under the headline "Don't judge us by your standards," Lee warned the U.S. media that, "The more you try to judge others by your standards, the more you show total disregard for their own circumstances."

And maybe this is unrelated but, in Singapore, Neuharth also sells 1,500 copies of USA Today and hasn't had any problems with the government. USA Today also is printed and distributed from Singapore to readers throughout the Far East.

A far more serious problem is Neuharth's strategy of not offending world leaders like South African leader P.W. Botha.

"I don't believe that the vast majority of copy that comes out of South Africa ought to deal with Bishop (Desmond) Tutu, who is not an elected official; who is a religious leader of a small minority religious group in that country, when there are elected representatives in that country, whether you like them or not," Neuharth lectured his peers.

Back to basics, Al. Botha was elected to head a government that does not allow blacks to vote. Blacks who talk to the press there have a way of being silenced. The gentlest forms are house arrest or banishment. There are other ways that are worse.

So journalists talk to Tutu, a black Anglican who speaks eloquently for blacks not allowed by Botha's government to speak for themselves. There are almost four times as many blacks than whites in South Africa. So, it's Botha who represents the minority.

After Neuharth's speech, journalists wondered aloud what would have happened if JetCat Al had conducted his "nonconfrontational" interview with Joseph Stalin? Or Idi Amin? Or Attila the Hun? Would it be bad manners to ask about the gulag? Idi, could you tell the JetCateers about your hobbies? Mr. Hun, what's your version of all those European villagers tilling their fields and how they got in the way of your plundering hordes?

Neuharth said that unless the media stops trying to offend these world leaders, they will oust us and ban our newspapers. Well, maybe not all of us and maybe not all of our newspapers.

If Neuharth has his way, they will always have time for him and space on their newsstands for USA Today.

New St. Louis Paper Off and Running

Eleanor Randolph, October 1989

Now that the hype is over and most of the television crews are gone, suburban newspaper baron Ralph Ingersoll II has begun the tough job of turning his three-week-old St. Louis Sun into a new daily newspaper that doesn't eat money.

History is against Ingersoll, 43, chairman of Ingersoll Publications Co., which owns more than 42 dailies and 200 weekly or semiweekly newspapers, including 43 free papers around St. Louis.

For the past four decades, starting a new metropolitan daily was considered a quick way to lose a fortune. Ingersoll's famous father, the late Ralph M. Ingersoll, who helped run Time and the New Yorker, started PM newspaper in June 1940. The experimental newspaper that has sometimes been called the precursor of the modern tabloid lasted less than a decade.

But on Sept. 25 the younger Ingersoll's $21 million experiment broke into the St. Louis market, and home delivery is already more than 64,000, Sun executives said last week. Publisher Thomas M. Tallarico boasted that sales are "in excess of 100,000" every day—a figure that Ingersoll had given out as the magic number he needs to succeed in his adventure. "We're going to make money in our first full year," said Sun President Robert M. Jelenic.

The enthusiasm from the new team—two of its members have experience with the Toronto Sun—cools somewhat beyond the clean, hushed offices of the St. Louis Sun (no relation to the Canadian paper).

The St. Louis Sun has been widely trumpeted as a futuristic newspaper that would lead the gray old establishment papers to new young readers. Ingersoll's scrubbed new staff and its shiny new equipment are still working out the kinks in front of the world. The question is whether St. Louis will be patient.

Advertised as a bright colorful tabloid, the Sun had early problems with wire service photos that looked like bad Polaroid shots when they were blown up to cover most of the front page. Then it seemed that the news staff of 80 reporters was a little too small for what they were required to cover. For example, there was no full-time police reporter or city hall reporter because the paper wanted all reporters to be flexible enough to move quickly on any subject.

And finally, the interest level was vastly higher than Ingersoll and his staff had expected. The paper got 168,000 calls the first day from potential subscribers. About 11,000 got through.

"It was just pandemonium," Ingersoll said of that day.

Some saw this as a sign of success, but Ingersoll, who recently expanded the Ingersoll newspaper empire into England and Ireland, saw it as a lost opportunity. "One's credibility hinges on promises kept," Ingersoll said. "I feel if I was a homeowner and I paid my bill for three months, and I didn't get the paper, I would look on that as a broken promise."

But if energy is what it will take to make good on those promises, Ingersoll and his young staff seem to have it. They already have moments when they show how it can be done. Columnist Kevin Horrigan, 41, who was hired away from the St. Louis Post, has written pieces that will grow yellow on peoples' bulletin boards.

Photographer Eric Williams, 23, followed an undercover drug operation and got a photo of a policeman pushing a shiny .44 caliber revolver into the belly of an accused dealer. Ingersoll ran the startling photo big on Page 1, and some other St. Louis journalists were critical.

"It was too good. You wondered if it was real," as one put it.

Ingersoll, who lives in Princeton, N.J., and recently added a home in St. Louis, said he began to think about creating a new St. Louis daily because of other newspapers that had been started successfully in recent years in Europe, Puerto Rico and Canada. He also said that he had a poll done that showed that two of three people did not read the daily newspaper in the St. Louis area.

Ingersoll, who wears suspenders and glasses and talks a lot tougher than his bookish appearance, sits in the glass-lined, 11th floor offices that have some of the best views in downtown St. Louis.

Everything and everybody at the Sun is new. "New, new, new," says James Bottorff, production director of Ingersoll Publications Co. He notes that normally when someone takes a new job, everybody else has been there for a while and knows the ropes. That wasn't the case at the Sun. "I wouldn't say we haven't had a bump in the road, but there was never a day when we were in danger of not getting the paper out," said Bottorff.

If the cost of starting a paper seemed high, some newspaper experts say it was probably lower than buying one. Ingersoll was not forced to accept staff members he did not want and then have to buy them off or fire them. He does not have to pay pensions, at least not yet, and the staff is young and healthy enough to keep medical expenses and other benefits at a minimum.

Moreover, the Sun staff is not unionized like the employees at the Post-Dispatch and many other newspapers.

"It is our understanding that some of the people in the pressrooms are working 90 hours a week," said Nicholas G. Penniman IV, publisher of the St. Louis Post-Dispatch. "We simply could not do that."

When asked how long people work, Sun executives say only that workweeks are long.

Penniman said that Ingersoll can also lean on his successful suburban newspapers for support. Classified advertising is being handled by the suburban journals. And the news staff of 160 to 170 is filing copy to the Sun as well as their normal suburban papers.

Although most of Penniman's reporters say they welcome the Sun because competition makes the job more interesting and more fun, Penniman views the arrival as bad news.

"There are just so many dollars," he said. "The appearance of another newspaper is not going to create new advertising dollars."

Penniman said that in the past few days he had been negotiating with two major real estate brokerage firms that have been rethinking their decisions about where to advertise. "Any dollars that go to the Sun are clearly coming from the Post-Dispatch or Ingersoll's own suburban journals."

The 111-year old Post-Dispatch, a Pulitzer newspaper that has a circulation of 378,225 daily and 560,618 on Sunday, has not taken the Sun lightly. The paper has been expanded. Sports coverage and use of color have been increased. The Washington bureau has been told to look for local angles.

The changes, according to Post-Dispatch managing editor David Lippman, were in the works and were merely "accelerated" by the new venture, adding that for all the "hoopla, when it came out, the Sun did not have any technological innovations that surprised readers in St. Louis."

Most residents interviewed at random at a shopping center said they hoped the Sun would survive.

Steve and Andrea Dent, a young couple walking their infant son at an upscale mall in the city, are the kind of people Ingersoll must win over. The Dents said they take the Sun and the Post-Dispatch. "It's pretty interesting. I like the way it looks, but it doesn't seem to be as in-depth,'" said Dent of the Sun. "But, we may dump the Sun at the end of three months."

"I read it first," said his wife. "Then if I have more time or I want to know more about something, I read it in the Post-Dispatch."

Part of the Ingersoll operation is an appeal to the basic human desire to show up the establishment—in this case the newspaper establishment that nationwide has not been gaining readers in recent years.

President Jelenic, a feisty 38-year-old who helped start the Edmonton Sun in Canada, laid out a copy of the Post-Dispatch on an office coffee table and sneered at the "foreign" news dominating the front page.

"East Germany, a Washington story, there's always a Washington story on Page 1. I don't think the paper's relevant to St. Louis," he said.

On other occasions, he has been more direct. He told a Chicago Tribune reporter recently that the Post-Dispatch is "the worst major newspaper in the United States."

Such talk may be 50 percent bravado, but it troubles people like Charles Klotser, editor of the St. Louis Journalism Review. Klotser, who praises the design and the staff, said that he worries about how short the stories are. "What they offer is television news in print," he said, noting the similarities to USA Today. "If he can tap into the non-reading public, more power to him, but if his paper is a substitute for the Post-Dispatch, it is a regrettable development."

Klotser and others cite a Business Week interview with Ingersoll as an indication that the Sun will not harp on racial tensions or desegregation problems in the city. "I see nothing constructive in continuing to lambast the white base in St. Louis for these perceived wrongs," Ingersoll said of the competition's tendency to address these problems.

But Ingersoll's well known conservatism isn't so noticeable yet in the Sun. In part, he said he allows his staff to rein him in.

Some analysts suggest that the reason for such restraint is that the politics of the Sun may not be as important as its numbers. Advertisers read circulation figures more urgently than they do the editorial page.

The philosophy and the style of the Sun have been widely described in advance as a tabloid version of USA Today. The front page, which emblazons the paper's name in white on a red band, features a picture and a headline. The cover story starts inside.

But for all its boldness, the Sun is careful so far not to be lumped in with the supermarket tabloids, as the paper demonstrated the day Tass carried Soviet reports of UFO sightings. The Post-Dispatch ran the story on its front page. The Sun had it inside.

"I think they just didn't dare run a picture of E.T.," said one Post-Dispatch reporter. "They don't have enough history yet to take that chance. They would be judged by that one picture."

The Problems with Sources

Richard Harwood, September 1989

This newspaper and other elements of the "media" last month gave an obscure carpenter named Randall Lee Breer his 15 minutes of fame. We said he was the probable murderer of 10-year old Rosie Gordon of Lake Braddock. He probably was not.

We—the "media," that is—had a dramatic explanation for the turret explosion on the battleship Iowa this spring: it was the result of a lovers' quarrel between two homosexual sailors, Clayton Hartwig and Kendall Truitt. Mr. Hartwig, we told you, was so soured over the end of the affair that he blew himself up along with 46 other sailors. Today, after exhaustive investigations by the Navy and the FBI, the "lovers' quarrel" theory has evaporated; it was unworthy of mention in the 1,100-page report on the incident. Sorry about that, boys.

We—the "media," that is—rhetorically lynched Marine Sgt. Clayton Lonetree and other guards at the U.S. Embassy in Moscow in 1987, informing the masses that they had given the KGB free run of the building's code rooms and other most secret places. This whiz-bang tale, it turned out, was fictional and, in its lesser elements, was "wildly overblown."

We—the usual suspects, that is—have elevated a State Department functionary, Felix Bloch, into the company of such celebrated villains as Aaron Burr, Alger Hiss and Julius Rosenberg. We told you he was doing treasonous business with the Russians. Peter Jennings and his colleagues in the ABC television news department even showed us a film of Mr. Bloch handing over a briefcase to his Soviet handler. The film was phony. The story may be, too. All we really know at this point is that Mr. Bloch remains on the State Department payroll, happily playing the role of Washington boulevardier with frequent appearances on the evening news shows.

Well, comme ci, comme ca; you can't win 'em all, Ma.

The interesting thing about these stories is that none of them was fabricated, a la Janet Cooke, and all of them originated with an "official source." Mr. Breer was fingered by the Fairfax police department at a news conference called expressly for that purpose. The Marine guards and the sailors on the Iowa were implicated by blunderers in the Naval Investigative Service with willing assists from imaginative reporters. The Bloch story may have first come out of one of the congressional intelligence committees but, in any case, was quickly given backhanded credence by the State Department.

Time magazine speculates that blind ambition is behind much of the defective history we've been producing of late: "Both networks and print have moved dramatically toward a star system. The fastest way to stardom is to produce pizazz early and often; the worst sin is being second." There is something to that. You can see it in The Post newsroom nightly as people huddle around television sets to monitor the news programs for scoops. If a hot item is broadcast, there is a mad scramble to somehow match it immediately. This is not peculiar to The Post. News organizations all over Washington anxiously await The Post's first edition each night and "borrow," shall we say, from any exclusive stories that appear. The scope of this type of thievery is one of the dirty little secrets of the news business in America. It helps explain why if one of us slips up, we may all fall down.

Another of our secrets is that we are neither as sophisticated nor as competent as we like to appear. We don't track down murderers, discover Tut's tomb or audit the Pentagon's books. We are pathetically dependent on "sources," especially "official sources," and very often we lack the knowledge or experience to evaluate what they tell us or, for that matter, to evaluate their motives for telling. It is rather obvious now, for example, that when it identified Randall Breer as its "prime suspect," the Fairfax police department was in part responding prematurely to community pressures to find Rosie Gordon's killer.

I think it is also probably true that the costs of being wrong have lessened. The courts over the past 25 years have freed us from many of the legal restraints and liabilities that once were in place. And we are very forgiving of each other's mistakes. When Dan Rather opens his news broadcast denouncing Tom Brokaw for a real blooper, the immunity shield will be broken. Don't hold your breath for that great day.

The Unnamed Source

Eleanor Randolph, July 1988

Editors who go to boring seminars, where news people talk about a lofty journalism that doesn't exist in real life, are fond of grumbling that journalists use too many anonymous sources.

These are the same editors who go home to their offices and ask the working reporter, not in a friendly way exactly, why their paper doesn't have yesterday's scoop. Occasionally, one of these editors will decree an end to use of accusations unattached to name and address. These decrees usually last about a month.

In recent weeks, for example, there has been much chortling among reporters in Washington about a dictum to the New York Times newsroom on the issue of quoting people without using their names.

The reason, for one thing, is the timing. The memo from Executive Editor Max Frankel came in the middle of the Pentagon procurement scandal, a story that rests each day on a bed of "law-enforcement officials" or "investigators" or just plain "sources."

Frankel wrote: "In the energetic and competitive quest for news about law breaking and official investigations, we want to avoid becoming the purveyors of anonymous and undocumented charges. We also don't want our competitors' choices to dictate ours."

Within hours after the memo was posted, Times reporters began complaining in Washington to their anonymous sources. Other news organizations began calling those sources and saying—not in precisely these words, of course—that, if the New York Times won't play, we will.

Granting sources anonymity can mean that someone needs to be protected, like the poor guy ratting on a mobster, for example. Sometimes a mid-level bureaucrat provides details that his boss, a political appointee, is trying to whitewash in whatever official release may be presented to an unsuspecting public.

If it seems that, in an ideal world, there would be no unnamed sources, think again. News stories would be full of carefully prepared statements. Or quotes would be attached to the names of people who would do anything to get their names in the paper. The result would be like Brezhnev's Pravda or the Congressional Record, a shred of the story at best.

Frankel's effort, however, is an admirable one. Too often in Washington, Mr. Y asks for anonymity because he wants to ruin Mr. X's reputation in the morning paper and still be able to commiserate with Mr. X at an embassy cocktail party that evening. Worse, it means that the reporter often didn't try very hard to obtain the same information on the record from someone else—if not a congressional aide, then perhaps a young member of Congress willing to take the heat in order to get the publicity.

Conservative columnist James J. Kilpatrick wrote earlier this year in Washington Journalism Review that an outlander who came to Washington during any of the various scandals of 1987 would believe that the city is inhabited by "officials," "sources" and "aides."

He called the phenomenon "trust-me journalism."

John L. Perry, combative editor of the News-Tribune in Rome, Ga., recently won the Lowell Mellett Award for media criticism in part for efforts to demand attribution by editors at the Philadelphia Inquirer and Associated Press. Perry was so enraged at the Associated Press at one point that he began deleting references to anonymous sources in AP wire copy in his paper. The result was that AP seemed to be making the assertions or accusations on its own. Perry noted recently that the AP wire included an item on his award, but failed to explain why he received it.

The problem for Frankel and other well-meaning editors is that their task is like shooing kids from a broken water hydrant on a hot August afternoon. The orders are obeyed, but only for a little while.

For all of the talk about how the press operates as a herd, reporters act like rogue elephants when they are searching for news. Washington Post editors recall that, when they tried to start a walkout from background briefings at the White House more than a decade ago, they found that another journalist simply moved in the briefing room and took the Post's chair.

"We found ourselves walking out alone, so it just broke down eventually," recalled Richard Harwood, former deputy managing editor and now the Post's ombudsman.

Similarly, Frankel's edict June 16 was slipping into the fat-chance category less than two weeks later. An article by Times reporter M.A. Farber in the paper's June 29 edition detailed questions about Samuel McClease, one of those entwined in the Tawana Brawley case in New York. Farber wrote: "Federal prosecutors and former employers, co-workers and relatives said McClease was at best an amiable braggart and at worst an unstable liar...."

The same article quoted an unnamed customer at a store where McClease worked as saying that McClease gave "fantastic discounts," then asked for "scratch-my-back money," which the anonymous customer paid McClease around the corner from the store.

So much for unnamed sources at The Times. Good try, Mr. Frankel.

CHAPTER FOUR

The Recording Industry

The Beat of a Different Drummer

Mark Jenkins, May 1990

"We are the world," sang America's glossy pop-soul aristocracy in 1985 in a noblesse oblige gesture toward starving Ethiopians. American musicians may still make the same global claim five years later, but surely with less justification. Decline-of-America commentaries frequently point out—sometimes with alarm, sometimes with pride—that the only way foreign companies can make movies with worldwide appeal is to buy Hollywood studios. But foreign interests have done more than buy control of most major U.S. recording companies (of the big six, only two are American-owned); they've created "worldbeat," a new internationalist form of pop music colored by Third World rhythms and instrumentation and one that doesn't resonate at all in Los Angeles, New York or Nashville.

Worldbeat is not about to do to Michael Jackson what rock and roll did to Eddie Fisher. Still, as a significant new pop-culture product that is neither produced nor inspired by America, the wellspring of Western popular music since World War II, worldbeat suggests a diminished role for Yankee ingenuity in the invention of international mass culture—and at the very moment that international doors are unlocking at a quickening pace. The U.S. recording industry, of course, is skeptical that the market for this mongrel music will either expand or endure.

But then that's just what another American industry thought about Japanese cars.

With its May 19 edition, the music-and-video trade weekly Billboard introduced a "World Music Albums" chart, a sign that the U.S. music business does at least want to keep track of the phenomenon. According to an article about African pop stars in that same issue, "though substantial radio airplay for them is still lacking, sales figures for these artists have increased dramatically, especially in urban areas." The piece quotes a Tower Records buyer who notes that "our floor space for world music has increased by 33 percent recently."

Despite such bullishness, Billboard's new-chart indicates that worldbeat has yet to become an especially volatile commodity in stateside record stores: Included on the 15-slot list are the last two records by the neo-Eurofolk band, the Gipsy Kings; a pair of albums by The Bulgarian State Radio and Television Female Vocal Choir that have charmed some of the New Age audience; a collection of Middle Eastern music compiled by English art-rocker Peter Gabriel while he was composing the score to "The Last Temptation of Christ"; and records by such long-established artists as Miriam Makeba and Hugh Masekela. Also included is an album by Beausoleil, a Louisiana gumbo-circuit band.

Few of these are recent releases, suggesting that in America worldbeat is still bought and sold like folk, classical or other semi-popular musics. To listeners here, music that is neither American nor British remains either novelty (as in the recent "lambada" hype) or specialty (as in reggae), just as it has been since the days of Desmond Dekker's proto-reggae hit, "Israelites" (which reached No. 12 in 1969) or the Singing Nun's "Dominique" (No. 1 in 1963). The charts are dominated by Americans and by Europeans (most of them British) playing American-style music.

Yankees have heard glimmers of worldbeat, of course. South African "township jive" or "mbaqanga" (literally, a sort of stew) found itself on everything from Top 40 radio to National Public Radio through the mediation of Paul Simon, who set his haute yuppie tales of Upper West Side parties to Soweto's "indestructible, beat (and in the process made South Africa's Ladysmith Black Mambazo mainstream enough to qualify for a gig selling 7 Up on U.S. TV). Longtime cult artist Peter Gabriel, who became a stateside chart-topper with 1986's "So," has also drawn heavily on African music. And that bellwether of trendiness, Talking Heads, recorded its most recent album in Paris.

Paris? Well, yes. The center of worldbeat is not Dakar, Soweto, Algiers or even Kingston, which does maintain a significant recording industry. It's Paris, axis of the Francophone world and presumably a much easier place to get a decent cup of cafe au lait than Abidjan. Just as America sold its musical primitivism to the world—well, some of it—as rock and roll, France is merchandising the beats of its former empire. Zouk, rai, soukous, juju and the rest of the trendy Third World music may come from the African diaspora, but it's become the soundtrack for Europe 1992 —freshly blended music for a newly unified market.

Though it is sometimes sold—especially in this country, where its commercial viability remains dubious—by record companies that specialize in folk music, worldbeat is nothing of the sort. Indeed, it could be argued that worldbeat was presaged by Giorgio Moroder, the German-based producer who helped invent disco some 15 years ago.

"Disco" became a bad word quickly, but Moroder's synthbeat didn't die. it can still be heard everywhere from the American hits of teen-pop princess Debbie Gibson to the new album by Yemenite-Israeli singer Ofra Haza. After becoming an English worldbeat sensation—a digital sample of her voice had been employed in a left-field hip-hop hit, "Pump Up the Volume," so infectious that it even sold in the hidebound United States. Haza's next move was to go to New York and make a Madonna-sounding album. Recorded in English, Hebrew, Arabic and even Aramaic, with such producers as Arif Mardin, Haze's album was probably best-known for producing the "Jive Talking" era Bee Gees sound (itself a New York take on Moroder's Eurobeat version of Motown soul, written and sung by expatriate Australians). Today, Paris has largely supplanted Munich as the continent's leading pop-music factory, but the beat is much the same: The synthesized pulse known as "Eurodisco" underlies much worldbeat. Traditional styles are often employed merely as exotic spices in a sound designed for European dance clubs from Paris to Ibiza. (The latter's "Balearic Beat," a brief craze transplanted by vacationing Brits to dance halls in the chilly, rainy Midlands where beachwear was de rigueur, is just more disco.) The "lambada," concocted in Paris from a loosely interpreted Brazilian recipe, is merely the most notorious example of French shamelessness in producing ersatz Third-World music.

French rock and roll was long known as the world's lamest—the French know how to sneer all right, but only at tourists, not at microphones. (French rock's reputation is finally being challenged by the rote rock of the Soviet Union, where bands are now free to copy the most banal of Anglo-American sounds.) French musicians seem ideal, though, for the flagrantly upbeat sound of worldbeat, which sounds impossibly cheerful even when its message is dour. (Witness Zimbabwean Thomas Mapfumo's recent "Corruption," which non-

Shona-speakers would likely take for joyous if not for the clue offered by its title.)

Somewhat disturbingly, worldbeat seems to appeal both to France's vestigial imperial notions (this is a country, after all, that keeps a Japanese flag in St. Louis-de-Invalidies as a token of its proxy victory over Japan in World War II) and its historic tendency toward "exotisme"—a willingness to see Third World inhabitants in this case as happy darkies. Imagine the American Revolutions being marked— as was the French one last year—by a parade in London or Washington in which dancing, drumming Africans were surrounded by Great White Hunter-types in pith hats.

African and Caribbean musicians are important to worldbeat, but not essential. Also in vogue in Europe is a polyglot pop that draws on everything from Parisian cafe music to Islamic chants to Gypsy ballads to American rap. Among its more straightforward practitioners are Les Negresses Vertes (who are neither black nor green) and the Gipsy Kings, but the movement also includes such self-consciously bizarre acts as 3 Mustaphas 3, a group of British-accented musicians who claim to be from "the Balkans"; Mano Negra, a rowdy France-based outfit influenced both by punk and ska (the good-timey predecessor to reggae) that sings in Spanish, English, French and Arabic; Nasa, an English hard-rock duo that draws heavily on Middle Eastern sounds and imagery; and Dissidenten, a German quartet that layers Moroccan protest poetry (sung in Arabic) over Eurodisco rhythms.

In one sense, it's difficult to generalize about this music. Yet, from the somberly traditional to the flamboyantly goofy, one thing is certain: It's not American.

The decline of American rock's European appeal, thus far more obvious among various avant gardes than with mainstream music consumers, could be a simple matter of oversaturation—of both the music and the culture. Last year, Joe Strummer explained in a Washington Post interview, why the anti-American anthem he co-wrote for the Clash in 1977, "I'm So Bored With the U.S.A.," no longer has any power: "Now a song like that is superfluous," he says. "There's a 7-Eleven or McDonald's on every corner in London. It's kind of boring to complain about those things now. It's kind of the province of people who write to the newspapers, you know? 'Why is there a McDonald's on every corner?'"

If American popular culture is no longer sufficiently exotic to Western Europeans to engender even gripes, neither is its subtext: affluence. American pop was not just a token of a freewheeling style that appealed to European youth constrained by traditional cultures and rigid class systems; it was also an advertisement for a bountiful consumer culture. Today, London, which was still under food-rationing when Elvis first went to Sun Studios, has 7-Elevens, Taco Bells, Pizza Huts, enormous American-style supermarkets and Londoners who can afford to patronize them. If shopping has become a "drama of consumption," as some contemporary sociologists put it, the stage is now erected in Bonn, Manchester and Lyon as surely as in Cincinnati or Tucson. The Warsaw Pact market may have opened up just in time, and not just for the sake of burger chains that have colonized every likely location from Van Nuys Boulevard to the Champs L'Eysees. Those Bon Jovi records gathering dust in Dusseldorf can just be loaded on freight trains heading east.

There's also another demographic at work here, one that bodes well for worldbeat's eventual success in this country. The aging rock generation has not abandoned pop music, but it betrays a declining interest in the teen-angst and young-lust that drives today's heavy metal bands and neo-disco divas. The search for a music that's upbeat and danceable without being angry or mechanical has created a market for zydeco, norteno, Tex-Mex, Cajun and other native exotics. Their good-natured energy does correspond to that of African highlife and Brazilian samba, so perhaps Billboard knew what it was doing when it included Beausoleil on the same chart with the interracial South African band, Johnny Clegg & Savuka. Certainly the magazine was correct in grouping the 'World Music' chart together with the New Age chart under the joint heading, "Top Adult Alternative Albums." If Zaire's Kanda Bongo Man does become a bestseller in this country, it will probably be the responsibility of the same generation that made chart-toppers out of such unlikely pop stars as Bob Dylan.

Toure Kunda, a Paris-based Senegalese trio, or Algerian Chaba Zahouania may never rival Michael Jackson's skill at moving "units," as the record industry sentimentally labels tapes, CDs and records. Certainly Arabic and Zulu are less well understood in Europe—let alone America—than English. Nor is worldbeat completely un-American: Soul and rock are staples in the worldbeat ragout. N'Dour's "Nelson Mandela" album, for example, interrupts its politics for a cover of the Spinners' "The Rubberband Man."

Still, Kunda, Zahouania and N'Dour portend a world in which American popular culture has no particular claim to primacy. In the pop-music marketplace as in so many others, the United States may have to get used to being just another country.

Rhythm, Blues & The Battle

Richard Harrington, May 1988

The recent news from Atlantic Records—that the company would recalculate the royalties due its original base of rhythm and blues artists, and would also fund a Washington-based Rhythm and Blues Foundation —marked the end of a long campaign for a singer whose career started on the corner of Seventh and T streets and a local corporate attorney reared on rhythm and blues.

For Ruth Brown, it was the culmination of a 20-year struggle to correct royalty inequities.

For Howell Begle, it capped a five-year effort in which he represented not only Brown, but other Atlantic R&B stalwarts including the Drifters, the Coasters, the Clovers and the late Big Joe Turner.

Brown, 60, the most successful Atlantic recording artist of the '50s, and Begle, 44, counsel to the American Film Institute and the Kennedy Center and a specialist in newspaper acquisitions, are an unlikely pair, except that she was one of his idols when he was growing up in Arizona.

Begle, who owns several thousand 78s, describes himself as "a longtime fan, going back to playing guitar in a band in high school and listening to R&B at night. When I was 11 years old, I dragged my mother to see Ruth Brown, the Alan Freed show with Sam Cooke, everybody. This music was the love of my life.

"And to have gone to law school, worked for a Wall Street law firm, to have acquired all these skills and to have an opportunity later in life to apply these things to something I loved is wonderful. Too often in one's professional career, you don't get a chance to be on the right side of the right issue."

At the root of the problem: royalty wrongs that Brown had been trying to get redressed since the late '60s, wrongs centered on faulty bookkeeping and underreported sales as well as diminished foreign royalty rates, and deductions for packaging and advances not called for in her original contracts. By the time Begle met up with Brown in 1983—a media client informed him of her problems—she'd been through four lawyers who'd had little luck penetrating corporate defenses. Atlantic's attitude was summed up in one letter telling Brown that "laches and statutes of limitations" barred her royalty claims.

It's not unusual for artists to try to undo bad deals made decades ago, often with small, independent companies that have long since folded or sold off their catalogues. Early rock 'n roll history is a litany of primitive business practices that seldom favored the artists.

But Atlantic was a company apart, not only because it has grown into one of the industry giants (as part of the Warner Communications Inc. conglomerate) but because the label, through founder Ahmet Ertegun, had always been perceived as a nurturer of black music. Ertegun continues to head the 40-year-old company, so Atlantic couldn't claim a lack of knowledge about its past.

"I'm still here so I feel responsible for anything that has to do with Atlantic," Ertegun says. "We were fans. Most of the other people were businessmen. We were more like amateurs, though it seems to have worked out well."

Still, it took years of prodding, cajoling, negotiating and compromise to reach an agreement. Begle—who had taken on the cases of another dozen artists with royalty disputes similar to Brown's—started by examining old contracts and lucking into some documents that seemed to show patterns of questionable bookkeeping practices. He enlisted the aid of the American Federation of Television and Radio Artists, and in 1985 persuaded CBS' "West 57th" to do a segment on royalty problems. A year later Brown was invited to testify about the issue before a congressional panel headed by Rep. John Conyers (D-Mich). Begle was also involved in a key 1986 meeting between Warner Communications Chairman Steven Ross and Jesse Jackson.

"I used every resource I had," says Eegle, who ultimately chose to pursue a path of negotiation rather than confrontation.

There were small victories at first. In 1984 Begle was able to get $10,000 for Joe Turner and $3,000 for the Clovers, their first royalty payments in 25 years. But there was also discouragement.

"I had written (the disputed royalties) off," says Sam Moore (of Sam & Dave), another Begle client. "I felt like no one ever really cared, and I think we all felt that way. We didn't work that much, and even if we did, we couldn't afford to get attorneys to fight the thing so we just gave up." (Verner, Liipfert, the Washington law firm where Begle worked when he started the chase in 1983, wrote off some $60,000 worth of legal time and expenses, and all of Begle's work has been pro bono; his current media and entertainment law practice at Johnson & Swanson has been rewarding enough to make this possible.)

During the long negotiations, just as he had as a youngster in Arizona, Begle found his inspiration in Ruth Brown.

"I never would have succeeded had I not had such confidence that this was a matter of principle with Ruth," Begle says. "What scared me so much was that some of the people I was representing were in such tough financial straits. They had valid claims for very substantial sums of money, but I knew Atlantic could have put $30,000 in front of them and they would have taken it—they couldn't have resisted. But Ruth was just rock solid. She was the one who kept me going, really."

Ironically, Atlantic's 14-record "Atlantic Rhythm and Blues" collection —released in 1985 and intended as a celebration of historic achievement—served as a checklist of potential plaintiffs. And at one point, Atlantic's corporate bookkeepers tried to bill both Brown and Joe Turner—who was undergoing dialysis treatments at the time and depending on benefit concerts to pay his medical expenses—for the mastering, editing and mixing done for that collection though they hadn't recorded for the label in 25 years. Begle protested, and when Ertegun heard about it, he immediately put an end to such practices; when Turner died soon afterward, Ertegun paid for his funeral and paid off the mortgage on his widow's home.

Such individual generosity was not new at Atlantic. In 1948, just after Ruth Brown signed with the label, she was on her way to recording sessions in New York when a car crash hospitalized her for nine months. "Atlantic paid my hospital bills and I had not recorded a note for them at that time, so they took a chance on me," she recalls. "In those days, we were all very close."

Still, almost all of Atlantic's original R&B roster had left the label by 1965—and almost all had left owing the label money for disputed packaging costs and advances. After a while, Atlantic simply stopped keeping up to date the accounts from which royalties are calculated, in essence writing these artists off the books because, Atlantic spokesmen say, they never envisioned recouping that money. Between 1969 and 1983, they even stopped mailing the quarterly statements demanded in contracts, claiming it was an administrative burden to post royalties and send out statements on closed accounts. No one envisioned the public's enduring interest in rhythm and blues, particularly overseas, or the popularity of reissues, or the development of CDs.

Yet compared with most of the other independent labels of the late '40s and '50s, Atlantic had an excellent reputation for fairness. Most labels "just knew they could beat black artists out of the money," says veteran songwriter Doc Pomus.

"It's a known fact," says Ertegun. "Independent record companies (then) were famous for not having good bookkeeping. I'd sometimes visit them and ask, 'Where's your accounting department?' They'd look at me and laugh."

Atlantic's royalty recalculations are based on post-1970 reissues and don't address the earlier period, in which the bulk of these artists' sales occurred.

The company says its records for this period are not complete, and that in any case, it has no legal obligation to audit such old accounts. Begle concedes that more is probably owed the people he represents, but says, "I don't know what's realistic to expect of corporate America at this point. Sometimes you have to temper action with reason."

That's probably why Atlantic took the extra step of committing at least $2 million, with another $150,000 for annual operating expenses, to the newly formed Rhythm and Blues Foundation (which Begle will head as unsalaried executive director). The foundation will make tax-free grants to pioneering rhythm and blues pioneers of the '50s and '60s as recognition for their artistic merit; initially, the artists will be drawn from the Atlantic roster, but if other companies kick in, as Atlantic hopes they will, that focus will expand.

"We hope people will follow our lead, but we can't force them to," says Warner's Ross. "We were always legally right, but we wanted to be ethically and morally right, as well."

Begle says the foundation will work to publicize the rhythm and blues genre in general and surviving artists in particular. Many of them, he points out, are still eager to perform publicly, but find opportunities limited.

"We're in good shape, in good mind," says Sam Moore. "What we should do now is put all of the past in the back, forget all the animosity and the hatred, and stick together and go back to work. We're good singers and performers. We had to be to keep the meals paid, the house rented."

And having served as counsel for the Kennedy Center Honors and AFI Tributes, Begle hopes he can put together some sort of television tribute, perhaps on a yearly basis.

"There's very few things in life I've invested as much time and energy in over such a long period of time," says Begle. "I'd love to have my legacy be watching this organization prosper."

"This is a fantasy really," says John (Buddy) Bailey, who sang lead on nine hits by Washington's Clovers. "It's a great feeling to know that. someone was in our corner, especially Howell...We were the pioneers but who in the hell cared? We had bad management, bad booking agencies, the whole nine yards. It was a complete rip-off and we didn't know it. We were just kids—I was 17, you know how that goes. I just wanted to sing.

"I'm 55 now," Bailey adds. "That's the settling-down age." Thanks to Ruth Brown and Howell Begle, it may be the settling-up age as well.

DATs, Fighting to Be Heard

Joseph McLellan, May 1988

There is something new in the May issue of the Schwann Compact Disc Catalog: a full page (Page 29) listing the first 52 digital audio tape (DAT) recordings available on the American market. Music lovers eager to sample the latest state-of-the-art technology in sound reproduction can choose between Bach's "Brandenburg" Concertos; five collections of baroque trumpet music; Chick Corea's "Light Years"; and the Glenn Miller Orchestra playing "In the Digital Mood."

The only problem (a temporary one) is finding something on which to play this music.

Some audiophiles in the northern states have been slipping across the border and coming back with DAT machines, which are available in Canada. In fact, these machines, introduced in Japan a year ago and in Europe six months ago, can be bought almost anywhere in the civilized world except the United States. That situation will probably end Wednesday, when at least one company (Marantz) and probably several others are scheduled to import the first machines to be regularly marketed in this country. On the same day, the Recording Industry Association of America (RIAA) will slap one or more lawsuits on the offending companies. Having failed to stop DAT in Congress, the record industry is now prepared to try the courts.

The most important thing about digital audio tape, like any form of digital recording, is what you don't hear. Digital sound recording is a medium (the first in history) that leaves no perceptible trace of itself —puts nothing between you and the music.

Next in importance, for the immediate future, are the reasons why we haven't been hearing DAT in the United States. The short answer is that it would remove state-of-the-art musical reproduction from total control of the recording industry.

DAT is the tape equivalent of the compact disc, the medium that has risen to dominate the recording industry in the last few years. DAT recorders look pretty much like the analog cassette recorders that have long been familiar. Their range of sizes is almost the same, down to the size of a substantial hard-cover book, and they are equipped with the same sorts of buttons and functions. They take a cassette that is about 1 1/8 by 2 7/8 inches—smaller than standard audio cassettes but bigger than microcassettes often used for dictation. The DAT cassette is shaped like a small video cassette, with a hinged front that drops down to protect the tape when not in use. The cassette cannot be spliced because there are consecutive location codes printed on it to allow the DAT player to find a precise spot on the tape—a significant advance over the old turn-counters on analog tape decks.

The DAT machine can be plugged into existing jacks on any standard audio receiver or preamplifier and operated essentially like any other tape recorder. Though some audiophiles eventually may want more powerful amplifiers and or speakers to accommodate the medium's wider dynamic range, DAT, unlike the quadraphonic systems developed and abandoned in the 1970s, will not threaten the other components in your system—particularly CD players—with instant obsolescence. It will merely complement them.

The CD, in fact, has been much more disruptive. Though the mopping up process will take time, the CD for all practical purposes has already killed the LP. DAT is not likely to kill CD in the immediate future. There is room for coexisting tape and disc technologies, which have enough different features and advantages to make them essentially noncompetitive.

Tape, which does not require the kind of precise tracking needed to scan a disc, will probably remain the preferred medium for car systems, Walkmen and other uses where portability is desired. There are portable CD systems, but their operation is not as trouble-free and shock-resistant as tape.

On the other hand, disc technology offers instant access to any part of the flat surface on which the material is stored, whereas even with digital tape, you still have to fast-wind through items A, B and C before you can play D. In a nutshell, the, disc medium is best for a collection of short items from which you may want to play one or two; tape (which has a much longer potential playing time than disc) is best for long works—operas or oratorios—or assemblages of shorter works that you may want to play frequently in a fixed order. Because of these differences, DAT may take a substantial share of the audiophile market (as analog cassettes have done with LPs), but it is not likely to eliminate CD.

The biggest difference between CD and DAT right now is that DAT is a medium for recording and playback, while CD is playback-only. If a system is ever perfected for home-recording on CD, the competition between the two will become much more significant and disc recording would have some strong competitive advantages. Research is underway, and Radio Shack has already announced plans to market a recordable CD of some sort this year.

On grounds of pure sonic superiority, DAT will certainly undermine the market for analog cassette tapes and recorders, but probably won't eliminate them in the near future. One key factor is price. It is expected that a blank DAT cassette with two hours playing time will cost about $10, approximately twice the cost of a top-quality analog cassette. As long as the tapes and hardware for analog recording remain significantly cheaper than DAT, there should be a market for music in the analog tape format. That market could disappear if DAT prices drop enough. But DAT is unlikely to ever become cheap enough to wipe out analog cassettes in the vast market where relatively low fidelity will do.

The chief physical difference between DAT and other tape recorders is one you cannot see unless you take the machine apart; its record and playback heads do not stand still while the tape passes by, as the heads do in an analog recorder. DAT heads, which either set down or pick up the magnetic signal on the tape, move across the tape like the heads on a videocassette recorder. When they go on sale in the United States, early models are expected to retail for $1,500 to $2,000. If they follow the trend of other electronic equipment from computers to CD players, the prices will go down fairly soon and the quality may go up.

While the DAT recorder does not look like a menace to our musical culture, the recording industry has pushed all its panic buttons to stop it. There has been intensive legislative lobbying, an enormous public relations campaign, technological proposals that would amount to mutilation of DAT hardware and threats of lawsuits against any company that imports DAT equipment for the consumer market.

If this opposition has not stopped DAT, it has certainly slowed it down here, compared with Europe and Japan. And the RIAA, despite lost battles, is not abandoning the war. "It is our intent to sue," threatens Jay Berman, president of the Recording Industry Association of America. He charges that DAT recorders will be used to "rob the American music community of the right to be paid for the music we create."

This attitude contrasts sharply with the industry's reaction to the arrival of the compact disc five years ago. CDs were welcomed enthusiastically by American recording companies and have given the industry a financial shot in the arm. The dollar volume of production and shipments in all forms of recording (as measured in list prices) rose 20 percent last year, from $4.65 billion to $5.57 billion. And the fastest-rising part of the industry was the compact disc, up 93 percent over 1986 from 53 million units to 102.1 million. These CDs had a list price value of $1.6 billion. LP sales peaked in 1980 and have been declining ever since—15 percent last year, when the list price value of LPs distributed was only $793 million, half of that for CDs.

But audio tape is still the backbone of the recording industry and still growing. Last year, 410 million professionally made cassettes were distributed in America, 19 percent more than in 1986 and four times the number of CDs. So the industry has nothing against digital recording per se or audio tape per se. Why the problem with DAT?

The problem with DAT, in a nutshell, is that it's too good. Some of its more enthusiastic fans claim that DAT sound is actually better than CD sound. It might be prudent to wait a while before jumping on that bandwagon, but DAT sound is likely to be exactly as good as CD sound, and that's too good for the RIAA. In Congress, in the courts and in the media, industry spokesmen have complained that DAT makes it possible to produce copies of commercial recordings that are indistinguishable from the originals. Copying at that level of quality "could be devastating to our already battered industry," says country singer Barbara Mandrell in a statement solicited by the battered $5.57 billion industry with production up 20 percent in the last year.

Home copying has been a significant activity since at least the mid-'70s, when analog audio cassettes (aided by the Dolby process for noise reduction) reached a level of sound quality satisfactory to most music lovers. And the RIAA has fought against analog cassettes, but not with the ferocity it has mustered against DAT. Part of the problem was that the audio cassette sneaked up on the industry. It began as a sort of toy—something for dictating letters and preserving baby's first words. Then the sound began to be refined, improved tape formulas were developed, noise was reduced, dynamic range expanded, and the industry was faced with an almost foolproof, high-fidelity home system that made every man his own recording company.

The proliferation of the analog cassette has undeniably led to a lot of record copying, and that may have had something to do with a temporary slump in record companies revenues in the late 1970s. But since 1979 the growth of prerecorded-cassette production (from $82.8 million to $410 million) has sparked the growth of the entire industry (from $3.68 billion to $5.57 billion).

The fairly satisfactory sound of homemade analog cassette recordings, when done with care on good equipment, has become better than ever. When copied from CDs, they are usually superior to most predigital commercial recordings on either LP or tape. The analog cassette sound may compare unfavorably with the crisp, clean, dynamically wide-ranging sound of the original compact disc, but the differences are hardly noticeable when heard on the kind of equipment available in most American homes. Still, the industry apparently feels it's too late to declare war against the analog cassette. Or perhaps it fears it could not win that war.

The DAT menace, however, is strong enough to rally the RIAA for a last-ditch battle. The superiority of DAT recording becomes crucial when one begins to make copies of copies of copies. In analog recordings, the quality of the music would decline each time it passed into a new generation of copies. Not only would the noise-to-signal ratio increase as the background hiss and other types of residual noise accumulated; various kinds of distortion, tolerable in the earlier generations, would compound themselves to a level where the music could no longer be recognized. Making 10 generations of an analog recording is something like typing a telephone number, making a photocopy of it, then copying that photocopy, then copying a copy of the copy for 10 generations. Try it and see how long the number remains legible.

Digital recording, on the other hand, is like typing the number over again the same way 10 times. With DAT, ideally, all noise and distortions would be eliminated. The system records sound as a stream of numbers (digits) rather than the physical wave forms fixed in vinyl or the magnetic patterns imprinted on a ribbon of iron oxide that constitute analog tape recording. The 10th-generation copy would be identical with the original. The potential for copying material through endless generations may worry the RIAA more than the prospect of one person making and selling multiple copies in a single generation. That is known as piracy, and it is already, quite properly, outlawed.

Ultimately, the reason for the industry's opposition to DAT boils down to dollars and cents. In popular music particularly, record companies usually enjoy a monopoly on a particular item—unlike in classical music, where most of the blockbusters have long been in the public domain. This monopoly position allows a level of price fixing that is undermined when the product can be easily duplicated. The ability to make your own recordings at home does not absolutely destroy the value of the professional product, but it introduces a competitive factor.

In practical terms, DAT will make it hard for the record industry to price its products much higher than the combined costs of the tape, your labor and the depreciation of your recording equipment. In other words, what DAT means in the long run is that the cost of CDs will have to come down below $10 to be competitive. That has already begun happening in classical music, which has a built-in competitive element. It is now possible to buy a complete set of Beethoven's nine symphonies, on five CDs, for under $20. And MCA has introduced a "Double Decker" line of classical CDs that will be sold in pairs for the price of a single midline CD (usually $8-$10). The pressure of DAT is likely eventually to force prices down similarly in the pop field.

So the RIAA has already tried to legislate the implanting of a "copycode chip" in all DAT equipment sold in the United States. The chip would prevent the copying of CDs on DAT, and it was seriously considered by Congress until the National Bureau of Standards criticized it on two grounds: It would degrade the signal put out by the DAT, and people with electronics skills could easily find ways to bypass it.

Lawsuits to prevent private copying of recorded material have already been fought all the way to the Supreme Court, and the right of Americans to tape proprietary material for personal, noncommercial use has been upheld. The recording devices primarily involved were VCRs, but the legal principle remains the same. This does not mean that the recording industry will not try again what has already been tried by the movie industry, but it does mean that changes of success seem slim. When the dust settles, there will still be the problem of arranging for equitable payments to artists whose material is being copied. But it doesn't look as though that can be done through attacks on the copying hardware.

Recording Industry Hits a Flat Note

Paul Farhi, April 1990

Here in the platinum-record lined offices of the music business, you can almost hear the sound of money.

At Geffen Records storefront shop on Sunset Boulevard, the label's boyish boss, David Geffen, is burning up the phone lines a month after selling his company for $545 million to MCA Inc. Geffen is reportedly spending a fraction of his windfall on a $47 million estate in Beverly Hills.

A few blocks away, at A&M Records, founders Jerry Moss and Herb Alpert, the trumpeter, are sitting on $500 million, the haul from the sale of their company in October to the Dutch-owned PolyGram Inc.

Shrewd operators all, Geffen, Moss and Alpert may have cashed out at just the right time. Fed by the starting success of the compact disc, the recording industry finished its best year ever in 1989—but is showing incipient signs of losing its groove.

As measured in dollars, record sales grew only 3 percent last year, less than the inflation rate and the slowest growth since 1985, according to the Recording Industry Association of America. Unit shipments were up 5 percent, thanks mainly to the CD, but cassettes—still the backbone of the business—actually experienced a slight decline. Even the CD explosion begins to look a lot less dynamic for record companies in light of the inexorable fall in CD prices and profit margins: The average disc sold for $12.49 last year, down from $15.63 in 1986.

Geffen, for one, sees no portents, confident that the industry's good times will last for the foreseeable future. "Music is considerably more important than it was to people 20 years ago," said the 47-year-old executive, an informal man whose business attire runs to T-shirts and loafers. "Listening to music is a way of shutting out the noise of contemporary life. Life is a lot less quiet than it used to be and people would rather replace it with sounds they prefer to hear."

Yet in a notoriously faddish business, prosperity can disappear faster than the Knack. In 1978, before video games and VCRS, the industry enjoyed one of its best years ever—then went into a tailspin. By 1983, one major label, PolyGram, had absorbed $200 million in losses and was threatening to pull out of the U.S. market. That year, however, the business was almost single-handedly rescued from its post-disco depression by a new sound: Michael Jackson's "Thriller", which sold 40 million copies, still the world record.

In 1986, in the midst of another slump, the compact disc came to the rescue. CDs not only have driven traditional vinyl records nearly to extinction, but also have been responsible for pumping up sales by almost 40 percent.

What tempers the enthusiasm of some record-industry executives now is that neither a new sound nor a new technology are in the immediate offing. Potentially revolutionary advances like digital-audio tape and an erasable-recordable version of the CD mostly scare music producers, who worry that sales will be clobbered by home taping.

An even more enigmatic problem lies here in Southern California, the creative heart of the worldwide music business. Even as the business grows more flush, some worry that the music itself may be growing stale.

"I'm not hearing anything out there now that's awe-inspiring," said Peter Paterno, president of Hollywood Records, Walt Disney Co.'s new record label. "Ultimately, that's going to have a direct effect on the business. In 1963, the music was horrible and no one was buying it. Then the Beatles came along. In the early '80s, the music was horrible and then "Thriller" came along. If things don't change, we're going right back to the bad old days."

For the moment, it's easy for the industry to hear only soothing sounds. The CD-fed surge has made Midases of the six multinational companies that have consolidated their control of the business since 1985. (The Big Six are Time Warner Inc. and MCA Inc. of the United States, Bertelsmann AG of West Germany, Sony Corp. of Japan, Thorn-EMI of Britain and the Dutch Philips Industries NV).

Bertelsmann, for example, bought the money-losing RCA and Arista records group in 1986 for a then-astronomical $330 million. Behind such star performers as Whitney Houston and Milli Vanilli, Bertelsmann has earned back the entire purchase in three years, said Michael Dornemann, chief executive of the company's music group.

Similarly, Sony's $2 billion buyout of CBS Records in early 1988 looked pricey. But after a brief stall and a management shake-up, CBS's Columbia label came roaring back last year to become the top-selling label with the pop group New Kids on the Block. Time Warner's record group, the biggest in the world, has been so profitable of late that analyst Alan Kassan of Shearson Lehman Hutton considers it the company's most valuable division ahead of Time Warner's formidable magazine, cable and movie units.

The drive by the Big Six to grab a bigger share of the growing market touched off "a frenzy" to acquire independent labels during the past few years, said Geffen. And with a dwindling number of major independents, recent deals have been at dizzying prices. For its $500 million, for instance, Philip's PolyGram got A&M, a label that had only one hit performer last year, Janet Jackson, and no distribution or manufacturing operations.

While Geffen insists MCA has given him total autonomy, others fret about the impact of the industry's consolidation on creativity and innovation.

"I believe the industry used to take greater chances," said Joe Smith, chief executive of Capitol-EMI Music Inc. from his office atop Capitol's headquarters, an L.A. landmark that resembles a stack of LPs on a turntable. "The bigger you are, the more cautious you get."

Noting that independents have traditionally pioneered musical trends in rock, pop and jazz, Smith added, "Everyone says they want to encourage entrepreneurialism, but these are all public companies."

Nevertheless, Smith said the next logical step will be "a collision of elephants"—a merger between two of the industry's six giants, perhaps Bertelsmann and MCA.

Until its next technological leap, the record business will have to rely on more people making the switch from traditional stereos to compact-disc players to fuel its momentum. On the surface, this is a fair bet: CDs were in only 18 percent of U.S. households at the end of last year; in Europe and Japan, the totals were 16 percent and 27 percent, respectively. That leaves huge portions of the market still untapped, and the falling prices of both the machines and the CDs seem likely to suck in many more customers.

But the CD picture also has a down side: As prices and profit margins fall, the record industry finds itself having to run harder to stay ahead. In other words, said Michael Dornemann, volume will have to keep growing to make up for falling CD profits, which are currently estimated at less than $2 per CD sold.

Dornemann and others are concerned that each new level of CD penetration will be less profitable than the last for another reason. The earliest CD buyers have been the most avid music junkies and the most willing to spend heavily to replace their aging vinyl LPs with CD copies of the same material. As Dornemann frames it, the question is whether the industry has already heard from its best customers: In other words, will new CD owners be as acquisitive as early buyers?

The next technical breakthrough could come from digital-audio tape, which offers the same sonic quality as CDs but gives consumers the ability to record and erase. But DAT's future is murky at best.

Its arrival has been delayed for years by an interminable squabble between hardware manufacturers and record companies over royalties and protection from home-taping. The record industry has effectively blocked DAT by refusing to license recorded music for the new format and by threatening to sue manufacturers that import mass-market versions of the machines to the United States. Record companies are concerned that home taping and counterfeiting on DAT could undermine both the CD and cassette formats.

For music fans, the most hopeful sign that DAT will soon be forthcoming was the tentative agreement struck last summer between the manufacturers and record companies. The agreement calls for a microchip to be inserted in all DAT players to prevent DAT copies from being copied. To have teeth, however, the agreement needs to become law. Even if that happens, the warring factions need to negotiate a royalty formula on the sale of blank DAT cassettes to make up for lost sales.

"DAT," said Geffen, "may never happen"—but not, he believes, because of industry infighting. "There's no real clear-cut advantage to it. It doesn't give you better sound (than a CD). It's smaller, but so what? It's a lot more expensive. Do people want another box?"

The hardware industry's reply to that is that people have always hungered for new and different ways to listen to music.

Of course, new technologies are on the horizon in other entertainment fields as well, and fickle music fans might someday stop loading up on CDs and start watching high-definition television. As always, it's the music, not the music player, that does the talking.

On the Beat; an Obscene Amount of Attention

Richard Harrington, June 1990

The music industry probably would be happy if 2 Live Crew simply disappeared. While the Recording Industry Association of America (RIAA), the National Association of Recording Merchandisers, ASCAP, BMI, the Country Music Association and other members of the newly formed Coalition Against Lyrics Legislation have been quite vocal about lyrics legislation, they have been curiously silent the past four months as judicial forces, mostly in Florida but in several other states as well, have gone after the Miami-based rap group on obscenity charges. Apparently it's easier to rally around free speech and First Amendment rights than it is to support a controversial group in obscenity issues.

Labeling and obscenity are two distinct issues, says Trish Heimers of the RIAA. "Even before voluntary labeling, we were always subject to obscenity laws. And even if mandatory labeling passes, we still would be subject to obscenity laws in those states where sound recordings are included in the obscenity statutes."

The court ruling Thursday in Florida on 2 Live Crew's "As Nasty as They Wanna Be" "is the first time a musical composition has been deemed to be obscene, so this is the first time our industry has been faced with the issue," Heimers points out. Like the National Association of Recording Merchandisers, "we did not want to get involved on the local level, but on the appellate level we anticipate filing an amicus brief in the civil case. In terms of the criminal charges, we are investigating every option. We will most vigorously defend 2 Live Crew's right to artistic expression."

As for the arrest of members of the group during the weekend, Karl Freed, executive director of the North American Concert Promoters Association, says, "Our stance is that it violates the First Amendment, restricting free speech of performers. One of the problems with the arrest was that it was an adults-only club, and was advertised as an adults-only show. This is a live performance—it's no different than some of the comedians that are allowed to perform live on the stage these days. As promoters, we think that any restriction of expression jeopardizes our business as concert promoters, especially because of the subjectivity of the people making the arrests. We're coming into a time when the government is telling us what we can and cannot watch as adults, and that's a severe infringement on our civil liberties."

Florida state Rep. Joe Arnall, whose mandatory lyrics labeling bill is one of those on hold as the industry implements its now voluntary stickering system, expressed surprise at the arrest of 2 Live Crew after its show last weekend. "The scope of my bill didn't pertain to performances at all," he says. (Bills in some states, including Missouri, do.) "If parents don't understand that some of these groups are X-rated in their performances, they're really not paying attention, but I don't think many minors go to 2 Live Crew shows. Let's put it this way: If adults want to go to that type of entertainment, fine."

In Florida, George Corlius, a spokesman for the Broward County sheriff's office, said yesterday that some thought had been given Saturday to arresting audience members who chanted the lyrics along with 2 Live Crew, but that it was "impractical." (Some fans wore T-shirts with the slogan "I Used to Live in America, Now I Live in Broward County.") He also confirmed that in the South Florida counties affected by last week's ruling, possession of "As Nasty as They Wanna Be" is technically a second-degree misdemeanor punishable by up to 60 days in jail and/or a $500 fine.

"We do not plan to actively (pursue), unless we receive a valid complaint from someone to the effect that harm is being done to the complainer through the possession or transmitting of the music, perhaps publicly," Corlius said. "Then we would respond just as we did to the complaint about the obscene nature of the lyrics (of "Nasty") by investigating it and asking the court to prescribe some remedy."

Meanwhile, 2 Live Crew is preparing a new album, "Banned in the USA," which Luther Campbell (whose former stage name was Luke Skywalker) says will be even "dirtier" than "As Nasty as They Wanna Be." The release date? The Fourth of July. The cover will feature 2 Live Crew leader Campbell standing in front of an American flag, offering a one-finger salute.

Perry Farrell, the lead singer and songwriter for the Los Angeles band Jane's Addiction, has had to provide two covers for the group's upcoming album, "Ritual de lo Habitual." The original cover, designed by Farrell, is a painting of him with two nubile women; all three figures are frontally naked and friendly. Warner Bros. Records executives subsequently informed him that, in light of growing conservatism among record retailers, such a cover would likely be banned from many stores, a situation Farrell probably understood beforehand: The cover of the band's debut, "Nothing's Shocking," featuring two naked nymphets, was shocking enough that nine of the 11 biggest record chains refused to carry it.

Subsequently, Farrell designed an alternate cover, though his original will be available to retailers on request when the album is released in August. The new cover is blank except for the title and, in small print, Article 1 of the Constitution, the one about Congress making no laws "abridging the freedom of speech or of the press."

The (Bleep) Goes On

Susan Baker; Tipper Gore, November 1988

Now that cable television has reached the District, many D.C. residents have realized that family programming is almost a thing of the past. By subscribing to cable, many viewers expected to lose commercials and gain the Discovery Channel and unlimited movies. Instead, they have discovered MTV, which features music videos that are often sexist and sexually explicit and a deluge of R-rated movies, many of which contain the dangerous ingredient of sexual violence. Women are most often the victims.

One dilemma that modern parents now face is this: how do we control our children's access to violent and sexually explicit entertainment without placing a childproof cap on the entertainment industry?

In 1985 we formed the Parents' Music Resource Center to grapple with this issue. We became aware that some music containing violent and sexually explicit themes was being marketed to our very young children.

As parents who grew up with rock 'n' roll, we weren't unfamiliar with the sound; it was some of the lyrics that shocked us. For example, the group Guns 'N' Roses sings to children of all ages: "Panties round your knees, with your ass in debris, doin' dat bump and grind with a push and squeeze." Their album, "Appetite For Destruction" spent weeks at the No. 1 spot on the Billboard Pop charts, has sold more than 5 million copies and features a graphic depiction of a raped, semi-nude woman in its artwork.

Our children are increasingly bombarded with violent, pornographic and pro-drug and alcohol messages. This forces us to become more involved with their listening and viewing habits.

We cannot be knowledgeable about every movie, video or song that is released, so consumer information from the entertainment industry is needed. If it is going to adopt the "sex and violence sells" philosophy, we want to know just what kind of sex and violence is being sold to our kids and bought with our money. The fact is that children aged 10 to 14 spend many millions of dollars every year on prerecorded music.

We met with representatives of the recording industry to stand up for our right as consumers to know the content of the music products we buy. As a result of these talks with the industry, a voluntary agreement was reached. Twenty-two of the major record companies agreed to alert the consumer to releases containing lyrics that are violent, sexually explicit or promote the use of drugs and alcohol by applying a warning label or printing the lyrics on the cover.

Since the agreement went into effect, there has been limited compliance on the part of the music industry. Some companies have shown a good-faith effort. However, most have not complied, or when they have, the warning labels are too small to be noticed or are hidden in the artwork.

Labeling is a form of information that consumers have come to demand for more and more products. Why should the recording industry be an exception?

U.S. consumers no longer want to buy their products blindly. Three recent national polls prove beyond a doubt that they want consumer information to facilitate their musical choices. The movie industry supplies this information through its voluntary rating codes. The video industry recently agreed to apply these ratings to its product. Even the television industry supplies copious programming information prior to the show. The music industry has yet to show that it will demonstrate good faith in alerting parents when recordings are violent or explicit.

Last month Congress passed the Child Pornography and Protection Act. This bill penalizes companies found to be selling written or auditory pornography deemed obscene by community standards. By unanimous vote (97-0), the Senate passed the bill as written. The House passed a revised version that dropped some of the more controversial provisions dealing with property seizure and forfeiture.

Passage of this legislation is evidence of the public's real concern about the popularization of pornography and its effect on society and how we raise our children. The inclusion of auditory pornography in this bill reflects the growing public awareness that the recording industry is not providing the tools parents and consumers need to make educated choices.

Years ago, the motion picture industry did not move to regulate itself until growing public concern activated statewide legislation. Faced with the prospect of hundreds of community rating boards, the movie industry decided to do the job itself.

The PMRC has never proposed or endorsed federal legislation, and we continue to work for voluntary measures. We hope that one day soon, the recording industry will understand that working for the public interest by answering the demand for consumer information is good business sense any way you look at it.

The Jukebox: A Century of Spinning Dreams

Richard Harrington, November 1988

It's been a long century for the jukebox.

Of course, the juke as we know it today is really only in its mid-fifties, approaching retirement age, but its prototype was introduced Nov. 23, 1889, at the Palais Royale in San Francisco, and today marks the beginning of the industry's centennial celebration. That primitive machine was actually a coin-operated phonograph with no speakers, four individual listening tubes—and a coin slot for each tube. Even then, the underlying principle was as much money as music.

Forty-five years later, they started building the classics, the kind where you slip your nickel into the dream machine and wait for the magic to happen. The nickel would drop down the slot—usually you could hear it join its brethren—and then came the sudden illumination of translucent plastic panels, sometimes creamy as unsunned skin, just as often rainbow-hued. There might be revolving color panels or oil-filled tubes, psychedelia before psychedelics.

You'd stand at the machine, not necessarily conscious of its soft shoulders and gentle curves, the subtle seduction of its finely crafted wood cabinets. Would look at the card titles—or flip through one of those little carousel remotes if you were sitting at a table in the malt shop—and press the buttons that matched your mood. You could peer through the glass window and listen for the whir of the motor as the chrome-plated mechanism searched out your selection, moving up and down or sideways, looking for connection. Then it would stop and the tray would swing out, the chosen disc flipping into position.

Then, the music.

During the golden age of the jukebox—roughly 1935 to 1950 for the manufacturers, another decade for the consumer—this scene was played out in front of 700,000 machines scattered across the United States in restaurants, bars, bowling alleys, soda shops, any place people tended to gather. Of course, if there was a jukebox, they would gather a little harder, often jitterbugging or whatnot to favorite songs of the moment—there to dance and make romance, as Chuck Berry would say.

The jukeboxes from this era are highly treasured now. They evoke a bygone era of innocence, which may be why baby boomers are willing to spend big bucks for them (into the low five figures for a 1946

Wurlitzer 1015, the Classic of Classics, and the most popular jukebox ever made). Having one in the basement—in working order, of course—creates an ambience in which people can conjure up their past. Some hip executives have even converted old Wall-O-Matic models into grand Rolodexes.

In the Swing Era of the '40s and even more in the early days of rhythm and blues and rock 'n' roll in the '50s, the jukebox was a symbol of independence—musically, socially, esthetically. You didn't hear a lot of classical music on the jukes; the emphasis was on American music rooted in American communities. Little wonder that during World War II, jukeboxes were often shipped to the troops overseas to give them a little taste of home. Rally round the juke, boys.

After the war, with America feeling its oats, there was a sudden national compulsion to make everything bigger and better. This was particularly true in the auto industry, arid pretty soon the big five of the jukebox world—Wurlitzer, Mills, Seeberg, Rock-Ola and AMI—were mimicking Detroit's option consciousness. They offered 100 or 200 selections where there had only been dozens before, and moved away from gracious curves, dark wood and colored plastics to angular shapes, metallic trim and a harsh fluorescent glare that reflected the more aggressive sound of postwar music.

Even in the late 1890s, when the sound was terrible, coin-operated phonographs were a familiar sight; there were "phonograph parlours," forerunners of today's video arcades, with dozens of machines, each with a linen towel to clean the earphone. Of course, back then, not only were phonograph players and records rare, they were so expensive most people couldn't afford to buy them. But they could afford to rent them, one play at a time. An industry was born.

Unfortunately, no effective selection system was developed until the 1900s. And even when the format moved from clumsy cylinders to the more convenient and longer-lasting 78 disc, the early models suffered from amplification problems, rendering them ineffective in public places. They competed with mechanical instruments (pianos in particular), and it wasn't until the mid-'20s, with the arrival of the Simplex multiselection mechanism and AMI's first electrically amplified phonograph, that people could gather to hear, and dance to, decently amplified music.

Then came the Depression, when even a nickel's worth of entertainment was a serious commitment. But with the repeal of Prohibition in 1933 and the return of alcohol and good times, people looking for cheap entertainment could turn to radio (which replaced the phonograph as the dominant musical medium) and to the jukes.

Some places would rent a jukebox for the weekend instead of hiring a band, and the primal relationships that still fuel the industry—operators and locations splitting the money, hot music being hyped—were reestablished.

The '30s also marked the emergence of the legendary manufacturers. Henry Ford-like characters came forth, foremost among them Homer Capehart, designer of 1928's Orchestrope, the first automatic machine able to play both sides of its 28 selections (it also spun off those remote control wall boxes). Unfortunately, the Orchestrope didn't work particularly well and it wasn't until after the Depression that the industry took hold.

Over the next 15 years, classic model after classic model was shipped out: Wurlitzer's Model 950 and its famous 1015; Rock-Ola's Rhythm King and Monarch; Seeberg's Gem, Crown, Casino Royal and Symphanola (in 1938, the first light-up jukebox); AMI's Streamliner, Singing Tower and Model A, a huge, garish machine dubbed "Mother of Plastic." Seeberg even had its Play-Boy, a juke that was wheeled around from table to table, much like a dessert wagon.

During World War II, and with jukeboxes hardly a vital commodity, the manufacturers converted to defense work. Since most of the world's shellac came from Japanese-controlled Southeast Asia, there was an immediate record shortage; new releases were few and far between. There was also a two-year musicians' union ban on recording, fueled partly by the popularity of jukeboxes and their ability to put musicians out of work (the head of the union referred to jukes as "Public Scab No. 10).

After the war, renewed competition between the various companies was marked by industrial espionage and one-upmanship. New models came out every other year, and when Seeberg brought out its M100A Selectomatic, for example—offering 100 selections where the norm has been half that—it vaulted to the top of the pack. Suddenly, anything with less than 100 choices seemed archaic.

The next advance was the introduction of the 45, and in 1950, Seeberg once again lead the way. Seeberg sensed that the smaller, lighter format was perfectly suited to the jukes, and could in fact expand the capacity to as many as 200 records per juke; its M110B was the first jukebox built strictly to accommodate 45s.

It took some of the other manufacturers two or three years to make the same commitment and, just as today's consumer has to choose among album, cassette and CD, early '50s jukebox owners had to choose among machines that played 78s, 45s and even LP's. Also in the 150s, the cost of a single play went from a nickel to a dime (it helped that the cost of a phone call went up at the same time). The last juke to accept nickels was built in 1951.

By this time, the classic art-decoish designs were a thing of the past. Instead, you could see the influence of Detroit in models like Rock-ola's Rocket, Comet and Fireball, some of which mimicked the grills and the tailfins of the autos du jour. Jukeboxes became symbols of the developing youth culture. In almost any youth-oriented film of the time, a jukebox figures somewhere in the action.

Then, without warning, times changed.

By the early '60s, the music industry focus had shifted to albums. A mass suburban migration meant there just weren't as many venues receptive to jukeboxes. Now it was car radios—and later, cassette players—that gave young folks their music. The '50s suddenly seemed hopelessly passé. Television took hold. Fast-food restaurants sprouted up, undermining the casual culture of diners, drug stores and malt shops. Restaurants shifted to Muzak, radio or tapes. Bars stuck televisions in the corner, often unplugging the jukebox. In the '80s came video games, stealing all the quarters.

Over these years, jukebox designs became more subdued and functional than grand and artistic; the jukes were consoles now, no longer dream machines. They are no longer the center of attention, but mechanical employees, often at bars and bowling alleys, working for tips.

Still, there are a lot of them out there (225,000 according to the Amusement and Music Operators Association, which estimates that 48 million songs are played each week, and that 78 million people hear them). Wurlitzer's last model came out in the early '70s—the 1050 was a nostalgic (but technically updated) version of the classic 1015, but it didn't take hold.

Seeberg went bankrupt, then went back into business in 1983 and now manufactures only the LaserMusic CD jukebox, the one with a thousand-plus selections, three for a dollar. You can play a whole album on the LaserMusic machine, which doesn't take coins: only dollar bills. AMI/Rowe manufactures a jukebox that plays both singles and CDs and there are several models of videojuboxes, though they seem only marginally more popular than the Mills Panorama models that failed in the '40s.

Rock-Ola's recent Nostalgia jukebox—with a bubble top, plastic panel, fancy grillwork and light shows based on a Wurlitzer design—didn't really catch on. But Wurlitzer's German division has started manufacturing the Wurlitzer One More Time—a faithful recreation of the 1015, with modern electrical components—and it has done well.

The new machines cost between $3,000 and $9,000; for quite a few dollars more, you can get the real thing at a place like Rockville's Home Amusement Company, which has hundreds of old jukes on its premises. A 1015 in top condition goes for as much as $12,000, though most models are priced considerably lower. Most of the refurbished classic models have changed their mechanisms from 78s to 45s, but for diehards, the Rhino label in California has started pressing 78s featuring the classic tunes you'd want on a jukebox. With the 45 format in serious decline these days, Rhino may have even more work in the 1990s.

What does the next century hold? Certainly not 1,200 options like the LaserMusic machine. Still, the jukebox will stick around as long as people keep feeding it. It won't occupy quite the same place in American culture it did from 1935 to 1960, but it will undoubtedly remain a resonant pop artifact—a machine that mirrors dreams and makes money in the bargain.

CHAPTER FIVE

The Movies

Voices of a Golden Age

Pat McGilligan, November 1986

They were originally poets, playwrights, journalists, songwriters or press agents, the generation of writers who streamed to Hollywood in the early sound era and created the storytelling rules that screen writers abide by today.

In a forthcoming book, "Backstory: Interviews With Screenwriters of Hollywood's Golden Age," some of the best screen writers of that era reminisce about the Golden Age of Hollywood.

Richard Maibaum (who arrived in 1935, and whose 50 credited screenplays include the Alan Ladd version of "The Great Gatsby"):

"Our trip West was our honeymoon. We were met at Pasadena—at that time the V.I.P.'s got off there. A limousine was waiting, so you didn't have to go through the crowd at the station in Los Angeles. An assistant of [MGM story editor] Sam Marx met us. He sat in front while Sylvia and I were in the back holding hands. As we passed the observatory, the guy says, 'The Griffith Observatory—see it before you go back.' Sylvia and I looked at each other.

"That night we strolled along Hollywood Boulevard, still holding hands. We got to Musso and Frank's and walked in. There was a place in the back where the writers gathered, and somebody was eating a salad with a lot of garlic at the next table. It smelled great, so we ordered it. A chiffonade salad. We still call it 'our salad.'"

Julius J. Epstein (in Hollywood since 1932, whose 50 screenplays include "The Male Animal," "Mr. Skeffington" and "Light in the Piazza"):

"I came out on a Friday and landed in the railroad station at ten o'clock at night. October 14, 1933. Twelve o'clock that night I was ghostwriting for two desperate people who shall remain nameless, because they had to take some stuff in [to Warner Bros.] on Monday and they had nothing to turn in. Sunday, one of them took me downtown to the Paramount Theatre—I think it was 'College Humor' with Bing Crosby and Mary Carlisle. He said, 'That's a fade-out. That's a dissolve. That's an iris-down.' That was my education in screenwriting. I think it's all you need.

"I learned by looking at other scripts. And I learned very early that directors pay no attention to that [technical language]. You just write: 'master scene,' 'cut to' or 'close shot'—which is very easy, you just mix it up. The master shots and the individual shots were all shot the same way. When I first arrived, I wrote an original story every night. In those days you didn't have to write a screenplay to sell, you could do ten or twenty pages of an idea. In about nine months one sold to Warners. I came in October and sold something in August. After a week Warners put me on a seven-year contract, and I was there under two seven-year contracts."

Philip Dunne (in Hollywood since 1932, he is the writer of about 40 screenplays including "How Green Was My Valley" and "The Ghost and Mrs. Muir"):

"I like to go to the movies. I liked to take a girl to the movies on Sunday. It was just something you did. But I thought movies were quite frivolous. The older generation of my time had no feeling of respect for movies. You have to pay respect now; it's an art. But to my parents and their friends, the movies were low-down popular entertainment. They didn't care much for movies.

"The only time I had movies treated seriously was when a Harvard professor of mine, a fine arts professor, took his Class of Six— it was a class in Renaissance sculpture, of all things—to see 'Flesh and the Devil' [1927] at the Paramount Theatre in Boston, so we could look on Garbo as a perfect Classical face. Very interesting. It was the first I could imagine a professor being interested in the movies. It had never occurred to me."

Allan Scott (who arrived in 1933 and wrote about 50 screenplays, including six of the 10 Astaire-Rogers musicals):

"My first office [at RKO] was in the newly erected building called 'The New Writers' Building'—very pleasant, large paneled woodwork offices with a room for one's secretary. Actually, I wrote mostly at home, which you were able to do after they realized you were really working. Between assignments, you'd come in, gossip, have lunch, wander around the lot, talk with the other writers, a nice life."

Epstein: "In those days, each studio had 75 to 200 writers. They did about 50 to 60 pictures a year, and there were about six studios—about 400 pictures a year plus independents. But if you look at the credits, the same names of about 150 to 200 writers kept popping up all the time, and they kept doing 90 percent of all the pictures. The same writers, the same names. You were given the assignments. Today, you write something; if you sell it, it's a picture. If you don't sell it . . ."

Niven Busch (in Hollywood since 1931, whose credits include the novel "Duel in the Sun" and the screenplays of "In Old Chicago" and "The Postman Always Rings Twice," for MGM):

"I was awed. I was accustomed to sitting and thinking a long time before I had an idea. Like doping out a 2,000-word short story might take me all week. But these guys—story ideas, plot, construction, motivation was the grist of their live. The way they bandied about ideas that streamed out, they all seemed like instant whiz-kid brains. Instead of being alone to plot something out, you might work on three stories in a week. You'd hear a shoeshine boy who'd been to the preview the night before say, 'Well, sir, I thought the third act was weak—wasn't really enough motivation.' What you thought was your craftsmanship coming from the forehead of Minerva was only the rules of the game."

Frances Goodrich (who arrived in 1932 and, with her husband Albert Hackett, wrote screenplays ranging from "The Thin Man" to "Father of the Bride" to Nelson Eddy-Jeanette MacDonald musicals):

"We had a wonderful table [at MGM] in the commissary. Just think of the people who were there! Dashiell Hammett, Ogden Nash, Sid Perelman, Laura Perelman, Dorothy Parker and Alan Campbell . . . a wonderful group of people!"

Albert Hackett: "When we got to California, if you were a writer, the only people you ever knew were writers. The actors, the big ones, all were friendly with producers. The only exceptions were Freddie March and a couple of stars we had known in the theater; a couple of times we'd go to dinner with them. But most of the time . . ."

Goodrich: "There was such a caste system out in Hollywood. There was never anything like it. There were layers and layers, you know. And the lowest layer was the writers."

Hackett: "Less than dust."

Busch: "Once I had become accustomed to Hollywood, I was very happy. Happier than I had been in New York. But I was doing the drudgery and I'd had the insecurity and the loneliness. A writer at that time was not an important person; you went from your little apartment to the studio, and you worked like a s.o.b. You didn't have time for much social life. You didn't meet many women. In my second year, I began to play polo because I was a good horseman. And polo was very fashionable. Horses were cheap and I could afford it. We had learned as kids to play polo on bicycles. That was my great relaxation. I played polo every day for ten years. I don't think it helped me hugely in my career, but it did afford me some good companionship."

W.R. Burnett (who arrived in 1930 and whose 60 screenplays include "Scarface" in 1932 and "The Great Escape" in 1963):

"[William] Faulkner was an absolute Southern gentleman, precisely dressed, when he was sober. Faulkner really looked like Poe. I would cast Faulkner as Poe. I really liked him.

"He was a very quiet man. One time, when I was standing outside the studio [Warner Bros.], Bill came out smoking his pipe, and we stood there for a few minutes, exchanging a couple of words. on the lot we had one of those overnight geniuses—a woman—someone who had published a book about her family or some silly thing and is suddenly a national celebrity and then you never hear of them again. They were making her movie at the time, and she was throwing her weight around the studio.

"Oh, she was a most unpleasant person. She began to raise hell with Faulkner because of his terrible influence on American writing. Faulkner smoked his pipe, and looked at her. People who were passing by looked embarrassed. I just stood there, what else could I do? He never said a word, never said a word, not to me, not to her. Just smoked his pipe."

Dunne: "I object to the notion that [people like] F. Scott Fitzgerald were ruined by Hollywood. People forget Fitzgerald wrote a perfectly terrible play—unplayable ['The Vegetable']—before he came to Hollywood and nobody says Broadway ruined him. Back in the 1930s, there were a lot of us who went around together—Ted Paramore, Nunnally Johnson, John O'Hara, the Hacketts, Arthur Sheekman, Joel Sayre. These were mostly fugitives from New York. And we knew, peripherally, Thomas Mann, Aldous Huxley, Lion Feuchtwanger, Fitzgerald, those people. Nobody was very excited about being at a party with them. Now, people are awestruck when you say you knew Thomas Mann or Fitzgerald. No, we were sorry for Fitzgerald; we were not awestruck by him."

Burnett: "I didn't think any of the studios valued writers very much. If the writer could fit the Warners system, it was far and away the best place to be. And I wrote every place. Metro—you might as well be out in the middle of a desert. Nobody ever knew you were there. You could sit there for four weeks, and draw your pay and not say anything and you never heard from anybody. Paramount was always hit-or-miss—they had people coming in and out. It wasn't a well-run place, ever. Columbia was a tight ship. Harry Cohn was tough, real tough. Republic was a joke. And Fox, I would say, was very well run under Darryl Zanuck. Very well run."

Dunne: "The script was king at Twentieth [Century Fox] because we had no stars to begin with. I think people started out at Warners by saying, 'Let's do a Bogart picture.' I know at Metro, Thalberg always worked from the star up. Zanuck never had stars in the early days, and apart from that whole group that worked mostly in musicals, he didn't have that many big dramatic stars.

"I'm not saying the great bulk of the product was great. The 'B' pictures were a big part of the program. I'm saying, for example, that in the 20 years Zanuck was at Fox, I think there were five Academy Awards for best director given to Fox pictures . . . In a discussion like this, I tend to think of the top pictures of each studio, and there I think Fox scripts were the best."

Scott: "At RKO, writers were treated generously. There was none of the committee writing so prevalent at other studios. [Producer] Pandro Berman permitted us to do what no other studio permitted at the time—for example, I was on the set constantly during shooting, something new for writers in those days.

"At other studios, those writers who were low on the totem pole were treated as a necessary evil but not for long once films began to talk . . .Hollywood was at its height, powerful, alone, dispensing its pictures all over the world, seemingly impregnable, and under no direct assault from outside sources. A small, almost inbred community. They kept referring to it as the "industry," and the heads of the studios kept thinking of themselves as the captains of industry."

Burnett: "I never had any idea of turning my novels into movies. Some of them just fell into movies and some of them didn't. I sold seventeen of them [to movies]. But it was just the reverse for me—I worked in pictures to subsidize novel writing. Novel writing was what I was interested in—not pictures . . . What happened to so many good American novelists when they came out here didn't happen to me. They got into the big money and quit writing novels. I published some 35 novels. I was actually subsidizing myself so I could write novels.

got into the big money and quit writing novels. I published some 35 novels. I was actually subsidizing myself so I could write novels.

"Films I never took seriously as an artistic endeavor. But I always did the best possible work I could do; I never brushed it off or anything. Under the circumstances, which are never any good; the circumstances are mostly poor, because writers have no control whatsoever. Screenwriting consists of rewriting, and I don't rewrite. I don't have to rewrite. I know what I'm writing when I write."

Scott: "The '30s was a great learning period for me, and what the studio was pleased to call my gift for first-class dialogue got me over the early days.

Busch: "When I made the move [to Hollywood], terrible adjustments had to be made. I don't know to this day if I did the right thing. I might have been an entirely different kind of writer—might have been a better recognized writer, might have been a more literary writer . . .

"Now, it might have been that without the Hollywood training I had I might never have been able to make a living—certainly not as good a living. Of course, I wrote quite a string of novels, all of which were successful. Some were praised by critics, some were denounced; but every one was a good story, and every one sold. And 'Duel in the Sun' and some of the others were very big. The story craft I learned and I put into them, I learned at the screenwriter's bench."

Norman Krasna (in Hollywood since 1931, he is the comedy expert whose work included "The Devil and Miss Jones," "Let's Make Love" and the Oscar-winning screenplay for "Princess O'Rourke," which he also directed):

"There are some people who are professional writers because they wear steel-rimmed glasses and look like writers and have a whole list of credits. You can live a whole life as a writer in Hollywood without ever having written a movie, and you can still be considered one of the great ones. Such writers will do either an original story or write the screenplay of someone else's story. The story can be so full that fleshing it out is not my idea of sensational; or they write the story, and somebody else can make something absolutely fabulous out of it. I don't consider that you're a real, real screenwriter unless is frail enough and the contribution is just marvelous.

"I claim that if you're been in the business 30 or 40 years and you look back, I would think that one of the things that ought to stick out is what pictures you did that reflect what you are, your experiences. You may only have had a few, two or three or four, but you're a writer. You write motion pictures. To make a living at adapting is a big trick; but out of 30 or 40 years, didn't you write anything that is yours? I use that word subjectively. I belittle the writers who took a great book and adapted it; that's all?

"I think I wrote what showed me off—romantic comedies. In the end they were never the big, big pictures; but they were mine. At the end of the whole picture, I'm the hero's witness."

Dunne: "I agree with my old friend Jo Swerling, one of the earliest screenwriters, who said screenwriting is not so much an art as like fine cabinetmaking. I think that's right. Nunnally [Johnson] used to use that analogy too. He picked it up from the same source I did, I'm sure. We never claimed to be artists, but we thought we were good craftsmen."

Krasna: "Here's the big change in storytelling [today]; they've given up the theme. Never mind the end! You see the most wonderful pictures today; scenes are just great, great, great. Then, suddenly, the crawl comes. I don't expect the crawl to come for another ten minutes— they haven't resolved anything. But you know, they haven't got any dull periods. They give you these great scenes, you've had a good time for two hours, and you've only had an unsatisfactory 30 seconds. People are accustomed to it. You go out and see this picture, which doesn't add up and is about nothing, and people say, 'I didn't like the ending, but...'

"Do you see all the thousands of books I've got here on the shelf? Since Aeschylus. In my generation they gave up plots with character formation. I had to be born now!"

Epstein: "The constant in Hollywood, which is a terrible thing, is pandering to what they think the public wants. Today they pander to the young kids who go see a movie four or five times—I'm not even talking about teenagers; I'm talking about kids who are nine, ten, eleven, or twelve years old. That's always been true of the studios. But not quite. In the days of the contract system, they all fought to get Ernst Lubitsch. His pictures never made it, they were all losers, but the studios all fought to get him. He could go from studio to studio. They wanted a little class in their program.

"But the pandering has never been as bad. In those days they wanted to make women's pictures—the four-handkerchief pictures with the Crawfords and the Shearers. So they were pandering to that; today they are pandering to kids. It's the pandering that is constant."

Krasna: "TV has taken up the motion of a beginning, a middle, and an end. I'm fascinated. It's child's play now. I look at "M*A*S*H," "Alice" or "The Jeffersons" every time I can put my feet up. I know what the rules are, and I couldn't do it as well. They're witty in what they do and how inventive they get. But when you are talking about a whole movie, I would think by now TV has used up all the plot twists, and you need something stark and wild. Maybe the art form has advanced. But if I was Vermeer, I would be sick to my stomach that Jackson Pollock is making all this money. I would say, 'Let me see you do a thumb!'"

Epstein: "What has changed the most? There's no more contract system. There's no more machine-belt production. There are no more clubs. There is no studio system, and the way of making pictures is entirely different. And much less fun. Pictures are better. I think pictures are much better today. People who say the golden age of movies was great, that's baloney. But they're not as much fun to make."

Having Fun with Hollywood

Richard Harrington, March 1987

It took Robert Townsend just 14 days and $100,000 to make "Hollywood Shuffle." Of course, the perils of independent filmmaking being what they are, those 14 days were spread out over 2 1/2 years. As for the hundred grand—which is probably less than Stallone spends on body oil in a single film—the fledgling mogul put a lot of it on his credit cards.

Townsend, who cowrote, produced and directed "Hollywood Shuffle," also plays a dozen distinct roles in this uproarious but bittersweet comedy. The film examines Hollywood's treatment of black actors and actresses—a process he's intimately familiar with. Anchored around a short Townsend made in 1984, "Hollywood Shuffle" slowly evolved into the feature now playing at area theaters.

Besides being extremely funny, "Hollywood Shuffle"—with its 83 speaking parts—is something of a demo reel for dozens of black actors and actresses (there are Hispanics and whites in it, as well) who, like Townsend, have been stymied by the dead-end stereotyping lampooned in the film.

"It's a lot of pain, but I didn't want to be bitter," Townsend says. "I have friends who are really bitter, and they go, 'Man, this industry is so rough . . . man, it makes me mad . . . if I was a white boy, they'd have me do . . .'

"And I'm not gonna get into that. I'd rather make a movie about it than just go, 'Woe is me, woe, woe.' I love people, so the only way I could do it is with love and being funny. I'm a comedian by nature."

The early word on "Shuffle" is that Townsend's comic touch comes through. 'Hilarious,' said Playboy. "Exuberant satire," said The New York Times. He's being heralded as the next Eddie Murphy (more on that later) or the new Spike ("She's Gotta Have It") Lee.

Townsend groans.

"It's just a shame because Eddie's style of comedy and my style of comedy are totally different," he says. "It's just that we're both young and black. And Spike's movie and my movie, we're just filmmakers who happen to be black."

For Robert Townsend, the acting end wasn't new—the 30-year-old is a gifted comic and mimic who's well known on the improv circuit and has appeared in a number of off-Broadway shows and Hollywood films. But he emerged as a potential behind-the-camera star through a distinctly unusual route.

And he couldn't have done it, he says, without Visa and MasterCard.

"I'd just done 'Streets of Fire' and 'A Soldier's Story' back to back," Townsend explains. Sitting on a hotel sofa during a recent Washington stopover, he leans forward and back, gesturing dramatically, barely able to contain his excess energy. "When I came home [to Los Angeles] I had all this money and my friends were saying, 'What are you going to do? You going to get a Porsche? A town house?' And my agent was saying, 'You should feel really lucky you did "Soldier's Story" 'cause they do one black movie a year and that's it.'

"And I'm going, 'Okay. Now what do I do?' I just wanted to work.

"So I decided to do a short. The way Hollywood is, there's always one black in every movie so I've got all these friends who are talented, even though none of them can get work. I said, 'Why don't we all get together and do a movie?'

"And they said, 'Who's going to direct us?'"

"And I said, 'I'll direct us.'"

The result was "Sam Ace," a grainy black-and-white spoof of Sam Spade, Mike Hammer and TV crime shows. "Then those TV critics blasted some movie I liked and it made me mad. So me and my partner, Keenen Wayans, rolled out 'Sneakin' in the Movies' to get back at them.'" In this short, Townsend and comedian Jimmy Woodard portray Speed and Tyrone, two streetwise appraisers of the cinema arts.

Despite the critical acclaim for the ensemble work in "A Soldier's Story"—Townsend played the jeep driver—he found himself, like many of the other black actors, back in Hollywood auditioning for the same old roles: "a slave on 'North and South,' a rapist on 'Hill Street Blues,' a mugger on 'Cagney and Lacey.' I said they need a school for this, and that's how the 'Black Acting School' piece came about." (It features black actors in class learning "jive" so they can get those plum roles as pimps, hoods and slaves.)

"We had all these little things together that looked good, so I said, 'Let's create a story around them,'" Townsend recalls. "We started writing and meanwhile I did four other movies, working on 'Hollywood Shuffle' in between. But I ran out of money and that's when I got desperate. I was like a junkie at that point . . . 'I gotta finish this film!'"

One day, early last year, his day's mail included an application for a preferred Visa and MasterCard.

"At first I was going to tear it up, but then I opened it and it said, 'Mr. Townsend, you have a credit line of $8,000 on one card and $9,000 on the other.' And I realized, 'Wait a minute, I could charge the film.'

"By the time I was done, I had a $40,000 bill.

"You'd be surprised, you can charge anything," Townsend says, gratefully. "Since I couldn't pay people, I'd do what I could do to help them out. I'd fill their tanks with gas, go to the Shell station and say, 'See those 20 cars out there? Put it on my Visa.'

"Catering? Me and my girlfriend went shopping at the supermarket—chicken, potato chips, pretzels, all those snacks—we'd put it on Visa. Same with wardrobe. The most important question when I was finishing the movie was 'Do you take Visa or MasterCard?'"

Everybody was working for free, though they've all got points in the film's potential profits. They did it, Townsend believes, because "at least I was trying."

"Hollywood Shuffle" was shot on the run. Equipment and wardrobe filled one van, actors another. Locations were scouted, invaded and vacated before the police could get there to ask questions about permits. When the cops did show up and ask who was the producer, who was the director, Townsend says, "everybody would point at me! We got through it, but it took nerves, trying to sneak and do stuff in broad daylight."

Of the 14 days of shooting, three were in 1984, six in 1985 and the rest last year. "My brother has a small role and I call my mother to check: 'How tall is he now?'"

And of course, Townsend was working with a budget the size of most films' insurance payments.

He would rent a camera on a Friday to be able to use it over the weekend for free. As for film stock, sympathetic directors from pictures Townsend was acting in would donate "shortage," the raw film left over from different scenes. "I got film from 'American Flyers,' and some of the shortage from 'Rat Boy,' and some from 'Odd Jobs.' When you have only a hundred feet of film, which is a minute, you're limited," he says. Which is why almost everything in "Hollywood Shuffle" was shot in one take, usually preceded by vigorous rehearsal.

Once armed with his credit cards, though, Townsend grew bolder. "We're talking 'Mission Impossible.' There's a place in Los Angeles that caters to film students and so I bought T-shirts that said 'UCLA.' And I'd go into the place with my UCLA T-shirt on—I've been out of school for years—and usually when students buy raw stock, they'll say 'Give me a can of film,' about a hundred feet for $200.

"I go into the place and the lady says 'How much film do you want?' and I say '10,000 feet.' But I'm cool. So she goes in the back room and comes back with cans and cans and cans and says, 'That will be $5,000.'"

"And I go, 'Okay . . . here, put it on my Visa.'"

"So I wait, and she takes it to the machine and it goes bdl-bdl-doop and I'm waiting and she's waiting.

"She looks at me and goes, 'Will that be all?'

"And I go 'Yessss.'"

Making "Hollywood Shuffle," Townsend says, "was like going to film school. I had to learn what it was to be a producer and a director, how to cut corners and edit in my head."

He had served an unofficial apprenticeship on the Arkansas location of "A Soldier's Story," where he'd find himself "drifting over by the camera because so many of my friends were working on the movie. Rather than go back to the hotel I just hung out around the set when my friends were shooting—Denzel Washington, David Alan Grier, Adolph Caesar. I'm on the side of the camera, Norman Jewison is directing, and then I hear the cinematographer, Russell Voight, go 'Get me an 85 lens out of there, I need an 85' and I say 'What's that?'"

Townsend and Voight became friends. "We would talk and I would look through his viewfinder, and he'd say 'This is a 20 here, look, and this is 35. If you want to go in close, this is a close shot.' And I'm just listening to him because I didn't want to go back to the hotel.

"When it came time for me to shoot my film, the first time I looked at a camera I didn't know what I was looking at because I didn't really understand composition and everything. I've got this whole crew together and I've never directed, when somebody says 'Townsend, come over here and look at this shot.'"

He was nervous, he confesses. But "I wanted to work as a director. And when you really want something, there's no obstacle."

Townsend got his first laughs in an unlikely spot—riding the bench of his high school basketball team in Chicago.

"That's where it all began," he says, admitting he was not an imposing ballplayer. "Everybody else would be wondering when they were going to get in the game and I'd be sitting there doing characters and dialect, like Walter Brennan." He slips into a perfect imitation: "'Dad gab, coach, I got a jump shot, I'll go to the basket . . .'

"And the team would be laughing. They'd tell me 'Townsend, you can't play—but you're funny.'"

Townsend's gift for mimicry developed early. "My mother kept us in the house a lot," he explains. "She had four small kids growing up in a tough neighborhood and she didn't want the gangs to mess with us. And so I used to watch a lot of TV.

"But I was a weird kid—I watched PBS, classic performances like the Royal Shakespeare Company doing 'King Lear' and 'Othello.'

"The first time I realized I had a special gift was when we were doing 'Oedipus' in my inner city black school. I played Tiresias, the blind prophet. The other kids started reading and it was 'Oedipus-you-shall-marry-your-mother' . . . He says the words in a flat, running monotone. "But when it came to my part, I went"—and here he begins to make like Laurence Olivier—' "Oedipus, it is your destiny thusly to go forth and to pierce an eye . . .'"

The drama teacher applauded, but "the kids went, 'Yo, man, where you learn how to talk like that?' At that point, I knew something wasn't right."

So he figured out how to use his talents in ways that didn't alienate his peers. Sometimes he'd be the class cutup (while teachers would be writing on the blackboard, he'd bark like a dog running loose in class, and they'd look for the hidden mutt). Other times he'd mimic parents' voices on the phone to school. "In the ghetto, I was like a double agent. I could be an employer, I could play the boss. It was a crooked way of doing things, but I had a gift."

At 16, he got his first good notices, playing half a dozen roles in an amateur theater production of a surrealist comedy. But acting was still an illusion, not an option. Townsend's grandmother—like the grandmother in "Hollywood Shuffle"—tried to get him to give up "the acting fantasy, to get a real job, go to the post office and get an application. My mother would catch me in the bathroom rehearsing scenes: 'Is someone else in there with you?' I didn't get encouragement, so I kept the dream to myself."

One time, though, Townsend brought down his guard and confided to one of his schoolmates. "Next day he was in school, telling everybody, 'Man, this dude want to be an actor . . . Robert want to be an actor, man . . . want to act like he got some money . . . wants a lemo-zine, not a Volks-wagen!'

"I felt humiliated.

"From that day on I said I'm never going to tell anybody my dreams.

I'm just going to do it."

He wouldn't even confide in Spike Lee, newly acclaimed for "She's Gotta Have It," when he paid Townsend a visit last year. "Spike came to house and he's an arrogant bastard," Townsend says, laughing. "'I am Spike, therefore I exist.' But I didn't say anything until much later. I kept my plans private."

One of the funniest and most caustic episodes in "Hollywood Shuffle" is a cattle-call of "Eddie Murphy-types," all struggling to be carbon copies of the original because that's what Hollywood wants. It's a scene that left Townsend just a little apprehensive when Murphy asked for a private screening at the Paramount studio.

"The day I had the screening his bodyguards, his father, his uncle, these people showed up. I get there and they're all there. And I go, 'Damn, I thought it was just going to be Eddie.' Then Eddie sat right behind me.

"And as soon as that scene came on, the room goes silent . . . everybody got real quiet, waiting to see what the King was going to do. Then all the Murphy types are on the screen . . . and Eddie starts laughing . . . and then everybody else starts laughing.

"Afterwards Eddie says, 'That scene you wrote about me, when you play it for other audiences, does it get a big laugh?'

"I go, 'Yeah.'

"And he says, 'I thought there was some tension in the room.'

Recently, Townsend directed an Eddie Murphy concert film for Paramount (it's due out this summer). And he is surprisingly good natured about the Murphy comparisons.

"To be compared to one of the biggest stars in Hollywood isn't so bad," he insists. "It's when they go 'He's the next Flip Wilson,' that I get nervous."

Robert Townsend's last credit card transaction was to rent the Writers Guild screening room for a distributor screening. Although a number of companies expressed interest, he went with the Samuel Goldwyn Co. ("Stranger Than Paradise," "Dance With a Stranger," "Repo Man") because "I felt they'd handle my baby special."

He's says he's not afraid of a professional backlash. "One of my friends said 'Oh man, you're going to get blacklisted!' I said, 'What?' 'For telling the truth.' But the industry people who have seen this so far have embraced it. A lot of times it's an education."

In Hollywood, he says, many black actors complain, "'It's the white man, the white man is doing this to us.' But a lot of times, just like in the movie, it's the actors themselves. I'll go in there and read a script— 'I ain't be got no weapon . . . wha's happenin' mama, sho''nuff . . .' And I'll go, 'Wait, I don't talk this way.' But the next guy will come in and say, 'Hey this is a great script, I'd love to do it.'

"A lot of times the studios didn't even know these problems existed because nobody was speaking up.

"Right now my deals aren't based on the amount of money I'll make but the amount of control I'll have. I like Woody Allen's situation. He does the kinds of movies he wants to do and they're always quality, he has that integrity."

Townsend likes Allen's role as a cultural interpreter as well.

"I used to go to Woody Allen movies and have a great time and then somebody'd say 'bar mitzvah' and the audience would fall out of their seats . . . and I'd be sitting there saying 'What's bar mitzvah?' I think 'Shuffle's' going to be an education. It's like a foreign film, and I love foreign films because you hear dialogue and see stuff that is unique. And that's what movies should be about."

Since "Hollywood Shuffle" was finished, the good word has gone out and Townsend's been approached with a number of projects and roles. But he's moving cautiously, to the point of turning down a television series that he says would have paid him $20,000 per episode. He still does the comedy clubs and just finished an episode of "Amazing Stories," though he's done little television comedy.

"I never wanted to be on TV just for the sake of being on TV," he says—particularly the kind of sitcom savagely parodied in the "Batty Boy" sequence in "Shuffle."

"You have to decide if you're in for the long haul or the short haul," he says. "If I do a TV series now I'd always be Batty Boy. At a Laker game not long ago Jimmy Walker sat a few rows in front of me and people walked by and went 'J. J.—Dyn-O-Mite!' And I heard somebody say, 'That's that stupid dude from the TV show.'

Would I ever want to be known as a stupid dude from a TV show?"

Townsend's quick to point out that he's not a snob. "I love doing street characters, but also Sam Ace, a tough detective who talks straight, and Bobby Taylor, a sensitive caring guy caught in the middle of it. I don't care—if there's balance. I wouldn't mind playing a pimp if I could play a lawyer or a surgeon the next week.

"When I think about the images and roles I want to do, I'm going to have to hold out, that's all. Hopefully now they'll look at me and know that I mean business, because a lot of times in Hollywood when you say no they think, 'How much more money do you want?'

"If the film hadn't got picked up, I'd probably be in some comedy club in Hoboken, New Jersey, paying off high interest rates on $40,000 in credit card bills . . . And now casting directors are going 'Where did you find all these people?' I say these are my friends, the same people who come in and you give them those cold shoulders . . .

"I'm just glad it all came together. My family's still going through hard times in Chicago and I couldn't even tell my mother I had

$100,000 invested in a film. I didn't tell her until we got ready to shoot the last day. I flew her out for a real small part. When I'm in the makeup chair, she's the one who says, 'Here's your jacket, Mr. Taylor.'"

For now, Robert Townsend has shrugged off Hollywood's straitjacket, and he's busy fitting himself for the future. "I want every movie I do to be classic," he says. "I want to work that hard. I want to write the rewrites, cast the cast, scout the locations, like the old studio movies. I've got to learn studio policy if I'm going to play the studio game or go back out on the streets with my credit cards again."

Then it hits him.

"Of course, now I'll have more credit cards and bigger credit lines, so I can do bigger films."

That's known as the Hollywood Option.

On the Cutting Edge

Desson Howe, March 1987

She's the one who lets Woody be Woody.

Susan E. Morse is the name on the credits. She goes by Sandy. She's tall, given to sheepish seventh-grader smiles, and has edited everything from "Manhattan" to "Radio Days."

She took over as Allen's editor from the esteemed Ralph Rosenblum, who left to make his own films and to write. And now, at 34, she's an Oscar nominee for "Hannah and Her Sisters." She took time off last week from a new picture to appear on a panel at the Women Make Movies film festival at the American Film Institute.

She's here to talk about being There.

"The best part of being nominated," she says in a silky, affable tone, "was telling my mother. She was so proud."

On the balcony of the Kennedy Center, the mood is balmy, languid. The mood of the cutting room, with daily rushes coming in, seems far away, closeted in some cinematic corner of Manhattan where Alvy Singer, Annie Hall and Danny Rose meander in clouds of urban doubt. Here where the bureaucrats trudge it's breezy and sunny. Planes fly over the Potomac. Daffodils push through sod. And Morse dressed nouvelle brunch in red sweater and flannel slacks, is talking about working for one of America's most popular living directors.

"Back in ancient Rome," she's saying, "they used to have triumphal processions for the conquering hero. He'd ride through the city in a chariot. And there'd always be a slave assigned to ride with him who'd whisper 'you're only a man' in his ear while he was being applauded in triumph."

That, she says, "is the role of the editor."

So what's it like to edit Allen?

She smiles that self-conscious grin, as if you had just screamed, "So tell us about your new boyfriend, Sandy," across a junior high school quad.

"It's not unlike a marriage," she says, her voice almost lost in the din of an overhead aircraft. "You're working for the same thing, and you're both aware early of the other's flaws. It's very interesting. You're both concerned with the end result. The key thing is honesty."

Part of that honesty is a cold-eyed detachment toward the material. "Your natural impulse is to dismiss everything that works," she says. "You immediately neglect what is good."

The director, she says, "has got built in how he wrote it, how it was conceived, the nuances of the performances he heard in his head, the problems he had in camera placement . . . It can distract him from really looking at it."

Being tactful about technical problems—being something of an ego stroker—is frequently part of the job description, says Morse, who edited Steve Gordon's "Arthur," Rosenblum's public television drama "The Greatest Man in the World," and assisted on Walter Hill's "The Warriors," Martin Scorsese's "Raging Bull," Jim Kouf's "Miracles" and Marshall Brickman's "Simon."

"You have to force yourself to talk about the good stuff more," she says. "It can be devastating to see someone not laughing at all your jokes . . . Although with Woody, you don't have to be as tactful as you do with others. He's more secure in himself."

Allen takes sobering news very well, she says. "He isn't married to the material in the sense some directors are." In fact, many of his films have been radically restructured in the editing room.

In "Annie Hall," which Morse worked on as Rosenblum's assistant, "Woody's original intention was to focus more generally on a midlife crisis," she says. "But it turned out to be about the relationship between Annie and Alvy. The film cried out to be restructured. But Woody's material permitted and even encouraged that. It was easy to move the material around."

And "Zelig," a technical tour de force that interweaves authentic and imitation newsreel footage, was finessed in the editing room over a period of two years, with Allen frequently rewriting jokes and situations for the evolving film.

Yet although "Annie Hall" received Academy Awards for best picture, direction, actress and screenplay, Rosenblum was not nominated for his editing. Indeed—and in keeping with the baffling vagaries of the Academy—of the 24 nominations Allen's films have received over the years, Morse's for "Hannah and Her Sisters" is the first in the editing category.

You wouldn't know what the editor does by reading the average film review or even by seeing the average film. Morse and her colleagues can only hope for a brief "and some fine editing by . . ." as public recognition. "Nobody knows what happens between any editor and a director," Rosenblum says, interviewed later. "It's the most hidden relationship in the movie business, because nobody's around."

But Morse gets gratification enough when colleagues recognize her work, she says. She hesitates to single out her contributions to Allen's pictures. "It's sort of like team sports," she says, referring to the collaborative aspect of making films. "It doesn't matter who passes the ball, whether so and so gets an assist, or who gets the goal. You just want to come up with the best end result."

What the editor does is transform thousands of feet of film and sound tape—sometimes up to 40 hours—into some 90 minutes of intercut image and sound. Consecutive 16-hour days can be spent pondering whether a sound effect precedes or accompanies a shot, whether a reaction shot helps or harms a scene, whether the second take is better than the twenty-second. Hard choices occur at every turn, all in the name of moving the story forward. This means junking the director's jokes, shots and scenes by the score. Morse remembers the unpleasant chore of cutting a friend's performance completely out of "Arthur." The weary cliche' "left on the cutting room floor" is, for her, a daily consideration.

One such outtake, from Allen's "The Purple Rose of Cairo," was a "beautiful, high, wide-angle shot which was envisioned as the last shot . . . Cecilia is retreating in front of the theater down the street, where she discovered the screen character from Hollywood had left and was not going to meet her. And that shot was a beautiful shot, poignant and evocative of the Depression of the 130s. It had a wonderful feel, but it was also devastating . . . because she looked so dejected and small as she walked off in this desolate setting. The end of the film was too devastating with that as the final image. So we went with something with an uplifting quality."

Some of Allen's jokes cut out of one film can be used again in another. "There was a joke that was part of the cocktail party scene in 'Annie Hall' which turned up as a recall in 'Manhattan,' then was cut and likely as not will show up again."

She doesn't want to give the joke away.

Morse learned her techniques mostly at Rosenblum's elbow. After a liberal arts degree at Yale, her interest in making films was piqued while she observed BBC and ITV productions in London. She enrolled at New York University's film school and, in fall 1975, answered a bulletin board ad for editorial help on "A Secret Space," a film for a public television dramatic series. She was then recommended to Rosenblum, who was cutting another film for PBS, originally titled "Remember Those Poker Playing Monkeys."

"He said he was Ralph Rosenblum," says Morse, who was sleeping in on April Fool's Day 1975 when he rang. "I was certain it was a joke and hung up on him. He called later and said, 'Are you awake now? Seriously, it's Ralph Rosenblum.'"

"Obviously, she had the intelligence and the background," Rosenblum remembers. "She was very in control of herself, and a bit anxious and a bit afraid, which told me immediately she wouldn't go to pieces when the pressure was on in the cutting room."

For Morse, working hands-on was a "wonderful experience for someone insatiable about learning filmmaking."

Rosenblum asked her to work on "Annie Hall" the following year. "I had the choice of paying for a film education or being paid for one," Morse says. She dropped out of NYU, and they worked together on that and "Interiors." And when Rosenblum accepted an offer to direct a film, there was a job open on Allen's upcoming "Manhattan."

"I think Sandy was timid about calling him and asking," Rosenblum says. "I encouraged her to call him. And she's been there ever since."

When Allen gave her the job, Morse was "terrified and elated at the same time. A natural question occurred—how did I become editor? You don't believe it was just a phone call. You feel there has to be something more to it than this."

There wasn't. Morse took "Manhattan." And "A Midsummer Night's Sex Comedy," "Zelig," "Broadway Danny Rose," "The Purple Rose of Cairo," "Hannah" and this year's "Radio Days."

Since "Annie Hall" there have been profound changes in the Allen oeuvre. He has evolved from "a wonderful, funny gag writer," as Rosenblum fondly remembers him, to auteur. And Morse entered the picture right at the pivotal stage. There are not only thematic differences in Allen's post-"Annie" pictures, but also the difference between Rosenblum's and Morse's approaches.

Morse says she is more concerned with "attention to detail," with things that "are probably not that important. It's like crossing t's and dotting i's." Rosenblum, she says, was "more concerned with the forest than the trees, and I'm concerned with both . . . I guess I'm a perfectionist."

"I have a feeling she spends a lot of time in the cutting room," says Rosenblum, "because she's painstaking, extremely painstaking."

"There are absurd moments when you think about editing," she says. Like the time she was looking out at the line between sky and ocean from a California beach and thought, "That looks like a soft edge wipe."

For Morse, her career has been "a fairy tale . . . I don't really to this day believe I've been nominated for an Academy Award." She

always figured she'd go the route of her older sister, who works at
Morgan Guaranty Trust and has two children. Instead Morse makes
movies and has been living with playwright Jack Richardson for
"eight or nine years."

Asked about the new film, she says, "I can't tell you anything
about it. That's the way Mr. Allen is."

Asked to describe the work she's proudest of, Morse says, "It's
funny, it's like the Prodigal Son. You think of the films which had the
worst problems to face. 'Zelig,' 'Purple Rose' and 'Radio Days' afforded
the greater challenges."

Indeed, "Zelig" was a concentrated collaboration among Morse,
cinematographer Gordon Willis and many others. Allen wanted to
insert his character into old newsreel footage, so Willis shot new scenes
through aged lenses and Morse superimposed Leonard Zelig in
available gaps in the stock film—such as next to Adolf Hitler and Babe
Ruth. The film was then washed out and the sound quality degraded,
and dirt and scratches superimposed for an archival appearance.

It was "a lot of trial and error and experimentation," Morse says.
"We went to extraordinary pains." The months of minutiae were
"excruciating, but also an enormous amount of fun . . . Film does come
together in the end." And in the end, Willis won an Oscar for his work.

Now Morse has to go downstairs to her panel presentation on "The
Cutting Edge: The Art of Film Editing." As she enters the foyer of the
American Film Institute, Washington's regular pack of autograph
hounds accosts her.

"Could I have your autograph?" asks one. (Shades of "Hey, it's
Alvy Singer!")

Morse points out that he is asking her to sign over the wrong
photograph in the program. "Does that bother you?" she asks politely.

It doesn't. It doesn't bother her, either.

Tom Davenport's Film Folk

Richard Harrington, March 1989

Steven Spielberg never had this continuity problem: Shooting began on "Soldier Jack" in the spring of 1987, but when director Tom Davenport had to go finish a documentary, production was suspended for almost a year.

"I had to wait around for the seasons to match," says the Delaplane, Va., filmmaker. Such are the fortunes of the independent filmmaker in America.

Still, "Soldier Jack" was finished, and the 40-minute feature, the eighth live-action film in Davenport's series "From the Brothers Grimm: American Versions of Folktale Classics," will receive its local premiere this afternoon at 2 at the American Film Institute, along with 1986's "Jack and the Dentist's Daughter." Both films—shot in the historic countryside of Fauquier, Clarke and Loudoun counties with local casts and crews—will also be shown at matinees next weekend at the Biograph. Davenport will be on hand for all the screenings.

"Things in real life can be as strange as they are in fantasy," says the director of his adaptations. "But all folk tales don't work in live action. A lot of times they couldn't even be done in animation. I have to choose ones that will fit my style."

"Soldier Jack, Or the Man Who Caught Death in a Sack," based on an Appalachian folk tale variation, is a mini-Frank Capra period piece in which a returning World War II vet (Michael Heintzman) is rewarded for his kindness to a stranger on a train through two magical gifts: a sack that can catch anything and a jar that shows whether a sick person will recover or die. After he rescues the president's ailing daughter and captures Death, Jack becomes a national hero; but after many years with his quarry strung up in a tree, Jack realizes he has upset the natural order of life and releases Death, much to the relief of many aged citizens.

Although it's just now playing here, "Soldier Jack" has already won first prizes at the International Festival of Children's Films, the New York Film and Video Festival, the Chicago International Film Festival and the AFI's American Video Conference, along with a citation from the American Library Association. One critic noted that it is "the amalgam of the mythic and poetic with the historical and human that makes (Davenport's) films work" and there is certainly

135

none of the patronizing, superficial ambience of Shelley Duvall's "Faerie Tale Theatre," a much more widely known series of adaptations (because more widely seen; Duvall's films were originally on cable and are now in syndication). While there has been scattered exposure on public television, PBS has so far shown little support for independent filmmakers of any stripe.

"I'd love for my films to be as well known and popular as hers, naturally," says Davenport, 47. "I think my films are as good as hers, and in some ways more serious in their attempts. It's like the tree that falls in the woods: You want somebody to hear the sound. Otherwise there is no sound."

There are some tales common to both series— "Hansel and Gretel," "Rapunzel" and "The Frog Prince"—and both are seeking to make the folk tale accessible. But where Duvall's hour-long versions starred the likes of Joan Collins, Robin Williams, Teri Garr and Ricky Schroder and were shot in a studio with exaggerated fantasy sets, Davenport's are period Americana pieces (set mostly between the Civil War and World War II) filmed with casts of unknowns (professional and not).

And while Duvall's versions play like television, Davenport's play like film, which has probably limited their exposure. In some circles, the darkness at the heart of a film like "Hansel and Gretel: an Appalachian Version," a stark, black-and-white, Depression-era retelling, is considered controversial because it is less a fantasy than a physical, gutsy and psychologically explicit realization.

Indeed, though many of Davenport's films play well to younger audiences "Kids see so much animation, they see these as 'real movies'"—they are perhaps more appropriate for middle and high school students as well as adults. Davenport concedes that certain elements—the three devils in "Soldier Jack," for instance—can be "more spooky live for younger children because they are more 'real.'"

"That devils scene is scary, like the flying monkeys in 'The Wizard of Oz,'" says Davenport. "But 'Oz' is a great kids' film because it has that element and it's not the Care Bears or Smurfs. 'Hansel and Gretel' had a dark feeling, and back then [the mid-'70s], you didn't show anything like that to children; it had to be hearts and flowers."

Perceptions began to change with the publication of Bruno Bettelheim's "The Uses of Enchantment," which "suggested maybe it was okay to show kids struggling through situations. And Joseph Campbell [the late cultural scholar] calls fairy tales and folk tales 'the primer of the picture language of the soul,'" adds Davenport, who had approached Campbell a decade ago about doing a series on mythology, long before Bill Moyers did his PBS series with Campbell.

Davenport, of course, has opted for versions of tales that were brought to the southern Appalachians by European settlers at end of the 18th century. It was a time when the art of storytelling was a chief form of recreation among people whose contact with the printed word was limited, when stories were told and retold aloud. Some of Davenport's earlier adaptations have Grimm roots—"Bristlelip" was an American version of "King Thrushbeard" set in 1815; "Bearskin, or the Man Who Didn't Wash for Seven Years" is set during the Civil War—but the director's last two films, the ones being shown at AFI and the Biograph, are drawn from "Jack Tales" and "Grandfather Tales," Appalachian folk tales collected in the '30s by Richard Chase.

In fact, the folklore connection runs deep in Davenport's work, which is split between folk and fairy tales and documentaries: PBS recently aired "A Singing Stream: A Black Family Chronicle," his warm and revealing portrait of a North Carolina family bonded by song and purpose. The documentaries are part of the American Traditional Culture Series and are tied to the folklore curriculum at the University of North Carolina. Davenport says the two kinds of films often draw on each other.

His overall struggles as an independent filmmaker are not that different from his compatriots', but working out of his 50-acre Delaplane farm for the last 19 years has certainly been beneficial. A Yale graduate, Davenport spent some time in China teaching English and learning Chinese before moving to New York and apprenticing with documentary filmmakers Richard Leacock and Don Pennebaker. In 1969 he met his wife Mimi while working on a film about maple syrup, and when they decided to make their own films—she is a coproducer—and to start a family, they moved back to Delaplane, buying the farm next to that of his parents.

"I owe a lot of gratitude to my parents," Davenport says. He bought the farm outright back in 1969 for $25,000, so he's not had to deal with mortgages; there was always plenty of food raised on the farm, and as a result, cash flow headaches have been minimized, if not eliminated. "We can survive even when we're not making films," he says.

Over the years, Davenport Films has become something of a self-contained cottage industry, and computers have made possible an effective distribution network. "It's no longer necessary for filmmakers to be in urban areas," he points out.

As Washington has developed as a theater city, Davenport has been able to mix professional actors with the community people he turned to for the early tales (the father in "Hansel and Gretel" was the local dog catcher, and beyond the occasional devil, most of Davenport's characters are portrayed as real people). Virginia's historic countryside has served as a superb background for films whose time frames range from the colonial ("The Goose Girl") to post-World War II ("Soldier Jack"). Not only is it cheaper to film this way, but Davenport has a homebred confidence about the rural settings that gives his work a certain authority.

Still, even with self-distribution and low overhead, Davenport says he couldn't make films without grants. "Soldier Jack"—made with grants from the National Endowment for the Humanities, the Virginia Foundation for the Humanities and the Virginia Commission for the Arts—is his most expensive film yet at $100,000, "and that's not a very big budget." It's about what a minute costs for an average feature film.

Since Davenport's Delaplane roots run deep, it's not surprising that he's turned his documentarian eyes on the region as well. In fact, his first film was "Upperville Horse Show," a candid look at the oldest such event in the country, and at the upper-crust society that runs it. He's also captured the 1973 National Country Music Contest in Warrenton in "It Ain't City Music" and sketched a local hunt master in "Thoughts on Foxhunting."

Davenport's documentaries are not all Virginia-focused. His definitive portrait of "The Shakers" has been shown on public television and won a blue ribbon at the American Film Festival; "Being a Joines: A Life in the Brushy Mountains" dealt with a traditional storyteller from North Carolina; "Born for Hard Luck" centered on Arthur (Peg Leg Sam) Jackson, one of few remaining veterans of the classic patent medicine show; "A Singing Stream" was the most recent folklore documentary.

"In some ways, documentaries are stranger than fictional films because often you just don't know what's going to happen in the background," says Davenport. But in both cases, "the key is to be true to the drama and not necessarily the facts of the thing." Although folk tales weren't really designed for children in the first place, the dramas often revolve around young adults struggling with basic issues (from life and death to vanity and peer pressure), overcoming obstacles and trying to gain control over their lives. Whether they are scary or not, they usually celebrate basic ingenuity.

"Unlike modern fiction, folk tales seldom end on a dire note," says Davenport. "They celebrate the best images of humanity, which is why they're good, or enjoyable, for all ages, because they present a picture of mankind that's not all hearts and flowers."

Next on the story board is "Ashpet," inspired by the Appalachian version of Cinderella published in "Grandfather Tales"; it's set in rural Virginia in 1942, and the emphasis is less on magic than human resourcefulness. That is something Davenport knows a lot about, but for him and his colleagues, outside recognition has rewards of its own.

"The AFI has been very supportive," says Davenport. Events like today's, he adds, mean a lot—they're "an opportunity for cast and crew to come together and for people to meet them and give them the sense that they've . . . accomplished something together."

Steven Soderbergh, After the Sex and Lies

Martha Sherrill, August 1989

Steven Soderbergh is waiting for his possessions to appear. His bed. His books. Moving vans are on their way. Aside from the worn-out 1960 Rambler parked out front—the one that he drove here from Los Angeles—he hasn't got much, except maybe all the stuff that's floating inside his head and some T-shirts.

This drowsy, tree-shaded town must feel like a monastic retreat in Mayberry RFD compared with Studio City in the San Fernando Valley, his last place of residence. The sweet, empty house that Soderbergh's rented is being fixed up. A couple of guys lounging on his stairwell turn out to be painting the molding. A telephone seems to be ringing in every room, but it's only echoes.

"Subconsciously, as soon as I get out of Los Angeles, I think there's a subtle shift," says the 26-year-old filmmaker. "I get a little more of the screw-it attitude. I do what I want to do—and that's worked well for me."

He'd been thinking about moving to Charlottesville even before January, before his movie "sex, lies, and videotape" astounded the audiences at the U.S. Film Festival in Park City, Utah. He'd been thinking Charlottesville—where he once lived as a kid—before May, when he won first prize at the Cannes Film Festival and was besieged by journalists.

He'd been thinking it before the world started crowding in, before the Hollywood types began handing him their business cards and using words like boy wonder and young genius and the next Woody Allen . . .

"I didn't want to live somewhere," he says, "that I had to escape from every weekend."

Soderbergh is a Swedish name—his grandfather was born in Stockholm—and it's hard not to carry the stereotype too far. He wants a spare life. An honest life. No smog. No movie people making deals. No furniture. Few compromises. There's no girlfriend around and he's got only one pal in town. He seems to want to be alone.

"I've tried very hard, with all the new people that I've met in the last six months, to keep everything in a business context," he says, "so that my social life and the people I'm close to does not change."

140

Thoughts of fame find him shuddering. He's already worried about privacy. In the short time he's been here—since July 14—he's become a minor celebrity. People have been nice and friendly, but he's also been asked for Jessica Lange's autograph and he doesn't know Jessica Lange—or any of the other movie people in the area such as Sam Shepard or Sissy Spacek. He wants to know if the newspaper can avoid mentioning the town's name at all, but it's already been printed in papers and magazines around the world.

A local photographer comes to take his picture. He's heard all about Soderbergh and is happy to meet him. Soderbergh, wearing a white T-shirt and droopy khaki shorts, stands uncomfortably by some mossy steps leading up to his house. He stands uncomfortably by a tree. Then he sits on the tail end of the Rambler, his hands folded in his lap.

"I don't have many facial expressions," he says in a listless voice.

His face isn't hangdog as much as his attitude. There's a certain amount of suffering going on, and wisdom at work. His features—the dignified nose and lined forehead of an older man, the blue eyes and soft lips of a kid—get upstaged by his brains and sobriety every time. He's got an adorable traffic jam of teeth—if only he'd smile.

"As Socrates said," he quotes, "'You make your own prison.'"

Watching Mr. Droopy Drawers leaning over a butcher-block table at a college hangout, behind a mountain of corned beef and bread, it's easy to see why people have found it remarkable that Soderbergh could have done the thinking and achieved the maturity required to make "sex, lies, and videotape." Maybe he's been fooling around with a movie camera since he was 13, but let's face it—he's still 26.

"Sometimes I feel 30," he says.

In the tradition of Woody Allen and Stanley Kubrick, Soderbergh never bothered to go to college. By high school he knew what he wanted to spend his life doing, and his parents—even his father, who was then the dean of the college of education at Louisiana State University—didn't get in his way.

"I was a pretty obsessive kid," he says. "That would have been futile—both for them to try to talk me into it, and for me to go."

One of six children, Soderbergh grew up all over, as his father moved from college to college. He was born in Georgia. Lived in Texas for four years and Pittsburgh for six, before moving to Charlottesville at the age of 10. During his three years there he pitched a no-hitter in Little League, which he says 'had nothing to do with why I came back.' At 13 he moved to Baton Rouge, La., where his family has stayed since.

His father enrolled him in an animation class taught by college students because he was good at drawing. "I quickly learned that animation bored me silly, and uhhhh, I took the camera and started shooting live stuff, which was more interesting. But all through high school, I had access to all this equipment. . . . I got to try and fail without anybody watching."

He left for Los Angeles at 17, and the instructor of his LSU film class, as it turns out, got him a job editing for NBC. When the show, "Games People Play," went off the air, he tried all kinds of things. He held cue cards. He was a game show scorekeeper. He worked for two years as a coin attendant in a video arcade.

"I did not—during that time—feel bad about myself," he says. "The qualities that I look for in a person have nothing to do with what they do as a job, and how successful they are."

He admits to being single-minded in his ambitions. He continued to make movies, when he got the chance. "Everything I've made since I was a senior in high school, I'm proud of," he says. "The three shorts that I've made . . . I'd stack up against 'sex, lies.' They are every bit as complex technically, and as grown up in their content."

One short made in 1986, called "Winston," was shown to producers to sell his "sex, lies, and videotape" screenplay. "It is very much a warm-up for 'sex, lies,'" he says. "It's about a woman who concocts rather complex lies to keep her suitors at arm's length, but it's very, very similar in style and tone to 'sex, lies.' I look at it now and see that I was getting ready at some subconscious level."

It came to him in eight days—mostly during a drive from Baton Rouge to Los Angeles. At night he stopped in motels and wrote out the screenplay to "sex, lies, and videotape" in longhand.

"It was like taking dictation," he says. "I mean, it really just fell out of my head. And I didn't know. I didn't know, when I started, how long it was going to be. I didn't know how it would happen. It just seemed to come. One thing would lead to another."

Soderbergh is obsessive and self-obsessed, he says, but he must do that when he's alone. Across a table, he asks as many questions as he's asked. He seems more comfortable the deeper and more personal the conversation gets. There's a spongy selflessness about him, like he's soaking up people, watching them, listening carefully. In his talky movie, the camera hones in close, fascinated—the big faces of his characters fill the screen.

There's the face of Ann (played by the gloriously beautiful Andie MacDowell), a repressed madonna who thinks sex is overrated. There's her lawyer husband, John (Peter Gallagher), a soulless philanderer.

There's Cynthia, Ann's little spitfire sister (Laura San Giacomo), who's sleeping with John. And there's Graham (played by James Spader, who won Best Actor at Cannes), who likes to watch videotapes.

Graham sits in a director's chair with the video camera rolling. He prods women, in the deadpan of a shrink or gynecologist, for their most intimate stories. Maybe it's the voyeur Graham—impotent by self-punishment and "a recovering pathological liar"—who's the most messed up, but everyone in the movie's got problems. Soderbergh's characters are sexually repressed or sexually careless. They are either uncomfortable or too comfortable with each other. They stutter and stammer out the revelations, but they're sure of their lies.

"I went through a period of my life, in my personal relationships, when I was lying," says Soderbergh. "I don't do that anymore. But there was a very long process of monitoring. . . . It's like—as Graham says—being an alcoholic. You have to watch yourself at first. And after a while, telling the truth becomes second nature. You don't have to monitor anymore. You just do the right thing."

Soderbergh's talking about the days when he was a creep. He has called himself, as Graham does, "a pathological liar." He hurt the people around him. He cheated on a girlfriend. "I became," he says, "someone I hated."

This whole business—Soderbergh's dark period—has been much discussed in print. Mostly because of his own big mouth. "I'm not sick of being interviewed," he says, "it's just when I say stupid things that hurt other people." He means the now-famous Rolling Stone interview by Terri Minsky in which he talked about sitting in a bar one night, spitting distance from three women he was sleeping with.

Soderbergh's guilt and regrets about this time in his life gave birth to "sex, lies, and videotape." And the movie's upbeat ending—three of the four characters are left transformed—reflects his philosophy now. "It's been my experience that after pain and suffering that you go through a period of healing," he says. "And I have a sense that you go through these things to get better."

He tries hard not to get preachy. "Making films is my job, and I love doing it. But my life's work is trying to be a better person," he says. "It's a continuing thing. It takes a lot of work . . . an unexamined life is not worth living."

In Rolling Stone, Soderbergh wasn't only revelatory about his past. He also mentioned not returning a recent phone call from Don Simpson and Jerry Bruckheimer, the producers of "Beverly Hills Cop." He told Minsky: "They're slime—just barely passing for humans."

"I just didn't think," he says now. "It's just part of the learning process and it's not Terri's fault. I know Terri liked me. And I know she wanted to write a piece that reflected that. I just said some stupid stuff."

He's since gotten more guarded, and somewhat less impressed with journalists. "I used to read a profile and believe that they could get people," he says, chuckling as if amused by his own naivete. "But no one's gotten me."

Once you've talked to Soderbergh, all kinds of things in his movie—which for starters takes place in Baton Rouge—start to seem very personal. There's even a detached deadness to the action that's reminiscent of the way he moves. And the character of Graham seems particularly close. He drifts into town. He lives alone. He has no furniture. No visible income. A history of lying and penitence. He sits behind the camera.

Toward the end of "sex, lies, and videotape," Graham says to Ann: You don't have the slightest idea who I am. Am I supposed to recount all the points in my life leading up to this moment and just hope that it's coherent, that it makes some sort of sense to you?

It doesn't make any sense to me, you know, and I was there. . . .

"Nothing in the film happened," Soderbergh said in Park City. "I have never taped women. But it's all true."

For $1.2 million, he made what's called "a little movie." The title appears in lowercase because Soderbergh likes it that way.

"There's something more quiet about it," he says.

His quiet movie was financed by RCA/Columbia Pictures Home Video. It was finished and shown at Park City just over a year after Soderbergh speed-wrote the script on the road. For its Park City premiere, the titles had been typed and blown up on a photocopier. "I spent all night doing them," Soderbergh remembers. "They were barely legible." The soundtrack was also homemade—cuts from Brian Eno records.

By the time it got to Cannes five months later, it was done. But Soderbergh still wasn't prepared to deal with the attention, the praise and fawning. "I thought we were going to get lost in the shuffle," he says. "I was hoping to just survive, and not be squashed."

He briefly returned to L.A. before the decisions were made on the awards, expecting that Spike Lee's "Do the Right Thing" would capture first prize. "For a while I wasn't going to come back," he says. "I was thinking somebody else could accept an award for me—if we won anything. I was so beat. But that's a pretty scary thought. What a bonehead thing to do. I shudder to think now—if I hadn't been there to accept it."

At Cannes, jury president Wim Wenders, the director of "Wings of Desire" and "Paris, Texas," said that "sex, lies, and videotape" was chosen for the Palme d'Or—and not just the Camera d'Or for best first-time directing—because it was "a film that gave us great joy, that surprised us all and gave us confidence in the future of cinema."

Not since "Apocalypse Now" split the prize with "The Tin Drum" 10 years ago has an American movie won the festival. And no director as young as Soderbergh ever has.

Since then, he's given even more interviews and been offered lots of movie deals. "When it became apparent that I had the opportunity to do what I wanted," he says, "I pulled three projects out from under my pillow—pet projects—and managed to get all of them set up."

Sydney Pollack will be executive producing Soderbergh's next movie, "The Last Ship," which he will write from William Brinkley's book about a boatload of men and women who survive the nuclear holocaust. (Soderbergh's still in negotiations with Universal Studios because he doesn't want the movie released in South Africa.) Barry Levinson's company will produce "Kafka," which Soderbergh will direct from a screenplay he admires. And he's agreed to write a script of "King of the Hill," an A.E. Hotchner memoir, and direct the film for one of Robert Redford's companies.

Meanwhile, he's been fighting off the usual ego problems.

"I assume, like most people, I have certain insecurities and self-image problems," he says. "And being in a situation where people are telling you that you're great all the time can screw you up on two levels. On the first level, you want to believe it. . . .

"And the other way it affects you is that you begin to feel unworthy of it. You know that you are not any better than anybody else. I just happen to do something that people have an inordinate fascination with. So it kind of gets you coming and going. Your ego wants people to say it, yet the other part of you says, This is really bad for you. It's going to screw you up."

He says he wants his success to be demystified. He was paid only $37,000 for directing "sex, lies, and videotape." Half of it was spent before he got it. Up until a month ago he was totally in debt, hadn't paid his taxes and owed his producer money. "People read that I won the Cannes Film Festival and think, 'Gaaaaad. He must be rich.' They just don't get it. . . .

"Sure, I'd rather be where I am right now than back on my buddy's couch, where I was for six months last year, but ahhhhhhh, the belief that my life is better than other people's is completely false."

Soderbergh's movie isn't really about the act of sex. It's pretty much about everything else. The sex scenes are also not like watching other people have sex, it's like being inside the sheets. There aren't really nude scenes—just sweaty face shots of people breathing hard.

"I could probably—when pushed into a corner—name maybe a handful of films where I thought it was dealt with with some sort of equanimity. Just, most of the time, the way sex is dealt with in films is really lame. It's not real. It's not interesting to me. And it seems to be specifically from a male point of view."

When pushed, he comes up with "The Last Picture Show."

"That still has elements of a male point of view," he says, "but that's kind of what the film is about—and what it deals with. . . . But still, it's a pretty mature, grown-up piece of work about men and women. I came out of there thinking that adults had made this for other adults—which is not the feeling I get from a lot of movies."

He's not planning on making a career of sex. Or relationships. "Certainly, I am very interested in men and women and how they treat each other," says Soderbergh. "And that's primarily what drew me to 'The Last Ship.' But 'King of the Hill' isn't primarily about that—neither is 'Kafka.' They just are good stories, I think. The strain seems to be people, and the human condition."

Are we entering an Age of Feelings?

"Yeah," he says. "But I hope it's not in a really wimpy way—like it gets really granola-head. I don't want to go through that. . . . I just don't want it to turn into this new age stuff—channeling our emotions. . . . I would encourage people to examine their lives—their lives, not just their feelings. That's why when I hear people talking about getting in touch with their feelings, I just want to duck and cover. Its just so warm and runny, you want to gag."

Comparisons to Woody Allen, he says, will stop after he makes his next film. "In the case of John Cassavetes, I think it's unfortunate because I've made one film, and this guy has left us a life's work—that was very hard earned. I just think it's premature."

These days, he tries to keep words like "slime" out of his running movie criticism, but it's not easy for him. There are a lot of movies he doesn't like. He will, however, reveal his all-time top 11 favorites, in no particular order: "Citizen Kane." "The Third Man." "The Godfather" I and II. "The Conversation." "Jaws." "Annie Hall."

"Sunset Boulevard." "All the President's Men." "The 5,000 Fingers of Dr. T." "The Last Picture Show."

At the end of a couple hours—answering questions and asking his own—Soderbergh starts to fade. He's got to get back to the house. His stuff might be arriving. He needs to go to K mart for a shower curtain. He's leaving the next morning for a week of television interviews to promote the opening of the movie. "I feel obligated to," he says. "And hey. I own a piece of this film. I want to see it do well."

Promoting, Soderbergh-style, isn't the usual stuff. He just sits there. His pale, one-expression face looks numb. He responds with great modesty, bordering on disdain, to all compliments. He smiles—once, maybe.

Back in Charlottesville, after cleaning the house a few times to avoid writing, he will retreat into his screenplay of "The Last Ship." He'll probably call his "closest friends on the planet" in L.A., then he'll put his phone machine on, with a new message: This is Steven. I am home. The fax machine is on. All systems are go, basically. . . .

CHAPTER SIX

On the Air

The Televisionary Forecast

Tom Shales, January 1990

Mural-size TV screens that hang on the wall like paintings! Two-way television conversations with your Aunt Hazel and Uncle Fritz! Banking and shopping via fiber-optic cable! These are some of the promises of television in the '90s.

Unfortunately, they were among the promises of television in the '80s and '70s, too. Mural-size TV screens have been just around the corner for about 30 years now.

The public deserves more practical predictions, nuts-and-bolts stuff, when it comes to looking into television's future. Of course, if the future is like the past, there will be many more nuts than bolts. But the point is, TV has changed greatly in the '80s and will continue to do so in the '90s.

Here are some of the things likely to happen in the first half of the last decade of this bedraggled old century of ours:

Dan Rather will turn over "The CBS Evening News" to Connie Chung by 1992. Rather, weary of the daily grind, will concentrate on "48 Hours" and specials.

As early as March, Tom Brokaw will no longer be sole anchor of "NBC Nightly News" but will be joined by a partner, probably Bryant Gumbel of the "Today" show. Bob Costas will take over Gumbel's spot in the chair next to news kitten Deborah Norville. Michael Gartner, the avidly disliked president of NBC News, will hold the job only a few more months.

General Electric will sell NBC and make a zillion trillion dollars. Disney may fulfill a longstanding rumor and buy CBS Inc., now that Laurence Tisch has left it in ruins. All three networks will become so heavily involved in cable that cable will no longer be thought of as the competition, only a subsidiary.

"Monday Night Football," an ABC fixture for 20 years, will move to CBS in the fall, as part of the new resurgence of CBS Sports. Where once CBS was known as first in news and ABC first in sports, the roles will reverse. CBS will become the No. 1 sports network and ABC will be first in news. NBC will be first in neither.

Sam Donaldson will be quietly dropped from the ABC News magazine show "PrimeTime Live," and producers will either leave Diane Sawyer the sole anchor or team her with another star, possibly someone from the entertainment side instead of the news side. Despite the cosmetic improvements, the show will not be around to see the light of fall.

Fox Television's "Married . . . With Children," the racy and foul-mouthed sitcom, will be the most imitated series of the next couple years. All the networks will try similarly raunchy shows of their own. Rear nudity could become fairly common, and so may bare breasts in late-night TV and the last hour of prime time. Stock up on videotape now.

Having abolished innumerable other rules already, the FCC will seriously consider lifting its ban on foreign ownership of domestic TV stations, clearing the way for the Japanese to buy an American network.

CBS will fold the disastrous "Pat Sajak show" early in 1990, and many network affiliates will replace it with syndicated programming, rejecting whatever lame replacement for "Sajak" CBS comes up with and thus costing the enfeebled network yet more millions of dollars.

At least one of the three major networks will cancel all its Saturday morning cartoons and fill the time instead with a news and informational service along the lines of "Today" or "Good Morning America."

Jim Bakker will begin live inspirational telecasts from a special studio constructed for him in prison. (All right—I admit it. This isn't a prediction so much as wishful thinking.) Oh, and Tammy Faye will drop by for guest shots.

In a fit of overconfidence typical of him, Arsenio Hall will try to bring his clattering late-night talk show into prime time, and fall flat on his fist.

Johnny Carson will still be on television on New Year's Eve, 1999.

Brandon Tartikoff of NBC Entertainment, Robert Iger of ABC Entertainment, and Jeff Sagansky of CBS Entertainment will all come to their senses sometime within the next two years and admit that they should have been paying more attention to TV critics all along and faithfully following their majestically intelligent counsel.

They will ply the critics with effusive apologies, and beg for forgiveness on bended knee.

But—I digress . . .

TV News at War

Eleanor Randolph, December 1989

When calamity strikes, even in the form of a little war around the Panama Canal, Americans are accustomed to clicking on their television sets and enjoying the latest historic moment from the front-row couch.

This week, they were deeply disappointed. The television news pictures—the same on every channel—all had the look of home videos. Here was film of a few helicopters, several transport jets and six soldiers standing lamely in the mud. Over and over, the same incomprehensible shots.

Amateur photographers subbing for the big guys? Not hardly. This was the "thin gruel," as some media executives called it, that came from an agreement between the press and the Pentagon that was supposed to have been worked out six years ago.

These videotapes were the first, and for a long time the only, information that came out of a "pool" of representative reporters who flew with U.S. troops to Panama and who were told that they would be able to film the operation as it occurred. The video recording of the invasion would then be released to other members of the media after everybody, even the enemy, had figured out that the American military had descended on Panama. It didn't work that way.

Instead of allowing the media to film the action, the military dropped the 16 members of the "pool" at the American Embassy and then proceeded without them. After the invasion was mostly over, the reporters were allowed to take a few pictures and write a few paragraphs that were sent off to thousands of reporters waiting in Washington and elsewhere for the news.

Once again, the "Pentagon Pool" was a failure.

Once again the U.S. military proved that the first casualty of a post-Vietnam era war isn't truth, as the saying went for earlier wars, but the videotape of it. The legacy of Grenada—when President Reagan invaded a tiny island in the West Indies and left the media at home sputtering in rage—lives on. Grenada-think remains at the Pentagon, even though the press and the military have spent the last six years in numerous seminars and practice runs trying to work out a way to wage a war and cover it at the same time.

Part of the problem is the media's. The Pentagon issued a statement that the reporters had been kept from the front line in Panama because it was dangerous. Of course it was dangerous. Any reporter who accepts a pool assignment and thinks it means going to a beach somewhere to combat nothing worse than mosquitoes is in the wrong business.

But news organizations appeared to agree with the Pentagon about the dangers in Panama. News executives had been calling the White House and the Defense Department demanding protection for U.S. journalists who were being harassed by Panamanian troops. These news executives were sending a strong message—backed with the bullhorns that they have at their disposal—that the safety of their reporters was top priority.

Apparently nobody made the point that Pentagon pool reporters were supposed to be different. They had signed on for combat duty. Some Pentagon press officials tried admirably to make this point within the military, but the issue was lost somewhere between the upper reaches of the Bush administration and the ground forces in Panama City.

Another part of the problem is that since Vietnam, this nation's soldiers have distrusted the nation's media. Their view is that television lost the war in Southeast Asia, even though many thoughtful military historians disagree. William Hammond, who is doing a series of books on "The Military and the Media" for the U.S. Army Center of Military History, has written that, "What alienated the American public, in both the Korean and Vietnam wars, was not news coverage but casualties."

Even if the commanders in Panama last week agree, they also knew that nobody but the media would complain if the press was kept in the dark. For many Americans, the media's complaints seem either silly or unpatriotic. So, the military commanders did the safe thing: They took the cameras to the war, but kept them away from the initial fighting.

Maybe we could go back to the old methods, where warriors try to win the battle and reporters scramble to cover it. The Pentagon Pool doesn't work.

Robert Johnson's Cable Vision

Paula Span, June 1989

It was a sweet day for Robert L. Johnson. The weather was perfect: brilliant spring sunshine, a slight breeze stirring the bouquets of mylar balloons. The sleek tiled building—Black Entertainment Television's new studios in Northeast Washington—gleamed impressively as Johnson pulled into the parking lot in his black Jag. Proud staffers, the press, his friend and ally the mayor and other city dignitaries were gathering to watch Johnson's 3-year-old daughter, Paige, scissor through the black-and-gold ribbon at the building entrance.

A decade back, the industry might have been offering only the longest odds that Bob Johnson's new cable network for black audiences would survive until 1989, let alone construct a $10 million production facility. But by this spring's ribbon-cutting, though BET still posed no threat to Ted Turner, it was growing and making money and keeping its president and founder in monogrammed shirts. He was a happy man, a vindicated man, though not a man content.

The first 10 years had merely been a prelude, to Johnson's way of thinking. In the early days, he had shown the necessary entrepreneurial refusal to recognize why a new venture can't succeed. Now, he was showing the entrepreneur's unwillingness to let the momentum stop here. His network was about to take on its biggest challenge since its launch: unleashing a blitz of new fall programs, wrestling with debt for its new building and increasing its staff by 60 percent.

Johnson wasn't about to bite his nails in public, however. That's not his style. "When I see BET, I don't see a cable network," he likes to say, perennially full of plans. "I see a black media conglomerate." He has always talked big. "I want to be a communications giant," he announced before Black Entertainment Television's debut. At its opening reception in 1980, he pointedly read aloud from the memoirs of CBS patriarch William Paley, though BET at the time amounted to a two-hour sliver of old movies on Friday nights. At BET's fifth anniversary, when it had only recently become a 24-hour network (and still didn't have enough of its own programming to fill the time), his prediction was that it would become one of the country's largest black-owned companies. He's still saying so: "From where we sit now—and I don't

153

think we're bragging when we say this—BET is positioned to be the preeminent black company in America in the '90s and beyond."

Johnson is bragging, of course, limitless enthusiasm and rosy predictions being part of an entrepreneur's stock in trade. At BET's launch, Johnson said he hoped it would break even within three years; it took six. Throughout the '80s, he has talked about the diverse programming he would offer his under-served black audience— "sensitive drama" and soap operas and variety shows—but, finances lagging behind ambitions, BET's weekday schedule this fall will still be two-thirds music videos. Washingtonians got a stiff dose of Johnson's brand of optimism a few years back when, as president of District Cablevision Inc., he parlayed his business and political connections into a winning bid for the right to wire the city, then disclosed that his company couldn't finance the elaborate cable system it had described. The system DCI is now installing is considerably scaled down. "Like everybody else in the industry, he overpromised," says Merrill Brown, editor of the television magazine Channels.

Johnson, universally described as a great salesman, acknowledges "a little bit of overconfidence" in some of his projections. "If you can't go out and paint a picture of what the world is going to look like six or seven years from now," he says, "you're not going to get (people) on board today." And if the picture he paints takes longer than expected to materialize, well, that doesn't make him or his company anomalous in the cable industry.

Bigger players than Johnson foundered during the '80s, wildcat years for cable programmers. As cable's "penetration"—the proportion of subscribers among all television households—grew from 20 percent in 1980 to 55 percent this year, it set off considerable scrambling to find something to put on all those channels. Lots of companies had swell ideas, but attracting enough advertising to pay for them proved dicey. CBS, to take a prominent example, abandoned its acclaimed culture channel in 1982, after little more than a year and losses of $30 million. Ted Turner, it is frequently forgotten, created a music video channel that survived barely a month before being steamrollered by rival MTV. MTV itself, the paradigm of how a cable network could make pots of money by targeting an audience largely ignored by conventional broadcasters, burned through $80 million before turning profitable in 1983.

Black Entertainment Television never had anywhere near that much to lose—Johnson launched it with a $15,000 personal loan from the National Bank of Washington and a $500,000 investment from cable giant Tele-Communications Inc. (TCI). Forced to start small, expand slowly and stick with cheap programming, BET was a poky tortoise in an industry hopping with hares. "It was created ahead of its time," says Char Beales, vice president for programming and marketing at the National Cable Television Association. Now, however, a number of major cities that could be fertile territory for the network— Washington, Baltimore and New York's outer boroughs among them— are finally being wired, and "BET is crossing the threshold," she says. While some of the hares dropped out of the race, BET is still here.

"You had to have a whole lot of confidence in Bob Johnson to stick around," Johnson says—and no one had more confidence in Bob Johnson than Bob Johnson. He was just 33; his Princeton degree was an MPA (Master of Public Administration) instead of an MBA; he'd spent his career in government—serving as press secretary for D.C. Del. Walter Fauntroy and City Councilman Sterling Tucker—and at the National Cable Television Association, where he was vice president for governmental affairs. That gave Johnson connections but no business experience to speak of since his boyhood newspaper route in Freeport, Ill., went bust. But John Malone, president of TCI, currently the nation's largest owner of cable systems, liked the idea Johnson brought him in 1979: a cable channel aimed at black viewers and the advertisers who want to reach them.

The trait most often ascribed to Johnson by those who know him, aside from a genius for networking in the non-electronic sense, is determination. "He's number 9 of 10 children," says his wife, Sheila, a music educator. "He grew up not having much . . . I think the word is, he's hungry."

He's also gregarious and graceful, given to loosening up audiences with jokes. He displays the badges of wealth—a thick gold bracelet, the custom shirts, the new XJ6 Jag—but avoids sounding imperious. It's easy to picture him campaigning for a congressional seat.

He seemed a man worth taking a chance on. Besides, BET gave TCI two things it needed: programming to entice subscribers (they'd be less likely to sign up if all that cable offered was the same shows they could get from over-the-air broadcasters) and a concerned-citizen image that would prove useful as TCI sought the rights to build new cable systems. With much of suburban and rural America already wired in 1979, the looming battles would come in urban areas, and both the cities and the governments who would be courted during the franchise fights were heavily populated by minorities. "Operators out franchising would want to tell city officials that they could serve a black audience," Johnson reasoned. Buying 20 percent equity for half a million dollars, Malone could claim not only that TCI carried programming of interest to blacks but also that it had made it possible. "He wrote the check," Johnson says. "He gave me only one word of advice: 'Get your revenues up and keep your costs down.'"

BET could hardly have kept costs lower, relying at first on cheap, slightly over-the-hill '70s movies like "Lady Sings the Blues" and so-called blaxploitation epics like "Willie Dynamite." It was probably overstating the case even to call BET a network, since it appeared on another cable network for two or three hours late Friday night, then disappeared, Brigadoon-like, for another week.

It was a big step when, in 1982, BET announced it would transmit over its own channel for six hours daily, adding music videos (more cheap—in fact, free—programming) and taped black college sports. "My first goal was to make it for 100 days," recalls Jefferi Lee, now vice president of network production, then 25 and nervous about the fledgling network's technological capacity. "Then I'd look for another milepost." The expanded schedule made its debut in August; Lee wrote the word "Done" on his calendar in late November. When BET had pulled it off, "I remember calling Bob up and saying, 'We've been up for 100 days.'" "Well, that's good, keep it going," responded Johnson vaguely; he was in the middle of a meeting. Anyway, he'd always had bigger things in mind.

By 1984, BET could claim 7.6 million subscribers and was transmitting 24 hours a day, though much of that time was (and still is) leased to product marketers selling things like hair care supplies and exercise equipment. But its equity had been reshuffled as its start-up debts mounted, TCI having been joined as an investor by Taft Broadcasting and Home Box Office, a Time Inc. subsidiary. It was taking BET longer than planned to reach profitability.

"You get into the realities of the business," Johnson says. "Cable operators don't give you the distribution you think you should have. You assume advertisers will jump in, and they're slower than you hoped . . . You don't get the subscription fees you think you should get." BET was supposed to be ad-supported but, like other cable services, found that Madison Avenue wanted to see Nielsen ratings before it committed ad dollars. Few cable networks had big enough audiences to earn any ratings at all (they got asterisks) in the early '80s; to bring in more revenue, they began charging cable operators a per-subscriber fee. BET got 2 1/2 cents per month, among the lowest fees of any programming service.

To stay afloat until its subscriber base grew large enough to generate ratings and attract advertisers, BET borrowed from its three equity partners, its debt eventually passing $10 million. Observers wondered if Johnson would lose control of BET; he wondered himself.

But 1986 proved a turning point: BET's subscriber base was nearing 12 million, it was finally showing up on the Nielsen meters, and it edged into the black. Johnson sent dollar bills encased in Lucite to his top managers to commemorate the occasion; he keeps one on his own desk at BET's corporate headquarters in Georgetown. "I give him all the credit in the world," says Bart McHugh, a senior vice president of DDB Needham and a leading media buyer. "He had to convince people that there was a need for black programming for blacks. I don't think anybody believed it."

Though BET will not disclose figures, industry analyst Larry Gerbrandt of Paul Kagan Associates estimates that this year the network will tally $4 million in operating cash flow on $23 million in net revenues. (Operating cash flow—revenues minus expenses, before interest, depreciation and taxes—is the measure the industry uses to gauge network health.) The big cable networks with mass audiences make that look puny—Kagan estimates that ESPN, the sports network, will have a cash flow of $100 million this year; CNN, $120 million— but "for a niche programming service, (BET) is doing quite well," Gerbrandt says. "They started out modestly and built . . . They did it right," agrees Gustave Hauser, a cable veteran whose Hauser Communications Inc. owns franchises in Arlington and Montgomery County. "And when they needed money, somebody stepped up and said, 'Here it is, before you go into Chapter 11.'"

Even more generously, the partners still owed $10 million by BET have contented themselves with 48 percent of the company's stock, each owning 16 percent and having a seat on the seven-member board. (Taft has since metamorphosed into Great American Broadcast Co.) Johnson, whose investment never increased past his $15,000 (except, of course, for 10 years of his life), remains the majority stockholder with 52 percent.

This is an unusual arrangement (Ted Turner, for instance, owns only 42 percent of Turner Broadcasting, though he retains voting control), but BET has always involved more than purely financial considerations. "Under traditional investment standards, the return on investment has not been what one would look for," says Bob Thomson, TCI's vice president for government affairs. What is trickier to assess, he says, is "how much goodwill we get from making a major attempt to provide programming of interest to the minority community."

TCI's involvement with BET came in handy, for instance, when District Cablevision was battling two other groups of investors for the

District cable franchise. In such slugfests, big cable operators who have the resources to build the system typically join forces with local investors who have clout and connections. "You find someone familiar with the city and the dynamics of the city, the economics and the politics," Thomson explains. "Bob Johnson was clearly such a person." Johnson, who invested $100,000 in District Cablevision and is its president and chief spokesman, likened the process at the time to a political campaign. Indeed, supporters and allies of Mayor Marion Barry figured prominently among District Cablevision's local investors.

But TCI—which through a limited partnership now owns 75 percent of District Cablevision—also benefitted from its role in launching the nation's first and only black-oriented cable programming service, according to Richard Maulsby, executive director of the D.C. Office of Cable Television. Minority input and influence were a City Council priority in awarding the franchise in 1984. "{TCI's} Malone coming in with that background, that was a real factor," Maulsby says of District Cablevision's winning bid for the franchise.

Johnson still mixes politics and business in ways that raise eyebrows. In April, Johnson, a longtime friend of Marion Barry's and a political supporter ever since his upstart 1978 campaign, agreed to serve without compensation as the mayor's in-house image consultant for four months. In May, in an effort to help Barry gauge his political standing, he convened an informal gathering of black business leaders and Barry associates, a number of whom wound up urging Barry not to seek reelection.

The announcement of Johnson's new role at the District Building came just days before BET unveiled its new studios, constructed in a city-owned industrial park. The Capital City Business and Industrial Park, 25 acres of what used to be Conrail yards off Brentwood Road NE, is meant to lure businesses to the District, or keep them there, with packages of economic incentives. BET's modern-looking studio, with its curved black-tiled entrance and impressive antennas, became the park's second tenant, after Washington Beef Co. Raymond Skinner, executive director of the city's Office of Business and Economic Development, said at the ribbon-cutting that the city had contributed $500,000 in site improvements for BET's building; Johnson says the city's package of incentives (including a below-market lease and tax abatements) totals $800,000. Meanwhile, Johnson continues to serve as president of District Cablevision.

Barry, responding to criticism of Johnson's appointment as his adviser, complained that the involvement of business people in city government ought to be welcomed instead of questioned. But he eventually said he'd avoid taking part in any decisions affecting Johnson. For his part, Johnson sees no conflict of interest, "none at all, none whatsoever," in his tenure as a Barry adviser. There has been, he points out, no financial benefit to either BET or District Cablevision.

Access, perhaps? "Access," Johnson says, "I had before." In studio A, the night of the ribbon-cutting, Public Enemy was rapping on the big bank of video monitors, waiters were passing the champagne, and every guest—Freddy Jackson, Tone Loc, Patti Austin—who stopped by the rec-room set of "Video Soul" to chat with amiable host Donnie Simpson was bubbling about how "fabulous" the new facilities were. It was fitting that the first show to emanate live from the new studios was "Video Soul"—highly rated, popular with advertisers, cheap to produce, therefore a significant BET bill-payer. It's just the sort of thing that Johnson's friend John Malone might have had in mind back when he instructed him to keep his costs down.

But it's not all that Johnson himself has had in mind. BET now reaches 22 million households and pulls a decent average rating, by cable standards, of .6 in prime time, meaning that a prime-time show is seen in more than 130,000 households, ahead of the audience for the Weather Channel or VH-1 though far behind Lifetime's or MTV's. It makes a profit. So Johnson recognizes that the financial excuses for the predominance of videos, sports, retread TV series and classic movies on BET's schedule are evaporating. He had promised more. "One of the things [Johnson] has got to face, like everyone else, is programming," says McHugh of DDB Needham. "He's going to run out of old movies and old sitcoms." Johnson feels the heat himself. "People are going to start saying, 'Okay, he came along, he struggled. Is what he's doing quality?'" he acknowledges. "The critical eye is on us now."

A few of BET's self-produced shows have now survived for several seasons, including the popular "Bobby Jones Gospel Show," the hour-long "This Week in Black Entertainment" and the half-hour "BET News," several of whose journalists have graduated to broadcast networks or their affiliates. But most of its attempts, excluding music videos, have been short-lived. A call-in psychology show and a cooking show were early casualties. "Portraits in Black," an arts interview show, was jettisoned after a year. More recently, three high-hopes entries for the '87-'88 season—a live call-in show on current events, a second gospel show and an ambitious public affairs program called "Urban Scene"—were canceled. And a quiz show launched last September lasted only until April. The common explanation for their demise is lack of advertising revenue. "They just didn't deliver the numbers," Johnson says.

In not allowing programming costs to spiral ahead of revenues, he has been relentlessly pragmatic. "We're not going to go out and try to make 'How the West Was Won II,'" he says. At various times he can sound proudly defensive, slightly regretful, sometimes quite cynical about that decision.

Like television programmers everywhere, he insists that his network will happily air programs that "the intellectual critics" loathe, as long as people watch and advertisers buy in. On the other hand, reminded of what he used to say about showing black viewers original dramas about black doctors and other role models, Johnson says that "that's still the aspiration . . . We've got to fill that void." He says BET is now ready to produce quality programming even if it doesn't turn a profit. At the same time, he is blunt about his expectations that some of the political leaders and intellectuals to be featured on BET's new fall shows will subsequently become helpful lobbyists, pressuring more cable operators to carry BET. "We tell the black playwright, 'The reason you can't see your work on BET is because your cable company doesn't care,'" he says with relish, looking ahead. "[Congressional Black] Caucus members can be critical to us in getting distribution."

"The first day I met Bob Johnson he was a very strong idea man," says James Ebron, vice president of network sales and a six-year BET veteran. "He was brimming: 'Why don't we do this?' 'Why don't we try that?'" Now, Ebron says, Johnson is "very bottom line. He still cares about creativity—as long as there's a rainbow at the end."

At last spring's NCTA convention, Johnson made a pitch to cable operators for increased fees to allow BET to expand and improve its original programming. They complied, doubling the per-subscriber fee to 5 cents a month, making roughly $7 million more available for the programming budget in 1989.

In November, Johnson and Jeff Lee and BET's new vice president for programming, Lynn Wallace, holed up in a suite at the Westin Hotel for a 36-hour brainstorming session. They emerged with plans for a record seven new shows for this fall, including a nightly live talk show, an on-location town meeting called "Black Agenda 2000," a Saturday hour for teenagers, half-hour profiles of movers and shakers in various fields and one-character plays by leading black playwrights. They're still not 'How the West Was Won II'—"Nothing we discussed is going to set television on its heels," Lee says—and some of the plans are already being scaled back. But Johnson says they represent a $10 million programming investment; he wants to be seen as putting his money where his mouth has been.

"It's a very big step for them," Beales of the NCTA says of the planned blitz. "There are no guarantees in the programming business." Gustave Hauser says that creating programming is "the sport of kings." It can use up cash at alarming rates. It is accompanied, ideally, by promotion to let audiences know about the new offerings, an additional expense that BET has undertaken only fitfully in the past. At the same time, BET must start repaying the $9 million note from the National Bank of Washington that it used to build its new Northeast production facilities (replacing leased studio space in Alexandria). The network's payroll will swell from 103 to 169 by September. And BET will be working until at least 1993, by Johnson's estimate, to retire the $10 million debt owed its partners.

"It's a very open question whether this operation's going to make it as a business venture," says Brown of Channels. "I don't think it's fair to pass judgment yet. I think it's fair to raise a lot of questions about its viability." BET is classic "narrowcasting" to a specific audience, but some of cable's recent success has been "big-time, big-budget stuff" that apes the broadcast networks in its mass appeal, Brown points out.

Johnson and his executive team believe that none of this threatens BET's success. BET is on "cruise control," Johnson maintains; only a serious recession or "pilot error" can endanger it now.

Once in a while, Johnson will air a gripe. He's unhappy, for instance, that only 22 million subscribers (just 20 percent of whom are estimated to be black) receive BET on their cable systems. Johnson thinks that after a decade the number should be higher by a third and recently lured Curtis Symonds from ESPN to sign up more systems. Some of those systems carry BET for only part of a day, including—the one that really hurts—the system that serves Harlem. The cable operator there said he lacked channel capacity to give BET its own round-the-clock channel. "Next thing I know, they put on Discovery and A&E (Arts & Entertainment). A&E in Harlem!" Johnson fumes. "If you can't get carried in Harlem, what chance have you got in Missoula, Montana?" The success story of the Discovery Channel has to rankle: Like BET, it was launched with cable operators' money; like BET, it serves a less-than-mass audience (those drawn to PBS-style documentaries); unlike BET, it broke even in four years and now has more than 41 million subscribers, perhaps a commentary on what Madison Avenue and the cable industry think about the demographics of documentary fans versus the demographics of African Americans.

But this is uncharacteristic of Johnson. He confesses that in the past, he suffered the occasional doubt that plagues any entrepreneur ("Am I believing my own rhetoric?") but adds that "if it ever gets hold of you, you're sunk." What he'd much rather talk about, and does at every opportunity, is his "vision"—of how BET and its rich corporate partners can vault past Percy Sutton and Berry Gordy and every other black entrepreneur, or maybe merge with them a la Time Inc. and Warner, to become a monster media business. "Why shouldn't BET produce feature films to screen on TCI's United Artists theaters?" he demands. "Why shouldn't BET produce television shows that Worldvision (a recently merged television syndicator and distributor) can syndicate? Why shouldn't BET and Time Warner produce a magazine? And I could go on and on and see the synergy."

He could, undaunted by the fact that BET has no experience with film or magazines and has an uneven record with its own shows. He does. "There's no reason," he says a bit later, returning to his favorite topic, "that we shouldn't start a radio network."

Talk Is Cheap

Tom Shales, November 1988

Talk Rot infests the airwaves and pollutes the atmosphere. Where TV's daytime talk shows once dealt, at least on occasion, with serious social and political issues, they now concentrate mainly on the trivial and the titillating. Hours and hours are frittered away on shock, schlock and folly.

The Reagan administration has insisted for eight years that increased competition helps television, and Reagan's FCC threw out many rules that once protected the public. Result: the worst television in America's history. Increased competition for audiences among talk shows and the stations that carry them has resulted in the wholesale degeneration of the form.

Even Phil Donahue's pioneering talk show has felt the pinch and lowered its sights. "We are dangerously close to being referred to as an intelligent talk show," Donahue says worriedly. "If that happens, we're doomed. Please do not call me 'intelligent.' Call me 'outrageous.' I'd rather have it be suggested that we occasionally go too far, and I'd rather be called 'sleazy' than to be identified as 'intelligent.'"

Isn't that a sad comment?

"Yes it is, but it's also a recognition of the reality of survival on daytime television today."

TV talk shows squander broadcast time on subjects that encourage viewers to think only about themselves or that tease them with reports from the outer limits of sexual adventurism. Viewing of nightly network newscasts, meanwhile, is at an all-time low, and the 50 percent voter turnout on Nov. 8 was the lowest since 1924, continuing a 30-year decline.

The American telectorate is becoming the most overinformed uninformed people on earth—a nation of boob-tube boobs spoon-fed nothing but low-fiber fluff.

"There's a crowding-out factor," says consumer crusader Ralph Nader, once a frequent talk show guest and now rarely invited. "They've taken very precious time away from real issues, public issues, and created two categories of subject matter: what I call the typology of the bizarro, and the soap opera stuff—'how did you feel?' and 'what did he say to you?'

"This is a country hurtling headlong into ecological and economic and other crises and this is what they're into on these shows."

Nader singles out the syndicated "Oprah Winfrey Show" for helping to sully the format: "They get all their ideas from the National Enquirer." Winfrey scored her best ratings ever this week with a show about her success at weight loss, "Diet Dreams Come True."

In recent weeks Winfrey topics have included subservient women, paternity fights, infidelity, man hunting, "threesomes," wife beaters and Joan Collins. A press release promised a show on "shopaholics" for Nov. 11:

"Among the shopaholics to be seen on the live show is Zsa Zsa Gabor with an extensive look via videotape of the voluminous closet in her Bel Air mansion."

"Geraldo," the barrel-bottom talk hour starring dauntless panderer Geraldo Rivera, has dealt in recent weeks with "transsexuals and their families," "teen prostitutes," "swinging sexual suicide," mud-wrestling women, Charles Manson, "serial killers," "kids who kill," "battered women who kill" and, of course, male strippers.

Eventually Geraldo will surely get around to male strippers who kill. With self-aggrandizing inventiveness typical of him, Rivera taped a show in New York this week that asked "Has TV gone too far?"

The answer is yes.

Rivera made headlines and got his broken schnozzola onto the cover of Newsweek recently with a show about "hatemongers" that turned into a brawl during the taping. When aired, it scored huge ratings. The Rivera program is advertised as "definitely more than just talk."

"Donahue" remains the most frequently substantive of the shows, but this week, Phil flounced around in a skirt for a peek at cross-dressing. November is a Nielsen ratings "sweeps" month when the talk shows get even tackier than usual.

From New York, Donahue concedes that competition from the other guys has forced him to do a stupider program.

"Yes. It gives me no pleasure to say yes. We used to be the only kid on the block, swaggering around the mountaintop, and so we could feature programs that interest me as a news junkie, things that our show was unique to present—public service and so on," Donahue says.

"We knew we could not keep the audience if we did not have variations on the theme of the male stripper. But we did not have the kind of competitive influences that we have now. Now that we're on the busiest street in television today, with more and more people running around a studio with wireless mikes, I have to say that we do feel the pressure."

Though "Donahue's" balance has tipped in favor of more froth, less substance, than it used to have, his show is still the one most likely to tackle bona fide news issues. On a Friday in late October, the lineup of talk shows and topics in most markets had Rivera interviewing ex-pimps and ex-hookers, Winfrey telling women how to "break the bad-guy cycle, get the losers out of your life," and Sally Jessy Raphael, another tiny-minded entry in the talk show race, offering makeup tips.

Donahue had Republican John Sununu and Democrat Jesse Jackson discussing the election.

"This is a nation with a seriously diminished interest in serious news," Donahue laments. "And the media is reflecting this. Time and Newsweek covers look more and more like People magazine covers.

"Against that observation has to be considered the enormous competition and profit squeeze that these fewer and fewer and larger and larger media companies feel. They're not unlike me in that they have no interest in being dead heroes. There's no sense talking if nobody's listening and there's no sense writing if nobody's reading."

At the "Oprah Winfrey Show," nobody's talking. Not about this subject. Winfrey may have shed a wall of fat but she is protected by a hefty squad of public relators. Not even executive producer Debra DiMaio would comment. "We don't put ourself in the same category as Geraldo and Morton Downey Jr.," a spokeswoman says, "so we are sticking to our policy of not commenting."

"It's easier to get through to Ronald Reagan than it is to get to Oprah Winfrey," says Nader, who's tried.

(Morton Downey Jr.'s syndicated talk show—more of a shout show in which the host and his guests heap shrieked abuses upon one another—airs late at night in most markets and is not of the same genre as Winfrey, Donahue, Rivera and Raphael.)

The race now in TV talk is to see who can stoop the lowest and make the most noise doing it. Donahue would rather be lumped with the lowly Rivera than be considered a host who treats viewers with excessive respect. That is not a selling point in the new talk market.

"All the media, it seems to me, are tap-dancing a mile a minute trying to figure out what it is this multiracial, multiethnic, apparently very fragmented nation will buy and read or turn on and watch," Donahue says. "And the evidence is pretty overwhelming that as we move into the 21st century, Americans have more and more interest in

Madonna and less and less interest in the Persian Gulf or Central America."

The cheapening of the talk shows is part of the larger trend in deteriorating standards—tabloid television, trash TV, whatever one calls it. Broadcasting seems to be going about the unenviable business of diseducating America—of hyping all that is trivial and frivolous, and hiding all that is real and relevant.

Talk shows lead the way.

Can the decline be pinned on deregulation, on the no-holds-barred competitive environment fostered by the Reagan FCC and its laissez-faire chairmen Mark Fowler and his successor Dennis Patrick? Andrew Jay Schwartzman, director of the Media Access Project, says that in part, it can.

"Deregulation has brought in a new breed of broadcaster to whom public service matters less. They're willing to close their eyes and say, 'Go ahead and put it on.' This creates pressure for broadcasters who know better and say privately they hate this kind of programming but have to do it to compete."

The new hot market in TV stations, fostered by the FCC's abolition of longstanding rules that prevented trafficking in broadcast properties, contributes to this, Schwartzman says. Talk shows proliferate because they are cheap to produce, and trashy talk shows dominate because they're a quick, easy route to big audiences and big bucks.

"There is little doubt that the emphasis on the more spectacular stuff has driven out the issue-oriented discussion," Schwartzman says.

Donahue insists talk shows have not rotted as much as it may seem. "I watch Geraldo and I watch Oprah and I watch Sally and if you give them one week, Monday through Friday, you're going to find that not every show is looking up somebody's dress and that 'sleaze' is a word kind of thrown out there in not a very precise way, and often without information."

Thursday's talk show topics, in most U.S. markets, according to USA Today: "Shopping for sex via cable TV" on "Donahue"; "Flirts" on "Winfrey"; "Sex for survival" on "Rivera"; and "Alien encounters" on "Raphael."

"These people are introverting the audience," Nader charges. "To do topics like this once in a while, that's fine, but they've gone off the deep end. If you suggest they do a show about how people are adversely affected by power—whether it's an abusive corporation, a bad workplace situation, government, whatever—they won't touch it."

Donahue says that when he does schedule serious shows, some of the stations that buy his series will shunt them away from ratings periods. "They collect the sex shows for the ratings periods. They can air the shows whenever they want. The customer is always right."

And so it continues, the daily parade: wackos, loonies, stars, celebrities, freaks, geeks and gurus. Much of it is appallingly entertaining. Little of it is remotely worthwhile.

On one of her few serious, outer-directed shows, Winfrey dealt with declining literacy among the young and the escalating crisis in American education. In promos she looked into the camera and asked, "How dumb are we?" There's every possibility that talk rot is making us dumber.

Lucy, Lost and Found

Tom Shales, December 1989

It's not the funniest episode of "I Love Lucy" you ever saw, but there's a 99.9 percent chance it's the one you've seen the least. A special that originally aired on Christmas Eve 1956, "The I Love Lucy Christmas Show" gets its first repeat telecast ever on CBS tonight, at 8:30 on Channel 9.

The program was not included among the 179 episodes of "I Love Lucy" that have been in syndication for eons. Except for the airing of a brief excerpt on an NBC special in 1981, there hasn't been a sign of it since that one and only telecast 33 years ago.

Lucille Ball and Desi Arnaz, the stars and producers, apparently withheld the show from the syndication package because its holiday theme dated it. The half-hour ends with the Ricardos and the Mertzes (Vivian Vance and William Frawley) looking into the camera and saying in unison, "Merry Christmas, everybody."

The episode was thrown together quickly and has only bare bones of a plot—trimming the tree, setting out presents for Little Ricky, and so on. But the chitchat is interrupted for three flashback sequences to earlier programs, including the 1951 show on which a pregnant Lucy marches into the living room and announces, "Ricky, this is it."

At that signal, Ricky, Fred and Ethel panic themselves into a fit trying to get Lucy and her suitcase out the door and off to the hospital for the birth of Little Ricky, the highest-rated blessed event in TV history.

Ken Ross, vice president of CBS Video, gets credit for unearthing the Christmas show and placing it in prime time. Last July, Ross was looking for Christmas-theme material for the home video market. CBS has been "extremely successful," he says, selling "I Love Lucy" episodes in stores and via a mail-order club.

Once Ross became aware that a Christmas "Lucy" existed, he had to find it in the CBS vaults. Then a print was made from the negative so Ross and fellow executives could take a look. "We said, wait a minute, this is so warm, because of the flashback sequences in it, that it would be a wonderful thing to share with the American public," Ross says.

All four of the principals are gone now, but it's a sentimental kick to see them in their prime again, both in the flashback sequences and in new scenes that are totally unfamiliar.

"It's a significant show only because it hasn't been seen more than once," says Bart Andrews, author of "The I Love Lucy Book," a definitive appreciation of the series. "For a 'Lucy' fan, it's like being a stamp collector and coming across some rare and valuable stamp."

Even rarer than this Christmas show, says Andrews, is the original pilot for "I Love Lucy" made by Ball and Arnaz, but without Vance and Frawley, who were cast later. It was long believed Arnaz himself owned a print of that show and kept it "under his bed," Andrews says.

But after Arnaz died, no film was found, under his bed or anywhere else. New York's Museum of Broadcasting has run magazine ads asking for information as to the whereabouts of this collector's item of collector's items. So far, no collector has come forward.

If the 'Lucy' Christmas show gets a decent rating—and it only has to do as well as "The Famous Teddy Z," the ill-fated flop it's preempting—the program may become a holiday perennial. "I don't see why not," says Ross. "It could be our 'Miracle on 34th Street.' This would be 'Miracle on 52nd Street.'" That's where CBS is headquartered in New York.

Ross and CBS refuse to say how many "Lucy" tapes have been sold in the home video biz. But Andrews has one indication. Those who join the mail-order club get a free copy of his book. So far, he says, at least 150,000 books have been bought by CBS for this purpose.

Ross sounded indignant when asked if thought had been given to colorizing the "Lucy" shows marketed on cassette. In fact, it's all but inevitable and—to judge from a brief colorized sample done for the introduction to the first tape in the mail-order series—it won't hurt a bit. After all, they're always talking about Lucy's dyed red hair. So dye it already.

CBS, which is awfully adept at missing the boat, could have colorized tonight's episode and thus added to its novelty and its audience appeal.

Even in black-and-white, the longevity of "I Love Lucy" and the popularity of Lucille Ball is like nothing else in the life and times of television. People usually speak of the show in terms of Ball's clowning, but in fact there was a solid dramatic heart to the series and to the relationships of the four main characters.

Here in Washington, two episodes of "I Love Lucy" air each morning, Sundays through Fridays, on Channel 5. The reruns recently reached the point at which the Ricardos move to Connecticut, which means the shows are from the last season of the series.

In some odd way, it's sad to see it ending again—even for the umpteenth time—but then it will all begin again, and the cycle will repeat itself. Lucy will get stuck in a freezer. Lucy will stomp grapes. Lucy and Ethel will steal John Wayne's footprints from Grauman's Chinese Theater.

And pregnant Lucy will march into the living room once more to make her big announcement. Watching "The I Love Lucy Christmas Show" is like looking at home movies of old friends. Ricky, this is it.

Radio Fills the Void

Eleanor Randolph, October 1989

Sometimes it takes a hurricane or an earthquake to remind us how much our high-tech communications system depends on a thin, little wire that plugs into the nearest power station.

Last week in California and last month in the Carolinas, Mother Nature severed electrical umbilical cords. The human beings living in these disaster areas were not catapulted back to the Stone Age, but they were instantly dependent on batteries and backup generators.

In the dark, literally, and in need of advice and information, they remembered the value of a long undervalued gadget—the portable radio.

"Most people don't have battery-operated television sets, and it's pretty tough to sit around your living room and watch television if your living room doesn't exist any more," said David Bartlett, president of the Radio-Television News Directors' Association.

"But almost everybody has a battery-operated radio or a car radio," Bartlett said. "Radio's new role in our world is portability, not immediacy."

In such times, people cared little for the latest trend or the price of hair dryers or vidwizardry that clogs up the broadcast airwaves. They wanted basic questions answered: Is my family okay? Where can I get help? Is there food or water nearby?

Easterners watching ABC network television shortly after the quake saw a local San Francisco newscaster explaining how fellow residents should turn the gas off in their homes to prevent fire. She noted the page in the telephone book where quake victims could find the information.

It all seemed an admirable public service until you realized that most of the people who could smell gas weren't watching television. They didn't have electricity.

Other media struggled to provide help after the quake. Newspapers, with borrowed generators and store-bought batteries, struggled to get slim editions on the street where they were hungrily bought for their value as news and souvenirs. The telephone service was better than anybody had hoped—unless, of course, you had one of those new, slim telephones that can redial or speed dial and play a tune when somebody's calling. Those phones run on electricity.

In areas where there was power, computer networkers instantly began networking. Subscribers to such computer networks as Prodigy and CompuServe tapped into their electronic-billboard systems to send messages to friends or relatives in California. One woman sent a message that the students at Mills College were all fine—a few lines that probably calmed an army of parents in the rest of the country. And a CompuServe executive compared the computer networkers to "what ham radio operators do, only it's on a computer."

But the medium that clearly won the race for getting more crucial news to more people who needed it in San Francisco was radio.

At Candlestick Park, when the concrete "rippled" and the big lights went down shortly before the start of World Series Game 3, people huddled around radios in hopes of getting the news about what was happening beyond the stadium walls.

"We have been on the air nonstop with no breaks since it happened," said John McConnell, news director for KGO Radio in San Francisco. With a damaged radio tower reducing by half its normal 50,000 kilowatts, McConnell said the AM station was off the air for about 20 to 25 minutes after the quake. Since then, it's been nonstop news and call-in shows at KGO. The first ad since the quake did not air until Friday morning.

San Francisco residents said they tuned to KGO, KCBS and KNBR for news of what was happening and where to go for food, water and safe buildings where they could sleep.

Music-format stations tried to be helpful as a disc jockey or two tried to give a little news in between the music segments. But most FM stations aren't designed for such things as information; the most they could provide was mental relief.

The news shows offered advice from traffic experts, psychologists and structural engineers. They gave residents tips on what to do when the water looks and smells funny.

At KGO, where listeners routinely call in and tell what's happening in their area, one resident described how strangely the family pets were acting before the quake. A woman who wanted to get to work at an Oakland hospital asked advice about the traffic pattern. The broadcaster told her how to get to work.

Last week in San Francisco, radio became more than a thing that plays music during the traffic jam. It was a utility because, in the beginning, at least, it was the only medium that worked.

The Primest Time

Tom Shales, March 1990

Sunday night, and America is watching television. For all that TV has changed in the decades since it arrived, and for all the societal upheaval TV has wrought, one central constant has survived.

On Sunday evenings, though they may have split up into factions during the day, family members tend to band together before the TV set as they do on no other night of the week. Monday nights are about tied with Sundays in attracting the largest number of TV households each week, but Sunday night shows have the highest ratio of viewers to sets.

Indeed, of the top 10 shows in the viewers-per-set rankings, all but one airs on Sunday night. Holding the top spot currently in this ranking is "The Simpsons," the new and sparkling animated series from Fox about a bizarre, hapless cartoon clan.

Its success underscores the fact that Sunday night is still family night in television.

The second-ranked show is also new this year: ABC's "America's Funniest Home Videos," the breakaway hit that is a model of economical programming; the show consists of spills and sprawls captured on tape by America's growing army of camcorder owners. It's ultimate family programming: families watching other families.

Although ABC's new biographical series "Elvis" has scored low in the overall weekly ratings, it's No. 10 on the list of most viewers per set. For TV watchers of a certain age, the presence of a surrogate Elvis Presley on Sunday night has an aura of deja vu, because on a Sunday night in 1956, the real Elvis Presley appeared on "The Ed Sullivan Show" and the world, as commentators love to say, would never be the same.

America had reached an unforgettable cultural crossroads. Another would occur on the same program on Feb. 9, 1964, when Sullivan introduced, for their first live TV appearance in this country, "these youngsters from Liverpool," as he called them then, the Beatles.

Such have been the Sundays of our lives.

Now, "Elvis" and "Videos" and "The Simpsons" join a long, long list of great American television programs that have been Sunday-night fixtures over the years. These are shows that both reflect and contribute to the night's distinctive flavor, which might be described as Extreme Middle of the Road.

In the '50s, in addition to "The Ed Sullivan Show," we watched "The Jack Benny Show," "Alfred Hitchcock Presents," "Lassie," "Maverick," "The Dinah Shore Chevy Show," "Mr. Peepers," "What's My Line?," "The Colgate Comedy Hour," "The Steve Allen Show," "Garroway at Large," and "The 20th Century" with Walter Cronkite.

In the '60s, it was "Candid Camera," "The Bullwinkle Show," "The Judy Garland Show," "Profiles in Courage," "The Rogues," "Perry Mason," "The Garry Moore Show," "The Smothers Brothers Show," "The Bill Cosby Show" and "Mission: Impossible." And, still, "The Ed Sullivan Show."

Sullivan went off in 1971, and the Sunday night ritual changed, mostly for the worse. The reigning Sunday hits of the decade included "Kojak," "The Sonny and Cher Comedy Hour," and "The Six Million Dollar Man." The television audience was fragmenting, and the idea of unanimous, all-family hits was already beginning to fade.

Instead there were such spectacular failures as ABC's "Battlestar Galactica," an attempt to capitalize on the popularity of "Star Wars," and NBC's "The Big Event," a landmark in hyped tripe.

Even public television got serious about Sunday nights as of Jan. 10, 1971—the premiere of "Masterpiece Theatre," the series of imported, high-quality, serialized dramas still on the air. The first offering was "The First Churchills."

And in 1975, Sunday night television took on a radical new character when "60 Minutes" was moved to the 7 p.m. spot it has owned ever since.

That was actually the ninth time slot for the CBS News magazine show, which had once aired outside prime time, Sundays at 6. "60 Minutes" premiered on a Tuesday night in 1968. In every slot it occupied until 1975, it had been a flop. But "60 Minutes" took its licking and kept on ticking.

In format, personnel and outlook, "60 Minutes" has changed hardly at all since the '68 premiere. The executive producer was and is Don Hewitt. But somehow the change in setting turned it from a negligible gadfly to a national institution.

Sunday has always been a good night for institution-making.

"60 Minutes" continued to dominate Sunday nights in the '80s as well, joined in 1984 on the CBS schedule by the still-running "Murder, She Wrote." But otherwise, blockbuster hits on Sundays were scarce. Cable arrived to take a bite out of the networks' share of the audience.

ABC, CBS and NBC retreated to the relatively safe (and boring) option of filling two hours with movies.

Meanwhile, really big network shows debuted on other nights. NBC built a magnificent Thursday out of "The Cosby Show," "Cheers" and "L.A. Law." In terms of revenue, it's the most profitable night in television. And ABC has put its stamp on Tuesdays, with "Roseanne" and "thirtysomething."

For a while, "Moonlighting" gave ABC a high Tuesday night profile. Curiously enough, when ABC moved that show to Sunday nights, it died. "Moonlighting" is just not a Sunday kind of show. It had zero appeal for children—perhaps Less Than Zero—and that, combined with an attack of creative burnout, may be the chief reason it failed.

"60 Minutes" and "Murder, She Wrote" have zero kid appeal, too, yet they are nothing if not evergreens. David F. Poltrack, the brilliant CBS vice president who charts ebbs and flows in viewing patterns, says the shows are such big hits it doesn't matter that they don't fit the traditional Sunday night profile.

"Certainly we know our strategy on Sunday night," Poltrack says. "We're not going to change that winning combination, and that winning combination is not going to get us any children."

Nevertheless, Poltrack knows what makes Sunday, and its companion night Monday, unique. "The lighter television viewer watches on Sundays and Mondays, and is not as likely to watch the rest of the week," Poltrack says. "That lighter viewer is by definition the better-educated, upper socioeconomic viewer, so you'll find programs that appeal to those viewers on that night.

"'The Incident,' the movie we just played (March 4), would not have performed anywhere near the level it did on another night of the week," Poltrack says. "Incident" was a fairly sophisticated TV movie, not the usual pulpy exploitation.

But the high viewing level for Sunday night isn't just because the programs are better (they're just as likely to be worse) or because light viewers supplement the regulars. Sunday night's high viewership is directly related to longstanding national habits.

"The idea that after the weekend, people are now faced with going back to work, going back to school, makes Sunday a natural stay-at-home night," Poltrack says. "There's not a lot of social activity going on, and the significant number of people who now work Monday through Friday evenings aren't likely to work Sunday evenings as well.

"According to the lifestyle habits and the leisure-time habits of the United States, more people are at home Sunday night than any other night of the week."

There's one other factor. On Sunday night, prime time lasts four hours. It begins at 7 instead of 8 as it does on other nights of the week. People plop themselves in front of the sets earlier—some are there all day as well as all night in football season—and of all the nights in the week, it's the one that is more likely to bring families together than to drive them apart.

"The Simpsons" is in the best tradition of Sunday night television, yet it seems a true departure from everything that has gone before. The cartoon saga of a bickering, downtrodden middle-class family began as little blackout sketches, mere exclamation points inserted before and after commercials breaks on Fox's "Tracey Ullman Show."

Now on their own, the Simpsons have consistently scored hugely higher ratings than Ullman ever got, becoming the first prime-time animated hit since the days of "The Jetsons" (1962-63), though "Simpsons" is light years beyond that show in wit and style.

The program sprang from the apparently warped mind of Matt Groening, a cartoonist whose drawings of "Life in Hell" attracted the attention of writer-producer James L. Brooks, a founding father of "The Mary Tyler Moore Show" and "Taxi," and writer-director of the acclaimed movies "Terms of Endearment" and "Broadcast News."

Brooks, with Groening and co-producer Sam Simon, oversaw the transformation of the Simpsons from page to screen and from short sketches to a weekly half-hour. He talked about the show recently in his cozy bungalow on the 20th Century Fox lot in Hollywood.

"We're learning our way with it," Brooks said. "One thing that struck me, a little signpost, is that with all this nutty stuff you hear about 'family entertainment,' I never know what it is or what it's supposed to be. Usually it's a show that tends to be so vanilla that—well, you know. But this I think is family entertainment in that no matter what age you are, something is challenging you, something is pushing you along, something is a little not-quite-what-it-should-be, but fun.

"I think that's what we're trying to do."

There are five Simpsons: Homer, the father, who works with plutonium at the local power plant (it's a nuclear family) and whose eyes are in a perpetual state of pop. Marge, the mother, has blue hair piled high on her head, like it was billowing out of a smokestack. Bart is the renegade son, Lisa the sister with whom he constantly fights, Maggie the baby who is never without her squeaking pacifier.

They're the flip, dark side of the Nelsons, the Andersons, the Bradys and all other sitcom families from the dawn of television. The show inhabits a rarefied realm that enables it to be both fiercely funny and absurdly poignant.

"The Simpsons" is sweet cynicism.

Brooks says it's not true that since the show is about human characters, not talking ducks or mice or bunnies, it could have been done as a regular sitcom with real live actors.

"I thought of that as something to shoot for," he says. "You know, forget that it's a cartoon—living people with relationships and something to say and all that, hopefully, and that would be like a great thing to do as an animated series. I thought, you would get involved, there would be actual story content.

"But the thing about the form is, it obligates us every once in a while to take a flight of fancy. Since none of us has done that so purely before, it'll be interesting to see where that leads us. Every once in a while we'll have an episode where the form pulls us into an area we wouldn't ordinarily be pulled.

"Certainly there are production things we couldn't possibly do if it weren't animated. We can be anyplace, go to any country. But it is about a family. And ducks won't talk. Ducks won't talk." He smiles broadly behind his beard. "But little girls will play great blues on the saxophone! And women will have their money hidden in their hair."

Brooks is particularly proud of the show to air next week. In it, Marge—a cartoon character—comes very close to having an extra-marital affair with a bowling alley gigolo named Jacques. "The parts of the show I like most is when there's actual emotional life," Brooks says, and absurd as the episode is, it does have that quality.

It all starts when Homer realizes he has forgotten to buy a present for his wife's 34th birthday. He rushes off to Springfield Mall, walks past the Jerky Hut, the Ear Piercery and the International House of Answering Machines, and finally comes up with the perfect gift: a bowling ball, with his name inscribed on it.

This, Marge notes when she sees it, is on a par with his past birthday gifts to her: a tackle box and a Connie Chung calendar. It leads her into a life of bowling that could involve a case of adultery. Will she? Won't she? As funny, satirical and stylized as it all is, you actually find yourself caring.

"Marge, darling," Jacques coos temptingly. "There are 10 pins in my heart. You've knocked over eight. Won't you please pick up that spare?"

On tonight's edition of "The Simpsons," a rerun, Homer pawns the family television—oh, unthinkable act!—to pay for a session at Dr. Monroe's Family Therapy Center. "Sometimes I think we're the worst family in town," Homer mopes.

"Don't have a cow, dad," says Bart.

"The sad truth is," says Lisa, "all families are like us."

These are the Simpsons. Crazed, wonderful and bitterly funny.

Perhaps the great success Fox Television is having on Sunday nights will help nudge the evening back toward lost luster. Because the Fox shows, crude as some of them are, are aimed squarely at young families, and young families are watching. Of the shows that draw the most viewers per set, four are from Fox.

In fifth place is Fox's coarse and corrosive "Married . . . with Children," which offers the American family a hideous distortion of itself to laugh at. At least, one hopes it's a distortion. Fox's "America's Most Wanted," whose overall ratings are on a decline, makes the list too.

It would be nice to think that another show with the broad appeal of Ed Sullivan's could come along in television someday, but both television and its audience have so fractionalized that it isn't likely. Attempts to revive the variety format, on any night of the week, invariably fail. We're not the homogeneous society we were.

And yet on Sunday nights, we're at least closer, as a television nation, than on most other nights. The pickings are leaner, but the field is not barren. In 1960, a viewer could leave the channel selector on CBS all night and not see a truly terrible show: "Lassie," "Dennis the Menace," "Ed Sullivan," "General Electric Theater," "Jack Benny," "Candid Camera" and "What's My Line?"

Today—that is, tonight—it's not that easy. But with the remote control zapper in hand, and most families have one, you can spend Sunday with "60 Minutes" (CBS), "America's Funniest Home Videos" (ABC), and "The Simpsons" (Fox), then hope for a good movie or miniseries on one of the three major networks, or opt for Fox shows like "Tracey Ullman" and "It's Garry Shandling's Show."

If you watched TV only on Sunday nights, you would come away with the misleading impression that the level of quality on American television is not all that low. Sunday night is American television.

CHAPTER SEVEN

The News Business

What's Wrong with News You Can Use

Eleanor Randolph, January 1990

At a gathering of Third World visitors here recently, an African stood to ask a question of columnist James J. Kilpatrick.

"Why is it that American journalists don't care about my country?" the African asked.

"What country do you come from, sir?" Kilpatrick responded.

"Uganda," the man answered.

"Why the hell should I care about Uganda?" said Kilpatrick, as diplomats around the room wheezed and struggled to catch their breaths.

This story, retold recently in an essay published by the Gannett Center for Media Studies in New York, is another case of Kilpatrick having the nerve to say what so many other journalists were thinking. The American news establishment too often looks at foreign news as something alien. Their rule: The farther it is from home, the less important it is to the readers.

As a result, news organizations over the years have shed foreign bureaus and scaled back costly foreign coverage. One survey shows that the amount of the nation's top ten papers devoted to foreign news dropped from 10.2 percent in 1971 to 2.6 percent in 1987.

With recent events in China, Eastern Europe and Central America, the percentage of foreign news in the nation's newspapers is probably up from 1987, when near-war had broken out in the Middle East and Persian Gulf, says one expert on this trend, Michael Emery, chair of the journalism school at California State University, Northridge. But the percentage of foreign news is still down from 20 years ago, Emery laments.

The problem is that publishers are busy giving readers what they think they want instead of what is important. This is the era of "News You Can Use"—the catch phrase for journalism that helps you with your taxes, cholesterol and yearning for the latest in car phones. All that is fine, but you cannot use this news to help understand what's going on—not in your neighborhood, not in your country, not in your world.

If that sounds like a boring flashback to Mrs. Morse's ninth-grade civics class, so sorry. As Mrs. Morse would say: "Informed people make good citizens." But the money men who increasingly run newspapers and television networks seem to think that good citizenship is registered most concretely in the profit margins. Their accountants have found that the numbers for foreign coverage—or Washington coverage, for that matter—aren't good.

Foreign coverage costs big bucks, about $250,000 a year for a one-man bureau. Moreover, unless Americans are involved in the story—from a plane wreck in Scotland to an invasion of Panama—the level of interest among many readers and most editors ranges from pale to pallid. Their interest perks up a bit if there are pictures of some major calamity, bloody pictures, such as the ones from Tiananmen Square. Any foreign story without blood or Americans or both has a tough time.

The Times-Mirror News Interest Index, which comes out monthly, noted that the big foreign-news event for most Americans was the one we engineered—the invasion of Panama. More than half of those surveyed said that Panama topped their list of important news events for December and January.

By contrast, the overthrow of the Ceausescu government in Romania ranked as top story for five percent of those interviewed. And although 70 percent of those interviewed knew that Romanian President Nicolae Ceausescu and his wife had been tried secretly and executed, 13 percent said they thought that U.S. troops had been involved in the Romanian uprising.

Many serious journalists, both reporters and editors, have been shocked at the lack of interest here in what has happened in Eastern Europe. Surveys of news consumers show that few people can recognize the name of the man who has suddenly became head of Czechoslovakia.

For most of us in the news trade, the crumbling of the Communist threat is the biggest story in the last decade. It will dramatically affect how America does business, maintains its military and reorders domestic priorities. To learn that this news is falling on disinterested ears and even that some news managers are beginning to scale back their commitment to the story in Europe feels like a punch in the stomach.

More than the overactive journalistic ego is being bruised here. We know that when people aren't interested in news beyond their own bank statement and spa schedule, they are ceding the major decisions in their lives to others.

"As knowledge of foreign affairs drops, the chances for clear decisions in Congress drops because there is less public awareness," said Emery. "They can get away with more and more and more."

The most basic instinct of governments both abroad and at home is to keep everything they do a secret, except for those things they want to advertise. If the press limits its coverage of foreign matters, then it's an all-clear for the people in charge. They like it that way. We shouldn't tolerate it.

The Media Diplomacy of Ted Koppel

Tom Shales, February 1990

That ancient Chinese curse "May you live in interesting times" has lost its relevance in the age of global media. Because now, interesting times are usually just a satellite link away.

For the past week, ABC News has been piping in extremely interesting times from South Africa. A series of special "Nightline" broadcasts has been bringing together opposing factions who seem not to have talked much to each other before—a feat "Nightline" accomplished previously with its week-long visit to the Mideast in April 1988.

However, there are limits to "Nightline's" diplomatic journalism. Koos van der Merwe, a Conservative Party leader in South Africa, walked off Wednesday's lengthy "Town Meeting" from Johannesburg because he refused to "debate" with members of the African National Congress, whose most famous member, Nelson Mandela, has just been released from 27 years in prison.

"My party is not prepared at this time in history to debate with the African National Congress and the Communist Party," van der Merwe said. He didn't exactly stomp off, however. Three times he announced he was leaving and three times he stayed to answer a question or lodge a tirade.

It was a sign that not even Ted Koppel can necessarily bring harmony where there had been discord, that sitting down for a dialogue is not a guaranteed temper cooler, and that the problems of the country in question are dauntingly Byzantine and confounding. In addition, though the town meeting aired live from South Africa (where it started at 6:30 a.m.), it was not televised live in South Africa, and only portions of it may eventually be aired there.

Still, what "Nightline" has been doing in South Africa is brave, enterprising and historic.

The most rancorous outburst of the "Nightline" town meeting—which didn't end until 1:48 a.m. Eastern time yesterday—came from a member of the audience who identified himself as a transplanted Australian, causing many in the audience to begin chanting, "Go home."

Expressing agreement with the white supremacist views of van der Merwe, the Australian man shouted to him, "Don't leave. Just don't talk to the sons of bitches." A few moments later, the man marched down the aisle, grabbed a tan briefcase from behind a chair, placed the briefcase on the stage near Koppel and opened it.

There was no sign of security personnel. But fortunately, the man had only papers in the case. He shouted something inaudible to Koppel, who told him to go back to the microphone at the other end of the aisle if he wanted to comment. "We're here to do a television broadcast, not to listen to you privately," Koppel said.

ABC News spokesman Laura Wessner said yesterday from New York that security agents—out of camera range—were moving toward the man as he opened the briefcase, but when they saw its contents, they pulled back. Members of the audience had to go through a metal detector for admittance to the hall, she said.

Security was provided by the University of Witwatersrand, which hosted the event, by ABC-hired private guards, and by the South African Broadcasting Corp.

Curiously enough, the closing credits of the program included this notation: "Studio Coordinator for South African Broadcasting—Koos van der Merwe." The same man? "It couldn't possibly be," said Wessner. "There are a lot of van der Merwes there. It's like 'Jones' here."

Indeed, there was another van der Merwe on the stage: South African Minister of Education Stoffel van der Merwe, a political opponent of the conservative.

Koppel remained his unflappable self even during the ruckus caused by the man with the briefcase. And he managed to bring in all sides to the complicated debate as the evening wore on. But his moderating had its immoderate aspects. He did not ask a substantive question of a single black participant in the program until the second half-hour, choosing instead to indulge the van der Merwes as they bickered about giving yes or no answers to questions.

Thabo Mbeki, an ANC officer, was standing by in Lusaka, Zambia, but because of satellite trouble, he couldn't hear the Johannesburg portions. So Koppel can be excused for being late in getting to him. But other black participants sat on the stage for a long time before being invited to contribute.

Among those who did were Keith Musa Zondi, a member of the Inkatha Youth Brigade, and Popo Molefe, general secretary of the United Democratic Front. Interesting times—interesting names. One also got a new appreciation of how many diverse points of view exist in both the pro- and anti-apartheid camps.

If the idea behind the town meeting is indeed to bring together disparate factions for face-to-face discussion, however, Koppel often dulled the impact by interjecting himself between debaters, sometimes stifling exchanges just as they were getting started.

Late in the program, a man in the audience asked a perfectly coherent question about the gap between rhetoric and results among white politicians. Koppel, his reading glasses now hanging from the end of his nose, needlessly rephrased the question for a member of the onstage panel.

Having admitted in the past to pomposity, Koppel also displays an imperious tinge. He's fond of telling participants to address not each other or the audience, but him, the great interrogator: "Tell me a little bit about," he'll say, or "Just give me an idea," or "Talk to me for a moment," or "Let me make sure I understand what you're saying."

Nor is he precisely a man of few words. When the conservative van der Merwe made one of his several departure announcements, Koppel said to him, "Let me ask you one question. I understand you're leaving, and you have already indicated to me that if we brought Mr. Mbeki on the program that you would, and I told you we would, and so you are of course free to do what you have to do, and I'm free to do what I have to do. But let me just ask you, before you go, why it is that you're so worried about talk?"

Considering such windy pronouncements as that, it was nervy of Koppel to say to one of the guests, "May I ask you to pose your questions somewhat succinctly?"

Of course, however much one may find to criticize in Koppel's performances, he's still the best at this sort of thing, at least among the competition on the commercial networks. And he proved again that he will not sit back and let guests get away with double talk, gobbledygook or outright evasions. He forces them at least to make a stab at answering the question.

ABC News has been promoting the broadcasts from South Africa as if they are certain to change things in that beleaguered country. This is not a sound claim to make ahead of time, even if it may turn out to be a side effect afterward. But it is difficult to imagine how the "Nightline" telecasts from South Africa could do anything but good.

The town meeting was supposed to mark the conclusion of the visit—a return for "Nightline," which first covered South Africa in 1985. On Wednesday, however, Koppel secured a 45-minute interview with Mandela, which was scheduled to air last night. The interview would focus more on Mandela the man than on Mandela the political force, ABC said.

At the conclusion of the town meeting, ABC pitched viewers a home video called "Mandela," which could be purchased via an 800 number for $19.98, plus $3.95 postage and handling. It seemed a tacky way to end what had been a largely exemplary and engrossing evening—and a testament to the stubborn persistence of interesting times.

The National News

Eleanor Randolph, November 1988

The national news media has an unspoken rule: If it happens in Texas, it's quaint. If it happens in New York City, it's serious.

For years, journalists stationed around the country for the news magazines, the networks or New York newspapers talked with frustration about a story being "BAMed"—walloped by an editor inflicted with Big Apple Myopia.

Some of the most classic horror stories about Eastern ignorance include a call from the boss in New York who thought Idaho was next to Texas, or a correspondent who found herself steaming down the highway because her editor was convinced that Denver was just a "hop and a skip from" South Dakota.

With cable channels eating into the networks and magazines suffering from lack of national advertising, however, there has been a lot of talk about how New York editors and news directors have "discovered America." That is, they have decided that there are smart people, good people, bad people and interesting people who do not live within a two-hour (day-trip) radius of Rockefeller Center.

Forget it, says David Shaw, media critic for the—ahem—Los Angeles Times. It's nothing but talk.

In a recent series that has yet to get much notice back East, Shaw explains how it works: Newsweek's Detroit bureau chief was in Houston last year and tried to convince her editors to do a story on ocean pollution. A whale had died from swallowing debris along the Gulf coast. Shellfish beds were off limits near Texas. Volunteers in one three-day period picked up more than 200 tons of debris.

Sorry, she was told, not national. Then, New Yorkers found syringes on their beaches this summer. Suddenly Time and Newsweek—simultaneously, of course—trumpeted the warnings in their Aug. 1 editions. "Our Filthy Seas" said Time's cover. "Our Polluted Oceans" echoed Newsweek.

Calls to reporters and editors who work for various publications around the country brought near explosions of frustration at the networks, the news magazines and the Eastern newspapers for their "arrogant" provincialism.

186

"The New York Times takes a particularly hard policy," said Dan Thomasson, vice president of the Scripps-Howard News Service. "They figure it's not news until they print it."

Thomasson; obviously speaking for many of his colleagues, says that even reporters from outlying areas who go to work for The Times or The Washington Post or The Wall Street Journal "suddenly think that they're more worthy. . . . If you work for those papers it doesn't matter who you are. You could call up and say you're Mickey Mouse from The New York Times and, bam, you get the interview."

Mike Magner, Washington correspondent for the Booth Newspapers in Michigan, says that the way news is covered affects the way legislation is enacted. After New Yorkers and their media discovered ocean pollution, miraculously, so did Congress.

"Michigan congressmen complained that Congress tried to ignore the Great Lakes," Magner said. "In this case, medical wastes were washing up on shores in Lake Erie and Lake Michigan, but Congress wanted legislation that dealt only with oceans."

Nick Horrock, an alumnus of Newsweek and The New York Times who is now running the Washington bureau of The Chicago Tribune, says that he believes the Eastern bias is dissipating. To help it along, he makes certain the Associated Press offices in Chicago or Washington know about a Tribune scoop.

But in other areas, such as foreign policy, it's still tough going. "I've had guys who say they don't care about being in The Chicago Tribune, even if we got there first and ask the most intelligent questions. . . . They just want to be in The Times."

Some relief comes during presidential campaigns when thousands of national reporters and a few editors are forced to follow the candidates out into the real world. Iowa, New Hampshire, Florida, Michigan and Oregon are all places that have three journalistic advantages: They are not Boston, not Washington and not New York City.

But, this is once every four years. And, too many national political journalists can go to Arizona and spend a lot of time hanging out with their friends from New York, Boston and Washington. When they sit in an Albuquerque bar and talk about the Indian problem this year, they meant the Washington Redskins.

A suggestion: National reporters for national publications should be required by their bosses to visit other areas of the country at least once per quarter—a real place where a press advance crew has not arrived a few days in advance and made sure the phones work.

Kennebunkport doesn't count. Editors should make a national tour every year to talk about crime in Texas or the state of the arts in Chicago.

Maybe then some would realize that when they moved to the East Coast, all the best people and the worst problems and the most interesting news stories in the country did not automatically move with them. Maybe.

No News for Consumers

Richard Harwood, April 1989

The bombing of Pearl Harbor was "news." The Woodstock "be-in" was "news." The resignation of Richard Nixon and the Redskins Super Bowl victories were "news." It doesn't take a rocket scientist or a newspaper editor to figure that out.

But in the absence of self-evident events, what is "news"? We in the news business often will tell you in that patronizing and arrogant manner we are prey to that "news is what we say it is." That is something of a delusion. Editors control what is and what is not published and broadcast, but what we publish and broadcast may be "news" only in our own minds or in the minds of important dinner companions. The great American audience may tune out completely, as countless bankrupt editors and publishers have discovered and as the network news divisions have learned from their competition with the game shows.

The serious editor (nonserious editors being virtually extinct) replies that he does not pander to public taste but publishes or broadcasts the things people "need to know." His priorities often are correct, as we should expect. But very often, these priorities are suspect.

Last week editors of The Post decided that a very important "news" event had occurred: the head lawyer at the White House whose name escapes most normal people had been chewed out by the head bureaucrat at the White House for grumbling aloud about the recent contra aid deal worked out between Congress and the president. The story was given the premier spot on the front page—the top right-hand column. Okay. A White House chewing out is good cocktail chatter on a slow night in this town, even if you don't know the chew-ee.

The following day on an inside page of the Style section one encountered the following story: 1.7 million customers (virtually every household in the Washington metropolitan area and every reader of The Post) are liable to be clipped for $17 million a year under a new insurance scheme dreamed up by the C&P Telephone Co. The telephone wires inside your house will henceforth be insured against damage for $10.20 a year—tacked onto your phone bill—unless you inform C&P that you don't want the coverage. Is that "news"? It seemed so to me but not to the front-page editors; it didn't happen at the White House.

There was another expose' in the Style section a week earlier that got no front-page attention. It was a story about who gets what from the fund-raising drives of local police and firefighter organizations, which have sacred cow status in the universe of charities. The Montgomery County Deputy Sheriff's Association raised $103,600 for a charity ball in January, of which $10,000 went to the association; the rest went for overhead expenses and into the pockets of professional fund-raisers. This sort of thing, reporter David Streitfield found, is commonplace. It affects virtually every reader of the newspaper. Is it as newsworthy as a chewing out at the White House?

On Page B15 last month, a seven-inch story reported that the "government . . . is investigating whether 1.9 million General Motors Corp. cars have defective cruise control mechanisms that can cause a driver to lose control of the car." An earlier item buried in the bowels of a long "roundup column" in the back of the financial section stated that "NHTSA (all readers know what that is, right?) is stepping up probes concerning more than 2.1 million 1987 and 1988 GM cars because of complaints about poor braking, faulty steering and doors that fall off." The agency identified by the alphabet soup is the National Highway Traffic Safety Administration. These cars are on the highways. You may be driving one. Are their potential problems "news"?

"Consumer" news is old hat in American newspapers, especially for our upscale clients. We have been evaluating ballet performances, symphony concerts, the Paris fashions and accommodations on the Riviera for years; our restaurant critic has been recently sampling Italian food in Boston for those who might wish to fly up this weekend. But the "new" consumer news involving ripoffs, commercial fraud, product safety and the like has tended to fall between the cracks. We haven't known how to handle it or where to put it in the newspaper.

A radical idea would be to look at it as "news."

The Panelists Are the Debate

Eleanor Randolph, October 1988

If there is any question about who won the vice-presidential debate, here's the answer: Judy Woodruff of PBS, Tom Brokaw of NBC, Brit Hume of ABC and Jon Margolis of the Chicago Tribune.

These journalists were chosen by the campaigns and political parties to question Democrat Lloyd Bentsen and Republican Dan Quayle. They were deemed docile by both parties; they were considered safe. The candidates' handlers expected to be able to predict their questions and had programmed the journalists into a format so stage-managed that the League of Women Voters refused to run the event.

Were the campaign wizards ever in for a surprise when they picked this particular quartet.

Its members engineered a little revolution: They refused to obey the script. They junked the rule that questions should be equally divided on foreign policy and domestic issues. They asked questions that lasted more than 45 seconds, a no-no in the campaign-debate rule book.

And worst of all, for the candidate handlers, this group dared to ask follow-up questions.

As Hume said in the first round: "I'm sort of the clean-up man in this order, and I've been asked by my colleagues to try to deal with anything that's been left on base."

There are reports that Bush's people began scrambling for their Rolaids when they heard Hume's comment. They, like Bentsen's boys, had been practicing two-minute responses per question, nothing more. Note here that we are talking about responses to questions, not answers to questions. There's a big difference.

More importantly, the two campaigns had devised a cagey format based on the often valid idea that the average journalist is driven by an oversized ego and a short attention span. For reporters, these debates offer a chance to move up the career ladder or to disappear to the real-estate desk, and nobody who's been picked for one of these things wants to blow it.

Here's how it worked: The debate rules said a panelist who did not receive an answer couldn't have a second chance, at least not until the panelist's next turn to ask a question. By then, the issue would have been forgotten, the party men figured.

Thus, another journalist would have to follow up for a colleague. Guessing within the campaigns was that no journalist wanted to mop up after another. It doesn't look good in the home office. It looks as though the poor hack can't think of any new questions.

But this panel recognized that, without follow-up questions, there would be no chance of getting answers that came from the gut, not from the floppy discs working on overdrive between the candidates' ears.

"It was such a restrictive format, the four of us agreed ahead of time that, in order to do a responsible job as journalists, we had to follow up after one another," said Woodruff, who appears on "The MacNeil/Lehrer NewsHour" and "Frontline" and was panel moderator. "This was the one occasion when you have to put competition aside for a moment and work together."

The most dominant question from the panel was the "Q-3," as some journalists are calling it—the Question of Quayle's Qualifications. Six times, he was asked about whether he was competent to take on the presidency. Six questions, of the 24 asked over 90 minutes, made this issue the focus of the debate, just as it has been the prime question in the polls.

But Bentsen also got his follow-uppance. Twice he was asked about the fact that he has more political-action committee money than any other senator and even invited lobbyists to $10,000-a-plate breakfasts. Three times he was asked about differences with his running mate, Michael Dukakis.

By repeating unanswered questions, the panelists found Bentsen elaborating on, and Quayle repeating, tutored responses. What they were looking for was something, as Hume put it, "that told us about these two fellows as human beings."

After post-debate polls showed voters leaning toward Bentsen, Quayle's handlers quickly retreated behind the most convenient and predictable complaint. As Quayle adviser Stuart Spencer said after polls showed that Quayle lost ground for the Republicans: "The media was unfair."

Wrong. This debate's four panel members deserve nothing but praise. Their persistent questioning, which means that none will be invited to an orchestrated debate again, also means that they acted in the best tradition of their trade.

They were asked to be part of the charade, but they turned it into a real, live political forum.

"Semantic Differences and the Press"

Eleanor Randolph, February 1990

Outlanders, people who watch the national news and the sitcoms, think this town is famous for sex, lies and videotape. Natives know we really specialize only in lies.

We don't usually call them lies. They are called "obfuscations." Or "misstatements." Or, here's a favorite: "semantic differences." But the truth is that they are lies, and we all know it.

For example, a group of reporters met with President Bush recently and asked him what has become a routine question: Were any of his aides on secret missions?

The question has been routine since the secret mission to China last July 4 by two key aides, Brent Scowcroft and Lawrence S. Eagleburger. At the time, the White House was decrying the recent violence in China and saying all "exchanges" between the United States and China had been summarily banned.

Six months later, Cable News Network found out that Bush's aides had been secretly exchanging views with the Chinese in China. The hue and cry was enormous, and the White House explainers came out to explain. Those were not "exchanges" last July, they said. Those were "visits." That's different, they explained to the media and the American people.

When the reporters asked Bush recently about other secret meetings, Bush said there were none. As he spoke, two top aides were flying back to Washington after meeting secretly with the European allies about troop cutbacks that Bush planned to propose the next night.

Reporters at the White House have treated this matter with unusual delicacy. Brit Hume, White House correspondent for ABC News, sent Bush a gentle, chiding note about the difference between what Bush said and what he knew. Bush sent a gentle, chiding note back to Hume about the whole matter. Both notes are considered private, so we don't know what was in them. We do know what was not in them: Nobody mentioned that the President had told the press a lie. That would be impolite.

A White House aide later tried to explain the "discrepancy." The visits to Europe were not secret missions but a "routine consultation with allies."

Of course. That's something else altogether.

For the record, even the tough, old White House press corps understands that presidents must have their secrets. Diplomacy, wars, intelligence, national security (genuine national security)—those things start in private and sometimes stay there.

For the record also, these White House veterans also will try to discover every little detail about every single thing that happens in the White House.

This "we-they" conflict, however, is not a tennis game. It is serious business. In a democracy, our leader needs to communicate his goals and persuade the public that he is right to pursue them.

When Bush keeps a meeting between his aides and the Chinese secret, a large question looms: From whom? In the case of the China visit, he is keeping it from the American people. The Chinese government already knows about it.

At a news conference in January, Bush was asked this question: "On the trust factor, I wonder if I can apply that to the American people, sir. What can you say to convince the people that the missions to China weren't secret simply to avoid the overwhelming public opposition to them?"

Bush answered, "I say, 'I think what I'm doing is correct,' and I say 'I think I was elected to do in foreign policy what I think was correct.'" He added that Congress provided any checks and balances that were necessary.

An East Coast patrician whose family has its headquarters in Maine, Bush is saying that he believes he knows best. Congress knows second best; and the guy on the street, well, he can learn later—like when Bush and his staff publish their memoirs.

This is the way George Bush operates. He likes secrets, a quirk that may be left over from his days as head of the Central Intelligence Agency.

But there are ways and then there are ways to face the nation and its press corps. When the media ask about things that Bush wants to keep to himself, he can refuse to answer. He could suggest, any time he's asked, that he doesn't talk about diplomacy until the knots are tied. Or, being George Bush, he could probably joke that there are lots of things going on that he isn't talking about—yet.

There are ways to keep things secret. Lying should not be one of them.

Clustering for the Summit

Eleanor Randolph, June 1990

Reporters, like seagulls, fly to the spot where somebody is handing out even dry crusts of news. So, when a cluster began forming recently in one corner of the news center set up here for the summit, it kept growing larger and larger as everyone hurried to get a crumb of the action.

Elbowing my way through notebooks and tape recorders to the source of all this excitement, I found a strange subject. It was a television set, tuned to Cable News Network and broadcasting the Soviet leader live from his embassy.

More often than not these days, covering a mega-media event means working feverishly to stay in front of the tube. The chance for most of the 6,800 credentialed journalists to see one of the participants in happenings such as the summit between President Bush and Soviet leader Mikhail Gorbachev is worse than their chance to win $1 million in a magazine sweepstakes.

The chance to watch somebody who actually watched the real participants is better. Occasionally, press spokesmen who were there come to the press center at George Washington University about six long blocks from the White House and even farther from the Soviet Embassy. But most of these events are televised.

A few reporters are chosen to "pool," or appear with a small group of reporters whose job is to represent everybody. But even those pool reporters would do better to see their targets electronically rather than in the flesh. For example, the group that accompanied Gorbachev to the embassy where he gave a speech to intellectuals, cultural leaders and movie stars was kept on a bus for two hours, then told at the embassy that there would be "no writers, no writers at all."

"We were allowed to look into the room from the doorway for about a minute," pool reporter Jerry Seib of the Wall Street Journal reported to his peers. Meanwhile, CNN broadcast most of the event live.

Peter Jenkins, a British journalist with a sharp eye for the absurd, observed his fellow news-hands feverishly taking notes from the television set and shook his head sadly.

"It never pays to get too far from the office, to try to go to the site of the event," Jenkins said. "It simply puts you out of position." Too far from the telly, he meant.

CNN or C-Span seldom receive recognition for providing this service. Neither do the Associated Press, Reuters and United Press International, whose skeletal news reports often give the key about what is really "news" to anybody troubled with doubt about what has happened here.

The White House provides texts of speeches. A briefing service provides word-for-word transcripts of important briefings, so that unless pressed for time, one can listen to the briefing and not even take notes. The best notes will be forthcoming.

That front-row seat that every reporter seems to have at these events? Little credit goes to the "pool" reporters, who dutifully write details of everything they saw, details printed up by government aides and passed out to everybody else. It is considered very bad form to be on a pool and then withhold even an adjective for oneself.

As a result, in many cases, R-2,D-2 could write a story on one of these big international mega-events. It isn't reporting; it's digesting. It takes stamina (a reporter has to wait hours for briefings and pool reports), but not much intellectual energy. Why some poor Southwestern radio station has to send a reporter to Washington to be on the scene is a mystery. Like virtually everyone else, he or she never gets anywhere near the scene. The most that reporter can expect is to be able to loiter under the same weather system as the summit principals and say with absolute assurance that the superpowerful were blessed with a few beautiful days.

Newsday columnist Murray Kempton decided that even sharing the sunshine wasn't absolutely necessary. "I can get that on the weather channel," said a frustrated Kempton, who said that this was his second summit without seeing a participant in the flesh.

It's vastly easier if you work for a network or The New York Times or The Washington Post. Calls go through quickly. A Harvard University expert or a mid-level bureaucrat with expertise in this area is on the phone in a few minutes. Moreover, most of these big organizations have at least a dozen people with credentials and can afford to have somebody else, even a telephone operator, sitting in the press center collecting "news."

Rare is the reporter from Utah or Texas who can find somebody with expert knowledge and a spare minute. If he or she gets a scoop, or even an elaboration of the briefing, it's time for a raise.

To cover this summit, a reporter is asked for his or her birth date, Social Security number and press credential. But the most important question may be: Is a working television set available?

Fox News, Live But Not Yet Lively

Tom Shales, June 1990

At WTTG, they don't just give you the news; they Fox it to you.

"The Fox Morning News," a 2 1/2-hour newscast airing at 6:30 a.m. daily and designed to compete with "Today" and the other early network shows, premiered yesterday. As a shakedown cruise, it wasn't all that shaky, but as an alternative to the established programs, it seemed largely an exercise in low overhead.

Certainly it's a welcome step forward when the station, owned by Fox and one of the most profitable in the nation, replaces "Woody Woodpecker" and other syndicated cartoons with a live, local news program. One must admire the effort and risk-taking that produced the show, even if the show itself, at this early moment in its life, falls clunkingly short of excellence.

Tim White, formerly of "CBS News Nightwatch," and Lark McCarthy, formerly of ABC News, make personable and efficient anchors, though McCarthy seemed stiff on opening day, and not always certain in which direction she should look. She did alertly correct White when he called Defense Secretary Dick Cheney "defense attorney Dick Cheney."

What "Fox Morning News" offers that the other stations don't is that the program is locally produced and local in outlook, and that it's a relatively no-nonsense, nuts-and-bolts news show. There's little gingerbread and folderol, and no interviews with actors or actresses explaining what drew them to this or that role in a major motion picture—and never admitting that what drew them was a ton of money.

Considering that Fox is the home of the nightly sleazefest "A Current Affair," it's almost a pleasure to report that the morning news show tends more toward dullness than tabloidism. Ungenerous wags might even be referring to it as "The Fox Boring News."

You do get a lot of Real News from the show, but on opening day, it was often without Real Pictures. "Fox Morning News" isn't all-news television so much as it is all-news radio. Local bank threatening to tear down row of historic town houses? No picture. Bride invites dozens of homeless people to attend her wedding? No picture.

Producers of the network morning programs have said that those shows are designed as much for the ear as the eye, since in the busy morning hours, viewers don't sit riveted to the screen. But "Morning

News" executive producer Steven Borden seems to have taken that idea too far. The program is a parade of talking heads whose visual monotony gets to be wearing.

There were plenty of live remotes on the premiere, but these mainly qualified as backdrop news: Pat McGrath popped up seven times, no less, to announce from the White House lawn that Nelson Mandela would be arriving there several hours hence. Briar Wilson materialized five or six times from Capitol Hill to say it wasn't going to be a very busy day up there.

It's symptomatic of the prevailing impulse in TV news to go live to the corner of Main and Elm even when there's nothing happening at the corner of Main and Elm except that a correspondent is standing there blabbing.

More valuable were the live interviews spaced throughout the program, the best of them a chat with Washington First Lady Effi Barry about the Mandela visit. McCarthy said Mrs. Barry had agreed to talk about that subject only, not about her husband's trial on drug and perjury charges, but McCarthy skillfully worked related questions into the segment in a way that didn't seem rude or unfair.

The only real problem with this segment was the inordinate amount of background noise on the handsome newsroom set. It sounded as if somebody were erecting a circus tent behind the weather map.

One of McCarthy's questions to Effi Barry ended with her asking, as many Washingtonians have doubtlessly asked about the mayor's wife, "Why do you stay with him?" Barry didn't answer that precisely but did say, "Getting through the trial is just something else to do." Both Barry and McCarthy came out of the sequence looking good.

If this interview was the best on the "Morning News," the worst was done by co-anchor White, a painfully misbegotten segment in which he interviewed three District citizens who did not make the Barry jury. They "almost became a key part of the Barry jury," White said in breathless anticipation, but in the news biz, "almost" really counts for nothing.

Also embarrassing was the show's gushy-mushy closing sequence, in which Angela Robinson read excerpts from Nelson Mandela's love letters over photos of Nelson and Winnie.

"Morning News" is in a constant process of recyclement. Few things are seen or said just once. We're told that we'll never be far from a weather or traffic report; that means those reports are duplicated over and over again.

Traffic reporter Cheryl Doyle stands in front of a rather intestinal-looking animated map in which all the little car-dots are in motion—hardly ever the case during Washington rush hours. Once, Doyle felt compelled to leap out of the shot when the voice of the "airborne" traffic reporter came on, leaving the screen all to the map. Her numerous reports could all be boiled down to two words: "Expect delays."

Dave Bender, the suspender-sporting weatherman, is from the Frisky Puppy school of telecommunication. He was beside himself with glee over what a "great day" lay ahead; it'll be fun to see how he handles the miserably sultry summer scorchers just around the corner.

At 7:05, Bender reported that an ominous high-pressure center was hovering over the East Coast but, he assured viewers, it was "not going to squish down and heat us up." At 7:22 he reconfirmed the sighting of the dread high-pressure system but said it was "not a really nasty high-pressure system that's going to squish down and heat us up."

Bender further clarified this tricky, squishy high-pressure matter during the 8 o'clock hour when he again reassured viewers it was "not a real nasty high-pressure system where it's going to squish the air down and heat us up."

Hey, somebody squish this guy's air down before he heats everybody up!

The format requires the two anchors to be on camera more than is fair to them. No wonder there were little goofs, as when White reported on a Washingtonian magazine poll about which congressman was "the hardest working—no, the hardest to work for! Big difference!"

Or when McCarthy, during the 8:13 edition of the headlines, announced, "Efforts in Iran this morning continue, including the first American private relief mission to that country in 10 years." Alas, the word "earthquake" was missing.

It is a Herculean effort, however, to produce such a long broadcast every day. The only packaged material on the first show was a tacky "Fox Entertainment News" report out of Fox's Los Angeles station; the lead item just happened to publicize "Die Hard 2," the big Fox movie release of the summer.

Otherwise, everything else, for better and for worse, was home-grown.

"We're pleased with the first outing," said producer Borden, 33, after yesterday's show. "I think we've embarked on the course we're trying to set. We're showing what we can do when we marshal our resources."

Additional marshaling is in order, and it wouldn't hurt to expand resources so as to allow a few more pictures to sneak onto this alleged television program. The staff and talent have the whole summer to get the show in shape, and with that in mind, they have made a decent beginning.

"We apologize to kids who expected cartoons," White said at the end. "Yes, but give us a chance, give us a chance," McCarthy added. Consider the chance given.

Safeguarding Our Freedoms As We Cover Terrorist Acts

Katharine Graham, April 1986

Picture a warm and sunny day, not in Athens or Cairo, but in Washington. The Israeli prime minister is in town and is scheduled to meet the President.

At 11 a.m., the leader of an obscure Muslim sect and several accomplices armed with guns and machetes storm the headquarters of B'nai B'rith. Three other members of the group seize the city's Islamic Center and two more fanatics invade City Hall, killing a radio reporter in the process. Altogether, the terrorists take 134 hostages in three buildings by gunpoint, force them to the floor and threaten to kill them unless their demands are met.

The news media, as one might expect, descend on the scene en masse. Live television pictures carrying the group's warnings and demands soon go forth over the airwaves. One hundred and thirty-four lives hang in the balance, as reporters compete to get exclusive interviews with the terrorists.

This crisis actually happened, on March 9, 1977, when the Hanafi Muslims staged a terrorist attack on the very day Prime Minister Yitzhak Rabin was meeting with President Jimmy Carter. Happily, it ended with the surrender of the terrorists and no further loss of life.

The Hanafi incident illustrated a troubling fact about modern terrorism: It requires an audience. The terrorist has to communicate his own ruthlessness—his "stop-at-nothing" mentality—in order to achieve his goals. Media coverage is essential to his purpose. If terrorism is a form of warfare, as many observers now believe, it is a form in which media exposure is a powerful weapon.

As terrorism increases, we in the news media are being encouraged to restrict our coverage of terrorist actions. British Prime Minister Margaret Thatcher, for example, has proclaimed: "We must try to find ways to starve the terrorist and the hijacker of the oxygen of publicity on which they depend." Many people, including some reporters in the United States, share her view. Most of these observers call for voluntary restraint by the media in covering terrorist actions. But some go so far as to sanction government control—censorship, in fact—should the media fail to respond.

I disagree. I am against any government-imposed restrictions on the free flow of information about terrorist acts. Instead, I am in favor of as full and complete coverage of terrorism by the media as is possible. Here are my reasons:

• Terrorist acts are impossible to ignore. They are simply too big a story to pass unobserved. If the media did not report them, rumor would abound. And rumors can do much to enflame and worsen a crisis.

• There is no compelling evidence that terrorist attacks would cease if the media stopped covering them. On the contrary, terrorism specialists I have consulted believe the terrorists would only *increase* the number, scope and intensity of their attacks if we tried to ignore them.

• Our citizens have a right to know what the government is doing to resolve crises and curb terrorist attacks. Some of the proposed solutions raise disturbing questions about how and when the United States should use military force.

In covering terrorism, however, we must also recognize that we face very real and exceedingly complex challenges. There are limits to what the media can and should do. Three critical issues, in particular, must be addressed. All touch the central question of how the press can minimize its role as a participant in the crisis and maximize its role as a provider of information.

Responsible behavior. The first issue involves knowing how to gather and reveal information without making things worse, without endangering the lives of hostages or jeopardizing national security. One television news executive bluntly explained to me: "Errors that threaten loss of life are permanent; others are temporary. If we have to make mistakes, we want to make the temporary kind."

In the early days of covering urban violence and the first terrorist attacks, the media would descend on the scene—lights ablaze and cameras rolling—in hot pursuit of the news. Sometimes we didn't know what could put lives at risk. And we were often less than cooperative with the police attempting to resolve the crisis.

During the Hanafi Muslim attack that I described earlier there were live television reports that the police were storming a building when, in fact, they were merely bringing in food. Some reporters called in on public phone lines to interview the terrorists inside the building. One interview rekindled the rage of the terrorist leader, who had been on the point of surrender.

These potential disasters led to discussions between the police and the media, and to a more professional approach and mutual trust on both sides. For example, most authorities now know that at the beginning of a crisis, it is best to establish a central point where reliable information can be disseminated quickly and efficiently. And the media, knowing that the authorities intend to help them obtain the information they need, are much more willing to cooperate.

I want to emphasize that the media are willing to—and do—withhold information that is likely to endanger human life or jeopardize national security. During the American embassy crisis in Iran, for example, one of our Newsweek reporters became aware that six Americans known to have been in the embassy were not being held by the Iranians. He concluded that these men must have escaped to the Swedish or Canadian embassies. This in fact had occurred. However, we (and some others who also knew) did not report the information because we knew it would put lives in jeopardy. Similarly, when a group of Lebanese Shiites hijacked TWA Flight 847 with 153 hostages aboard last year, the media learned—but did not report—that one hostage was a member of the U.S. National Security Agency.

Tragically, however, we in the media have made mistakes. You may recall that in April 1983, some 60 people were killed in a bomb attack on the U.S. embassy in Beirut. At the time, there was coded radio traffic between Syria, where the operation was being run, and Iran, which was supporting it. Alas, one television network and a newspaper columnist reported that the U.S. government had intercepted the traffic. Shortly thereafter the traffic ceased. This undermined efforts to capture the terrorist leaders and eliminated a source of information about future attacks. Five months later, apparently the same terrorists struck again at the Marine barracks in Beirut; 241 servicemen were killed.

This kind of result, albeit unintentional, points up the necessity for full cooperation wherever possible between the media and the authorities. When the media obtains especially sensitive information, we are willing to tell the authorities what we have learned and what we plan to report. And while reserving the right to make the final decision ourselves, we are anxious to listen to arguments about why information should not be aired.

The danger of manipulation. A second challenge facing the media is how to prevent terrorists from using the media as a platform for their views.

I think we have to admit that terrorist groups receive more attention and make their positions better known because of their acts. Few people had even heard of groups like the Hanafi Muslims or Basque Separatists before they carried out terrorist attacks.

The media must make every attempt, however, to minimize the propaganda value of terrorist incidents and put the action of terrorists into perspective. We have an obligation to inform our readers and viewers of their backgrounds, their demands and what they hope to accomplish. But we must not forget that terrorists are criminals. We must make sure we do not glorify them, or give unwarranted exposure to their point of view.

We often think of terrorists as unsophisticated. But many are media savvy. They can and do arrange their activities to maximize media exposure and ensure that the story is presented their way. As one terrorist is supposed to have said to his compatriot: "Don't shoot now. We're not in prime time."

Terrorists have taken the following steps to influence media coverage: arrange for press pools; grant exclusive interviews during which favored reporters are given carefully selected information; hold press conferences in which hostages and others are made available to the press under conditions imposed by the captors, provide videotapes that portray events as the terrorists wish them to be portrayed, and schedule the release of news and other events so that television deadlines can be met.

There is a real danger, in short, that terrorists hijack not only airplanes and hostages, but the media as well.

To guard against this, the television networks in our country rarely—almost never—allow terrorists to appear live. They also resist using videotape provided by terrorists. If there is no alternative, our commentators continually report that the material is "terrorist-supplied" so that viewers can evaluate its veracity and meaning. Likewise, when terrorists make hostages available for interviews, our commentators repeatedly indicate—or they should—that the captives are speaking under duress.

When one network reporter interviewed the hostages in the recent TWA hijacking by telephone, he said: "Walk away from the phone if you're under duress, or if you don't want to talk." One of them did walk away. Even when there is no evident coercion, the networks repeat that terrorists are standing by, although they are not visible on the screen. We also try to identify carefully and repeatedly the backgrounds and biases of the people we interview, including the hostages themselves.

Forbidding terrorists their platform goes beyond using specific techniques. It is more an issue of exercising sound editorial judgment.

Over the years, the media constantly have been confronted with attempts at manipulation. In the days of the Vietnam war, for example, we would get calls from protest groups saying, "We're going to pour chicken blood all over the entrance to Dow Chemical Company. Come cover this event." We didn't. But we did cover a Buddhist monk who wished to be filmed setting fire to himself.

How did we make the distinction? Here it was a question of trivial versus serious intent and result, of low versus high stakes. Clearly, the suicide was of cataclysmic importance to the monk.

The point is that we generally know when we are being manipulated, and we've learned better how and where to draw the line, though the decisions are often difficult.

A few years ago, for example, a Croatian terrorist group in a plane demanded that its statement be printed in several newspapers, including The Washington Post, before it would release 50 hostages. In the end, we printed the statement in agate, the smallest type size we have, in 37 copies of the paper at the end of our press run. Now I'm not so sure we would accede to this demand in any form.

The heat of coverage. That brings me to a third issue challenging the media: How can we avoid bringing undue pressure on the government to settle terrorist crises by whatever means, including acceding to the terrorist's demands?

State Department officials tell me that media coverage does indeed bring pressure on the government. But not *undue* pressure. However, I believe there are pitfalls of which the media should be exceedingly careful.

One is the amount of coverage devoted to a terrorist incident. During a crisis, we all want to know what is happening. But constant coverage can blow a terrorist incident far out of proportion to its real importance. Overexposure can preoccupy the public and the government to the exclusion of other issues.

During the TWA crisis, our networks constantly interrupted regularly scheduled programming with news flashes of dubious importance. And one network devoted its entire 22-minute evening newscast to the crisis. Many important topics were ignored.

The media have become aware of these dangers. The network coverage of the Achille Lauro incident was much more restrained. Some say it was only because it was difficult to cover and the crisis ended quickly. But the networks got better notices from the critics and the public.

Interviewing the families of hostages is another pitfall. There is a natural curiosity about how those near and dear to the captured are reacting to the life-or-death event. And the hostage families themselves often are anxious to receive media attention and present their views to the public.

But there is a fine line between legitimate inquiry and exploitation of human sentiment. The media can go too far. Tasteless invasion of privacy can result. The ultimate horror is the camera that awaits in ambush to record the family's reaction to the news of some personal tragedy.

There is also a real danger that public opinion can be unjustifiably influenced by exposure to the hostage relatives and their wives. The nationwide television audience becomes, in a sense, an extended family. We get to know these people intimately. Our natural sympathies go out to them. We often come to share their understandable desire to have their loved ones back at any cost.

This can force a government's hand. Last May, Israel released more than 1,000 Arab prisoners in exchange for three Israelis being held in Lebanon. It was an action that ran counter to Israeli policy. But the appearances of the families of the Israeli prisoners on television apparently made the Israeli government think it was a necessity.

I believe the media must be exceedingly careful with the questions they ask the relatives and, of course, the hostages themselves. When we ask if they agree with the government's policy or its handling of the incident, what they would do if they were in charge, or if they have messages for the president, we are setting up a predictable tension: Hostages and their families are, understandably, the most biased of witnesses. The media must exercise the same standards with them as they would with any other news source.

A final pitfall for the media is becoming, even inadvertently, a negotiator during a crisis. But it's tough to avoid. Simply by asking legitimate questions—such as "What are your demands?"—the media can become part of the negotiating process. Questions that ask "What would you do if . . ." are particularly dangerous. The question put to Nabih Berri, the Amal Shiite leader, during the TWA crisis by the host of one of our morning news shows was completely out of line and is so acknowledged. He asked: "Do you have a message for the president?"

As much as we abhor terrorism, the media cannot be diplomats, negotiators or agents for the government. If terrorists or urban rioters believe we are—if they believe, for example, that we will turn over our unused tapes, or pictures, or notes to the police—they will not give us information. They may even attack us.

Technology intensifies our problems. Before the advent of satellites, there was usually a 24-hour delay between the moment news was gathered overseas and the moment it was broadcast. Indeed, what appeared on the nightly news often had been in the morning paper.

This meant that television news executives had at least some amount of time in which to reflect, discuss and decide on whether a story should be broadcast and how it should be presented.

Today our networks have the technological capability to present events live—any time, any place. As a result, the decisions about what to cover and how to cover are tougher. And they must be made faster, sometimes on the spot. The risks of making a mistake rise accordingly.

Intense competition in the news business raises the stakes even more. The electronic media in the United States live or die by their ratings, the number of viewers they attract. As a result, each network wants to be the first with the most on any big story. It's hard to stay cool in the face of this pressure.

This has created some unseemly spectacles and poor news decisions. During the TWA crisis, for example, the U.S. networks ran promotion campaigns on the air and in print touting the scoops and exclusives that each had obtained. This commercialized aid trivialized a dangerous and important event.

The most dangerous potential result of unbridled competition is what we have come to call the lowest-common-denominator factor. I believe that all of the serious, professional media—print and electronic—are anxious to be as responsible as possible. We want to do nothing that would endanger human life or national security. But, unfortunately, high standards of professionalism do not guide every media organization and reporter. And I regret to say that once one of these less scrupulous or less careful people reports some piece of information, all the media feel compelled to follow. Thus it is true: The least responsible person involved in the process could determine the level of coverage.

These problems of covering terrorism are serious. But in spite of them, I believe the benefits of full disclosure far outweigh any possible adverse consequences. I believe the harm of restricting coverage far surpasses the evils of broadcasting even erroneous or damaging information.

American democracy rests on the belief, which the centuries have proven true, that people can and do make intelligent decisions about great issues if they have the facts.

But to hear some politicians talk, you wouldn't think they believed it. They appear to be afraid that people will believe the terrorist's message and agree, not only to his demands, but to his beliefs. And so they seek to muzzle the media or enlist their support in the government's cause.

I think this is a fatal mistake. It is a slippery slope when the media start to act on behalf of any interest, no matter how worthy—when editors decide what to print on the basis of what they believe is good for people to know. It's dangerous if we are asked to become a kind of super-political agency.

I believe that terrorism is ultimately a self-defeating platform from which to present a case. Terrorists, in effect, hang themselves whenever they act. They convey hatred, violence, terror itself. There was no clearer image of what a terrorist really is than the unforgettable picture of that crazed man holding a gun to the head of the pilot aboard the TWA jet. That said it all to me—and, I believe, to the world.

Publicity may be the oxygen of terrorists. But I say this: News is the lifeblood of liberty. If the terrorists succeed in depriving us of freedom, their victory will be far greater than they ever hoped and far worse than we ever feared. Let it never come to pass.

CHAPTER EIGHT

The Image Makers—
Public Relations Today

The Image Makers

Peter Carlson, February 1990

Part 1: Clint Eastwood as Federal Bureaucrat

Robert Weed is rolling.

He has shifted into oratorical high gear and now he's roaring toward the stirring emotional conclusion of his speech. He stands behind the podium in the unofficial uniform of the Serious Washington Insider—a blue pin-stripe suit and red power tie—while his shoulders bob to the rhythm of his words and his left fist pumps with passion. He has come to launch a crusade to liberate a despised minority group from the yoke of ancient prejudice. It is a minority group mocked by comedians, attacked by demagogic politicians, scorned by its fellow Americans. A hard-working, generous, 3-million-member minority group unfairly maligned as lazy and greedy.

Weed is talking about federal bureaucrats.

He doesn't call them that, though. He prefers the term "public servants." He says his crusade is designed to change "the public image of public servants." It is a crusade that Weed, who is the director of public affairs at the Office of Personnel Management, has been assigned by no less a public servant than the president of the United States. "This is a presidential initiative," Weed tells the crowd. "The first

210

milestone assigned to OPM by the White House is to strengthen the image of public service."

And on this nasty December morning, Weed has braved a blizzard to travel to Rosslyn to tell the annual convention of the National Association of Government Communicators how he plans to give Americans warm, fuzzy feelings about federal employees.

First he unveils the brand new logo of his "Public Service Celebration Team." It's red, white and blue, of course, and it carries the official slogan of the campaign: "Serving America Today for a Better Tomorrow." Then he reveals his plans for an elaborate public relations campaign that will kick off on March 1 with receptions in six cities and then usher in a "year-round cycle of events," including "Public Service Recognition Week," which is the first week of May.

Meanwhile, Weed says, he hopes to persuade the Ad Council— the public service advertising group that gave us Smokey the Bear and McGruff the Crime Dog—to come up with an ad campaign that will "reinforce the image of public service." Weed hopes the ads will star Clint Eastwood. After all, Eastwood did an ad urging Americans not to litter on federal land, which practically makes him a federal bureaucrat himself.

Meanwhile, Weed outlines his "Federal Heroes" program, which is designed to publicize federal employees who have done amazing things, like the air traffic controller who helped save a crippled plane in Iowa and the Social Security Administration worker who delivers checks to the homeless in Boston. Weed plans to pick up the phone and pitch stories on his federal heroes to the producers of TV talk shows and the editors of magazines like People and Parade—"just like any PR guy for anybody would do."

But Bob Weed can't do all this himself. Persuading Americans to love federal employees is too tough a task for Weed and his staff of 18 and his budget, which is only a measly million bucks a year. That's why, he told the crowd, he'd come to this convention of Government Communicators, a group composed entirely of people doing public relations work for government agencies. He desperately needs their help, he says, and he beseeches them to fill out an official Public Service Celebration Team volunteer card. He promises to reward them if they do.

"Let me tell you what you'll get," he says. "First of all, you'll get our OPM newsletter, Image Update, that talks about this campaign. And secondly, you'll get another newsletter that doesn't yet have a name that will be good ideas from different parts of the image campaign. Third, you'll get advance information on specific image-building activities in your area. And finally, you'll get a bumper sticker with our handsome logo and slogan . . ." Wait a minute. Hold it right there. Bumper stickers? Image Update? People magazine? Clint Eastwood?

A public relations campaign to polish the image of federal bureaucrats?

Sure. Why not?

Washington is a city full of government bureaucrats. It's also a city full of professional image-polishers. It was inevitable that they'd find each other.

Part 2: How Big is a Pound of Fog?

The National Solid Wastes Management Association has a PR team in Washington.

So does the Salt Institute. And the Sugar Association. And the Future Homemakers of America. And the Natural Resources Defense Council. And the House Education and Labor Committee. And the Federal Grain Inspection Service. And the Retired Officers Association. And the Selective Service System. And United Technologies. And the Air Force's Art and Museum Branch. And Saudi Arabia. And Angola. And Rhode Island. And the American Association of Motor Vehicle Administrators. And . . .

. . . And on and on it goes. In Washington, every government agency, trade association, trade union, congressman, foreign government, corporation, public service group, private interest group and ad hoc coalition to save the world—in short, everybody who's anybody in this town, or who wants to be—has a PR person or a PR department or a PR firm plotting out a PR campaign.

In fact, some Washington organizations were created by PR people and exist only as PR entities, as we shall see in this little tour through the world of Washington public relations, an ethereal realm where teddy bears lobby Congress, where dubious guerrillas become freedom fighters, where Army officers teach generals how to stand and how to sit.

"Public relations," says Ray Hiebert, professor of journalism at the University of Maryland and publisher of the Public Relations Review, "is the art and science of informing, influencing, neutralizing or changing public opinion." Edward Bernays, the oft-proclaimed "father of public relations," coined several other definitions. Some are sardonic: "to make large pedestals for small statues." And some are Orwellian: "the engineering of consent."

Any way you define it, public relations is a gargantuan industry in Washington. But nobody knows just how gargantuan. Part of the confusion stems from the fact that it's awful tough to specify exactly what constitutes public relations.

"It's a foggy business," says Jack O'Dwyer, the publisher of numerous PR industry trade publications. "How much does a pound of fog weigh?" he asks, sounding a bit like a Zen monk. "How big is a pound of fog?"

Another source of confusion is an absurd incongruity: The city's largest producer of public relations—the federal government—spends absolutely no money on public relations. Not one nickel. This is because the federal government is forbidden by law from spending money on public relations. Robert Weed's campaign, for instance, would be classified as "public information" or "public affairs" or "public-affairs-related activities." How much money do federal agencies spend on those activities? then-Sen. William Proxmire asked the General Accounting Office back in 1986. The GAO had the same problem as O'Dwyer: "Federal agencies do not uniformly define 'public affairs,'" it complained. Still, it managed to cough up some estimates: $337 million for "public affairs," $100 million for "congressional affairs"—defined as "day-to-day contact with the Congress"—and a whopping $1.9 billion for "public-affairs-related activities."

Which comes to more than $2.3 billion.

And that mammoth figure only includes federal agencies. It doesn't reflect the PR efforts of Congress, which are massive and eternal. Congressional offices are, as anyone who has ever worked in one can attest, giant machines for the greater glorification (and reelection) of the pol. The average congressional staff churns out a steady stream of constituent newsletters, computer-generated letters, daily press releases, weekly newspaper columns, one-minute radio spots called "beepers" and regular "video news releases" filmed in Congress's own TV studios and beamed by satellite to TV stations back in the home district. Which helps explain why the representatives' reelection rate approaches 99 percent.

And then there's the White House PR operation, which does everything the members of Congress do and a whole lot more.

"In the Washington area alone," says Eiebert, "there are at least 10,000 federal employees whose primary duty is what we'd call PR work."

The federal government's gigantic PR apparatus also serves an unofficial function: It's a farm team for Washington's gigantic private-sector PR industry.

PR prospects who prove their stuff in the federal government can generally find a warm place to park their Rolodexes when they head for the private sector. PR firms, like law firms, are the cushy nirvanas on the other side of Washington's legendary revolving door. So Jody Powell, who was Jimmy Carter's press secretary, goes to Ogilvy and Mather Public Affairs. And Elaine Crispen, who was Nancy Reagan's press secretary, goes to Hill and Knowlton. And Maj. Philip Soucy, who was among the Defense Department's 1,000 public affairs officers, becomes manager of military public affairs at British Aerospace. And Barbara Gleason, who was director of public affairs for the President's Commission on Industrial Competitiveness, becomes assistant director for public affairs at the Nonprescription Drug Manufacturers Association. And . . .

Watching the government's $2 billion PR industry intermarry with Washington's immeasurable (but huge) private-sector PR industry, a cynic might be tempted to conclude that virtually everything that happens in Official Washington is part of a PR campaign.

But that would be exaggerating. Slightly.

Part 3: What Do PR People Do, Daddy?

What does your daddy do? Rachel Swanston was asked one day when she was 5 or 6 years old. He's a public relations man, she replied. What does that mean? her friend asked.

He talks on the phone and gives parties, she answered. "And that's pretty accurate," says her father, David Swanston, president of Stackig/Swanston Public Relations.

Indeed it is. The little tyke came a lot closer to describing what PR people do than most PR people do.

If public relations is a "foggy business," as O'Dwyer put it, then it's at its foggiest in Washington, where PR people are generally pushing abstractions—ideas, opinions, images, influence. Which might account for the fogginess of the prose that Washington's PR people churn out when trying to describe what they do. The sentences in their promotional brochures sound like this: "The Canzeri Group focuses its efforts on developing and implementing programs that integrate its clients into the national decision-making process." Or like this: "The KSK PR Department is tightly niched into business to business communications for companies with high technology emphasis."

As the jargon flies, the fog deepens: "designs and carries out strategic communications plans" . . . "creates and manages image enhancement campaigns" . . . "issues management" . . . "issues tracking,"

... "communications audits" ... "strategic communications" ... "crisis communications" ... "audience research" ... "consumer image building" ... "comprehensive communications program design ... "

Burn through this fog of words and you find that what PR people do is this: They send out press releases and audio press releases and video press releases. They teach their clients how to appear on television without looking foolish and how to appear before congressional committees without looking foolish. They write speeches and brochures and congressional testimony. They ghostwrite editorials and op-ed pieces and then try to persuade newspaper editors to run them. They lobby Congress and they run grass-roots campaigns to persuade constituents to bombard Congress with letters. They stage press conferences and other media events. And they serve as the Washington equivalent of matchmakers, introducing their clients to the movers and shakers of government and the media: "That's really what we do," says Frank Mankiewicz of Hill and Knowlton. "We get clients time in the right forum to present their point of view."

And, yes, Rachel, they do spend a lot of time talking on the phone and giving parties.

They also do some secret stuff that they won't talk about.

Take, for example, the "nationwide grass-roots campaign to combat restrictive laws in 50 states" touted in the Susan Davis Companies's rather voluminous self-promotional brochure.

Susan Davis won't talk about that campaign. Davis—who is the chairman and CEO of the Susan Davis Companies, which includes Susan Davis Communications Group and Susan Davis International and Susan Davis Events Group and Susan Davis Advertising Group—will only say that it "could be tobacco-related." Why the secrecy? Especially about something as noble as a "campaign to combat restrictive laws?" "We really are behind-the-scenes players," she says, "and I'd like to keep it that way."

Very modest. Admirably self-effacing. Particularly coming from a woman who has named five companies after herself.

Part 4: Dueling Visuals on Capital Hill

Pamela Kostmayer is standing in the closet, looking for her jeans.

Kostmayer, a veteran Washington PR woman, uses the closet at Kostmayer Communications as a warehouse for the props—"visuals," she calls them—that she uses to attract the attention of politicians and TV cameras.

She pokes around a bit but can't find the jeans, which she'd silk-screened with statistics and used as a visual in her campaign against a bill limiting textile imports a few years back. But she does find a shirt, an Izod shirt that she used as a visual in a PR campaign for a bill to stop the counterfeiting of designer clothes. Still rummaging through the closet, she tells that story: She invited members of Congress to a lunch where her clients touted the bill, and then she invited the pols to take a souvenir shirt. "And on the day of the vote, we sent them a letter saying, 'If you got a white shirt, it was phony. If you got a colored shirt, it was real. You have the benefit of knowing what is counterfeit and what is not. The American consumer does not. Vote yes on HR-blah-blah-blah.'"

The bill passed too, she says. "And we'd get calls from the members' secretaries, saying, 'The shirt doesn't really fit.' And I'd say, 'It's not really meant to fit. It's supposed to be a visual.'"

Kostmayer is the queen of the Capitol Hill visual, which is a major PR art form in this era of photo-op politics. A former TV reporter and Senate staffer, she is also the wife of Rep. Peter Kostmayer (D-Pa.), who is himself a former PR man. But Pam Kostmayer learned the art of the visual at that ancient fountainhead of PR gambits—the circus. Promoting Ringling Bros. and Barnum & Bailey in the early '70s, she'd show up before the circus hit town, arrange a local contest and stick the lucky winner atop an elephant in the circus parade. Inevitably, the TV cameras loved it. "The best visual of all," she says, "is somebody on an elephant."

Back in Washington in the '80s, she quickly realized that the same rules apply in political PR. "National network news is what I'm aiming for," she says. "There are 22 minutes of news; the rest is commercials. Out of that, maybe five or six minutes comes out of Washington. And I've got to compete with everything else that's happening. So what can I give them that will almost guarantee that cameras will show up? A visual. Because that's what they need. Who wants to see another chart?" So Kostmayer gives her clients—and the cameras—visuals. For Mothers Against Drunk Driving, she parked a wrecked car against the backdrop of the Capitol dome. That "made air." For a group of undertakers, she put caskets and funeral urns in a Senate conference room. That made air too. But those were mere warm-ups for her epic textile bill campaign. For that, she had a college kid dressed as a teddy bear pulling a wagon through the halls of Congress, delivering little imported teddy bears with labels informing the pols how much more these cuddly critters would cost the parents of America's toddlers if the textile bill passed.

The "textile bear" got so much publicity that Kostmayer sent it back out every week to deliver other little goodies—like jeans that said, "The textile bill's got America by the seat of the pants" and socks saying, "Don't let the textile bill sock it to America."

Pretty soon, the groups supporting the textile bill responded with visuals of their own—"the world's largest jeans," which were four stories high; a 60-foot red-white-and-blue zipper labeled "Win one for the zipper"; and life-size cardboard photos of workers who would allegedly lose their jobs if the bill was defeated.

It was dueling visuals on Capitol Hill.

Which is not unusual. These days, Capitol Hill frequently plays host to the sort of goofy visuals and pseudo events that made the 1988 presidential campaign so, well, memorable. A congressman attaches a five-pound bag of sugar to his "dear colleague" letter about a sugar subsidy bill. The American Association of Retired Persons sends members of Congress baseballs with the slogan, "Don't throw consumers a curve." A band of representatives clusters around a casket to denounce a particular bill as "dead on arrival." Another band of representatives vandalizes Toshiba products to display its displeasure with the Toshiba Corp.'s selling of sensitive technology to the Soviets.

"This is what we feel about Toshiba," said Rep. Helen Bentley (R-Md.) before swinging her sledgehammer into a boom box as the TV cameras churned.

Sometimes, the search for the perfect visual goes a tad too far, as in the now-infamous incident when the Drug Enforcement Administration lured a crack dealer to Lafayette Park—where there had never been a crack arrest—so that George Bush could hold up a bag of dope for the TV cameras and say, "This is crack cocaine, seized a few days ago in a park across the street from the White House . . ."

In fact, these dueling visuals have gotten so out of hand that even Pamela Kostmayer's carefully planned, quasi-official pseudo events can be upstaged by goofy guerrilla pseudo events. Which is what happened last fall, when Kostmayer put on the official groundbreaking ceremony for the National Law Enforcement Officers' Memorial in Judiciary Square. "I had President Bush," she says. "I had gold shovels. I had crying widows. I had the president of the United States and the attorney general and the director of the FBI. I mean, it was a stellar lineup, it was a great visual. I had 28 television crews, I had 54 news organizations, and I didn't make network. What made network? A flag-burning on the steps of the Capitol with about six people."

That's the cruel law of life in Washington's PR jungle: You live by the visual and you die by the visual.

Part 5: When the Media Comes Banging on Your Door . . .

"We tell them how to sit," says Col. Gordon Bratz, "and we tell them how to stand."

Bratz has a bizarre job. He's a special assistant in the Secretary of the Army's Office of Public Affairs, which means that he's the guy who trains America's generals to face their most frightening enemy—the television camera. These are three- and four-star generals, towers of power, guys who fought the ChiComs in Korea and the VC in Nam, guys who can kill you with their bare hands. But when they see a TV camera, fear freezes them into man's most primal defensive pose.

"In that first stand-up interview, most of the generals are going to stand like this," Bratz says. Feigning terror, he stiffens up and cups his hands over his crotch.

His audience howls with laughter. Bratz is at the convention of the National Association of Government Communicators, leading a seminar titled "How to Put Together a Media Training Program for Your Agency."

"So we're going to tell them how to stand," he continues. "Put your feet about a foot apart with one ahead of the other. That typically prevents them from going like this"—Bratz rocks from side to side. "I tell them, if you do want to rock, rock forward because that engages the audience . . . In sitting, I'll tell them to sit in a straight chair and sit bent away from the camera, not into the camera with the knees, because that elongates the upper thigh."

"Say that again," a woman calls out. She's sitting in the back of the room, furiously scribbling notes.

Of course: This is important stuff. In an era of sound-bite politics, anybody who has power, or covets it, needs to know how to use television.

"How ready are you," Lew Brodsky, director of public affairs for the Selective Service System, asks the government communicators, "for the day when the media come banging on your door wanting an on-camera interview about a controversial situation?"

Pretty ready, they respond: About three-quarters of the assembled communicators reveal that they or their bosses have already hired PR people to teach them how to stand and how to sit and how to speak in sound bites and how to react when Mike Wallace barges in.

They are hardly alone. In 1986, when the Senate decided to televise its proceedings, the Republicans hired media whiz Roger Ailes to teach the senators how to look senatorial on the Senate floor.

Which is not surprising. These days, to paraphrase Chairman Mao, political power grows out of the tube of a television. In the Third World, revolutionaries don't attack the palace anymore, they seize the TV station. In Washington, things are slightly different: People don't seize TV stations, they simply build their own studios.

Official Washington is crammed with TV studios. The U.S. Chamber of Commerce has one. So does the U.S. Department of Commerce. And the House. And the Senate. And the RNC. And the DNC. And the National Education Association. And the AFL-CIO. And . . . And those institutions that don't have studios rent them. Why? So they can create the technological version of the old press release—the video press release. Some of these are full of video razzmatazz, but most are simply interviews. The Head Honcho is fed questions by his PR man and the result is beamed up via satellite to any TV station that might want it. The stations sometimes splice in questions asked by their own reporters so it looks as if they interviewed the Head Honcho themselves. Despite the fraudulence factor, these are known, believe it or not, as "actualities." Members of Congress love actualities because they enable the distinguished statesmen to appear on home district TV stations that can't afford a Washington bureau. But it isn't just members of Congress who use them. The U.S. Army Reserve Office's Individual Ready Reserve Campaign did a great video news release, which featured rumbling tanks and guys in camouflage and lots of shooting. The Nonprescription Drug Manufacturers Association did a less theatrical one. So did the Association of Flight Attendants and the Postal Service and . . .

In fact, these days, you're not a real Washington mover and shaker until you've beamed your image out to a waiting world via satellite.

But first you have to learn how to stand and how to sit and . . .

". . . Thirdly," Col. Bratz tells his seminar, you have to be interesting. I think this is very difficult for military people. They're very dull . . ." A woman in the audience raises her hand and says that at her agency, they give TV training to four or five honchos at a time and then let them criticize one another's performance.

"We don't 'do that," Bratz says, "because a lot of senior officers would just as soon have their training be private. They've told me that. A four-star general doesn't like to fall on his face in front of a one-star . . ."

Part 6: To Preserve and Protect the Widget

Gary Nordlinger is pretending to hold a phone up to his ear.

"Is this Mr. Smith?" he asks.

"Yes, it is," he answers. "I'm Gary Nordlinger from the Widget Manufacturers of America," he says. "We have a real problem going on. Congress is going to be voting tomorrow on HR-12, a bill which would ban the sale of widgets. We need to kill this right away. Mr. Smith, may we send a letter to your member of Congress and sign your name to it?"

And that, says Nordlinger, head of Nordlinger Associates, a Washington political PR firm, is the way you do "grass-roots PR."

"Grass roots" is the big buzzword in Washington PR these days. It's also the third stage in the evolution of lobbying. In the beginning there was the lobbyist. He got friendly with pols and tried to persuade them to vote the way his clients wanted. But now everybody has a lobbyist. "Your lobbyist cancels out my lobbyist," Nordlinger says. "So where else do you turn?"

To a PAC, perhaps. You augment your lobbyist with a political action committee that donates money to the polls campaign. "But as PACs rise and more and more people give money," says Jack Bonner, head of Bonner & Associates, another local grass-roots PR firm, "your $5,000 check to him isn't going to buy you a hell of a lot."

So what's a PR guy to do? "You create a situation," says Mankiewicz of Hill and Knowlton, "in which public opinion back home either is or appears to be on your side of the issue."

Which is a pretty good definition of grass-roots PR.

The prototype of the modern grass-roots effort was the American Bankers Association's 1982 fight against a bill to compel banks to withhold 10 percent of their customers' interest, just as employers withhold taxes on workers' earnings. ABA lobbyists fought the bill, which was backed by President Reagan, but failed to beat it. So the ABA tried a grass-roots effort, sending 15,000 "repeal kits" to member banks. The kits contained pre-packaged letters to members of Congress; pre-written op-ed pieces, which bankers were to re-type and submit to their local paper; and posters to display in their banks. Meanwhile, the banks inserted millions of protest postcards in their customers' monthly statements, along with the suggestion that they send them to Congress.

The result was a deluge of mail that succeeded in killing the bill.

Since then, grass roots has become much more sophisticated. Pre-printed postcards, for instance, are now considered passe: too obviously a mass mailing. The new thing is laser-printed letters complete with ersatz individual letterheads. "What you're able to do now," says Nordlinger, "is come up with 25 or 30 different messages, combine that against 10 different colors and sizes of paper and 10 different typefaces and"—he starts tapping the numbers into his pocket calculator—"and you're already up to 3,000 combinations there. It's not like getting a ton of postcards with nothing but a signature."

To find those voters most inclined to sign letters on a given issue, grass-roots PR people turn to direct mail experts who can produce lists of voters in virtually any demographic, geographic or special interest group. "They have the country broken down into little grids—everything from BMW owners who are yuppies to people who own Fords and go fishing on Sunday," says Bonner. "It's mass marketing. It's the same way that they sell Time magazine. Literally." Sometimes, of course, grass-roots PR people are less than completely upfront about who is behind their campaigns. When the Natural Gas Supply Association tried to mobilize public support for ending price controls on natural gas, the trade association didn't use its own name, it invented a group called the Alliance for Energy Security. When a collection of utility and coal companies battled a bill to control acid rain, they invented the Citizens for the Sensible Control of Acid Rain, which sent out a mailing of 800,000 letters.

Perhaps the most infamous dubious grass-roots campaign came in 1985, when the Environmental Protection Agency debated permitting the burning of toxic waste in special incinerator ships off Brownsville, Tex. Rollins Environmental Service, which operates land-based incinerators, thought that proposal might hurt its business, so it hired Robert Beckel, who was Walter Mondale's deputy campaign manager the previous year, to run a grass-roots campaign against it. Beckel created an ersatz environmental group called Alliance to Save the Ocean, which phoned Brownsville residents and urged them to fight the plan. The tactic raised some criticism, but Beckel defended his actions as standard operating procedure in Washington: "Why does Walter Mondale call his committee the Committee for the Future of America as opposed to the Walter Mondale Committee?"

Predictably, the result of all this grass-roots organizing is a huge increase in mail on Capitol Hill. In the early 170s, Congress received about 15 million letters a year. By last year, the total was more than 300 million. And the vast majority of those letters were inspired by PR campaigns. "Never, other than the mega-issues of our day, is mail truly spontaneous," says Bonner. "All the rest of the mail is prompted by somebody."

Does this avalanche of manufactured emotion bother the politicians who get buried under it? No way. It just gives them additional ammunition for their own postage-free direct mail PR campaigns.

"They love it," says Nordlinger. "When you send me your computer-generated letter, if I'm a member of Congress, I can send you my computer-generated letters. At that point, you're going to start getting two to three targeted letters a year on what Congressman X is doing to preserve and protect the widget." He grins. "Dear Mr. Smith: Bringing you up to date on what I've been doing about widgets . . ."

There's a term for this on Capitol Hill: Our computers answering their computers.

PART 7: A Nutritionist Named Meryl Streep

"We got rolled," says Frank Mankiewicz. "When you're dealing with a nutritionist named Meryl Streep, you haven't got a chance."

Mankiewicz is talking about how his company, Hill and Knowlton, the largest PR firm in Washington, got clobbered, got creamed, got its proverbial clock cleaned last year by a little environmental group in a big public PR battle over Alar and apples.

"It was a very good example of what the hell can go wrong," he says.

Alar is a chemical used to keep apples on trees longer, thus producing a brighter red color. In 1973, the chemical was first identified as a carcinogen, and in 1985 type EPA began taking slow steps toward banning it. Ralph Nader and the Natural Resources Defense Council, a Washington-based environmental group, lobbied for an immediate ban. But the issue never really caught fire—until the NRDC hired a PR man named David Fenton.

Fenton was hired to publicize an NRDC study called "Intolerable Risk: Pesticides in Our Children's Food." The report alleged that apples sprayed with Alar represented a dangerous cancer risk for children because of the huge amounts of apple products kids consume. Usually, reports like that live for a day in the media and then fade forever into the ether. Not this one. Fenton engineered a PR campaign that was the worst thing to happen to the apple since Eve.

First, he arranged to keep the report secret until the CBS show "60 Minutes" could "break" the story to 40 million viewers on February 26, 1989. Using the show as an ad, the NRDC released the report the next morning at 13 simultaneous news conferences around the country. The result was enormous publicity. But Fenton wasn't finished yet. A week later, just as the first media blitz was fading, he launched his second: Actress Meryl Streep held a Washington press conference to announce the formation of an NRDC spinoff group, Mothers and Others for

Pesticide Limits. Streep also testified before a congressional committee and did 16 satellite TV interviews with local news shows across the country. The Hollywood angle fueled another blizzard of publicity: the "Today" show, "Donahue," "Entertainment Tonight," People magazine, USA Today (the newspaper), USA Today (the TV show) and . . .

"Our goal was to create so many repetitions of NRDC's message that average American consumers (not just the policy elite in Washington) could not avoid hearing it," Fenton wrote in a memo about the campaign. "The idea was for the story to achieve a life of its own."

Which it did, much to the dismay of the apple industry and its PR firm, Hill and Knowlton. "I knew as soon as '60 Minutes' was over," says Josephine Cooper, a former EPA official who now heads up H&K's Environment and Energy group, "that we had a problem." Cooper and her cohorts snapped into action. They rounded up scientists and doctors who declared that apples were safe. Then they spread that information via countless press releases, video press releases and audio press releases. They took out full-page ads in newspapers around the country. They held luncheons to brief House and Senate staffers. They also lobbied the federal agencies responsible for food safety—the EPA, the Food and Drug Administration and the Department of Agriculture—begging them to defend the beleaguered apple. Finally, three weeks later, the agencies did, announcing jointly that apples were safe to eat and that Alar was not an "imminent hazard" to children. Immediately, Hill and Knowlton dispatched that statement via mailgrams to state and local officials around the country. They sent similar messages to thousands of grocers and pediatricians.

But none of it did much good. Apple sales plummeted, schools booted the fruit out of their cafeterias, and editorial cartoonists had a field day making apple jokes. Finally, Uniroyal, which manufactures Alar, withdrew it from the market. A few months later, the EPA announced a plan to phase it out entirely.

PR had killed Alar.

"NRDC and their hired PR counsel did a superb job of playing the news media like a Stradivarius," says Jack Borner. "The industry did not get their message across and they took punches and went down for the count."

Ironically, though, the Alar battle will probably make Hill and Knowlton—and other corporate PR firms—lots of money in the long run. "I think a lot of industries said, 'My God, there but for the grace of God goes us,'" says Cooper. When those industries find themselves in environmental fights of their own—which will happen more often in the '90s, many PR people predict—they'll turn to PR firms for help.

Which is why Hill and Knowlton is setting up environmental divisions in its offices around the country.

"It's very good for business," says Cc-oper, "and I think we're well-positioned to maximize the opportunities."

Part 8: A Guerrilla with a PR Firm

In Angola, government soldiers aided by Cuban troops were killing and being killed by guerrillas aided by South Africa. Meanwhile, in Washington, the battle was fought on a more lucrative—and more ludicrous—level: It was a PR War.

The war began on September 16, 1985, when Paul Manafort, head of Black, Manafort, Stone—the PR firm that gave America Lee Atwater—flew to Angola with Christopher Lehman. Three days earlier, Lehman had left his job as special assistant to the president for national security affairs to join Manafort's firm. Three days later, Lehman and Manafort persuaded Jonas Savimbi, head of Angola's UNITA guerrillas, to sign a $600,000-a-year contract with Black, Manafort.

A guerrilla with a PR firm?

Why not? Right-wing Guatemalan guerrillas have had PR reps here. So have left-wing Salvadoran guerrillas. And such dubious characters as Ferdinand Marcos, the shah of Iran, Manuel Noriega and the Sandinistas, among many others.

Savimbi wanted to get American weapons for his war against the leftist government of Angola. Unfortunately, he didn't have the greatest reputation. Trained in guerrilla warfare in Red China in the '60s, Savimbi had espoused a strident blend of Maoism and Black Power. After his rivals took over Angola in the '70s, however, Savimbi jettisoned Maoism and Black Power and found a new patron—the apartheid government of South Africa. Now, gunning for American arms, he needed to create a "freedom fighter" image. So he hired Black, Manafort, a firm with close connections to the Reagan White House.

And Black, Manafort engineered a brilliant PR campaign. It opened with an exclusive interview with "60 Minutes"—filmed in the Angolan bush and timed to air when Savimbi came to Washington on a private jet in January 1986. Meticulously coached in the fine arts of TV repartee and Hill lobbying, Savimbi spent the next 10 days doing interviews, meeting with pols—including President Reagan—and being cheered by conservatives at a banquet at the Capital Hilton. By the time he flew off—in a private jet loaned by an anonymous Texas millionaire—Savimbi had won assurances that his guerrillas would get American arms.

Obviously, the other side—the Angolan government—needed some reinforcements on the PR front. So it hired Gray and Co. for a reported $50,000 a month. The firm, which has since merged with Hill and Knowlton, was headed by Robert Keith Gray, a former Eisenhower administration official with close ties to the Reagans. Gray's media whizzes tutored Angolan foreign trade minister Ismael Gaspar-Martins in the art of TV repartee for his debate with Savimbi on the "MacNeil-Lehrer NewsHour," advising him to wear a nice conservative suit so he'd look more respectable than Savimbi, who favors funky Third World Nehru jackets.

But Gray's campaign reached its absurd apogee when Daniel Murphy—a retired admiral and George Bush's former chief of staff, who was handling the Angola account—touted the deep religious convictions of his Marxist clients. "I was very surprised to learn that everybody goes to church on Sunday," Murphy told the Wall Street Journal. "At least one-third of the Politburo members are practicing Presbyterians."

By then, the Young Conservative Foundation had gotten into the act. Irate that a fellow Republican like Gray would undercut the beloved Savimbi, the group launched a PR campaign. of its own. First, it picketed the Powerhouse, as Gray called his office, but that protest fizzled when the activists failed in their efforts to ignite a hammer-and-sickle flag. A few days later, however, they returned, storming the Powerhouse and handcuffing themselves to a banister. Four of them were arrested, which inspired the media coverage they we're seeking.

"They didn't want to talk," Mankiewicz, then a Gray vice president, complained to The Washington Post. "They wanted a media event."

A PR man complaining about a media event? It was the sound of defeat. A month later, after reams of bad publicity, Gray dropped the Angola account.

"It was too difficult," Mankiewicz recalls. "We were becoming the issue instead of Angola."

Ironically, Angola's PR efforts are now masterminded by David Fenton, the man who beat Mankiewicz in the Alar battle.

But Mankiewicz still has plenty of foreign clients. This fall, he traveled to Hungary to advise the Hungarian Communist Party—which recently changed its name to the Hungarian Socialist Party for obvious PR reasons. "That wasn't my advice," Mankiewicz says. "But it would have been if they hadn't done it already."

Part 9: 'Sodom and Gomorrah Was an Attention-Getter'

The room was packed with PR people.

A couple of hundred of them gathered in the Capital Hilton last December for the monthly luncheon of the Washington chapter of the Public Relations Society of America. They drank white wine, ate lukewarm chicken, applauded at least 10 past presidents of the chapter and then listened as the current president introduced the guest speaker—Harold Burson, chairman of Burson-Marsteller, one of the largest PR firms on God's green earth.

As Burson stepped up to speak, a protester dashed to the podium and draped it with blood-stained rabbit fur. "Mr. Burson represents the fur industry," she exclaimed, "and on behalf of the millions of animals that have been killed—the foxes, the lynx, the minks, the rabbits, chinchillas, who have been electrocuted, who have been beaten to death—we bestow the Public Relations Hall of Shame award . . ."

The audience groaned and hissed.

PR people catch a lot of flack. Not just from animal lovers and Savimbi supporters but from skeptics and scoffers in all walks of life who feel, for some reason, that PR people are somewhat less than totally, honest.

"Somehow, if you say the words 'public relations,'" says Soucy, who does PR for British Aerospace, "folks want to rush off and take showers because they've just been in the presence of something contaminated."

It's the great irony of PR: The public relations business, which is composed entirely of experts in the art of manufacturing public images, has a terrible public image. On the popularity scale, PR people are no doubt right down there with lawyers and politicians. Maybe almost as low as journalists.

How come?

"'Cause we ain't all choirboys," says Louis Priebe, who handles PR for the Salt Institute. "Joseph Goebbels practiced PR for Adolf Hitler."

True enough. But it probably isn't Goebbels' "big lie" that Americans associate with PR. It's all those little half-truths and weasel words and slick image campaigns. It's the sight of New York City disguising gutted buildings with decals that make them look occupied. It's the stories about the PR guys who help elect the pols and then traipse off to do PR work for people who want something from those pols. It's candidates campaigning in flag factories and presidents who won't make a speech until their personal pollster checks the public pulse. It's the negative ads and the spin doctors and the staged events and the symbol-mongering. It all combines to produce the vague feeling that nothing in politics or government is really real anymore.

These days, the fog produced by the "foggy business" is so dense that even the so-called "insiders" have trouble telling image from reality. Ronald Reagan compared the contras to our Founding Fathers so often that he actually seemed to believe it was true. Remember all the pundits who said that Mikhail Gorbachev was just a slick PR man? Gorby turned out to be the real thing. Or did he? Could tearing down the Berlin Wall be just another PR stunt? It's tough to tell these days. And that's the problem: We've seen so many slick visuals that we don't trust our eyes anymore. We've heard so many soothing slogans that we can't believe our ears. Nonstop PR has left Americans sated and jaded.

"PR," says Soucy, "has come to mean 'to take the unpalatable and make it palatable.'"

Of course, PR people don't see it that way. Quite the contrary. They consider themselves members of an honorable profession, descendants of a long line of people who have educated and elevated public opinion for centuries. In the speech that was interrupted by the fur protester, Harold Burson traced that lineage back to Thomas Jefferson and Alexander Hamilton. Soucy traces it back even further, to some even bigger names:

"For what did Christ perform miracles?" he asks. "I'm not comparing us to Him. I'm simply saying that when you use the term 'public relations gimmick' or 'attention-getter,' well, I'm sorry: Sodom and Gomorrah was an attention-getter. Man responds to attention-getters."

So why haven't any of America's estimated 150,000 PR people produced an attention-getting PR campaign to improve the wretched public image of the PR business?

Ray Hiebert, publisher of the Public Relations Review, thinks he knows why.

"They don't want to," he says with a sly smile. "They like it the way it is. They want to be seen as the custodians of some kind of sinister magic."

Part 10: Federal Bureaucrats Redux

Robert Weed is still rolling.

When we left him, Weed was exhorting the National Association of Government Communicators, pleading for help in his official campaign to enhance the "public image of public service," promising free copies of Image Update and free bumper stickers.

And now his voice is rising to a crescendo as he launches into his stirring conclusion: "We have truth on our side. We're going out saying to the American people: 'We want you to take a fresh look at your public employees, at the system that puts them into place, and we know that when you look at these people, you'll trust them' . . . If they take a fresh look at us, they're gonna recognize that we have truth on our side and they'll say, 'Yes, I can understand why you're proud to be a public employee.' And I'm proud to be a public employee. And I'm proud to be with you this morning. Thank you very much."

He gets a polite round of applause. Then he entertains some questions.

The first questioner notes Weed's rousing endorsement of public servants and then inquires why federal employees hadn't gotten a decent raise lately.

The second questioner launches into a diatribe, lambasting government-bashing presidents who appoint political hacks to boss around dedicated, experienced public servants.

Wait a minute. Hold it right there.

Here is a crowd composed entirely of government PR people and they don't seem terribly excited about a government PR campaign in their behalf. They aren't agog about receptions and Image Updates and ad campaigns and bumper stickers. They want something else. They want the one thing that PR just can't provide:

They want substance.

Don't they know what city they're in?

PR: Pay for Play

Eleanor Randolph, January 1989

So you want your face on "60 Minutes?" Plan to fork out a mere $45,000. Need to be interviewed by The New York Times? It costs about $12,000. USA Today would be more, almost $16,000, and a mention in the Wall Street Journal recently went for a scant $1,000.

This is not the price that networks and newspapers are charging for publishing your story. This is what one publicity agent has been charging if those networks and newspapers succumb to his sales pitch.

The technique is called "pay for play" and the concept, as it is being promoted by a 43-year-old Californian named Reed Trencher, has the publicity industry in a dither. The nation's image makers are worried that Trencher will do for public-relations what J.R. Ewing did for oil.

"It's really gross and offensive and tacky," Frank Mankiewicz, a prominent public-relations man in Washington, says of the Trencher system.

Many journalists believe that being gross, offensive or tacky is part of the job description for a purveyor of the public-relations trade. But such views, while pure and lofty, are not very straightforward.

Some public-relations people are sleazy, but others are smart, useful and even honest. Some see their job as that of matchmaker between reporters and clients. Some are selling a point of view, often acknowledging to a reporter that there is another side, often even giving the other side and then, of course, trying to knock it down. For virtually every story in the daily newspaper, reporters have consulted, trusted and often quoted people who are called spokesmen, information specialists and press secretaries—known generically in the newsroom as "flacks."

Others who practice flackery—may they rot in their pastel office suites along with their busy, little FAX machines—are paid to obfuscate. They earn their lucre by throwing their bodies between the reporter and the truth.

For the journalist, of course, it's not supposed to matter how a PR person earns a living, whether he charges a $6,000 a month retainer or $10,000 a story. It's his information that is supposed to count.

George Cotliar, managing editor of the Los Angeles Times, told the Columbia Journalism Review recently, that "fee structure is not

229

germane to us." When he was told that Trencher had succeeded in placing a story in the Times and billed its client, The Sharper Image (which sells expensive gadgets), for $8,830, Cotliar said: "That's none of our business. Our business is reacting well to stories that come from PR or reacting negatively, depending on the value of the information."

Clearly, that's the correct answer in today's journalism. But the realization that a big fee turns on my news judgment gives me the creeps. If I knew the person on the phone would earn his company $8,800 if I agreed to do a feature about his client in the Washington Post, I'd be tempted to pass the receiver to my bad ear.

But there is some question whether reporters ever know the caller's place of business.

A call to the New York number of Trencher's company, Primetime Publicity and Media Consulting in New York, brought a response from Louise Russell, vice president of operations in San Francisco. Russell said that it is "company policy" for employees to advise reporters that they are from Primetime.

Trencher, who is president and CEO of Primetime, apparently sees his company's policy on this matter a little differently. He told a reporter recently that part of his success has come from hiring ex-journalists to pitch stories to their former colleagues. "When Primetime people call," he said, "these are known journalists, and the name Primetime is probably not even mentioned."

Trencher told me that he has "some fairly big journalists" working for him, but he won't name them. Also, he said these people don't always acknowledge they work for Primetime when they call a reporter because "we're doing some pioneering here. . . . What is still unknown is how the media is going to react to this."

Obviously, this is a crucial part of Trencher's operation, and most established public-relations people I interviewed said this buy-the-story system has surfaced occasionally through the years but never caught on industry-wide. Trencher contends that the time has finally come and that a growing number of business executives "want to see their publicity first and then pay for it."

"Wherever you drop the seed," he said. "It grows."

The same can be said of dandelions.

Speakes's Kamikaze Rhetoric

Eleanor Randolph, April 1988

So Larry Speakes made up a few quotes. We were horrified. We were appalled. But why were we surprised?

If there are members of the news media who were shocked that a press secretary fabricated his boss's words, they should go in for vocational rehabilitation, Here in Washington, press secretaries routinely "clean up" quotes, which can mean anything from matching subject and verb to obliterating anything that makes their employer's words sound less lofty than Winston Churchill's.

Anybody gasping in horror at Speakes's admission should have been gasping instead that he admitted it. This was a very dumb move for a public-relations man, as Speakes learned last week when he was forced to separate himself from a very posh job as vice president of communications for Merrill Lynch.

Once a flack admits he makes up quotes, he's like a car salesman who acknowledges that he ups his prices by 40 percent. His usefulness to his employer is, shall we say, limited.

The whole flap begs for a word here—not about Speakes's dishonesty in 1985—but for his confessions in 1988. Speakes's book, "Speaking Out: Inside the Reagan White House" is one of those tattle-tale Washington exposes that everybody hates except the readers.

But Speakes was not just attacking the press in a gossipy way with this book, he was issuing a bon-voyage telegram as a flack. Although most of the media nave concentrated on how Speakes made up Reagan's quotes, privately they are steaming about what Speakes wrote about them in his book.

Here are a few favorite examples:

"NBC's lead White House correspondent, Chris Wallace, combined the worst qualities of Sam Donaldson and Lesley Stahl," Speakes wrote. "He was both obnoxious and a bit slow on the uptake."

Wallace, whose father is Mike Wallace of CBS's "60 Minutes," is now the moderator of NBC's "Meet the Press." Stahl is moderator of CBS's "Face the Nation." Donaldson is a heavy contender for all kinds of lofty positions at ABC News. In two sentences, Speakes has lobbed grenades over the walls of all three networks.

Well, maybe Speakes could have peddled his news elsewhere? To Dan Rather, maybe?

Speakes tells the story about how he got Rather to apologize to the President and Mrs. Reagan on the "CBS Evening News." Speakes said one night Rather accidentally called President Reagan "President Nixon." Speakes thought it was funny, a slip, and wanted to let it slide. But the Reagans were outraged and wanted Dan to say "I'm sorry."

When Speakes called Rather, the anchorman understandably argued that an apology would make it bigger than it already was. Speakes said: "'Dan, you're playing to an audience of two.' His reply: 'Good advice leads to good decisions.' And he came on and apologized for it."

That story has to make Rather wince; it makes him look like a patsy.

Okay, he's offended television; there's still the print medium. And not just any print medium, but the Knight-Ridder chain—which includes some of the most prestigious newspapers in the business. "There's something about Knight-Ridder reporters that makes them hot dogs, 'show-off' questioners, performing for their colleagues," Speakes wrote.

Speakes accuses Washington Post reporter Lou Cannon of revealing a source to Speakes who then fired the guy for talking to Cannon. Cannon vehemently denies that he revealed a source and says Speakes "does not even quote the Washington Post story correctly."

Reagan's former spokesman also writes about besting Bill Kovach, formerly Washington bureau chief of the New York Times and now editor of the Atlanta Journal and Constitution. Kovach got mad at "background" briefings which stipulate that stories can only be attributed to a high White House source, and his Times staff walked out of one such session.

Speakes sent Kovach a copy of the Times with all the unattributed sources circled in red ink—"administration officials" or "high White House sources"—and added: "'When you guys stop picking up information from mid-level bureaucrats on street corners, then you can walk out of officially sanctioned government background briefings.' I never had any more trouble with the Times failing to attend background briefings after that."

"Whaaat?" said Kovach, when he heard the story. He said that the Times boycotted those briefings three or four times after that and Speakes knew it. What happens when Speakes wants to talk to the Atlanta Journal? Or the New York Times?

The Wall Street Journal? "Although the Journal is a great paper, I was disappointed by the low-caliber reporters they assigned to the

White House." Ouch. Newsweek, Time, U.S. News & World Report? "I just didn't think the newsmagazines were worth my time."

Maybe Larry Speakes shouldn't have made up a few quotes for President Reagan; maybe that damaged Reagan's credibility. But the one who really suffers because of Larry Speakes's revelations is Larry Speakes. He left a wake of fury in Washington press rooms that would have relegated his phone messages to the twilight zone for years to come.

This book may be a best-seller when it comes out in a few weeks. But, for a man in the public-relations trade, it was kamikaze.

CHAPTER NINE

Advertising

The Rise and Fall of Saatchi & Saatchi

Glenn Frankel

Charles and Maurice Saatchi liked to tell their colleagues the story of the blind beggar in Central Park who sat on the sidewalk with a sign that read: "I am blind."

One fine morning in early spring, an advertising copywriter passed by on his way to work, bent down and wrote something on the sign. When he stopped by that evening and asked how the day had gone, the blind man replied, "Fantastic. Never done so well. What did you write on the sign?"

The copywriter replied, "I added a few words to make it read: It is spring and I am blind."

Even a beggar needs an adman, or so the Saatchis believed. During two frenetic decades of hyperactive deal-making, they set about, to make themselves admen to the world—nothing less than the biggest, boldest, most creative and most profitable advertising and marketing agency that ever existed.

Or, as they themselves put it in one annual report: "It's good to be big, it's better to be good, but it's best to be both."

For a brief moment, some would say, Saatchi & Saatchi Co. was both. Starting only 20 years ago, Charles and Maurice Saatchi transformed their six-man agency on a London side street into the largest advertising conglomerate in the world. Just as the Beatles took

234

American popular music, refined it and brought it back across the Atlantic, so too did the Saatchis lead the British conquest of Madison Avenue with a quintessentially American weapon: the ad.

They did it by a combination of British chic and British cheek. They hit London with a series of stylish, hard-edged ad campaigns—a pregnant man to advertise family planning, a pack of lemmings to illustrate the dangers of smoking, a long unemployment line with the slogan "Labor Isn't Working" to promote Britain's Conservative Party—shaking up an industry that despite its worship of innovation had grown stale and self-satisfied.

By 1979 they were the biggest ad agency in Britain. By 1986 after a corporate buying spree, they were the biggest in the world, operating on five continents and servicing more than 50 of the world's 100 largest companies. Among their clients: Toyota, Honda, Procter & Gamble, British Airways, Colgate Palmolive and Live Aid.

"Charles saw the world as a big supermarket—you go in and buy what you want off the shelf," says a former senior officer at the company, one of many who left on less-than-friendly terms, yet speaks of the brothers with a wary affection. "Everything is for sale. The only question is can you afford the price. Things had to get out of hand—and inevitably they did.

Among the corporate refuse of the '80s from Boesky to Milken to Campeau to Trump, the Saatchis stand out for many reasons. Perhaps the Saatchis were victim to their own hype, believed too deeply in their own infallibility. Meanwhile a chastened stock market caught up with the incredible game of buy and buy and buy with borrowed money that was the key to their breathtaking annual growth in sales and profits.

Their tale is in large part the story of Britain in the era of Margaret Thatcher, when entrepreneurs armed with cash and insouciance set out to reassert British influence in a changed world. Their climb was one of the most swift, their fall one of the most sudden.

The Saatchis helped pioneer the concept of globalization. Thanks to computers, satellite television and films, they reasoned, markets were shrinking, national identities slipping. If everyone was buying the same products, then everyone could be sold in the same way. And a few large, fearless corporations could practically run the world.

Neither of the Saatchis would speak for this article, and many of their closest associates and former colleagues insisted upon anonymity. Once the darlings of the press, the Saatchis now believe the press has turned vicious and unfair. Yet like those former associates who parted on bad terms, journalists remain fascinated, even when appalled, by the brothers and the world they built.

"They had a terribly low boredom threshold and a momentum they felt they had to maintain—they didn't want to do this year what they did last year," says financial journalist Ivan Fallon, author of, "The Brothers," the definitive British book on the brothers' rise.

"You say your bottom line is to become the biggest in Britain, and then in Europe and then in the world, and before you've even arrived there, you're asking, 'What do we do after that?' You keep forging a philosophy to fit whatever pleases you. And all the time you're succeeding, you reinforce your own view that you're infallible. They came to utterly believe that there were no ceilings for them."

Advertising may have been an American invention, but the British have always been masters at image making. A few weeks ago they celebrated the 50th anniversary of one of the most humiliating defeats in their history, the evacuation at Dunkirk, as if it were a triumph, a fable of small boats and brave men. Three generations of Britons believed the myth. They also believed that the gruff, steely voice that entreated them to stand tall during the darkest hours of World War II belonged to Winston Churchill, perhaps Britain's greatest image maker, rather than to the actor who read Churchill's lines over the wireless.

In the 1970s, the British had their chance to assert those skills anew. Like Washington after the Cold War, Madison Avenue had grown uncomfortable with its own vast powers, wary of its own instincts. For all of its explosive growth, the advertising business was still something of a cottage industry—a few giants, but lots of small agencies, and not much attention to bottom lines.

Enter Charles and Maurice. "They arrived at a time when rising American domination had been accompanied by a pervasive blandness and repetition in the actual creative work of advertising," wrote Robert Heller, editor of Management Today. "It gave British agencies, mostly new, the chance to become the Greeks to the Romans of Madison Avenue. A rolling tide of brilliant British advertising reset the standard and the style.

"The Saatchis shared in the flood. The difference was that their ambitions were Roman in scope. They wanted an empire."

The Saatchis were born in Baghdad, the sons of an Iraqi Jewish merchant who fled the country with his young family in the late 1940s. Their place of birth was a fact the Saatchis, keen to be seen as insiders, sought to conceal as they made their way up the mountain of British business.

Maurice went to the London School of Economics while Charles, bored, gifted and restless, skipped college and went directly into the ad business as a copywriter. He made few friends, fewer allies, but gathered a small circle of devotees. Eventually he decided that the only way to get where he wanted to go was to open his own shop. And he persuaded his younger brother to join him.

The Saatchis launched themselves with a typically self-engineered attention-getter—a two-page ad in the London Sunday Times titled "Why I Think It's Time for a New Kind of Advertising." It was bold and arrogant and it cost them a quarter of their start-up money.

They soon became London's hottest ad shop, a place for talented, difficult people. And the most talented and difficult, friends say, was Charles Saatchi himself.

William Muirhead, who now is chairman and joint chief executive of the original Saatchi ad agency on London's Charlotte Street, recalls his first glimpse of Charles Saatchi's witheringly high standards. Muirhead had been dispatched to a client with an ad he had never seen before and didn't quite understand. The client loved it, however, and Muirhead came back pleased.

Charles was not. "Charley said, 'It's crap,' and he ripped it into little pieces." says Muirhead. "I had to call back the client and say, 'You know that ad you really loved? Well, we've done something even better.' That's how Charley operated."

Friends say Charles Saatchi bullied everyone—his clients, his employees, but most of all his younger brother. Now 47, Charles remains a harsh, relentless, profane, reclusive, intensely competitive man with a take-no-prisoners approach—the adman as existential hero. Maurice, now 44, is a charming, quieter but no less assertive person, the ego to his brother's id.

To outsiders they were Rambo and The Nerd, a carefully honed brother act. Charles had the restless energy, the impulses and the intuition; Maurice, the know-how to translate the raw energy and ideas into a strategy for the 80's.

Charles was the spark, but Maurice handled the cash. He was the one who convinced London's tightfisted financial markets that an ad agency was a good investment, one worth backing with millions in share issues. And while Charles would skulk and hide from clients, Maurice would turn on the charm.

Between the two, friends recall, there was chemistry and there was terror. Sometimes there was blood as well when Charles lit upon

Maurice. "They are Cain and Abel," says a former friend. "You have to remember that Cain loved his brother.

"Even in a hysterical rage, Charley could be very funny. I can remember him one day, red in the face, screaming at Maurice: 'I can't believe you came from the same womb as me.'"

Friends say today Charles still brings his pet schnauzer to work each morning, still plays board games like chess and Monopoly as if they were life-and-death struggles, still dominates the psyche of the company with his brooding presence.

But it is at most a spiritual presence—most employees these days say they never see Charles Saatchi, who has long made a point of avoiding direct contact with clients and the press. After Saatchi & Saatchi went public in 1977, Charles never attended a shareholders meeting. There has been only one official photo in the past decade.

Both brothers tend to hover on the edge London's social scene, a world friends say they have never felt part of.

Maurice is married to Josephine Hart, whose career is as a West End theatrical producer. While less reclusive than Charles, friends say, Maurice prefers the privacy of the vast English garden he has designed for the multi-million-dollar country home where he and his family live in Sussex, south of London.

Charles's marriage to Doris Dibley, an American and former ad copywriter, broke up three years ago, but he still maintains houses in London's Mayfair area and in Long Island, still pursues the art collection he and Doris initiated together. It is now considered one of the world's largest collections of contemporary art—worth more than $100 million, by some estimates—and a small portion is displayed in a stark, white-walled former warehouse turned gallery in north London. Most of it, like Charles himself, remains behind closed doors, sealed off from view.

Among the best and brightest hired by the Saatchis in those early days of the agency were Tim Bell, who started as media director and ended up managing the day-to-day operations of the agency for the increasingly remote Charles; and Martin Sorrell, who did the same on the financial end. Sorrell and Maurice Saatchi together created a management system that monitored the company's financial condition daily and imposed rigid budgets on its new acquisitions yet allowed the new purchases wide-ranging autonomy in conducting business. The system impressed financiers in the City, London's version of Wall Street. They provided the cash that fueled the new acquisitions and made Saatchis the City's top glamour stock.

Both Bell and Sorrell left the Saatchis with bitterness, and their departures are considered among the key reasons for the company's subsequent decline. Sorrell bought a small firm, known as WPP, and began acquiring larger companies until last year he surpassed Saatchi as the world's largest advertising group. Bell has opened his own firm to develop corporate strategies and lobbying campaigns. He is also considered one of Margaret Thatcher's most intimate admirers. Yet friends say Bell, despite the rancor, still stands in awe of Charles Saatchi.

"Tim was great on a surfboard," says Muirhead, "but Charley made the waves."

The Thatcher account in many ways was the key to the Saatchis' reputation and acceptance. They won it in 1978 in typical fashion, according to Fallon—neither brother showed up for the meeting at the Conservative Party's central office. But Gordon Reece, then the party's communications director and a member of Thatcher's inner circle, was eager to import American-style techniques to help defeat the ruling Labor Party and he believed the Saatchis could help him do it.

The best ads were sharp and bitter—a slick, fast-moving television spot depicting everything in Britain moving in reverse, and the famous poster campaigns. One depicted an unemployment line above the simple message "Labor Isn't Working"; another showed a young black man with the line, "Labor says he's black—Tories say he's British."

The ads were aimed not at specific policies or issues but feelings, what Bell called "the emotional meaning" of voting for Thatcher. Labor was caught off guard—every time its leaders criticized the ads, the result predictably was more publicity, which made the Saatchis and the Conservatives look even more clever, and Labor more clumsy. Thatcher won a substantial electoral victory in 1979 and the Saatchi legend was born.

But by then the Saatchis were already moving on to bigger battles. Clever ad-making was not enough—they also wanted to be known as the top marketing company. And so the Saatchis had started buying. The first big acquisition was Compton in 1975, a blue-chip ad agency that was twice as big as they were. The Saatchis convinced Compton's owners that the two companies should merge. They even added Compton's name to their own. But within a few days, the headline in Campaign, the London ad weekly with a direct pipeline to Charles, read "Saatchi swallows up the Compton Group." Many of Compton's senior managers left quickly.

After that, says a former employee, the pattern was established. "Charley and Maurice would tell the prospective sellers anything they wanted to hear, invent an ideal version of what life would be like after the deal was signed. And afterward we would just do exactly whatever it was we wanted."

It was the biggest acquisitions binge the London stock market has ever seen. By 1985 the Saatchis were buying companies, most of them American, at the rate of one a month. In the spring of 1986 they paid $100 million for the New York ad firm of Backer & Spielvogel, the largest sum ever paid for an ad agency. A month later they smashed that record by paying nearly $500 million for Ted Bates Worldwide, the third largest agency in the United States.

Bates was the deal that made Saatchi the world's biggest agency, yet it also marked the beginning of the end. Analysts said they paid far too much for Bates and bought a company whose conservative approach to the business was the virtual antithesis of their own. The deal also cost them big amounts of business from major clients upset that Saatchi had grown so large its many little arms were servicing rivals. Procter & Gamble, the Saatchis' biggest client, Colgate-Palmolive and Warner Lambert reportedly removed more than $300 million in business after the Bates deal.

There were other problems. Searching for new worlds to conquer, Charles and Maurice decided that the consultancy business was as ripe for acquisition as the advertising business. As usual they formed a theory to justify the instinct—the Saatchis would become a full-service company that could offer clients not only advertising, but public relations, research, even financial services.

Beginning in 1984, they bought a dozen small agencies, only to discover that their expertise in advertising did not extend to the specialized world of consultancies. The new agencies proved a big drain on corporate profits.

The 1987 British general election was also a minor disaster—Saatchi still designed the ad campaign for the Conservatives but played a much reduced role. The brothers resisted Thatcher's plea that Bell, who had just left the firm, be hired on as a consultant to run the campaign. As Thatcher's lead in the polls melted away, she grew more and more panicky and increasingly inclined to blame her predicament on the Saatchi campaign, which looked lack-luster compared with the crisp new Labor Party ads produced by Hugh Hudson, director of the movie "Chariots of Fire." Hudson's ads personalized the campaign and portrayed Labor leader Ned Kinnock in the same heroic terms as the protagonists of the film, and included the inspiring Kinnock lines about his coal-mining ancestors that U.S. presidential candidate Joseph Biden later got caught plagiarizing.

Unbeknown to the Saatchis, Thatcher started quietly consulting with another agency, Young & Rubicam, then secretly called in Bell. When it was over, less than a month later, and the Conservatives had won another landslide, the Saatchis accused Bell of attempting to undermine them. Weeks of recriminations followed—insiders say Charles Saatchi phoned prominent newspaper editors and businessmen to accuse Bell of drug addiction and criminal wrongdoing—before both sides agreed to an uneasy truce. The brothers formally resigned the Conservative account a few months later. Thatcher, Conservative insiders say, was fed up with the Saatchis.

By then Charles and Maurice were adrift in even deeper waters. They tried to buy Midland Bank, one of Britain's largest, then Hill Samuel, a smaller merchant bank. In both instances they were rebuffed by the owners but word got out around the City, whose financial mandarins viewed the bids with awe and anger.

"Here they had just paid a ridiculous sum for Bates, had had difficulties with consulting, and the next thing you know, Maurice wants to buy a bank," says Emma Hill, an analyst with Wertheim & Co. in New York.

The drain on cash flow of the massive acquisitions began to eat into profits. After Sorrell left in 1986, the financial monitoring system fell into disrepair.

There was also a deep sense of alienation among newly acquired employees in the United States, where people never really caught Saatchi fever. Clients too sometimes felt unloved or ignored. Charles and Maurice increasingly removed themselves from day-to-day operations and turned them over to subordinates who were said to lack Sorrell's brilliance and Bell's feel-good style of inspiration.

After the Midland bank fiasco, investors grew wary and the share price of Saatchi stock tumbled. At the same time, corporate spending on advertising was shrinking as British interest rates soared and sales tailed off. Suddenly the dream was over.

It ended officially last October when Maurice announced that the brothers were relinquishing their roles as joint chief executives and appointing French businessman Robert Louis-Dreyfus to sort out the mess. He has been trying to sell off the consultancies, keep investors from bailing out and ward off the takeover artists who are hungrily eyeing the bloody remains like birds of prey after a massacre. Last week Saatchi sold, for only $2 million in cash, plus royalty payments, a Chicago legal consultancy called Peterson that it paid $116 million for only three years ago.

Louis-Dreyfus has quickly forced out a number of the brothers' longtime associates and allies and installed his own people. He has also lowered the company's sights. The new Saatchi image, says an insider hired by the new team, is that of "a company run by mature adults rather than a bunch of young creative guys playing with someone else's money."

The brothers each have accepted a 30 percent cut in their salaries. Maurice is still actively involved but appears to outsiders to have been reduced to a front man, accompanying Louis-Dreyfus when he goes to see fund managers to plead for more time and money, and taking senior clients to lunch. "His name is over the door," says an insider, "and he's not going to walk away from the mess."

Charles still plots and dreams, friends say, but is more reclusive than ever and often deeply depressed. They say he attributes the blame for his downfall to others, never to himself. "Charley is never wrong, he is never ever wrong," says a former associate. "It's the investors' fault for getting cold feet. Or it's Maurice's fault for failing to replace Tim or Martin."

Some of the glory remains. Bill Muirhead, the Saatchi loyalist who runs the original Charlotte Street agency, points out that his shop is still the biggest in Britain and last year was voted tops in the business by clients in an independent survey. It won more creative awards than any other firm and was the first agency to place a billboard on the eastern side of the Berlin Wall.

But even as Muirhead recites those achievements, a certain weariness creeps around the edges of his optimism. "It's a very competitive business," he says. "You've got to have an edge all the time and you can't stop competing, because once you stop, you're dead. I don't worry about the big guys. I worry about the guys who are just opening their doors. They're hungry and they want the money and they're ready to take the risks."

Sometimes the nerve endings show. When Paul Cowan, an accounts manager, and seven other staffers left last month and opened their own shop, boasting that they were the true "keepers of the Saatchi creative flame," Saatchis fired back with derogatory comments in the press and threats of lawsuits. It all looked rather heavy-handed and it contributed to another drop in the share price.

What it all comes down to is not just the loss of money, but of something almost as valuable in the ad business—aura and mystique.

Without those two characteristics, the Saatchis are just another pair of hustling admen, Supermen who lost their capes.

"The Saatchi magic was a huge plus factor, and now it's gone," says author Fallon. "These were the people who could do no wrong. But just as the gilt has gone off the Thatcher image, it has gone off Saatchi image as well. And they themselves are terribly conscious of it.

"They still have basically a very good advertising business. But is that enough?"

Magazine Advertising Up Close and Personal

Paul Farhi, December 1989

Magazine ads don't just sit there anymore. They play electronic jingles, light up, spew perfumed scents and even simulate human speech. They come dressed up with holograms, three-dimensional pop-ups and moving displays.

And now, in another marriage of technology and publishing salesmanship, a magazine ad will address readers by name.

Each of 9 million subscribers to Time, Sports Illustrated and People magazine will find their names emblazoned on an ad for American Isuzu Motors in Jan. 15 issues of the magazines.

Thanks to a sophisticated printing process, the advertisement not only will place the names on a special card but will also include the location of the Isuzu dealer nearest the reader's home.

"We call it a page-stopper," said Jon Bucci, who supervises the Japanese automaker's account for advertising agency Della Femina, McNamee WCRS in Los Angeles. "As you're reading the magazine hopefully you'll do a double take. We think this works a lot harder than a regular ad."

Beyond simple attention-getting, officials at Time-Warner Inc., which publishes the three magazines, hope personalized ads will lure national advertisers away from direct mail and newspapers.

Such ads will give advertisers the ability to promote their local outlets in national magazines, just as they can do now through local newspapers, said Bruce Judson, director of marketing for Time-Warner's magazine unit. The mass circulation of the magazine ads also will allow marketers to offer premiums and incentives the way direct-response advertisers do. Isuzu, for example, is offering a free phone or movie video to readers who take the card accompanying the ad to a dealer.

While innovative, the special Isuzu ad isn't unprecedented. Direct-mail advertisers have been producing personalized pitches for about 10 years, and several smaller magazines, such as American Baby, have carried advertising featuring subscribers' names.

Time's primary competitor, Newsweek, said it ran an ad for L.L. Bean, the outdoor-gear company, imprinted with subscribers' names in

2.5 million copies of Newsweek's Sept. 4 edition. "We can do anything Time can do," said Diana Pearson, a Newsweek spokeswoman.

Time-Warner, however, said the Isuzu ad will reach one in 10 households in the United States, making it the broadest use of ink-jet technology to date.

On the strength of the magazines' mass circulation, the company expects to collect about $25 million in 1990 by selling personalized ads to retailers, hotel companies, insurers and other companies that market their services or products through local dealerships or stores.

"This goes way beyond just another gimmick," Judson said. "If something works, people will use it."

Bucci isn't so sure. He points out that the novelty of the ads could make them short-lived, much like the scratch-and-sniff ads of yore. "Once our ad hits the market, interest will wane for others," he said.

The cost of imprinting ads may also discourage some advertisers from playing the name game. Neither Time nor Isuzu will reveal precisely how much Isuzu will pay, but Judson said ink-jet printing costs 35 percent to 60 percent more than the standard rate of $310,000 for full page ads in Time, People and Sports Illustrated. That's a big bite out of Joe Isuzu's wallet, especially for an ad that will appear only once and considering the automaker's total annual ad budget is $12 million.

As a complement to ink-jet printing, Time-Warner and Newsweek next month will both introduce a process called selective binding. This will permit advertisers to place their ads in only those copies of a magazine that reach a specific target audience.

By culling its subscription lists and reconfiguring its press runs, for instance, Time-Warner will be able to offer editions that reach high-income senior citizens, people who have recently moved or those who have bought a product from a catalogue.

Yet as with the name-dropping ads, someone already has beaten the magazine giants to selective binding: A farm publication began tailoring its editions last year to enable an advertiser to target readers who grow wheat with one message and those who grow corn with another.

The Smell of Money

Eleanor Randolph, May 1988

I don't mind advertising that pops up when you open the page. I don't mind advertising that plays a little tune. I don't mind when it quivers in a way that is supposed to look like 3-D. But when it smells, I mind.

Last week, I opened a copy of Vanity Fair, one of those expensive magazines wrapped in plastic, and a perfume so strong it could overpower a sulfur factory suddenly filled the living room. My family's noses turned up in unison, and the cats scattered.

Flipping through the pages (which made it worse), I found that the culprit was an advertisement for a new scent called Eternity, which was about how long it seemed before I could shut the magazine and carry it outside where it belonged.

Okay, so everybody's nose is different. One man's stink is another's cologne. I know that. I once knew a naturalist who swore he thought that skunk musk smelled terrific.

More to the point, some people probably also think that Eternity should stick around for a long time. At Vanity Fair, for example, they probably think it has the delicious smell of big bucks.

Scent strips, as they are called, are a boon for the magazine industry. Most magazines charge close to the cost of two pages for simply inserting the strip that has been produced elsewhere and given to the publisher during the printing process.

If this is good news for the magazine industry, these ads have been an even bigger boost to the perfume industry. Before the strips, if somebody wanted to promote a new olfactory flavor, he or she hired perfume guerrillas to perch on the ground floor of department stores and spray customers as they walked to the shoe department.

But in those days, if you shouted; "No, No, I'll have an asthma attack and scare away customers" or something equally threatening, all but the most aggressive would back off.

A magazine reader has no such option. Even though technically these strips are supposed to be activated only when the reader pulls a tab or opens an envelope or some such, the process doesn't always work. The odors waft out of their containers so mischievously and so often that some magazines—Vogue is one—make certain that there are fewer than three smells per issue.

The technology has been around for years since 3M and NCR developed something they called "microencapsulation," a process of making little bubbles of smell that burst upon contact. Most of us know this process from the scratch 'n' sniff children's books that have little patches of Christmas trees or violets or peanut butter. Each patch is full of millions of microscopic capsules that open under the grating of tiny fingernails.

Scratch 'n' sniff was, according to a 3M spokesman, an earlier generation of scent stripping. The makers of the next generation have improved the process dramatically: They have kept the sniff and removed the time-consuming need to scratch. The advance came about in part because merchandisers found that women would not activate the microsized capsules.

"Women don't like to scratch," explains Annette Green, executive director of The Fragrance Foundation in New York City. "They find it unpleasant to use their nails like that."

Giorgio seemed to be the first perfume that adapted the new no-scratch process to magazines and, when its sales soared, others "immediately saw the potential," as Green explains it. Now the ads are a $40 million a year business, and as Washingtonian magazine's advertising director, Ed Mansfield, put it, "We'll take as many of them as we can get."

Some magazines don't like the ads. The New Yorker, which has dramatically modernized its marketing and advertising techniques since Newhouse purchased the grand old matron of the magazine business in 1985, has held the line against smells.

"It was a question people asked when the new management came in," said Kim Wilson of the New Yorker. "The fragrance advertisers were hoping to open some new doors. But the management decided in favor of the readers."

Well, it's nice to know that somebody has standards, at least for now.

A recent New York Times article had some ominous news in the other direction. Those who make sniff strips are looking for new marketing territories. Some advertising executives have even suggested that inflight magazines and airline ticket jackets might be good carriers for the advertising technology. Imagine, for a moment, what would happen if a man wearing Old Spice stuck a ticketful of Aramis in his coat pocket? He would have to sit in the smoking section.

Clearly, what we've got here is a mere whiff of the future in "fragrance advertising." Only a consumer revolt would stop them from invading our homes with their smells like so many high-powered polecats. Failing such a reader rebellion, some magazines are best read outdoors. And then only in a stiff breeze.

Political Pitches Called Insult to Advertising

Paul Taylor, March 1990

It used to be that when people compared selling politicians to selling soap, the politicians were offended. Now the soap sellers are.

"Political advertising is so wretched that most of it wouldn't be approved by our own self-governing boards," Alexander Kroll, chairman and chief executive officer of Young & Rubicam, said at a recent ad industry luncheon here.

"I think we need to ban political ads," Jay Chiat, chairman and chief executive officer of Chiat/Day/Mojo, which creates advertisements for Nissan and Reebok, said in an interview.

"The worst thing that has ever happened to the advertising business is political advertising," said Malcolm MacDougall, chairman of the MacDougall Co.

To political consultants, being called names by Madison Avenue is like being called ugly by a frog. Yet with public outcry over political commercials mounting and new calls for regulation reverberating in Congress, the political consultants are beginning to explore borrowing an idea from their critics in product advertising by establishing a voluntary self-review system.

Bradley O'Leary, president of the American Association of Political Consultants (AAPC), said his group will hold its first ethics symposium "within three months" after the elections this November. The goal, he said, is to adopt a "self-regulating enforcement mechanism that everyone in the industry is comfortable with"—a mechanism that would allow a panel of political consultants to censure the makers of deceptive political ads.

The product advertising industry has had such a panel—the National Advertising Division of the Better Business Bureaus Inc.—for two decades. It reviewed 104 complaints against product ads in 1989 and, in 76 cases, negotiated a voluntary agreement with the advertiser to modify or discontinue the offending ad.

O'Leary made it clear that product advertisers are the last group he will look to for ethical guidance. "They have no morals whatsoever," he said. "They don't care whether they believe in a product or not. All they care about is making money."

Yet the same dynamic that drove product advertisers toward self-regulation appears to be taking hold among political consultants: the desire to fend off meddling outsiders.

Bills to regulate the format and content of political ads have been introduced in Congress for decades, only to gather dust. But in the aftermath of the 1988 presidential campaign—riddled with more negative television commercials than any other presidential race in history—there is new interest in legislation.

"Political campaigns turn the stomach of the average voter," Sen. John C. Danforth (R-Mo.) said in a recent speech on the Senate floor. "Oftentimes, negative commercials have nothing to do with, or little to do with, reality. They are substantiated by the thinnest amount of truth and accuracy and fairness."

Danforth said he supports a proposal that would require candidates to appear on the screen at the end of their attack ads to vouch for their veracity. Other bills have been introduced that would give targets of attack ads free response time. Still another approach is to give all candidates free time on television, with the proviso that they appear on screen in a "talking head" format—a way to encourage reasoned discourse over visual demagoguery. Many democracies around the world impose such restrictions.

Most people in the consultant community and broadcasting industry oppose these approaches, but it is an index of how seriously they take the threat of regulation that the AAPC has finally decided to hold an ethics symposium. It has been resisted for years by some members of the consultant community who argue that self-regulation is not feasible.

"One concern everybody has is how to keep politics out of it," O'Leary said. "If you put six people on a review commission, and three are Democrats and three are Republicans, you're going to get a lot of tie votes."

In product advertising, industry self-review is only part of a web of regulatory mechanisms. Before an ad appears on television, it must be approved by censors at the three major networks who are on the lookout for unfair comparisons or deceptive claims. Many times, product advertisers submit their ad for approval while it is still in the early phase of conceptualization so that they do not spend money producing an ad that cannot get on the air. Of the 50,000 product ads submitted to CBS for approval last year, about one-third required substantiation and/or revision, according to Matthew Margo, the network's vice president for program practices.

Once product ads appear on the air, aggrieved consumers and competitors can make complaints to the Federal Trade Commission or to a state attorney general.

Political ads are subject to no regulation of any kind and are generally thought to be protected as free speech under the First Amendment. They are specifically exempted, in communication law, from censorship by broadcasters.

MacDougall, a product advertiser who has had political clients in the past—including President Gerald R. Ford in 1976 and, briefly, Gov. Michael S. Dukakis in 1988—said this absence of regulation makes political ads "fundamentally corrupt."

"When you attack the other guy in a 30-second spot, distortion almost has to be the rule," he said, "because what political advertising does is find the one thing in a politician's career—and there is always going to be a Willie Horton, there is always going to be some dumb statement or vote cast—that is outrageous to a majority of the people. And then you blow that one thing all out of proportion.

"I'll give you an analogy," MacDougall continued, describing what product advertising might be like without regulation. "Suppose I'm Lipton and I find out that once, way back in 1948, a watch strap fell into a can of Campbell's soup in a factory in the South somewhere. It was found and no one was hurt and it never happened again. If I said all that in an ad, no one would pay any attention. But suppose I ran an ad with eerie music in the background and I had some poor woman screaming as she discovers the watch strap and I had a grotesque close-up of the Campbell soup container and my tag line said: 'Do you want a soup like this? Or do you want Lipton? We check every can.'

"It would be pretty damn effective. But of course there's no way I could get it past the network censors."

In political campaigns, this kind of advertising has become the coin of the realm. Did Rep. Jim Courter (R-N.J.) pollute his own property with toxic waste? Was Lt. Gov. L. Douglas Wilder (D) a slum landlord? Did former Texas governor Mark White (D) use ill-gotten gains to buy a million-dollar mansion after he left office? These were the 30-second spots that ran in gubernatorial races last fall in New Jersey and Virginia and this spring in Texas. All had a modicum of truth, but all—at least in the opinion of the targets—were blown far out of context.

Many political consultants argue that ads of this sort must pass muster with the toughest and fairest regulating body of all—the voters. "If people think you are running dirty ads, there's a 100 percent chance it'll backfire on you," said Republican National Committee

Chairman Lee Atwater, who helped devise the attack ad strategy that was used so effectively against Dukakis in 1988.

But more and more consultants privately say that the cross-fire of 30-second innuendo is causing voters to tune out of politics altogether. In the 1960 election, when political advertising was still in its infancy, voter turnout in the presidential contest was 63 percent. By 1988, it had fallen to 50 percent—the lowest of any industrialized democracy. This decline is a complex phenomenon with many causes, but one of them— say some consultants—is the attack ad.

"This is not something people in my business like to talk about, but attack ads are designed to depress turnout," said Neal Oxman, a political media consultant from Philadelphia. "It's very difficult in a campaign to get a voter who supports the opponent to switch over and vote for you. It's less difficult to create enough doubt about the opponent that some of his supporters stay home. That's what the attack ad is all about."

"In product advertising, if some people got so turned off by the ad that they didn't come into the store, everybody loses," Chiat said. "It's not that way with politics."

Connecting with the Black Consumer

Paula Span, December 1986

Like any ad agency, Lockhart & Pettus has its showcase reel. "Lockhart & Pettus' Greatest Hits," one might call it.

The first commercial on the reel shows actress Debbie Allen wearing plastic gloves and combing white goo through her hair. Dark & Lovely Permanent Creme Relaxer, she confides, "makes me feel like dancing"—and a few seconds later she's pirouetting in slow motion across a bare stage. "And there's no offensive odor," she points out.

There's no dialogue in the Wendy's spot called "Morning Message," just a lone saxophonist in a brick-walled loft, his arpeggios conjuring up visions of fast-food breakfasts, omelets and French toast swirling on the screen. It's one of Ted Pettus' favorites.

"Playback," another Wendy's ad on the reel, is set in a recording studio (except for the occasional shot of an airborne tomato slice or lettuce leaf), where Kool & the Gang are grooving happily to their hit song "Fresh" with slightly revised lyrics: Conversation all over town/ People talkin' fresh and where it can be found/ It's at Wendy's (FRESH!) . . .

Quick, what's different about these commercials?

Everyone in them is black. The audience at which they're aimed is black. The partners in the ad agency that made them—Keith Lockhart and Pettus, watching the tape unreel in their conference room and grooving a little themselves—are black. So are most of the 23 employes at Lockhart & Pettus.

There remains some skepticism in the ad industry about the sort of ethnic targeting—known broadly as "segmented marketing"—that Lockhart & Pettus' Greatest Hits represents. Take Pepsi's two flashy Lionel Richie ads by contrast, intentionally "mainstreamed" enough to transcend age and ethnic categories. "Our approach is to look at the way to reach the most people with the minimum amount of customization," says Gary DePaolo, executive vice president of BBDO, which made the commercials.

Lockhart hears such arguments all the time. "'Hey, we're all in this together,'" he mimics. "Isn't it divisive to have marketing segmented, to admit there's a difference between black and white?" . . . 'Don't people respond to the same stimuli?'

"Of course they don't" is his response. "Different people have different triggers."

Lockhart, 53, is the lanky one—6 foot 2—and the writer in this partnership; he once studied playwrighting at the Yale Drama School. Pettus, 39, broader and with the more intact hairline, is the visual specialist, a product of Harlem and Jamaica, Queens, and an art school grad. Both wear beards. "We're the principals, but we're also the creative department," explains Lockhart. (For clean-shaven chins, see the account side.)

They set up shop almost 10 years ago, in a single room with rented secretarial services near Grand Central Station. Both had shifted through a number of agencies, large and small, and they were a creative team at Foote Cone & Belding when a Savannah-based manufacturer of hair products made them an offer they couldn't refuse.

Carson Products, maker of Dark & Lovely, wanted to know if Pettus and Lockhart would take on its business. It was worth about $600,000 in 1977, enough to pay two salaries if not to hire secretaries. The partners took the plunge.

Lockhart & Pettus has since added Hiram Walker, Con Edison, Cameo Beauty Products and Wendy's to its client roster. It had, as a subcontractor to N.W. Ayer, a piece of the vast U.S. Army account (though that's now in doubt as a result of Ayer's recent suspension by the Army's Judge Advocate General office). It's entered the creative shoot-out for a major automaker's account. Last year Lockhart & Pettus reached $15 million in billings, according to the Directory of Advertising Agencies.

Though the partners resigned one account during their first decade, they have yet to lose one, a respectable record in this volatile arena. Pettus, pointing this out, immediately looks around for something wooden to knock on; in his glass-and-chrome office downtown (the Grand Central days are long gone) it's not easy to find.

Enough advertisers have accepted the notion of tailored-to-fit campaigns to support about 10 agencies that specialize in black-targeted national advertising, plus several aimed at Hispanics. Compared with the dominant "general market" firms, these agencies are still young and spindly legged: The largest, Chicago's Burrell Advertising, rated only 124th in size in Advertising Age's latest ranking. Lockhart & Pettus placed 400th. The seven biggest black agencies (all headquartered in New York or Chicago) combined pulled in less in billings last year ($187.3 million, according to the Directory of Advertising Agencies) than Coca-Cola alone spent on TV ads.

They compete not only against one another but, increasingly, against the big guns. The soulful radio spot in which Aretha Franklin sings the praises of Dial soap was done by a general market agency, Needham Harper Worldwide. And about two years ago, a vice president at giant BBDO noticed "a hemorrhaging going on . . . accounts being siphoned off because (we) aren't specialists in minority markets." So BBDO formed an in-house "special markets group" that runs the "Gilbey's Gin & Jazz" promotion for National Distillers, creates Spanish radio commercials for Lever Bros. and beat out several black-owned agencies to snare the new Venus Cosmetics account.

Still, executives at the top minority agencies are sounding fairly sanguine. They've survived the '70s shake-out that saw several minority shops fold, including the one where copywriter Lockhart first met art director Pettus. For a time, "companies were throwing around conscience money—not a lot, but enough to attract people," notes President Frank Mingo of Mingo-Jones, which vies with UniWorld Group for the No. 2 ranking among black agencies. Now Mingo sees "a healthier interest in the effects on the bottom line."

"It's business," echoes Tom Burrell, chairman of Burrell Advertising. "It's about $200 billion out there in the black consumer market."

Those consumers spend heavily on certain kinds of products, market research shows. Surveys demonstrate, for example, that blacks are frequent patrons of fast-food restaurants, which explains why UniWorld makes ads depicting black studio musicians taking Burger King breaks (that's Richie Havens on the sound track).

Leading distillers and brewers, similarly, earmark slices of their ad budgets for minority-targeted campaigns. A recent Mingo-Jones radio spot features a doo-wop group harmonizing about friendship. "You run into one of the guys," adds the announcer, "you can buy him a Miller Beer . . ."

Sometimes the differences between the big national campaigns and the ads aimed at minorities seem to come down to casting and sound tracks. But Pettus and Lockhart talk about their "sensibilities" and "gut feelings," ingredients almost as important as the research and focus groups they also rely on.

Canadian Club, for example, was fond of a print campaign devised by its mainstream agency around the theme "Be a Part of It." One ad showed a young white woman pulling a man along behind her by his necktie; in another an evening-gowned woman stood in an arched doorway, the man behind her.

Those ads didn't work for blacks, Lockhart says. "We don't live in a totally integrated society. When you see white people in a social situation, the black person knows 'I'm not really being invited in.' The black consumer didn't relate to that environment."

"They didn't want to be part of that scene," adds Pettus. Focus groups backed up the partners' skepticism.

The Lockhart & Pettus response for Canadian Club—running in black newspapers, in magazines like Ebony and Jet, and on billboards in 15 cities—is called "Fashion Show." It features a black couple clinking glasses at a cafe, table and ignoring three models posturing on a runway. "Forget About the Rest," says the slogan Lockhart wrote.

Like a number of Lockhart & Pettus ads, this one carries a subtext: Besides advising consumers to forget about competing liquors, "it means you have something already; you're not needy," Lockhart explains. Instead of urging blacks to become part of an ill-defined "it," the message asserts that "we're not going to get it down the road, we've got it now."

Sometimes Lockhart's copy plays on black speech, Pettus says, as in the references to "fresh" on Wendy's behalf, and in the line for a Hiram Walker product called Amaretto & Cognac ("It's Amaretto. It's Cognac. It's Together.")

Musical cues are also important; even when they use a jingle a mainstream agency has written, Lockhart and Pettus reorchestrate for a grittier sound that "lets people know, 'Hey, this is meant for you,'" Lockhart says.

Compared with lots of mainstream ads, though, the agency's are short on humor: The partners think it can evoke stereotypes. "It's tough to be funny about minority groups," Pettus says.

"They couldn't have done 'Where's the Beef?'"—the famous spot done by DFS Dorland, then Wendy's agency for the general market—"with an old black woman," Lockhart agrees.

And there's another agenda being followed. Lockhart & Pettus wants to sell its clients' products but, like other black agencies, it also wants to serve up "positive images." The Dark & Lovely campaigns, for example, subtly preach self-acceptance by featuring models of various sizes, ages and skin tones—"because black people do come in all colors," Lockhart says. The ads emphasize black families whenever possible and fathers' roles within them.

Last summer, on the other hand, the agency found itself in the pleasant position of creating a campaign—the campaign—for the general market. Wendy's was unveiling its Crispy Chicken Nuggets and, though the product had obvious antecedents, it was "our first foray into chicken finger foods and we wanted to make a splash," says Paul Raab, Wendy's manager of corporate communications. Both its ad agencies submitted scripts and storyboards.

Lockhart had come up with another Kool & the Gang connection: with the Liberty Weekend hoopla looming, their old hit "Celebration" had come to mind. This time copywriter Patricia Wright was assigned to transform the lyrics. (So take your good friends/ And your family too/ Wendy's got Crispy Chicken Nuggets for you . . .)

In the end, Wendy's thought the three "Celebration" spots would "make the cash registers ring" (Raab's phrase). It put Lockhart & Pettus' ads (two with integrated casts, one with a white gymnast daughter and mother) on network television instead of those proposed by DFS Dorland. That $10 million launch, by Lockhart's estimate, was the agency's first real taste of crossover advertising.

But not its last. Lockhart & Pettus' contribution to Wendy's current Big Classic ads was shot in the Rose Bowl, with a coach bringing bags of Big Classics to a famished, integrated football team. Besides being aired on black cable networks, it represents 15 to 20 percent of Wendy's current network advertising.

The burger chain, losing millions and in the midst of a "realignment" that involves closing or selling off 164 restaurants, has since replaced DFS, but has stuck with Lockhart & Pettus.

Still, the partners say they see plenty of unenlightened or downright offensive advertising around them, despite the toehold they and their colleagues have made.

Sometimes it's the token minorities sprinkled into an essentially white ad that raises their hackles—or worse, the depiction of an all-white world. Pettus recently noticed a commercial for a financial services company, set in an office peopled with perhaps 25 workers. "Not one was black or Hispanic," he says, wincing. "Not a secretary, no one."

Even integrated ads sometimes ring false. Levi Strauss ads, for instance, feature both blacks and whites sashaying along the street in 501 jeans. "Not offensive," Lockhart says, "but those blacks probably go to Choate. That's the image writers who live in Greenwich (Connecticut) have of blacks."

Misguided attempts at humor also rankle. "You'll see a black person with facial expressions exaggerated," Lockhart says. "The southern accent is overstated; the eyes pop . . . It's the laughing, smiling black person . . .

"We'd handle it differently," he says.

Ads Not Fit to Print

Richard Harwood, April 1989

Michael Gartner, an Iowa newspaper publisher who recently became president of NBC News, takes the screwball view that the First Amendment to the Constitution ought to mean what it says: that speech is immune from government regulation.

He would overturn the federal law against tobacco advertising on radio and television and let the whiskey makers buy as much TV time as they like. He would allow brokers to sell stocks and bonds through the mail. He would allow prostitutes to freely advertise their services in Nevada, where prostitution is legal. He would allow handgun retailers in North Dakota to put signs in their windows saying: "Handguns for sale." He would repeal the bans on liquor advertising in Mississippi, Utah and other states. He would allow women interested in surrogate motherhood to advertise that fact and would allow lawyers to stand on their heads in television commercials if that's what they want to do.

The Supreme Court of the United States, The New York Times, The Washington Post and right-thinking people throughout the land no doubt also believe in the First Amendment and its free speech guarantees. But in the case of the court, The Times, The Post and uncounted legions of citizens there are limits to their toleration.

The Times last week—after a bit of censorship—published a full-page ad with a rather provocative, vertical headline containing such words as "gooks," "kikes" and "niggers." The ad was paid for by the National Committee Against Religious Bigotry and Racism. It damned Mortimer Zuckerman's magazine, U.S. News and World Report, for a critical article on the Unification Church. The article referred to church members as "Moonies," prompting this language in the ad: "Today it's the 'Moonies.' What epithets will you use next, Mr. Zuckerman? Will it be 'gooks,' 'kikes,' 'niggers,' 'papists,' or 'holy rollers'?"

The Post wouldn't print the ad. It would not be surprising if other newspapers refused it as well because the censorship of "commercial speech" is commonplace throughout the United States. At least 300 newspapers, according to a study by the Los Angeles Times, have formal guidelines stipulating the kinds of ads that are and are not fit to print.

The censorship of speech is even enjoying a certain popularity among students at various universities including Stanford, Michigan, Wisconsin and Emory. They seek, according to The New York Times, to outlaw or banish "racist, sexist and anti-homosexual epithets, jokes and other kinds of harassment that occur in small-group settings, when one student intends to make others uncomfortable." There is a particular irony in this; the first shot in the cultural revolution of the 1960s was the student demand at the University of California at Berkeley for "free speech" including speech thought by authorities to be obscene.

The universities, however, are not the principal locus of anti-First Amendment sentiment. The Supreme Court is a far more significant culprit, along with legislatures and other courts throughout the land. The media, with their self-censorship policies, play a large role, too.

Mr. Gartner has produced an eloquent essay on this theme for the Twentieth Century Fund, an essay written before he got a job at NBC and before he had an interest in the network's advertising revenues. His argument is simple: "commercial speech," meaning advertising, is entitled to the same protection under the First Amendment as the editorial content of a newspaper or the ravings of a street-corner orator. And in his view, the censorship policies of the media are as obnoxious as those of the government.

On that point, I disagree. There is nothing in law or logic to require a newspaper to publish whatever garbage comes over the transom or a network to put on the air every foot of film or recorded bite of sound available to it. The idea of selection is a central idea and a necessity of the news business, the idea that human intelligence is at work in deciding what is and what is not to be published or broadcast. That is what news and editorial departments do. That is what advertising departments should do as well. If we do not discriminate, if we have no values and render no judgments, it is a game for idiots. But on the main point Mr. Gartner is right: these things are not the proper business of judges and politicians.

Advertising in the Classroom

Eleanor Randolph, March 1990

Every day, your average kid watches a week's worth of television. Every days, he or she sees ads for chocolate cereal and cookies spun from pure sugar and for plastic turtles that come with a greaseburger at the local drive-in.

So, we now need advertising in schools?

Ads-in-class is the latest idea from Christopher Whittle, the hotshot entrepreneur from Tennessee. His company has produced Channel One, television news for schools, complete with advertising. In a recent test at Union High School in Union, N.J., youngsters watched news about the Berlin Wall, elections in the Soviet Union and new Army enlistment requirements. They also saw commercials for Cheetos, M & M's and Gillette razors.

Ads encouraging teenagers to buy junk food? Commercials pushing razors on a young man who has been waiting for whiskers like a farmer searching for the first buds of spring? They need this?

Whittle's proposal is ingenious, of course. He loans the schools $50,000 worth of video equipment. Many schools, especially in rural areas, desperately need such equipment. Equipment in exchange for commercials, some educators say. What's the big deal?

Samuel Fortunato, Union High's principal, told a reporter recently: "Kids see plenty of TV commercials before and after school, and they can walk into our library and pick up a magazine with a dozen ads in it. So, this doesn't bother me."

Here is why it should bother Fortunato: In return for the equipment, the school agrees to show Channel One to 90 percent of the student body every day. Is this the way to get more money for schools? If Tylenol financed the school gym, would the administrators agree to start passing around capsules every morning?

Sanford Ungar, dean of the school of communication at American University, is like many in the media. He sees nothing wrong with the commercials, saying, "To be outraged by commercials in American society is to be outraged that there is gambling in the casino." But the promise by teachers that 90 percent of their students will view it every day "smacks of force-feeding," he said.

Exactly. What we have here is a captive audience. Okay, class? first we will pledge allegiance to the flag, and then we will watch 12 minutes of Whittled news. No talking.

The whole scheme is reminiscent of Whittle's proposal for another captive audience: patients stuck in doctors' waiting rooms. His plan was to clean up all of the messy magazines in doctors' offices— those People magazines that featured Cary Grant or last decade's Newsweek. If doctors would cancel all but two other magazines, he promised to provide a little rack and a series of large magazines—like publications called "Special Reports". These reports would have articles especially for people in waiting rooms. Of course, they also would have ads for people in waiting rooms.

Having found myself in a doctor's waiting room recently with only "Special Reports" to read. I can say with authority that they are hazardous to my mental health. They are filled with warm, mushy stories, like printed Muzak. They make my blood boil and just in time for a blood-pressure check.

Like many of Whittle's ideas, Channel One has sparked debate that sometimes seems to border on verbal war. Some educators are outraged and several states—including California, New York and North Carolina—have banned the enforced daily viewing. Many of these schools have opted for a plan from Cable News Network, which allows teachers to tape a news program, play the cassette in class and talk about the news while using teaching aids providing by CNN.

Also, there is no agreement that teachers must use the CNN cassette in order to acquire the teaching tools provided by the network. The CNN show has no commercial advertising, although technically it does advertise for one product—CNN.

One thing is certain: If a goodly number of schools accept Whittle's deal, he will become stupendously rich. He won't say how much his company will make from Channel One, even though he told reporters that he has sold more than $200 million worth of advertising for the first three years at a cost of $150,000 a second.

One television executive who has been watching Whittle's moves toward teenage customers said that, when it comes to the price of advertising, "if it works, each day will be better than a Super Bowl."

No one can blame Christopher Whittle for trying to sell his idea to the schools. The tragedy is that too many educators are willing to buy it.

CHAPTER TEN

Media and Society

People Do Understand the Media

James R. Dickenson, February 1986

We in the press have been sensitized for years now to the fact that many conservatives believe that there is a liberal bias in the media. We understand that while few really think that many of us actually are subversives, they do harbor deep suspicions that—at the least—we have more than our share of irresponsible opportunists who are a burden to democracy and weaken the national security.

A number of recent polls are even more unsettling to reporters. They appear to reflect public support for everything from the military excluding the media from the Grenada operation to libel suits against major news organizations. And they have reinforced the concern of many of us in the news business that there is a serious problem with Americans supporting or even understanding a free press.

It wasn't always like this. My recollection of 25 years ago, when I started out in the newspaper business, is that most of my friends and relatives thought I was working in a conservative institution, albeit a raffish and disreputable one.

But a number of factors—including the deep national divisions over the Vietnam war and Watergate, the emergence of network television as a national institution and the rise in journalists' educational levels—have changed the public's perception of us over the last two decades.

Whatever the reason, we tend to worry about the First Amendment and maybe feel just a little bit sorry for ourselves. A new and provocative study of public attitudes toward the media by the Times Mirror Co. suggests, however, that our biggest mistake may be our misunderstanding of what the American people think of us.

A national sample of more than 2,000 who were interviewed and re-interviewed in depth by the Gallup Poll indicates that the citizenry is much more supportive of the media in general and news organizations and individual journalists in particular than we realize. It also shows that the public is more discriminating in its attitudes toward the press than many of us think and that its opinions cut across ideological, social and economic lines much more than we thought.

The public thinks we are too much influenced by and dependent upon government, special interests and other institutions we cover and by the need to attract a mass audience. They also think we are often biased—liberally biased more often than not—and unwilling to admit error.

Thus, the major fault the public finds with us, according to this study, is that these shortcomings get in the way of our proper function of acting as a "watchdog" on the government and other powerful institutions. One of the most striking findings of the study is the high value most people place on this function and their criticism of our weakness in performing it.

Only a third of the respondents are aware that freedom of the press is guaranteed by the First Amendment. But in nearly every question involving government control or interference in disseminating the news, a majority—mostly two-thirds or more—support the media against the government.

The percentage of those who believe that "press criticism keeps political leaders from doing what should not be done" ranges from a low of 61 percent (non-whites) to 75 percent (college graduates). This approval cuts across every age, educational, occupational and political group "strong conservatives" agree with it by 66 percent, "strong liberals" by 75 percent.

When asked about the controversial publication of the "Pentagon Papers," the documents outlining the U.S. involvement in Vietnam, a whopping 66 percent approved publication while only 21 percent were opposed. Nearly 80 percent believe that a reporter sometimes "should be allowed to keep his source confidential if that is the only way he can get his information."

But when the conflict is between the press and individual rights, the press loses ever time.

Forty-nine believe that the growing number of libel suits is a good thing because they help keep the press under control and from becoming "less responsible" in dealing with individuals.

Only 23 percent define freedom of the press as the freedom to "report what it chooses." Sixty-one percent define it as the "public right to bear all points of view."

All of this is a remarkably discriminating view of the media, even where contradictory.

The study turned up other surprises for journalists. One is that for all the criticism we feel, people really don't think or talk about us much of the time. Only about 20 percent talk about us some of the time, which ranks us in interest behind, in this order, political leaders, entertainers, doctors, athletes, lawyers, clergymen and businessmen. The only group that stimulates less conversation than journalists is scientists.

Another is that for all the criticism and lack of talk about us, people like us to a remarkable degree.

About 70 percent are generally favorably disposed toward the media. Only about 15 percent find little or nothing good about us. Ten percent of these feel alienated from every major institution and the other five are our informed, vociferous, predominantly conservative and Republican critics—who question our morality, patriotism, competence, honesty and independence.

But most people like us because, for all the criticism, they think we're competent and believable—and they like the news. They like being informed. One of the most interesting findings is that during the TWA hostage crisis, which brought our critics out in full voice, the public's positive attitudes about us increased.

What conclusions can we draw from all this?

One is that we may be better off in terms of public support than most of us realize but that we still have a long way to go. Another is that the best way to counter our critics is simply to do what we pride ourselves in most—being fair, competent, accurate, thorough, independent and tough. And to never forget that we can always do the job better.

Bart Simpson:
Underachiever and Proud of It

Eleanor Randolph, May 1990

Bart Simpson is a jerk. Simpson, for those who have been in a time capsule the last few months, is a cartoon character who has become the mascot for a whole generation of teenagers and pre-teens. He and his slug of a family appear as part of the Sunday evening fare provided by Fox Television. This National Enquirer of networks, with three of the least-watched shows on television, has a winner with "The Simpsons."

Each week, the show brings about 10 million families together around the television set to watch little Bart, whose name could be spelled Brat with the slide of a letter. Bart is an offensive, 10-year-old loser who says things like "Eat my shorts"—not to his sister but to his father.

At school, he's worse and proud of it. He's the kid who sasses the teacher, plays tricks on the substitute, digs a hole for himself and jumps into it, while the whole class and most of the country laughs.

Here in this tourist city, Bart is everywhere. The favorite T-shirt this year features the little geek whose face is so misshapen that he would need plastic surgery to become ugly. Along with it is Bart's golden rule: "Underachiever: And Proud of It, Man."

Okay, okay. Bart Simpson is a cartoon character. Don't have a cow, as Bart would say to anybody as big and old as I am. This is fun; it isn't real.

Unfortunately, the problem with Bart is that he is real. In a recent Washington Post article, a black youth who wanted to do well in school said his worst problems came during his teens. He was called a bookworm, uppity. "There were a few times when I did almost succumb to the pressures," said Michael Coles, who had just won a scholarship. "But, at those times, I decided that, even if I had to walk alone, I should give my future the best shot that I can."

Alone? Through an army of proud underachievers, through a mass of mean little Bart Simpsons? How did we let this happen?

Newsweek magazine, which recently featured Bart and his family on the cover (the Simpsons sell more than T-shirts), said that during a focus group of boys between ages 10 and 14, Bart was their main man, equal in popularity to Michael Jordan and Bo Jackson.. "They see him as a misfit but cool," researcher Selina Guber told the magazine. "They think, 'There's a guy like me.'"

Not quite. Cartoon characters don't have to grow up. Bart's creators have talked about a fast forward to the little beast's adult years, but whether the viewers would go for such a depressing segment is anybody's guess.

The Bart Simpsons in real life are a lot of fun in junior high and high school. When the rest of the world goes off to college or computer school, Bart snarls around looking for a job. He can keep a few at minimum wage but, as a man without motivation, he will stay there.

At Bart Simpson's 20th high-school class reunion, the guys who laughed loudest at Bart will be back to talk about their new jobs and their new rec-vees and their new children. Where is that Bart Simpson? What a card he was? Didn't make it to college? Didn't get a good job? Aw, that's too bad. Sells scuba gear. Hey, how's it going for him? Drinks too much and gets rowdy, sort of a sad case, our Bart. Aw, that's tough. Keep him on the other side of the room, ya hear.

Some experts figure that Bart's popularity comes from the way he mirrors the lives of so many people who are having a tough time in this society. Fine. But Bart does more than reflect. He also teaches. He teaches kids that they can fail at school and still be cool.

When teachers began protesting that Bart's philosophy is contrary to that of most educators, the protests brought sniggers from Fox. Bart is the big ticket for Fox, where most of the rest of the programming barely registers on the Nielsen scale.

So, it comes as no surprise that Sam Simon, co-executive producer of the show, told the Associated Press recently: "I don't think it's the job of elementary school principals to pick the role models for their kids."

Well, maybe Bart won't grow up to be a loser after all. Maybe he can be a co-executive producer for a Fox Television show.

Director Spike Lee's Wake-up Call

Donna Britt, June 1989

Fresh off the red-eye from L.A., Spike Lee wheezes and sneezes over waffles and lemon tea at a downtown restaurant. The incendiary director-writer-actor—known for his righteous, brother-with-a-mission ire—looks doused. He's as sick as sin and tired as a toddler after a two-hour tantrum Lee blames his current malady on a too-tight schedule and an addiction to chocolate malteds ("Dairy products and white sugar," he sighs, "are worse than cocaine"). But anybody who knows him might suggest he's always sick and tired:

Of people who assume that Oprah's, Cos's and Eddie's popularity means all blacks have made it. Of "bourgeois, BMW Negroes" who decry his cinematic interpretations of black folks' failings. Of whites who won't give him his propers—like the jury at the Cannes Film Festival, which snubbed his critically praised new film, "Do the Right Thing," by denying it any of the 10 prizes awarded "We got robbed, gypped, jerked around—they gave us the okey-doke," he says now).

The creator of "She's Gotta Have It" and "School Daze" is particularly put out by critics who diminish or suspect his work, such as those who suggest that the glossy and powerful "Right Thing"—in which blacks angry over a police killing incinerate a neighborhood landmark—could actually incite race riots this summer.

"People don't need my films to make them angry," says Lee, pushing aside his tortoise-trimmed glasses to dab at big, damp eyes. "My films are designed to provoke thought and discussion about the number one issue in my eyes: racism. People are under the illusion that racism is gone, dormant, a thing of the past."

He shakes his head.

"Did they show 'Do the Right Thing' in Miami during Super Bowl week? I mean, the black folks in Liberty City must have it on videotape, on cable." His laugh, a high, Muzak-shattering cackle, is unexpected. "They must have it on Black Entertainment Television?"

But suddenly, he's serious.

"It's cops killing innocent black people," he says quietly. "That's what makes a riot."

That's exactly what happens in "Right Thing." It happened, Lee says, over the past several years to the six black New Yorkers to whose families the film is dedicated. But despite Lee's obvious rage, despite the title of his already controversial film, Lee has no intention of telling anybody—even the folks who, "by saying the film incites violence, are belittling its audience"—what the "right thing" is to do.

"I don't want anyone to come to my films thinking Spike Lee is gonna give them the answers," he says. "I just think black people need to wake up. It's no coincidence those were the last words in 'School Daze' and the first in 'Do the Right Thing.' Wake up!"

Jarring a drowsy movie-going public is Lee's particular mission. At 32 ("young and tender, like a Perdue chicken," he jokes), the man's a skinny, 5-foot-7 alarm clock. He's planning a special screening of "Right Thing" for two of his least-favorite sleepyheads, New York Mayor Ed Koch and black Police Commissioner Benjamin Ward ("I can't invite them to the regular screening—they'd be hooted out of there").

Certainly nobody slept through Lee's first feature. "She's Gotta Have It" detailed one woman's unapologetic sexual exploration with three wildly different partners and gave many audiences their first glimpse of frank black sexuality on screen. "School Dazes'" depiction of coeds and coolsters squaring off over skin color during homecoming weekend at a fictional black college generated a rumpus regarding African Americans' centuries-old schism over the issue. He says his next film, "Love Supreme," will star Denzel Washington in a jazz-tinged exploration of the relationship between black men and women.

"Do the Right Thing" takes on the world—or a Brooklyn-based microcosm of it. The action takes place on one Bedford-Stuyvesant block on one sweltering day, a day so hot that one character gives his girlfriend an ice-cube massage; so hot that a neighborhood disc jockey warns local residents with jheri curl perms to stay indoors or they could end up with "a permanent plastic helmet on yo' heads." Inflamed by the heat, African Americans, Koreans, Hispanics and Italian Americans step warily around each other, hurling rap-tinged litanies of racial epithets. The film climaxes in flames, rioting and a death.

Lee does make efforts to balance "Right Things'" violence with the notion of peaceful protest. The film closes with eloquent quotes from both nonviolence advocate Dr. Martin Luther King and the more inflammatory Malcolm X—men whose messages Lee calls "equally valid." Critics' too, are divided. In an unusual move, the current Newsweek features dueling reviews of the film—one praising it as "honest . . . bracing and necessary"; the other denigrating it as "an evasion of the issues" that irresponsibly places "dynamite under every seat."

Of course, Lee heartily disagrees with the latter. But that doesn't mean he feels African Americans shouldn't be angry."Black people have every right to be angry—if anything, we're not angry enough, let too much stuff slide," he says. "We forget . . . the injustices that have been done to us. We could learn from Jewish people—from here to eternity, there will be plays to be produced, books to be written, movies to be made about the Holocaust. It will be dealt with and that's great.

"Now we say"—his voice lowers to a weary drawl. "'We-ell, let bygones be bygones. Don't worry, be happy. We are the world. Thank you, Jesus.'" Again, his cackle reverberates through the restaurant. Then, just as abruptly, it stops.

"But we've got to turn that thing around," he says slowly. "In D.C., these ignorant brothers have got to stop killing each other; selling this crack. They're doing it for the money; these kids aren't going to work at McDonald's for minimum wage anymore. As the saying goes, they wanna live large.

"But what it comes down to," he says, "is recognizing the difference between right and wrong. And acting on it."

For Lee and for many of the people who inhabit his movies, what's right is obvious; acting on it is a given. As a child, he has said, he knew there was nothing right about the way black folks were portrayed in movies—when they were portrayed at all. So it felt quite right to the grown-up Lee when, as a New York University student, he used his Super-8 movie camera to record the slices of black life that nobody else seemed terribly interested in depicting.

His award-winning 1982 student film, "Joe's Bed-Stuy Barber Shop—We Cut Heads," was followed by the movie that made him something of a media sensation—1986's "She's Gotta Have It." Made for an almost unheard-of $175,000 (raised through friends, grants and anybody he could get to contribute), the movie garnered critical valentines, crossover audiences and an eventual $7 million gross.

It felt utterly appropriate to the director to make a movie loosely based on his experiences as a student at Atlanta's all-black Morehouse College. "School Daze," he decided, would shine an unsparing light on blacks' discrimination against each other on the basis of hair texture and skin color.

And though he's glad to have instigated the ensuing controversy. "This film is going to cause havoc," he gleefully told The Washington Post several months before "Daze's" release), some black folks' reactions, he says, couldn't have been more wrong-headed.

"All the criticism I've ever gotten on the film was from those bourgeois, chicken-and-biscuit Negroes who say, 'Why are there no positive images of Negroes? . . . Why open up a can of worms, reinforce what white people think of us?' If all my films were like the Huxtables, they'd be happy."

For somebody whose only knowledge of Lee has been gleaned from interviews focusing on his angry commentary on racism's effects, Spike-the-man is a bit of a surprise. Maybe it's the cold he's nursing; perhaps it's the effect of those striking, leap-out-at-you eyes, or his pigeon-toed gait. But in person, Lee's sincerity buffers the sting of his words.

His intensity also is tempered by his humor, that wild man's laugh. It ricochets around the room when he refuses to answer questions about his love life. ("I'm married to cinema," he snorts), and when he recounts an article he read about Redskins quarterback Doug Williams's recent marital problems. Suddenly, he's inspired. Certain prominent black men's experiences with "skeezers"—beautiful women with dubious motives—could be incorporated into black vernacular using the men's names: "A man could say, like, 'Man, she Douged him,' or 'Watch out, that woman tried to Tyson me."

But however much he jokes, Lee seems incapable of betraying his special vision. Hailed as a feminist for writing "She's Gotta Have Its'" independent heroine, he was excoriated by some for "Daze's" portrait of black coeds as whiners obsessed with hair and skin, and largely controlled by skirt-chasing men. "When I went to school at Morehouse, men ran stuff," he explains now. "I think some critics thought that I feel about women the way those men did. I don't—but there are men who feel that way."

Lee refuses to write movies that put a happy face on what he sees as black folks' challenges. In "Right Thing," certain characters are chided for their lack of initiative, their empty bragging. Mookie, the pivotal character played by Lee, is, by the director's own admission, "irresponsible, lazy . . . the type who'll bring children into this world without taking care of them." He shrugs. "All of my characters are flawed."

But they're much more. In this movie, Lee does what no filmmaker in recent memory has managed: goes into the ghetto, the 'hood, and honors its residents by showing them as worthy of more than fear, contempt or pity. Lee's creations generate affection, laughs, even respect—while remaining true to their real-life counterparts.

Where African Americans are concerned, Lee sees himself as a loving brother whose criticism is balanced by his regard; in fact, his barbs are a natural extension of it. "The baseball coach . . . is gonna be harder on his own son or daughter than anybody else. I'm harder on my siblings than I am on other people I know. It's love of black people that

motivates me. That's why I get upset when we do all that other stuff—
the jheri curls, nose jobs, crack."

Like many minorities aware of racism's nuances, its endless
variations, Lee has a hypersensitive antennae that has the potential
to both better and betray him. He sometimes seems suspicious of the
best-intentioned criticism. Early on, he tended to dismiss even the most
thoughtful blacks' concerns about "Daze" as misguided rantings.

Yet, when Lee's eagerness to explore black life in its tiniest detail
fuses with his appreciation for the beauty in the everyday, something
marvelous can emerge: a celebration of the race; a validation of
things—as he and pal Wynton Marsalis jokingly put it "negroidal." It
happens in "She's Gotta Have It" when its heroine lovingly oils the
hair of one of her amours. It happens in "Right Thing" when three
street-corner philosophers "woof," or bluster, about everything from
their conviction that they could soundly beat Mike Tyson's butt to
Koreans' seemingly effortless success at corner-store marketing.

For many black people, seeing slivers of their real, heretofore-
invisible lives on screen can be startling. That's why dozens of black
women, says Lee, effused to him about "Have Its'" hair-oiling scene.

"It's that 'negritude'—whites will never understand that," Lee
muses. "Every black woman in life has massaged her boyfriend's scalp,
greased it with some of that Posner, that Sulfur 8," he says, laughing.
"And every black man with some sense has gone back to her again and
said, 'Grease my scalp.'"

Conversely, he's averse to putting what many whites assume
about black life in his films. Recently, he's been questioned by some
critics about the lack of drugs in "Do the Right Thing."

"I made a conscious decision to leave drugs out—that's another
movie," he explains. "This film is about racism. . . . When white people
asked me about that at Cannes, I said, 'Look—drugs permeate all of
society. You didn't ask Barry Levinson on "Rain Man" where the drugs
were.' They say things like, 'The streets [in "Right Thing"] are too
clean—where's the garbage, the murderers, the teenaged mothers
throwing their babies out of the window?' "When you don't give them
that pathos, what they expect, they say you're not being realistic."

What's real, says Lee, is that despite their failings, despite how
far they have to go to meet his and their own expectations, black folks
really are "a great people."

"We produce the greatest artists in the world; put our imprint on
music, dance, the art world. Definitely on sports. Film and TV are next.

"For me, it's about loving blacks and then pullin' their coattails. .
. . I've said that Eddie Murphy could flex his muscles more. He has

made a billion dollars for Paramount—do you know how much money that is? And there's only two black executives at Paramount."

The criticism, the righteous taking to task, swings both ways, he says. Not only is Lee capable of being hard on himself. "I can't even watch 'She's Gotta Have It' now—the acting, the directing," he says—but those he loves best also keep him in line.

"Shoot, black people keep after me. They say, 'Why you do dat, Spike?' 'I didn't like that one—do another movie about that.' And I listen."

He sneezes again. And smiles.

"Oh, yes, I listen."

The News About Women

Eleanor Randolph, April 1989

To a group of about 400 people, mostly women, who were talking about their problems getting ahead, Joseph Ward of Marymount University in Arlington asked a tough question. He wanted to know how he would fare in the scramble for jobs in the newspaper or television industry.

Describing himself as a "young white male" at the conference on Women, Men and Media yesterday at the National Press Club, Ward addressed his question to Carole Simpson, a black senior correspondent at ABC-TV in Washington.

"Why did you ask me that?" groaned Simpson, who then began to wrestle with the tough answer. "I feel sorry for you right now," said Simpson. "I think we're at a period of time where there is some compensatory time due. I suffered discrimination for many years; many people I know did. Thank God we're at a position now where people are saying, 'Hey, let's open this up' . . . Perhaps you are going to be at a disadvantage. That's new to you white males. And you'll see how it feels. And maybe you'll be more sensitive about the kinds of things other people go through." Janet Chusmir, executive editor of The Miami Herald, disagreed. "I don't think it's a question that he's at a disadvantage. I think it's . . . that he doesn't have such a blatant advantage."

The exchange, which came early in the day-long conference, suggested progress for women in the news business—even at the expense of some white males.

But two studies released as part of the same conference reinforced another view that, "Baby, women have a long way to go," as Junior Bridge, a communications consultant who formerly worked for the National Organization for Women, put it.

Bridge, who studied the nightly news coverage by the three major networks in February, found that women correspondents reported 22 percent of the stories at CBS, 14 percent on NBC and 10 percent on ABC.

Bridge's study, which she called a "kitchen table study," also surveyed 10 major newspapers for March. She showed that women reported 27 percent of the stories, appeared in 24 percent of the photographs and were mentioned 11 percent of the time.

Bridge said that of these 10 newspapers, Gannett-owned USA Today had the most representation from women on its front pages (41 percent of the bylines) and The New York Times had the least (16 percent).

Yesterday's conference was funded primarily by the Gannett Foundation, but Bridge said that money for the study itself came from sources other than media companies.

A second study, part of an ongoing analysis of women in the media being conducted by Jean Gaddy Wilson at the University of Missouri, was unveiled yesterday. It indicates that women who work in the media suffer from "a pay gap and a power gap," Wilson said.

Wilson determined that a female employee earns 64 cents for every male employee's $1 in media companies, which parallels the national average for all industries of 65 cents for every $1 paid to a man.

The Wilson survey of 1,599 daily newspapers, 1,219 television stations and 1,091 radio stations, also funded primarily by the Gannett Foundation, showed that 3 percent of television presidents or vice presidents are women. Six percent of newspaper publishers are women, and eight percent of radio presidents or vice presidents are women. The Gannett Foundation in Rochester, N.Y., is legally separate from the company that owns the newspaper, according to a spokesman.

Diana Meehan, director of the Institute for Study of Women and Men at the University of Southern California, said that other studies show that "what's missing here is critical mass."

Women, minorities and others, she said, "cannot do anything in lone positions. It takes about 35 percent of your own kind to effect change."

Television Violence

Eleanor Randolph, June 1989

"'Sledgehammer!' The toughest cop on the airwaves explodes into television, and he's aiming to be Number One with a bullet in your programming lineup. A proven winner . . . among men and kids. . . ."

This is an advertisement in Broadcasting magazine this month from a group trying to sell this show to the television industry. There are other ads like this throughout the television trade press, many others. Violence sells. On television blood is green, the color of money.

But any pediatrician, educator or discerning parent can tell you about a growing mound of data suggesting that the murders, suicides and fearfulness among the young are encouraged by their most forceful teacher, the television set. Consider:

—Outgoing Surgeon General C. Everett Koop found that television violence promotes aggressive behavior. The National Institute of Mental Health said in testimony in 1984 that a "sizable number of studies did support the inference that there was a causal connection between the viewing of televised violence and later aggressive behaviors." Translated, that means that, if a kid sees the Equalizer angrily blowing somebody's head off, he might think that is how adults solve their problems.

—The American Academy of Pediatrics in June 1985 said that "repeated exposure to televised violence promotes a proclivity to violence and a passive response to its practice."

—Imitation is not out of the question. More than three dozen boys or men, ranging in age from 8 to 31, have killed themselves while imitating a scene from a movie often shown on television, "The Deer Hunter." The scene showed young men playing Russian Roulette.

—Some researchers find that violence on television makes children fear the outside world. It also makes them less sensitive to the pain and suffering of others.

Most of these studies have been around for a while, but what is their effect on the television industry? TV executives weighed the evidence and weighed the money. Let's just say there was no contest.

The networks like to argue that televised violence is widely recognized as fantasy, nothing more. NBC, for example, did a survey some time ago that showed that violence on television doesn't really cause violence in the streets. If you believe that, we have several interesting studies on smoking from the tobacco industry.

The government isn't much help in this matter. The Federal Communications Commission has all but abandoned control over content on grounds that such control is unconstitutional. The networks, apparently trying to save money and compete with cable television, last year began scaling back on the people who were supposed to oversee program standards. The bad-taste testers are being retired. They're out of date; they didn't pass the ratings tests.

What this means is that the person who controls what your kids see on television is you. The networks like it this way, of course. For them, it has the ring of the Liberty Bell.

But parents know that they can't be there every minute, ready to throw their bodies in front of the big screen to blot out such midday offerings as female wrestlers who claw, bite, scratch and kick each other in the name of entertainment.

So, a modest little bill is making its way through Congress and could staunch some of the blood that flows every evening during what was supposed to be family hour.

Backed by a senatorial odd couple of Paul Simon (D-Ill.) and Jesse Helms (R-N.C.), it gives the networks and cable companies a three-year break in one small section of the antitrust laws. This loophole would allow the television industry to meet and devise its own regulations about violence on the tube. The Senate passed the Television Violence Act, 91 to 0.

In the House, where the legislation stalled in the past few years, the new Judiciary Committee chairman, Jack Brooks (D-Tex.), has supported the proposal. There are now modest hopes for this modest bill.

The huge lobbying arm of the television industry is not waving the flag on this one. To oppose this anti-violence bill directly is like being pro-violence. But the moguls say they are worried about liability—for instance, can they be sued by a writer if they cut out the gory murder scene? Some civil libertarians suggest an implicit threat that, if television doesn't clean up its own house, Congress will move in soon with the industrial-strength lye soap.

Congress can't do the housecleaning. Most of the bill's backers agree that such legislation would be unconstitutional. But even Congress is ready to provide guidance.

By age 16, an average child has watched more than 20,000 hours of television. If all of those murders and exploding cars are pure fantasy and children don't believe it, somebody forgot to tell the television advertising salesmen.

The industry boasts that a 60-second ad sells soap and cars and senators. Okay, but that means 20,000 hours sells a lot of blood and guts.

Jim Henson and the Truth of Children's Television

Eleanor Randolph, May 1990

How are we going to break it to the kids that Kermit the frog died last week? And Miss Piggy too. And those two old geezers sitting in the balcony, and that rock-and-roller who seemed to be nothing more than ostrich feathers and a pair of shades?

They all caught a rare kind of pneumonia and died last week with a person the kids never saw but nevertheless knew named Jim Henson. Like a lot of parents, I have tried to think of ways to be upbeat about this departure, but I can't. Two reasons loom larger than the rest.

First, Jim Henson brought joy and light and education to children's television. Second, when you take away Henson from the TV lineup for kids, you're talking intellectual junk food. Starving young minds have just been robbed of their meat and potatoes.

There are plenty of choices for our children who learn, from us, that entertainment comes in a tube. Like chips off the old couch potatoes, the kids quickly pick up our habit. Children aged 2-5 watch television 27 hours and 49 minutes a week, according to a recent Nielsen annual report. The older ones, aged 6-11, watch a little less, because many of them are in school. They average 23 hours and 39 minutes a week, the report said.

What are they watching?

If they are tuned to a broadcast network, the chances of getting something even slightly educational are minuscule. Squire D. Rushnell, former head of children's television at ABC from 1974-89, wrote recently that in 1980 the networks had an average of 11 hours and 15 minutes a week that could help educate kids (teaching them their ABC's and how to cross the street). Public broadcasting offered 20 hours a week.

Now, he noted, the three major networks offer a total of about an hour-and-a-half a week. PBS delivers 12.

The reasons are not hard to figure. First, Ronald Reagan deregulated the television industry. Broadcasters celebrated this deregulation. It meant that the marketplace would determine what we see. You and I would have more control over what to watch, not some committee in Washington.

But the market theory doesn't work for a three-year-old.

Little Samantha doesn't really know when she's being educated and when she's been rocked to a state of near somnambulism by the cartoon characters in front of her. She is not going to say; "Mommy, change the channel. I'm not improving my mind." "Marketplace competition is never going to give educational television its due," Rushnell told me the other day. "It's kind of like news. If broadcasters started broadcasting news for a profit motive, there would have never been any news."

Rushnell, who has started his own production company and hopes to produce the kinds of educational shows that will makes these figures improve, said that most broadcasters were surprised that the television networks have stopped providing educational programming for children. "When I looked at these figures, I said, 'Holy cow, folks, we haven't been watching what is happening to us.'"

But he also says that he doesn't see any way for educational programming to return to the airwaves unless the federal government starts threatening to make moves on broadcasters.

"Kids don't pick up their socks unless their mothers tell them to do it," said Rushnell. "Broadcasters won't do it unless Mother Washington tells then to do it."

Mother Washington, it seems, is fairly bored with the kids issue. There are lots of other problems more absorbing to the Federal Communications Commission whose chairman, Alfred Sikes, works in an office with this telephone number—(202) 632-6600—and whose board members receive mail at 1919 H St. N.W., Washington, D.C. 20554, for those who are interested.

People like Jim Henson were such geniuses that their television characters could entertain and educate and even sell commercials, if necessary. But Jim Henson was a special person who felt that children deserved more than a movie about a bunch of silly little ponies—a full-length commercial really that has one main purpose, to get mommy to go to the nearest drugstore and buy all the plastic superstars.

The Muppets and Kermit the Frog could also be bought in the drugstore. But Kermit also had a soul and a great character. I loved Kermit, the reporter, on the scene when Humpty-Dumpty fell off the wall or trying to interview the first teacher in his cave-man costume. I loved him when he sang about being green.

He was more than a gimmick. He was Jim Henson's hand in a frog suit.

We have the tapes, of course, but Henson was only 53-years-old when he died and Kermit's future died with him. Kids who watch television—that is, all kids—will miss him. More than they know.

'The Media Made Me Do It'

Meg Greenfield, April 1986

A couple of weeks ago the director of the Kennedy Space Center bitterly complained about the pressure the news media had put on NASA to get on with the launch of the Challenger space shuttle. "Every time there was a delay," Richard Smith told The Washington Post, "the press would say, 'Look, there's another delay . . . here's a bunch of idiots who can't even handle a launch schedule.'" Smith was certainly right. The nagging and ridicule were merciless, unrelenting and unfair, day after day in the papers and night after night on TV. Yes, we should have been ashamed. Yes, it must have been extremely unpleasant. And yes, it was its own kind of dirty pool. But should it have entered for one second into the official calculation of when it would be safe to launch?

You can't quite tell from Smith's statement whether he is saying it did or didn't play a part: "You think that doesn't have an impact? If you think it doesn't, you're stupid." Conceivably, Smith's just saying here that the ragging humiliated NASA workers, demoralized them. But he does come close to offloading some of the blame for the launch on—who else?—the dear old media. I was still pondering this the other day when I heard a poignant young woman on TV describe her bout with bulimia; she was valiant and impressive, but she did attribute her ailment in part to the fact that—you guessed it—the media were always telling people they should be slim. I got to thinking about all the times that I as a journalist had heard official government acts that bordered on insanity and/or felony justified by a government spokesman this way: "But what would you people have said if we *hadn't* done something?"

What all this says to me is that in yet one more respect our fitting out as the great Satan of America is being completed: *the media made me do it.* It wasn't enough that we reported only the bad news, blew secrets, intruded on privacy and forgot or (worse) declined to take off our cap in the presence of our betters. We have become, as well, the Devil that didn't just tempt but actually seduced you. We are what people blame for weaknesses and failures and catastrophic lapses of judgment and integrity these days instead of "root causes," which went out with sandals and guitars. We are the new root causes. Our attention compels governments to do things they know to be risky and unwise; our revelations prompt adolescents to harbor forbidden fantasies and commit destructive acts; the celebrity we bestow entices people to terrorist crimes—or so it is said.

Maybe you will have noted that governments have been doing imprudent things and teenagers thinking unwholesome thoughts and brigands and bullies committing despicable acts since long before there were newscasts or editorial pages. True, since at least the lament of King David ("Tell it not in Gath, publish it not in the streets of Askelon . . .") leaders have been wishing they could put bad news off the record, and at least since Agamemnon chewed out Kalkhas, the pundit of his day ("You visionary of hell, never have I had fair play in your forecasts. Calamity is all you care about, or see . . ."), they have been complaining about their coverage. Moreover, history and literature are full of tales about people who met their doom by responding to a false report. The published account has always had its peril, and certainly in our time there has been plenty of reckless journalism. But none of this is quite the same as saying that what is blared out over the media megaphone represents either a taunt or a temptation too overpowering for the hapless victim to resist.

Actually, we who are the ones with tails and horns in this tableau should probably be grateful for our new opprobrium and take comfort from it. For we have become a great intellectual convenience, a national treasure, something indispensable for those who get into trouble, which is of course practically everyone. So we are safe. "Media" is a plural form and you are supposed to say media "are," yet I can't help thinking of it in the singular, since that's the way most people conceive it: as a huge, intrusive, lumbering, amorphous and amoral beast heaving around the national landscape and despoiling it, always a source of sorrow and a primary contributor to the downfall of whatever we are deploring today. I need hardly point out that none of this either addresses or excuses our true faults, which, though large, remain irrelevant to our usefulness as a blame bag.

You need to understand that this rap against us is quite different from the more common, old-fashioned complaint that we are always printing things that cause national embarrassment. The science writer John Noble Wilford cites a wonderful remark by a 19th-century paleontologist in extenuation of his going to the press with complaints about the ethics of a rival: "When a wrong is to be righted, the press is the best and most Christian medium of doing it. It replaces the old time shot gun & bludgeon & is a great improvement." This is what people used to say about the electric chair, too: as punishment went, it was humane. But what is different now is that exposure to ridicule or pressure from the press is regarded by people in our P.R.-obsessed society not as a lesser threat than that of death, but as more or less the equivalent of it. Thus the abandonment of sense and principle. The alternative was extinction: the media made me do it.

There is to be sure, a notable exception, Ronald Reagan does his share of griping about the press, and he also has been known to yield to insurmountable political opposition. But, importantly, he has built his career precisely by daring to hold out against overwhelming press admonitions and advice. From budgets to Bitburg and back again, time after time, he has withstood media derision and imprecations and also our moral certainty that he will fail if he doesn't change his tune. Not always, but usually, he prevails. It seems as though the Devil doesn't make him do anything he doesn't want to. Other blamers and hand-wringers take note: it may be the secret of his success.

Why We Aren't in Vietnam

Henry Allen

People keep telling me, "You should see 'Platoon.'" They say, "I'd love to know what you think of it."

I was a Marine in Vietnam. Every time there's a big new movie about Vietnam, people tell me I should go see it. They tell me I should read novels, memoirs and magazine articles about Vietnam, too, and see the documentaries and television shows, and tell them what I think. They've been telling me this for 21 years, ever since I got back.

"You really should read what The Times had to say about the Tet offensive last Sunday."

"You should see 'The Deer Hunter.'"

"You should be watching this Vietnam series on ABC. I'd be curious to know what you think of it."

Why?

My father was in World War II, but I don't remember anybody telling him that he really should see "The Sands of Iwo Jima" or read "Catch-22." He was interested in the war—he loved "Mr. Roberts," and "Victory at Sea"—but I don't think anybody was giving him suggested-reading lists the way they've given them to me for half a lifetime.

It's often men who missed the war who do this. They aren't looking for catharsis, tribute or memorial, like Vietnam veterans; they seem to be looking for reality, the war itself. Do they think they can find it in a movie?

Male or female, I'm talking about the crowd that got important from the middle 1960s to the middle 1970s—lawyers, college kids, journalists, academics, dinner-party hustlers. They had enough clout to stay at one remove from both reality and the draft board, and enough money to protect their naivete, which is a major asset of any ruling class. They believed life is what you think and feel. They wanted to be hip, and they thought irony would get them there. They smoked marijuana even if it made them anxious. They saw a lot of movies and believed in the media. They were the people who come to mind when somebody says that art is the religion of the upper middle class.

Since I was among the first men back from Vietnam, I assumed these people would have a lot of questions for me. They didn't.

They'd squint at me for a while, like physicists studying a stray decimal point that wandered into an equation, and decide I was

283

irrelevant. After a while, they'd tell me about Vietnam—the books they'd read, the columnists they favored, the movies they'd seen.

"I was there in 1966," I'd say.

"Have you read 'Going After Cacciato?'" they'd say. "I'd be interested to know what you think of it."

Clearly, I was no expert on Vietnam. I'd been a corporal on a pacification team in Chu Lai for three or four months before my enlistment ran out. Days, we won the hearts and minds of the Vietnamese people. Nights, we'd catch a little carbine fire and the occasional grenade. I supported the war because the best and the brightest said they thought we could win it. Later on, I changed my mind when I saw they'd been lying.

For the war or against it, people meant well.

Right after I got back home to Connecticut, the curate from my parents' church stopped by. He was fresh out of Yale Divinity School and very concerned about the war. He wanted to know how the guys in Vietnam "felt" about it.

"I don't understand," I said.

"You know, when they talk about the war, what do they say?" "I don't understand."

It turned out he wanted to know our moral positions on the war. I told him we'd been too busy to have any, where I was. He couldn't grasp this. He seemed to have a picture of us debating ethics and geopolitics under the mortar flares. Maybe he'd gotten that idea from a book, like "The Naked and the Dead."

There was the future lawyer who told me I wasn't on a pacification team in Vietnam.

"Why not?"

"Because it's a contradiction in terms."

They meant well. I've wondered if it was like this for blacks back when white liberals would start talking about reading James Baldwin, or going on a poverty-agency bus tour of Bedford-Stuyvesant; back before the black power movement told them to sit down and shut up. It's worth noting that "they meant well" is one of the worst things you can say about anybody.

The media coverage of Vietnam meant a lot to these people. They were concerned citizens. They told me that television was "bringing the war into America's living rooms." These were people who wouldn't go to a foreign movie dubbed into English—it wasn't authentic—but they thought they could know what a war was like by watching television.

They told me I should read the stories in this or that newspaper. They talked as if they made a huge difference. So I read them.

These were stories about how the ambassador contradicted himself in a press conference or Navy jets screamed north for the ninth straight day. They weren't about the war, they were about officers and politicians keeping their jobs, as far as I could see. This was sad. If ever there was an enlisted man's war, it was Vietnam, but the media—with exceptions like Michael Berr and Jimmy Breslin—kept hanging around the officers. You get better quotes from officers, and mixed drinks with ice. And the higher the officers get, the more their war is like something you can discuss at a dinner party—a theory, a movie of sorts.

Then the movies started coming out, such as "Apocalypse Now," "Coming Home," and "The Deer Hunter." People said I should go see them. They wanted to know what I thought.

I'd tell them.

"But it's such a good movie," they'd say. "How isn't it like Vietnam?"

I'd try to explain that it was just a movie, it was colored light moving around on a screen. It wasn't that these folks couldn't tell the difference between a war and a movie; they didn't want to. They were going to movies the way some people might go to church. When they liked what they saw, they wanted me to tell them that art's truths were The Truth, The Word, the war itself.

In their way, I think, they wanted to be veterans, too. They had their field jackets, their marches. One movement slogan said: Bring the War Home. This was as silly as saying that television put the war in America's living rooms, but as Kurt Vonnegut wrote in one of the most oft-quoted lines of the war era: "You are what you pretend to be."

Now we've got "Platoon." A young man who was in grade school when I was in Vietnam tells me it's "authentic." Time magazine published a cover story about it and the headline said: "Vietnam As It Really Was."

This is silly and decadent, this willful confusion of life and art. And it's dangerous. War is too wildly stupid, glorious, hideous, huge and human for us to think that art can tell us what it really is. War is a little like God—when we start thinking we understand it, we're heading for trouble.

I'll probably see "Platoon," but I can tell people what I think already—that it's a movie. I hope it's a good one.

CHAPTER ELEVEN

Media and Politics

Crossing Over from Politics to Journalism

Eleanor Randolph, May 1988

From about 5:30 p.m. until the early morning hours of the New Hampshire primary, Bob Beckel stood on an icy hotel balcony in Concord while a camera crew taped him analyzing the political scene in the state below.

News anchors from around the country, one by one, announced to their local audiences that they were about to hear from their very own political analyst. On their city's screens flashed the face of Beckel—a professional political consultant who was former vice president Walter F. Mondale's campaign manager in 1984. Beckel, as of 1988, converted to journalism, at least part time.

"I was really worried about him; it was so cold, we were pumping coffee down his throat just to keep him breathing," said Rebecca Bell, deputy Washington bureau chief of CONUS Communications, which has been transmitting Beckel coast-to-coast this political year.

"I said, 'You must be wiped out, frozen,' and he said, 'Are you kidding? This is much easier than what I did four years ago,'" she recalled.

The unwritten rule in journalism in the last three or four decades was that signing up with a political campaign jeopardized any future plans to be a journalist. With few exceptions, a journalist who started

286

working for a politician was considered to have dropped the mantle of objectivity.

Now, as several former political advisers said last week, the taboo has been lifted—especially for television. Television hires former political aides as consultants, advisers, technicians and, in a few cases, correspondents.

"The wall is gone," said John Buckley, a former press secretary for Rep. Jack Kemp (R-N.Y.) and now political consultant for CBS News. ". . . There are now a lot of people who have been active in partisan politics who have made the transition into journalism."

The wall was never solid. Pierre Salinger went from being President John F. Kennedy's press secretary to ABC News, and Bill Moyers became editor of Newsday after he was President Lyndon B. Johnson's press secretary.

But those were the special cases. What is happening now is on a broader base, and for some jobs in television, political experience or government work even seems to help get employment.

"We use the consultants mostly as brainstormers," said Thomas R. Bettag, executive producer of the CBS Evening News. "The point of consultants is that politics has gotten so damn specialized that (the media) can avoid some of the manipulation by having these guys around saying 'Wait a second? Don't you see what's going on here? They're just trying to sell a bill of goods.'"

For the political consultants, it's a chance at a second life in the campaign. "First they make a run with the candidate and, if that doesn't work, they go with the media. If their horse doesn't make it, they jump off and go into the press box," Bettag said.

CBS hired Democratic delegate expert Thomas Donilon that way. Donilon was available after his candidate, Sen. Joseph R. Biden Jr. (D-Del,) bowed out. Buckley became available after Kemp bowed out of the Republican race. Democratic pollster Peter Hart advises the network, but the favorite Republican pollster for CBS in past years, Bob Teeter, is busy. He is working for Vice President Bush.

Kevin Sweeney, who was former senator Gary Hart's press secretary before Hart left the presidential race the first time, has tried a variety of jobs including being a waiter in a posh California restaurant. As of next week, he is scheduled to be a political consultant for the CBS affiliate in Atlanta, WAGA, according to news director Mark Hoffman.

Hoffman said Sweeney has been commenting for some time on this year's presidential race. "Most of the time he is identified as a political analyst. Not every time though."

If these consultants are temporary, NBC News Vice President Timothy J. Russert and Dorrance Smith, President Gerald R. Ford's staff assistant and now executive producer of ABC's weekend news, are not.

Russert, a lawyer who was press secretary for Sen. Daniel Patrick Moynihan (D-N.Y.) and New York Gov. Mario Cuomo (D) before joining NBC in 1984, is an executive whose influence is felt in the news operation, especially during a political season.

"Having been behind closed doors, having made some of those decisions, means that when you step out of the room, you can look behind those closed doors," Russert said, adding that as a professional he's accustomed to stifling his personal views in the practice of law as well as journalism.

Newspapers seem to be more reluctant to hire people from politics or government. As Bill Kovach, editor of the Atlanta Journal and Constitution, put it: "I'm not sure that the values of a political animal and a journalist mix that easily because they are, in effect, propagandists."

But there are print exceptions. Leslie Gelb, who was a diplomatic correspondent for The New York Times, left to become assistant secretary of state during the Carter administration. He returned to The Times in 1981 and is now deputy editorial page editor. Claudia Townsend left journalism to work in President Jimmy Carter's press office. After the White House, she went to The Washington Star and then to The Washington Post, where she was city editor until she took a leave.

Reagan's former director of communications, David R. Gergen, is editor of U.S. News & World Report, and, in still another medium, former Ford press secretary Ron Nessen is vice president/news of Mutual Broadcasting System.

For those who have jumped back over the wall from politics to journalism, there are different groups of "poli-porters" or "media-pols." There are the consultants like Beckel and Buckley, who keep one foot in the political business while helping out the networks. There are the columnists, who leave politics but retain their political leanings, such as William Safire and George Will. And then there are those who make what one of them, Christopher Matthews, calls "the complete leap."

Matthews, who had been a speech writer for Carter and press secretary for House Speaker Thomas P. (Tip) O'Neill, is now a columnist and Washington bureau chief for the San Francisco Examiner. "I've wanted to be a columnist a lot longer than I wanted to be a political aide . . . . This caravan of consultants. I don't mind these guys;

I just don't want to be confused with them," said Matthews, who prefers to be linked with Safire, Will and Democratic consultant-turned-columnist Mark Shields. "I made a major change to become a columnist, a deliberate and complete transition."

Others who have made the full transition from politics into television as reporters include NBC News chief political correspondent Ken Bode, who was an aide to Rep. Morris K. Udall (D-Ariz.) in his 1976 presidential campaign, and Diane Sawyer, who worked in President Richard M. Nixon's press office before going to CBS News.

"Diane Sawyer had to overcome enormous organizational skepticism and some resentment," Bettag said. "And she did it by hard work, diligence, scrupulous fairness."

The conversion that so easily brings charges of bias sometimes works in reverse. Matthews, for example, says the Democrats often think he's tougher on them as he proves his independence.

For Beckel, it's trickier, because he could go back to politics sometime in the future. He gets criticism from both worlds.

"I get some flak from you people," Beckel said of his friends in journalism. "'This is our world,' they say, 'and you're not supposed to be stepping into it.'"

Democratic friends also get angry, he said, when he suggests as he did last year that "If 1987 were a bottle of wine for the Democrats, it would have been a miserable year."

That brought calls from people he worked with in the past and could be working with in the future who said, as he put it, "Why are YOU, of all people, raining on our parade?"

Media Consultant Fights 'Bad Boy' Image

T.R. Reid, July 1989

After building a prosperous career on his talent for tearing down Democratic politicians, New York media whiz Roger Ailes now has launched an aggressive campaign to shore up a political reputation: his own.

Thanks to his prominent role in George Bush's hard-hitting campaign for president last year, the 49-year-old Republican consultant has become a lightning rod for public dissatisfaction with negative political advertising. Ailes's adversaries are starting to use his reputation against him, a tactic that makes him fighting mad.

So Ailes is fighting back. In recent months he has threatened several political operatives—including three fellow GOP consultants—and. at least two newspapers with libel suits for criticizing his ads. Meanwhile, according to senior White House officials, he has asked his friend Bush for a more visible role as a presidential adviser to help offset his slash-and-burn image.

It's unclear whether the turmoil surrounding Ailes has had any impact on his business or on his clients' political fortunes. He said he lost the chance to land one 1990 Senate candidate, Colorado Republican Hank Brown, because of bad publicity concerning his work in a recent Denver referendum. Overall, though, "we're turning away business," Ailes said.

Political strategists for the Democratic National Committee are betting they can use Ailes's reputation against his Republican clients.

"We encourage [Democratic] state chairmen, when . . . Ailes shows up, to call a press conference and remind people of his track record," said Michael McCurry, the DNC's communications director. "The level of outrage about negative ads is great enough . . . that Ailes has become an issue everywhere he goes."

Ailes's personal level of outrage about all this is high. "I was attacked personally. They're calling me a liar," he said heatedly. "The Democratic National Committee would like to put me out of business. But not because I'm negative, because I keep beating their people."

Recently, Ailes has threatened to sue his critics. After he became the focus of sharp criticism for his role in last May's referendum on a new Denver airport, his lawyer sent letters to both Denver daily newspapers and to four political consultants warning of libel actions.

Ailes has sent both Denver papers editorials he wants them to run retracting their criticism. The proposed editorial says 'Roger Ailes has had a distinguished career as a media consultant, and it was unfair and inaccurate for us to criticize him personally.' Neither the Denver Post nor the Rocky Mountain News has agreed to run the editorial. Both papers have said their coverage of Ailes was accurate.

Ailes argued in an interview that the whole basis for the attacks—his reputation as a master of gut-punching negative ads—is mistaken. "I probably make more positive ads than anybody," he said. "I won the top award for a positive ad from the Political Consultants Association last year, the spot where Bush is picking up his granddaughter at the end. How come nobody reports that?"

James Mazzarella, executive director of the American Association of Political Consultants, said Ailes won a first-place "Polly" award—the group's version of an Oscar—in the presidential category for the 1988 campaign. Mazzarella said Ailes won for a set of three ads he submitted.

Two were positive, including the one that pictured Bush with his grandchildren. The third was the well-known "Tank Ride" ad, which showed Democratic nominee Michael S. Dukakis riding a tank in an ill-fitting helmet. The commercial derided Dukakis and misstated some of his positions on weapons systems.

Kathleen Hall Jamieson, a University of Texas scholar who studies political advertising, said Ailes relies predominantly on positive commercials. "I would guess his percentage of ads that are positive is higher than it is for a lot of the people in the business."

For better or worse, however, Ailes is best known for his attacks. "There are candidates who want to hire him just to scare other people out of the race," Jamieson said.

Ailes's negative ads often are effective. Sometimes they backfire, and those instances have led Democrats to conclude they can score points by making an issue out of Ailes.

In last year's Senate race in New Jersey, for instance, Ailes wrote an ad for Republican nominee Pete Dawkins that said Sen. Frank R. Lautenberg (D) would serve in the Senate "as long as he can make a little money on the side." The resulting furor forced Dawkins to repudiate his own commercial and helped Lautenberg to win reelection.

But the most dramatic evidence that Ailes can be turned against his clients came two months ago in the Denver referendum, when Ailes was hired to help defeat a proposal for a new airport.

"We took him on directly, made Roger Ailes the issue and it was a terrific asset for us," says John Frew, the aide to Sen. Timothy E. Wirth (D-Colo.) who ran the pro-airport campaign. "We met him in the street and shot him right between the eyes—and it worked."

Ailes's first ad for the anti-airport side in Denver appeared on television on a Thursday night. First thing Friday morning, pro-airport leaders held a news conference to deplore the arrival of a "New York media manipulator" and to warn that "the other side is going to play dirty." That Sunday, both Denver daily newspapers published editorials calling Ailes a liar and excoriating his work. The next day the pro-airport side launched television ads of its own attacking Ailes as a "master of the slick and sleazy."

In the end, Ailes's side lost overwhelmingly. However, polls had shown a majority of voters supporting the airport before Ailes went to work for the opponents, so it is difficult to measure what impact he had.

Since that referendum, Frew said, he has been deluged with calls seeking advice on how to deal with Ailes. Frew concluded that his attack on Ailes worked mainly because Ailes gave him an opening. The first anti-airport ad Ailes made included factual errors. Among other points, it put the proposed airport site in the wrong county.

Ailes today seems defensive about his work in the Denver referendum. "You can say that Ailes Communications did sloppy research," he said. ". . . But that's different from Roger Ailes is a liar, which is what those editorials said."

Whether or not Democrats can score points by attacking Ailes, there does not seem to be a general voter backlash against all consultants or their negative ads.

"I don't think the voters give a hoot who brought up an issue or who the consultants are," said John Kurzweil, communications director of the California Republican Party.

Other party leaders agree. Several state chairmen cited Dukakis's much-criticized "handlers" commercials in 1988 as evidence that attacking the other guy's consultants generally won't work.

Still, political experts can sense voters' disenchantment with negative campaigning, and they almost surely will try to capitalize on it.

In the New Jersey gubernatorial primary this spring, for example, Republican Jim Courter bought television ads reminding voters of the nasty tone of the 1988 New Jersey Senate election, when Ailes was a key player. "We had enough of that last year," the ad said.

And which consulting firm produced Courter's ad disparaging negative campaigns? None other than Roger Ailes's.

TV Marti

Eleanor Randolph, April 1990

The idea sounds terrific. Instead of ferrying troops the 90 miles from Florida to Cuba, we send Alf. We bombard the beaches with Kate and Allie. We undermine the hearts and minds of the Cuban people with American television.

The problem is that TV Marti isn't simply American television. It is U.S. government-issue television. The telecasts being tested and scheduled to start any day now will be run by the United States Information Agency (USIA) and paid for by the American taxpayer.

If TV Marti picked up network programming and rebroadcast it to Cuba, that would be one thing. But there are indications that the news and public-interest programs will be overseen by powerful forces in the Cuban-American community in the United States before they are beamed to their former homeland.

In short, the United States is spending $40 million over the next two years to air American propaganda. The last thing the poor Cubans need at this point is more propaganda.

This is how we got here: Radio Marti and TV Marti were pet projects of Charles Z. Wick, USIA director under former President Ronald Reagan. Wick believed that if the U.S. government owned a news operation, it had bought the ability to fix the news.

For many journalists working at USIA, remolding the news to fit the government line was a scandal. They wanted Voice of America and other U.S. broadcasts to be as straight as possible—as straight as the British Broadcasting Corp., which is still trusted around the world. In most cases, the VOA journalists were arguing into the wind.

When Wick began pushing Radio Marti and TV Marti, many members of Congress objected to what they believed would be overt propaganda aimed at Cuba. As a result, Radio Marti began its programming cautiously, airing soap operas, sports information, music and a popular program that allows Cubans in the United States to send voice-messages to people in Havana.

In short, Radio Marti has been better than expected. One reason is that the man who ran it, Ernesto Betancourt, resisted efforts to skew his broadcasts in favor of Cuban exiles in Miami, most of whom are Republicans.

No more. Betancourt was summarily yanked from Radio Marti a few weeks ago. A USIA spokesman said that he was needed in the research department of the agency. Sure he was.

Betancourt, a man known for straight talk, said he was ousted for two reasons. First, he refused to hand over control of Radio Marti to Jorge Mas Canosa, who is in charge of the most powerful Cuban exile organization in Miami and who is also a friend of President Bush's son, Jeb. The second reason is that Betancourt opposed TV Marti.

The Betancourt matter does not bode well for the news content of TV Marti, but there are other problems. The broadcasts appear to be in violation of international telecommunications law, which says that one government should not use more power than is necessary "to maintain economically an effective national service of good quality within the frontiers of the country concerned. . . ."

Moreover, technologically, TV Marti sounds like something out of a high-school science lab. TV Marti is scheduled to be broadcast from a mini-blimp that looks a little like an old World War II barrage balloon. It is a big gray thing that will float above one of the Florida keys. Some reports suggest that power is supplied to the balloon by a 10,000-foot cable.

"It's Buck Rogers," as one broadcasting expert put it recently.

Broadcasters are worried about whether Cuban President Fidel Castro will see this little blimp as a big target and start blasting away with his radio and television equipment at the U.S. mainland.

Castro already has fired up his big Soviet-made radio transmitters to send off a warning shot. On March 23, he gave a three-hour speech (a mere sound-bite for him) and beamed it toward Miami. All over the South Florida coast, listeners were hammering their radios trying to figure out what was happening. Fidel could be heard as far away as Nashville inveighing against the Yanquis and their electronic invasion.

Castro and his people also say they can easily jam broadcasts aimed at their island, a move that may disrupt television stations in Florida as well. Turning a television picture into a snowstorm is not particularly difficult. Anybody who has aimed a vacuum cleaner at the television set or turned on the microwave oven knows how delicate the whole system can be.

Finally, TV Marti sounds like a bad idea that became a lot worse when communism changed from the Red menace to a kind of ideological roseola.

Fidel Castro is isolated, a lonely pillar of hard-line Marxism watching the roof falling around him. The promoters of TV Marti suggest that they can speed up the demolition. They could do just the opposite. So far, the old revolutionary sounds like a man revving up for a good, long fight.

For this President, the Medium Is Not the Message

Ann Devroy, April 1989

No one is quite sure whether it was a tongue-in-cheek comment, but when White House aides recently received the routine internal memo that describes the public theme of President Bush's week, it wasn't cutting the deficit or preserving the peace or fighting drugs or promoting volunteers or enhancing competitiveness or negotiating on Central America.

It was all of those and more. The president's public message that April week, the memo noted, was "Diversity in Government."

With Bush settled into a pattern that aides say essentially reflects what Americans will see the next four years, the "Diversity in Government" phrase captures, more than anything, the scattershot style of the presidency.

The read-my-lips, fly-the-flag, jail-the-criminal campaigner of 1988 with a tightly controlled, simple message tailored for television has vanished.

In its place is a president whose day often offers a jumble of public events, tumbling over and into each other with no apparent theme and little success in dominating the news. The Bush presidency, said one analyst, will test a conventional media wisdom begun with John F. Kennedy and perfected with Ronald Reagan. It holds that a president who fails "to establish a relationship" with the nation by dominating television cannot succeed.

That Bush gets himself and his message on television significantly less than previous presidents is undisputed. The Center for Media and Public Affairs, a Virginia-based organization that monitors the nightly television news, reports that in his first 60 days in office, Bush was the subject of stories on television news 265 times, compared with 399 times for Reagan and 520 for President Jimmy Carter when their presidencies were new.

Robert Lichter, director of the center, said much of the coverage Bush does get is "reactionary," showing him reacting to events rather than initiating action. Lichter said his impression of Bush after watching the campaign and early coverage of Bush's presidency is: "The guy knows he's no good on television. You get the impression he held his nose and did it during the campaign because he was convinced

297

he had to. But now that's over and he's back mumbling and babbling and cutting off his words in mid-sentence."

One of Bush's most senior advisers, who has seen him through years of ups and downs, said Bush is an "old-fashioned politician who believes the best way to govern is from the inside . . . " by working with the parties involved to reach agreements and seeing the agreements are implemented.

"He doesn't think of television in terms of governing," the adviser said. "He thinks it's for entertainment."

Bush stated a central foundation of his presidency: That the goals he sets and the successes he thus far claims are based not on successful communication but successful negotiation.

"When I took office," he said recently, "I told the Congress that the American people hadn't sent us to Washington to bicker. They sent us to govern, to work together to solve urgent problems . . . . I think the work we've done these past three months demonstrates the value of tough, principled negotiations between Congress and this administration."

White House officials readily agree that Bush and his team make none of the Reagan-era efforts to put what one called "hot language" into a routine speech for the sole purpose of getting on television. Nor do they attempt to stage elaborate events for the television pictures they produce, or work for days on the perfect Bush utterances for television. House Minority Whip Newt Gingrich (R-Ga.), a media-age politician, said of Bush: "This is a print administration, not a television administration."

"It's not like we're trying not to get coverage," said White House communications director David F. Demarest Jr. "Not having a message of the day or a theme of the week is not necessarily a problem. I always believed that the impression a president makes is not a daily impression; it is a mosaic."

White House chief of staff John H. Sununu made much the same point, insisting that television is a part, and not a major part, of presidential communication. It is "results" and not "media manipulation" that count, he said.

There are many who suggest that even if it tried, the White House team, which has few of the key players who staged the campaign, lacks the organization and skills to use the media to its maximum advantage.

The critics cite, for example, an announcement on joining an international effort to control chlorofluorocarbons, a move hailed by environmentalists and taken by a president trying to establish his environmental credentials. Bush made the announcement in the middle of another ceremonial event, and it got virtually no television coverage. One official working on the issue noted sarcastically that while the Reagan team worked to put out its bad news in the "dead of the news night," the Bush team "seems to put its good news out that way."

One Republican strategist used a savings analogy to describe how a successful president can use television. Every nightly news appearance that helps the president, he said, is like "putting a dollar in the bank . . . You build up a lot of good impressions with frequent deposits, so when the bumps come, and they will, you got something there to withdraw. It's not that Bush is making withdrawals. It's just that this is the honeymoon, and he should be making more deposits."

Exhibit No. 1 cited in support of that thesis is the four-day trip Bush completed Thursday. It involved more than a dozen events in six states with themes that were supposed to range from competitiveness, to drugs, to the economy, to the legislative agenda. Speeches were given; crime scenes viewed; a tree was planted in North Dakota.

The trip got spotty national coverage at best, with many of the major events never broadcast on television. The most consistent media theme to emerge was a string of reports on television and in print noting the themelessness of the trip and highlighting wacky moments or Bush's mangling of the language. It was a kind of Murphy's Law trip, perfectly symbolized by radio reports Friday that the tree planted in North Dakota on the first day was, by the fourth day, infested by gypsy moths.

The trip was so roundly criticized by the traveling press, and grumbled about by some White House aides, that Demarest and White House press secretary Marlin Fitzwater held what was described as a "spirited discussion" with Sununu aboard a returning Air Force One on what went wrong and who was to blame and whether personnel changes were in order.

Participants declined to discuss the session, and Sununu defended the trip as successful and himself and the president as well satisfied with their team. But the fact that few agreed with this assessment was not lost on Bush. Reacting to the media ridicule and criticism of the trip, he said, "It is a very important thing for a president to get outside the White House and move around the country. And some of the friends that were traveling with us didn't seem to understand that, but I can tell you, I learned a lot and it was a good thing to do and I'm going to keep doing that."

White House officials, growing increasingly defensive about charges that the president has little to say and his staff has limited ability to focus a message to capture public attention, take comfort from Bush's high standing in public opinion polls. But Lichter offers a counterargument.

"The president's popularity now may be a mile wide, but it is an inch deep," he said.

"You build a lasting relationship with voters and a reputation for leadership night by night in people's living rooms. When you need to get people behind you at difficult points, you need to have formed that relationship and you need to use the media. It's not like riding a bike where once you learn how to ride it, you can forget it until you need it again and hop on. When Bush needs the media, when troubles come, he's going to try to hop on and fall on his face."

Media on a Red Leash

Richard Harwood, February 1990

Nothing is more uncertain than the nature of the "media" that will arise out of the revolutions now taking place in Eastern Europe and the Soviet Union. It has been a cardinal principle in those societies that organs of mass communication exist to serve the state. They are instruments of the ruling class, the nomenklatura, operated according to doctrinal guidelines no less inflexible than those of the Holy Roman See.

In the U.S.S.R., for example, all media assets—buildings, printing machinery, delivery systems, office equipment, newsprint, broadcasting facilities—are the property of the state, meaning, in shorthand, the Politburo. The media managers are party officials, their "journalists" acolytes and altar boys.

Today, in the warming climate of glasnost, it is tempting to say that the Soviet press somewhat resembles the United States in 1860: half-slave, half-free. But that is not quite right. Some of its elements simply have been allowed to operate on a longer leash than others. Opposing pictures of the world begin to emerge; there is ideological conflict and intellectual debate often of a higher quality than you may find in the pages of American newspapers, including this one. But this is not a product of "freedom"; it is a product of "permissiveness" that will continue only so long as it suits the purposes of those in control of the state. The father of glasnost, Mikhail Gorbachev, made that clear in October when he warned Soviet editors that the publication of "provocative" or "irresponsible" material is comparable to "a man striking a match while standing in a pool of gasoline." He subsequently fired the editor of Pravda, the official party organ, and denounced the editor of Arguments and Facts.

A "free" press requires financial independence and the protections of a legal system that has acquired social and political legitimacy. Legislation to satisfy partially one of those requirements is under consideration. It would relax some party controls over the news media, abolish censorship prior to publication and give citizens the right to create their own newspapers. If these measures are accepted, the problem of financial independence will remain.

Years after adoption of the U.S. Constitution with its Bill of Rights, American newspapers, by and large, required government or political party subsidies to survive. And in accordance with the folk wisdom—"whose wine I drink, his song I sing"—they were essentially propaganda sheets with brief life spans. The papers that found success in the marketplace emphasized news over political groveling. They attracted large audiences, which attracted much advertising, which produced large revenues and the financial independence characteristic of the American newspaper industry today. This is possible only with popular support in the marketplace.

That is being demonstrated today in the difficulties of the Morning Star, the Communist Party newspaper in England. Its circulation has shrunk during the past 40 years from 143,000 to 24,000. Its annual income has been about $2.8 million. Of that sum $1.3 million was a subsidy from the Soviet government in the form of 12,000 subscriptions. An additional $300,000 subsidy comes from a "fighting fund" supplied by Britain's Communist Party, the British Labor Party, various trade unions and the "peace movement." Last Christmas the Soviet subscriptions and subsidy were cut in half at a cost to the paper of $660,000 a year. It is now running a deficit in excess of $25,000 a month and is appealing to the public for contributions. The People's Daily World in New York—circulation 55,000—lives a similar existence. Unable to succeed in the marketplace, it survives on contributions and party subsidies.

If the press in Eastern Europe and the Soviet Union is to be free, a democratic marketplace must be created in which capital is raised and private ownership is achieved by individuals purchasing shares in media enterprises. This system, Soviet economist Boris Fyodorov recently has written, is "a human invention on a par with the wheel," a "perfect" system that balances the interests of the state in taxes, the interests of shareholders in dividends and the interests of employees in payrolls, a system that must take account in the market economy of "competition and supply and demand." It is a system in which there are losers as well as winners. That, in the Soviet Union, may be hard to take.

Swift Justice for a British Newsman

Eleanor Randolph, March 1990

My friends in the British community say that Farzad Bazoft, who wrote for The Observer, worked like a madman. What he wanted, they said, was the big scoop that would send his name clattering over the international wires.

His name came over the wires, but not the way he wanted. Bazoft was executed (March 15) by the Iraqi government. The Iraqis said he was a spy for Israel and Britain. Maybe he was overzealous. Maybe he was a little reckless. Maybe he committed a few journalistic sins. But he wasn't a spy, and he didn't do anything bad enough to die for.

Bazoft, 31, was a young man without a country. An Iranian by birth, he had been exiled by his native land. He went to London, hooked up with the news rowdies on Fleet Street and started covering the Middle East for several publications, including The Observer.

Iraq's foreign ministry invited Bazoft to visit in September to cover the Kurdistan elections. While he and other journalists were there, an explosion rocked a secret military area southwest of Baghdad. Bazoft and the rest of the media crowd tried to get to the site. They had heard that it was a chemical-weapons explosion or maybe even a nuclear plant.

At first, it seemed the foreign ministry was going to take them around the place. There were rumors that a car would be sent. The car never came.

Some of the other journalists set out for the site. They were turned back. Bazoft made it. He got there because he charmed a British nurse into driving him to the area in an ambulance. He had disguised himself as a doctor.

According to the canons of good journalism, this isn't done any more. Disguises, once considered a necessary skill in the trade, are considered disreputable. In the United States, reporters can be fired for it. Clearly, it's not a hanging offense.

When Bazoft got back to the hotel, he showed other journalists drawings he had made and shared some of the news he had found. He also called his London office to tell about his scoop. How many spies who had cooked up a disguise to get to a secret military operation would then brag about it on a phone that probably had more ears than a cornfield?

What happened after that call is not very clear. Perhaps Bazoft got word that he was in trouble. Some friends said he was acting strangely. At any rate, his adventure didn't end as well as Mel Gibson's in "The Year of Living Dangerously." Bazoft was arrested on his way to the airport.

After weeks in solitary confinement, he "confessed" that he was a spy. According to the state-run papers in Iraq, it is an elaborate confession, full of details about a mysterious spymaster named "Michael."

Later, Bazoft told British officials that he made up the spy story because he thought that it would help him to get out of jail. At his trial March 10, he said the confession wasn't real. He didn't mean it, he said. But it was too late in the kangaroo courtroom that allowed him no witnesses, no British lawyer, no defense.

The British tried mightily to get him back. Prime Minister Margaret Thatcher protested. Britain's Foreign Secretary tried to see the Iraqis to protest and was told in polite diplomatic language, to buzz off.

Then, when the global outcry seemed to be increasing, the Iraqis apparently became irritated about it. So, they proved that revolutionary justice can be swift. Bazoft was hanged shortly after dawn, and his body was carried to the British Embassy. The chief spokesman for Iraq told reporters: "Mrs. Thatcher wanted him alive. We gave her the body."

On one level, this serves to remind that being a foreign correspondent isn't all that Mel Gibson made it out to be. It's dangerous. Terry Anderson, an American correspondent for Associated Press, has been in a basement somewhere in the Middle East for five years. The Committee to Protect Journalists reported on March 16 that a record number of journalists died last year trying to do their jobs.

It also serves to remind the world of something that the Iraqi government has been trying to veil in recent months: Iraq has a long way to go before it arrives in the 20th century. For years, the country has been criticized for its prehistoric human-rights record. Dissent is stifled by means of the ultimate censorship: torture and death. State Department officials, in their latest catalog of human-rights abuses throughout the world, called Iraq's record "abysmal."

They were being nice.

The President's Public Events Man Attempting 'Moments,' Not Messages

Ann Devroy, April 1990

The day after President Bush's trip to Toronto last week, Sig Rogich, the man in charge of how Americans see the president, told a reporter how pleased he was with the day-long visit. "Good news coverage," he said.

When it was pointed out that no news of the Bush visit had appeared on the network television news shows, Rogich replied, "Oh, I didn't see the news. I read the papers."

In Ronald Reagan's White House, where Michael Deaver's theme-of-the-week, message-of-the-day and sound-bite-of-the-hour approach dictated the president's activities, such an admission would have been heresy or a lie. But in the Bush White House, the evening news is not required viewing, mainly because the president is only infrequently on it. There's only occasionally a theme for the week, much less anything like a message of the day, and Rogich, the man who holds what could be called the "Deaver job," says that what he does are "moments," not messages.

Six months into his tenure as the man in charge of Bush's public events, Rogich, a 45-year-old Las Vegas advertising executive, exemplifies a major difference between the past and current administrations. While Rogich has a chunk of the "image-making" part of Deaver's job, his role is far more narrowly defined.

If Deaver's job was to make sure Reagan got on television with a message scripted for him, Rogich's job is to make sure that when Bush has something to say, the setting enhances the message. "I oversee and coordinate events for the president," he said, "I make sure that the setting is right so that it amplifies what he is going to say or do. The president, after all, is the one who decides the message and delivers it."

This administration, Rogich said, "does not contrive events to get news coverage."

As one of the most traveled presidents, Bush gets massive local coverage wherever he goes. As for striving for routine national exposure of the president's views, "I don't think we consciously think about it one way or another," Rogich said. That is evident in the result. According to the Center for Media and Public Affairs, which monitors the nightly news shows, in his first year in office Bush was the subject of only one-third the number of television news stories that Reagan was during his first year.

A senior official who served in the Ford, Reagan and Bush administrations said, "While Reagan used the media, most presidents are used up by it. Bush is aware of that and has taken a different tack."

In what one outsider mockingly described as the "hi-where'd-you-prep" administration, Rogich adds an exotic flavor. Clothed in elegant designer suits and exhibiting an unabashed joy at being part of the White House, he stands out among his tightly controlled colleagues in their crumpled, indistinguishable blue and gray suits.

When earnest aides earlier this month were debating the latest Soviet moves in Lithuania or the status of the Clean Air Act, Rogich was headed to Denver to watch "his" team, the University of Nevada-Las Vegas Runnin' Rebels, win the NCAA basketball championship. Rogich recruited UNLV's controversial coach, Jerry Tarkanian, 13 years ago when he was part of an alumni group working to build a sports program at the school.

Most of Bush's top aides have spent their lives in government or politics, and mostly in the East, making Rogich sometimes seem like a visitor from another world. He has spent all his working life in Nevada, acquiring part ownership in casinos, a seat on the state commission that oversees boxing and friendships with glitzy show business personalities and famous sports figures.

When Steve Studdert, the first assistant to the president for events and activities, left the White House, Bush and White House Chief of Staff John H. Sununu turned to Rogich, who built a $40 million Las Vegas-based advertising business on his skills at creating television advertising. Although not originally a Bush partisan (he worked on Reagan's 1980 advertising team and for Paul Laxalt in the 1988 primary season), he became a key player in Bush's 1988 campaign.

Roger Ailes is given the credit—or blame—for many of Bush's highly successful television ads, but Rogich, by the accounts of many involved in the campaign, was vital in turning many of Ailes's ideas into effective television and provided many ideas of his own. 'He's an artist with a camera,' said Peter Teeley, Bush's campaign press secretary. He is described as a man "who knows everything there is to know about light, camera angle, movement, composition."

Rogich is credited with conceiving and producing one of the most mocking ads of the 1988 campaign—the so-called "tank ad" that used news film of a helmeted Michael S. Dukakis riding in a tank looking more like the comic strip character Snoopy than a potential leader of the free world. The ad also listed weapons programs Democratic nominee Dukakis was said to oppose and was criticized as inaccurate by Democrats and others.

Rogich said he does not regret that ad or any of the others he was instrumental in producing, including one on pollution in Boston Harbor that suggested Dukakis would be bad for the environment and another that showed a prison with a revolving door to suggest that Dukakis would be soft on criminals.

An official of the campaign described Rogich as "not necessarily a content person. He is a guy who captures the dynamic. If you define what you want to say, there is no one better in the country at finding the pictures to say it."

Ailes, who is not well-known for sharing credit, said, "I would have to give a lot of credit to Sig. I had the vision and he implemented it."

At the White House, working with Sununu, communications director David Demerest, press secretary Marlin Fitzwater and others, Rogich offers ideas for locating and staging the president's events. "I've offered about 1,000 ideas and the White House has had the good sense to reject most of them," Rogich joked. He said the process is much like brainstorming a commercial or campaign ad.

"He has a lot of good ideas," said Bush adviser Robert M. Teeter, who worked with him in the campaign and talks with him regularly in the White House. "The president really likes him. He has a good feel for what Bush is comfortable with. His job really is to think about the things the president is doing and creative ways to do them."

But Rogich is not without his critics. A senior White House official said Rogich is having some trouble adjusting to a setting in which everything is "staffed out" to dozens of interested parties. "He's a man who has been paid all his life for having wild, crazy, creative, impulsive ideas," the official said. "It is not easy to be impulsive in the White House. Having the president do something wild and crazy is always not the best idea."

An official said Rogich has a tendency to "ignore the system" and have his plans questioned or squelched in mid-stream. "We have the tendency then to look over his shoulder to make sure he doesn't get us 56 percent into something we just can't do," he said. "He has promised 'exclusive rights' to one television network for public events, something you just can't do," one official noted. Some of his ideas, said the official, "are pretty weird, and definitely unpresidential."

Beyond the purely creative aspect of the role is the complex technical part that involves running the advance office that is in charge of setting up events. Bad lighting can ruin a speech. A snubbed local politician can blow up and destroy a carefully staged tour. An oversight can publicly embarrass the president. "If anything goes wrong, I'm responsible," said Rogich.

One senior official, who described Rogich as "a sort of glorified director of advance," said, "That's not a criticism. People want to say he's our Deaver. Well, we don't have one of those. You don't see Sig at staff meetings promoting the great idea and the grand strategy. He's this guy where they say, 'Sig, we're going to Utah and we need an event.' And he comes up with an event. And its done right and it looks good."

Rogich is credited with creatively expanding the use of presidential public service messages, such as the anti-drug messages that appeared during the televised NCAA basketball tournament and other major sports events. The norm for such messages was to have the president seated in the Oval Office while he spoke. In the NCAA spots, Bush strolls across a softly lighted basketball court to deliver his message.

Rogich's mark on the Bush White House can be seen more in the delicate television touches such as the basketball anti-drug messages than in any grand contrived scenes, officials say. Unlike many in the White House, Rogich expects his tenure in Washington to be relatively brief. He owns a million-dollar home alongside a golf court in Las Vegas and returns there often, particularly when his 17- and 20-year-old daughters are home from school. Divorced for several years, he has raised the two girls.

His business is being run by a partner and he expects to rejoin it when he returns from what he views as an interlude in his life. He is a millionaire several times over and laughs at the suggestion his White House connections will be useful in private life.

One longtime friend of Rogich said, "My real question about Rogich is whether he can tolerate White House staff work. He's an open-shirt, West coast kind of guy used to running his own operation. He's in an image-making job with a president who says he won't tolerate image-makers. What do I think he's doing there? The first thing he's doing is having a good time."

Journalism, Colombian-Style

Eleanor Randolph, October 1989

Luis Gabriel Cano does not look like a hero. He is small and white-haired, the grandfather of 13. His voice is soft. His English is stiff and measured as he talks quietly about his life and his business.

Without the Superman whiz-bang we have come to expect in our champions, it quickly becomes clear to any listener that Luis Cano and his family are brave people. They publish a newspaper in Colombia called El Espectador; their editorials say no to drugs.

Three years ago, Cano's brother, Guillermo, suggested in print that Colombian drug lords should be extradited to the United States for trial. As Guillermo's car pulled away from the newspaper's office in Bogota one evening, three people on two motorcycles suddenly appeared from the line of traffic and opened fire. After Guillermo's death, the three other Cano brothers continued running the paper. They also continued to push for locking up what Luis Cano calls "the mafia."

Thus, the revenge by this mafia continues.

On Sept. 2, a truck laden with 200 kilograms of dynamite exploded next to the Espectador building. One person was killed, and damage to the building was estimated at about $2.5 million. The explosion destroyed the phone system. It wrecked the computer network. One-third of the newsprint was ruined, and the presses were damaged. Insurance doesn't cover terrorism in Colombia. The cost of the explosion came out of the company's hide.

At the same time, drug traffickers began calling Cano's advertisers. They suggested that when they saw ads in El Espectador, they would come around to visit the advertisers. Not to buy the merchandise they explained. Not hardly.

The big businesses shook off the threat. A lot of the smaller advertisers were not so blase. They canceled their ads. Some apologized, and Cano, a man who understands fear, said he understood theirs. But, for a newspaper like this one, whose circulation is about 200,000, dynamite is mightier than the printing press. Cano, president of the newspaper company, came to the United States last week to look for help.

"If we don't receive support, we cannot continue," Cano explained as he asked about journalistic organizations that support newspapers such as his.

That Cano wants to continue is what is so astonishing to most people. There are easier ways to make money. He explains the reason: His family has run El Espectador since 1887 and is proud of its role in Colombian society.

"We have a tradition of being always against any group or any person that violates the law," he told a group of reporters and editors at the Washington Post last week. After Cano talked last week? he left us subdued about the "battles," as I often misidentify them, in the American media.

We howl when a government agency denies us information. That's legitimate, of course, but we also howl when the agency gives us information too late for our deadline. The public is not being deprived of the data, at least not eventually, but we scream anyway.

We hunker down when somebody files a lawsuit—about libel, newspaper boxes on the corner or the way newspapers compile circulation figures. Each prompts newspapers and their lawyers to decry the "chilling effect" on the First Amendment right to freedom of the press.

You want to talk about the chilling effect? Like journalists in China and South Africa and too many other places around the world, Luis Cano can talk about the real chilling effect. His newspaper, what's left of it, is crawling with guards and policemen to protect him from the live weapons of the drug lords. Haven't the drug thugs infiltrated those police or even your newsroom? he was asked.

Cano shrugged. "How could you tell?" he replied.

Bodyguards ride in his car with him. "I feel very, very uncomfortable," Cano explained. "The guard sitting next to me has a very long machine gun, an old one, and I said? 'Why don't you ask for a shorter one so that you can (move) it more quickly?'" He knows, like we know, that the guard probably cannot move quickly enough if the drug lords really want to get him. What a way to live.

Speaking to people accustomed to worrying about cholesterol and the cost of braces on kids' teethe Cano admitted: "We are worried. We are afraid. I always worry about the future of my children and my grandchildren." Then, he added: "I think that's why we have to fight the problem of drugs. If not, I don't know which world they are going to live in."

Thank you, Luis Gabriel Cano and El Espectador, for reminding us that the presses are there to fight corruption and to try to tell the truth. We've got it so easy here, we sometimes forget.

CHAPTER TWELVE

Media Law and Regulation

The Great American Cable Tangle

Tom Shales, June 1990

If the '80s were cable's decade of growth, the '90s will be cable's decade of reckoning.

From 14 million subscribers in 1980, the cable industry has grown to a current 53.9 million, about 58 percent of all the nation's TV homes. After years of delay, cable has even come to the District; nearly 53,000 of D.C.'s 252,700 TV homes have been wired.

With the growth, however, has come a revolution of collapsing expectations. In a relatively short amount of time, cable has compiled an awesome record of customer dissatisfaction: skyrocketing rates, atrocious service, and a seeming indifference, if not outright hostility, to the plight of consumers.

Sports fans have seen baseball, football and basketball games they formerly watched on free TV siphoned off to cable as greedy leagues and team owners sign lucrative cable deals. Public television has lost high-quality imported programming to higher-bidding cable channels. And the cable industry has shown itself to be not only a lethal lobbyist, but also Godzillian in its ability to stomp out competition.

There are compensating innovations that have helped give cable a degree of social worth, like the global newsgathering presence of

311

CNN, or the dogged diligence of C-SPAN, which transmits the proceedings of the House, Senate and congressional committees.

But by and large, cable has become a synonym for crumminess—an unsavory mix of R-rated movies, tattered reruns from broadcast TV, 800-numbers for buying Zamfir records and ginsu knives—and cable operators have achieved an image of public-be-damned indifference that makes broadcasters look like philanthropists by comparison.

But hey, relax. Relief is just an incredibly complicated legislative donnybrook away. A cable reform bill was approved overwhelmingly, 18 to 1, by the Senate Commerce Committee on Thursday, with ranking minority member Jack Danforth (R-Mo.) hailing it, prematurely perhaps, as "a major victory for the American public."

A House bill—expected to be weaker than the Senate's—is being forged from drafts now making the rounds on the Hill, and is expected to be ready for mark-up the week of June 25.

And a study on cable from the Federal Communications Commission (FCC) is supposed to be ready next month, though no one should expect too much from that.

It's fitting that Congress should finally, if reluctantly, try to untangle cable because Congress helped create the mess in the first place. In 1984, at the height of Reagan de-regulation fever, with the FCC obsequiously quiescent and the anti-trust division of the Justice Department in voluntary coma, Congress passed the Cable Communications Policy Act, a bonanza of goodies for the cable business and a hearty whack across the face of the viewing public.

"It was dream legislation, from the industry's point of view, the biggest giveaway in recent history," says Andrew Jay Schwartzman, executive director of the Media Access Project. "Cable operators were given an opportunity to make as much money as they could grab, and they went out and did so."

Among other provisions, the bill forbade local communities from regulating the rates cable systems charged their customers. Since January 1987, when that provision took effect, average rates for basic cable (without premium services such as HBO and The Disney Channel) have increased by 29 percent, and Danforth's office estimates that prices for basic cable have jumped 40 percent for a quarter of the nation's subscribers since deregulation kicked in.

Among the latest gimmicks by cable operators to disguise rate increases is the "tier" system in which customers are offered a choice between low and high tiers of service. Low-tier corresponds to the old basic cable, offering of local channels plus commercial-chocked cable channels such as USA and TNT.

But as ESPN and other sports channels bid huge prices for league contracts, these once-basic channels are being pushed by some systems into the second tier. Even though they still have commercials, consumers have to pay added fees to get them.

Then there's the growing pay-per-view market, channels dedicated to super sports events and pop concerts for which subscribers must pay extra. A horrifying prospect that even Congress can grasp is that treasured national rituals like the World Series and the Super Bowl could end up on pay TV, denied to huge sections of the American public. The combination of rising fees and a wretched service record would seem to spell failure for most businesses, but as an unregulated monopoly, cable has been able to enjoy a wild ride. "Cable TV has replaced the phone company as the monopoly everybody loves to hate," says Schwartzman. "If Lily Tomlin were doing her telephone operator bit now, she'd say, 'We don't have to care; we're the cable company.'"

In the late '80s, people started to get royally fed up. At a New York cable hearing last year, then-Mayor Ed Koch railed against the cable companies who were depriving some New Yorkers of, among other attractions, their beloved Yankees. "Deregulation is a fraud and a farce," Koch fumed, "and an attack upon the consumer that leaves him totally unprotected."

Rep. Charles E. Schumer (D-N.Y.), who convened the hearing, said, "Cable no longer needs the protection of congress or anyone else. The question now is, do we need to be protected from cable?"

Emblematic of the myriad grievances against the industry are those concerning Manhattan Cable, one of the systems serving New York, which had to be mandated by law to answer the telephone— within four rings—after consumers complained they could not get a response when they called.

"Manhattan Cable Television stinks," wrote Amy Pagnozzi, a columnist for the New York Post, after days of dickering with her cable company over the installation of service. "The employees are surly, the programming is dismal, the service nonexistent," she wrote. Manhattan Cable is a subsidiary of media monster Time Warner, Inc.

Rep. John Dingell (D-Mich.), chairman of the House Commerce Committee, has been among the leaders for reform. In January, he told the U.S. Conference of Mayors here that since the 1984 bill, "the rapacious cable industry has ratcheted rates-higher and higher," and as far as responsiveness to subscribers goes, Dingell said, "In the cable business, 'customer service' is an oxymoron."

When USA Today opened a 900-line to cable comments, the newspaper got more than 3,600 responses, leading it to conclude, understatedly, that "cable discontent seems to be on the rise." One caller, Steve Sutton of Bethesda, said, "Cable is the greatest argument against monopoly in America. The only way they could make more money is to go up and down the street with a mask and a gun."

Commendably attempting to deal with this mounting resentment and with a mammoth image problem, the cable business is taking some steps to upgrade service, though it remains to be seen how effective it will be. In February, the National Cable Television Association (NCTA) unveiled "industry-wide customer service standards" due to be implemented by July 1991. Systems that pass muster will get a "Seal of Quality Customer Service" from NCTA.

Among the standards: "telephone answer time by customer service representatives shall not exceed 30 seconds." New installations are supposed to be performed within seven business days and outages—when all the channels disappear—are supposed to be corrected "immediately in most cases, but in no event later than 24 hours."

Customer complaints did not seem to be uppermost on the minds of cable operators when the NCTA held its 1990 convention in Atlanta last month, however. Prior to the convention, a press release announced the agenda: "Cable industry leaders will address such issues as factors involved in building a stronger business for the long term, how to better promote and market cable television, and how to more effectively position cable in the increasingly competitive entertainment marketplace."

Jeez Louise, how much more effectively positioned could it be? Not only are most cable systems monopolies in their communities, but the national cable lobby has done a highly efficient job of keeping competitors and potential competitors locked out of the game.

Congress' pending legislation may force cable programmers to sell their products to the fledgling 'wireless cable' industry (which delivers multiple channels over the airwaves) and the young Direct Broadcast Satellite (DBS) business. Until now, wireless cable and DBS have been largely shut out of acquiring programming that is partly owned by the cable industry. Legislation might also give a break to the nation's 3 million home satellite dish owners who've been able to get some of the premium services only by paying outlandishly high fees.

The legislation also addresses the problem of vertical integration by which the largest multiple-systems operators (MSO's) also have controlling interests in the production of programming and the channels that buy it.

Unfortunately for the public, the cable industry has reached that vaunted corporate state of being able to dictate to the government how much regulation it will accept. Schwartzman says the NCTA has proven itself a potent lobby. "They've been unbelievably effective and unbelievably sophisticated," he says. "They can turn on a dime."

No sooner had the Senate Commerce Committee marked up its bill last week than NCTA President James P. Mooney declared his opposition. The bill "goes too far," he said in a statement. "We cannot accept legislation that hampers the ability of our industry to continue to grow, and to serve our subscribers."

One of the major whines of the cable biz is that if a cap is put on the rates it can charge subscribers, it will have to cut back on the generous banquet of channels it provides. In fact, many of the channels are there primarily as revenue-producers for cable systems.

Cable TV Arlington, in suburban Virginia, has increased its channel capacity in recent years, but services added include two shopping channels, three pay-per-view movie channels (one offering soft-core pornography), and the ridiculous Movietime channel, recently rechristened E! Entertainment. Twenty-four hours a day E! spews plugs and promotions for current theatrical films and pay TV offerings. One must almost admire the ingeniousness with which cable operators dream up new sources of revenue. Last year, the Time Warner cable system in Rochester, N.Y., started its own TV station and gave it a choice location—Channel 5—on the dial. The old Channel 5 was shunted off to Channel 31, a much less prominent location.

Preston Padden, president of the Independent Television Association (INTV), noted in an angry letter to the FCC and to House and Senate committees that as a major program supplier, Time Warner "sold itself its best programs" for airing on its own new channel. He also said that Time Warner had the technological capacity to program all the cable boxes in the system so that when they were turned on, Channel 5 would automatically pop up.

If this kind of enterprise were applied to programming and service, cable TV might not need the reregulation Congress now proposes.

Dennis Fitzgibbon, a spokesman for the House Commerce Committee, sounds optimistic about passage. "Our target is a bill this session, definitely," he said Friday. "There's a fair amount of momentum behind it. We have broad public support in the form of cards and letters and phone calls."

As for the Senate, its bill could reach the floor in a few weeks. With summer recess scheduled to begin Aug. 3, it really has to. The bill would re-empower local communities to regulate basic cable rates; reinstitute a "must-carry" provision requiring cable systems to allocate channels to local broadcast signals (thus preventing, among other things, a lock-out of public TV stations); and limit the growth of the giant companies that now control cable TV.

The bill essentially forces the FCC to get back in the regulation business it abandoned under Reagan-appointed chairman Mark S. Fowler, the man who said TV sets were just appliances like toasters. Albert Sikes, the current FCC chairman, is considered less of an ideologue. He is also a friend of Danforth's.

One hurdle for both bills is the very touchy and complicated matter of allowing telephone companies (or telco's) into the cable TV business in order to increase competition for existing cable systems. Naturally the NCTA, which opposes all competition for cable systems, is wildly opposed to the idea.

Of course, the legislation faces many other hurdles, one of them, potentially, the White House. In a letter to Senate Commerce Committee Chairman Ernest F. Hollings (D-S.C.), Secretary of Commerce Robert A. Mosbacher declared, "The administration opposes the current legislative proposals for re-regulation of the cable television industry."

The letter was cosigned by James F. Rill, assistant attorney general of the Justice Department's so-called antitrust division. Rill could not be reached for comment Friday. A spokesman said he was not familiar with the content of the letter.

Much more than cable rates and reruns of "The Patty Duke Show" are involved in the re-regulation movement. This, we are forever being told, is the information age, and as the wiring of the nation continues, cable operators will function with increasing authority as gatekeepers, controlling access to data, opinions and ideas.

Ideas considered threatening to the economic welfare of the cable business already have a hard time getting through. On the other hand, Ted Turner's CNN runs occasional features that point out ratings drops and other economic woes befalling the nation's broadcasters.

Information is power, and cable represents an ever-increasing concentration of that power. Reregulation is an attempt to return some of it to the people who watch and buy and vote.

Prospects for the legislation are anything but rosy, despite the momentum and the public outcries. The NCTA's statement on the Senate bill indicates a dig-in-and-fight mentality. "By the end of June, the whole thing may be dead," notes Schwartzman sadly. "At this point, it's anybody's guess. But there's still a 50 percent possibility that the last major cable legislation of this century will pass in the next six weeks.''

Fox Launching a Campaign to Ease Curbs on Networks

John Burgess, January 1990

Fox Broadcasting Co. likes to cast itself as a spirited upstart that is fast building the nation's fourth national television network. But there is one important part of network status it would rather do without—federal regulation. Next week, Fox will go on the offensive in Washington to try to keep the company free of this load.

With filings at the Federal Communications Commission, Fox hopes to reopen a debate that has divided the entertainment industry for two decades: what to do with rules that were enacted in 1970 to limit the role of networks in the lucrative ownership and syndication of programming.

Fox Chairman Barry Diller said yesterday his network, which provides programming for 129 stations, will ask the FCC to ease the limits on all networks in view of changed market conditions. The network also will ask to be exempted from the rules while the FCC considers the issue.

"Public policy has been for 40 years to increase competition for the networks," he said in an interview at WTTG Channel 5, Fox's Washington station. "We have started to provide that." But now, he said, "these antiquated financial rules" are hindering Fox's ability to grow further and provide a concerted challenge to the three major networks.

The rules were intended to rein in what the FCC and Justice Department saw as monopoly abuses by NBC, CBS and ABC. With their control of access to the airwaves, the networks routinely demanded a financial interest in shows they aired, allowing them to profit from any subsequent syndication or, critics said, to withhold shows to keep them from airing on competing independent stations. The rules barred the networks from taking financial interests in independently-produced shows and from granting syndications to non-network stations. Proponents said the rules have broken the networks' grip, helping to create programming diversity and bring large numbers of independent UHF stations onto the air.

Fox, however, argued that the rules should be changed because the market has changed, not only by its growth in the over-the-air broadcast business, but also because cable television reaches more than

318

half the households in the country and satellite dishes have become common.

Leading the fight to keep the rules has been the Motion Picture Association of America, which represents film studios. MPAA president Jack Valenti said yesterday that despite advent of cable, networks still dominate national television. The combined ratings of 76 cable networks, he said, fail to match that of the lowest-ranked broadcast network, CBS.

Valenti said he met Wednesday with FCC commissioners to argue against the Fox proposal, which is to be filed Monday or Tuesday. "It would be a travesty of justice if this rule were re-opened," he said. ". . . It's the only barrier between competition and total domination by the networks."

Fox's immediate concern is to push back the day on which it is officially designated as a network, at which point the rules would kick in for it. The rules create a dilemma for its parent, which has a large and very profitable syndication business: Should it keep the system small so that it is not designated a network, or keep it growing but rein in the syndication business?

The only FCC criteria for network status that Fox doesn't meet at present is that there must be 15 hours of programming or more per week. But it plans to introduce new children's shows this fall, which would put it over the top and bring the rules into play—unless they are changed.

Diller said yesterday it is unfair to treat Fox like the three networks, noting its annual revenue of $480 million is 4.5 percent of the total for Fox plus the three. "We're not in their world yet," he said.

In 1983, the FCC recommended easing the rules, but it never followed through, after the Reagan administration asked for a delay, and members of Congress suggested the problem would best be settled through talks between the networks and Hollywood. Talks have continued intermittently since, but produced nothing.

Capital Cities/ABC Inc., owner of ABC, said last night it would oppose any special waiver for Fox. "Fox is no fledgling company that needs every little bit of help it can get," said company spokeswoman Julie Hoover. "It is part of the third largest media corporation in the world."

The debate has been largely dormant since the mid-1980s. If it is revived now, it would be with an important shift in alliances, however. In the past, the lines were clearly defined, with networks on one side and independent TV stations and the MPAA on the other. Now, one of the association's most important members—Fox Broadcasting's parent company, Twentieth Century-Fox Film Corp.—has switched camps.

The Truth about the Fairness Doctrine

Tom Shales, April 1989

American TV stations were supposedly being freed of prior constraints when the Federal Communications Commission (FCC) summarily repealed its 38-year-old Fairness Doctrine in 1987. The rule, which required stations to give balanced treatment of "controversial issues of public importance," supposedly inhibited them from tackling troublesome hot potatoes.

In fact, says a study released yesterday, those uninhibited stations now give less time to public affairs than they did before the rule was thrown out. Comparing programming aired on commercial stations in 1988 with a similar period in 1979, Essential Information, a public interest research group, found a 51 percent decrease in the amount of time devoted to "issue-oriented public affairs" material.

Consumer advocate Ralph Nader, who founded the group, said in a statement, "This study refutes FCC predictions that repeal of the Fairness Doctrine would remove an impediment to presenting issue-oriented public affairs programming on television."

On Capitol Hill this morning, Rep. Edward Markey (D-Mass.) and his telecommunications subcommittee will begin marking up legislation that would restore the Fairness Doctrine and make it law. Markey said yesterday that the study "underscores the importance of Congress reinstating the Fairness Doctrine as soon as possible" and reveals the "intellectual bankruptcy" of the FCC's rationale for killing it.

Both the House and Senate voted to make the doctrine law in 1987, but President Reagan vetoed the bill. Reagan and his FCC clung to the idea that marketplace forces would compel stations to good citizenship, but the fallout from deregulation has been a tawdry new trend to trashy and tabloid television.

When the FCC subsequently killed the Fairness Doctrine, many in Congress considered the move intolerably sneaky, and it's been open warfare between Congress and the commission ever since.

For its study, Essential Information looked at programming on 217 TV stations in 50 markets from January through April of last year and compared it with a similar period nine years earlier. Jim Donahue, the staff researcher who wrote the report, said yesterday that local TV

Guides were used to gather programming data because the FCC no longer requires stations to make their program logs public.

"I have a feeling the FCC may not even respond to the study," Donahue said, "because they didn't collect any data to confirm that repealing the doctrine increased issue-oriented programming." Donahue said that the FCC couldn't care less about the public interest and that its decision to repeal the Fairness Doctrine was "based totally on ideology to enhance corporate interests rather than the interests of the audience."

But Sally Lawrence, a spokeswoman for FCC Chairman Dennis Patrick, did respond. "This report is nothing short of outrageous," she said. "There is nothing in my data file that corroborates this study." Lawrence said networks and local stations are doing more public affairs programming than ever under deregulation, though she conceded she did not have figures to support the idea that such programming increased once the Fairness Doctrine was abolished.

Some aspects of the doctrine remained in force after 1987, mainly those concerning ballot issues such as referendums and propositions. A report released in February by the Public Interest Research Group found many stations unaware that such provisions remained in effect. Of those that acknowledged such a requirement, the study found, 98 percent "agreed to present opposing points of view" on such issues as California's voter crusade to cut insurance rates.

But among stations that considered all Fairness Doctrine obligations to be extinct, the report said, only 56 percent were willing to give time to opposing viewpoints.

"This conclusion stands as powerful evidence that the Fairness Doctrine works," the report said, adding that the FCC "overreached its authority" when it threw the doctrine out.

According to Donahue, Patrick wants to abolish the ballot provision of the Fairness Doctrine, too, which would free stations to give completely lopsided coverage of such issues and refuse requests from opposing viewpoints. Patrick could not be reached for comment yesterday.

The report from Essential Information singles out Fox Broadcasting for criticism. Fox, owned by Rupert Murdoch, has achieved success—and some notoriety—with tabloid shows like "America's Most Wanted," "A Current Affair" and "The Reporters."

After Fox bought Washington's hugely profitable station WTTG-TV (Channel 5), the study says—quoting a former news producer at the station—"the whole public affairs staff was fired and given two weeks to find new employment elsewhere."

Told of this remark, Thomas Burwitz, vice president of Fox Television Stations Inc., said yesterday from his office at WTTG, "I really don't know what this person's talking about. To my knowledge, we have the same public affairs director and staff as when I joined."

Camel Ad Ignites Opposition

Brooke A. Masters, July 1989

"Bored? Lonely? Restless? What you need," according to a recent R.J. Reynolds Tobacco Co. advertising campaign, is a Camel cigarette.

R.J. Reynolds is anything but lonely and bored now because consumer and feminist groups are fuming about the four-page ad, saying that it encourages minors to smoke and promotes violence against women.

The pull-out—featuring a sexy blonde on the cover and the face of Camel's mascot, Old Joe, inside—offers tips on "how to impress someone at the beach." One suggestion is to "run into the water, grab someone and drag her back to shore, as if you've saved her from drowning. The more she kicks and screams, the better."

The ad also includes a coupon for a free pack of cigarettes with the purchase of another pack, and urges would-be coupon users to "ask a kind-looking stranger to redeem it."

In a May letter to an R.J. Reynolds attorney, Rep. Gerry Sikorski (D-Minn.) called the suggestion "thinly veiled advice on how to redeem the coupon if you are underage."

R.J. Reynolds's new chief executive, James Johnston, wrote Sikorski last month apologizing for the ads. He wrote, "It would not have run had I been at Reynolds when it was proposed. . . . I can assure you that it will never run again."

A company spokeswoman said the series was intended to be "tongue-in-cheek."

But the issue has not died.

In testimony before a House subcommittee yesterday, several witnesses cited the ads as justification for a bill to ban all cigarette advertising that might be seen by young people.

And Public Citizen, a Washington-based consumer group, yesterday asked Health and Human Services Secretary Louis Sullivan to publicly condemn the spread, which appeared in the May issues of Rolling Stone, National Lampoon and several other magazines.

The National Organization for Women (NOW) also attacked the advertisement at a workshop on smoking at its national conference last week, said NOW President Molly Yard. "We are totally irritated by them. We have been recommending that people write to whatever magazine they see the ads in."

The Washington-based Advocacy Institute also has asked its members to write R.J. Reynolds. The ad "is basically advocating date rape," said Phil Wilbur, director of the institute's Health Advocacy Resource Center.

Consumer groups, including Public Citizen, plan to ask state attorneys general to prosecute R.J. Reynolds on charges that it violated state laws against selling cigarettes to minors, said Sidney Wolfe, Public Citizen's director.

Since many states have laws that make it a criminal offense to sell cigarettes to minors, the attorneys general could prosecute the company on the ground that the ad is "aiding and abetting in the crime," Wolfe said.

R.J. Reynolds spokeswoman Maura Payne said the ad was supposed to appeal to men aged 21 to 34, and the ads were placed in magazines whose readers are about that age. The suggestions for having a friend turn in the coupon were included because young men rarely use coupons, she said.

The advertisement was a one-time-only installment in Camel's ongoing "smooth character" campaign, Payne said. It will not appear again, she said. "It was meant to be humorous. . . . It was never our intention to advocate unseemly behavior toward anyone."

National Lampoon Publisher George Agoglia said he thought the consumer groups were "making a mountain of a molehill. . . . We were happy to get the ad." He said his magazine rejects "raunchy" ads and has turned down ads from Hustler magazine. The average age of a National Lampoon reader is 27.2, he said.

Gary Miller, spokesman for the Tobacco Institute, said the anti-smoking groups are exaggerating the possible effects of the ad on minors. Studies have shown that young people are more likely to smoke because of peer pressure or because they are imitating parents or siblings than because they are influenced by advertising, he said.

However, studies show that teenagers can identify brand names from ad campaigns, said Ronald Davis, director of the U.S. Office on Smoking and Health.

The anti-smoking groups said the ad demonstrates that a ban on cigarettes is necessary because the industry will not police itself.

Wilbur said the ad obviously violates the tobacco industry's advertising code of ethics, which states, "Cigarette advertising shall not suggest that smoking is essential to social prominence . . . or sexual attraction."

He pointed to the ad's "foolproof dating advice" that one should "always break the ice by offering her a Camel."

"This ad tells us that if we think there's some kind of regulation of cigarette advertising, we're wrong," Wolfe said. "What kind of morals do (the tobacco companies) have that they think this is acceptable?"

John McGrath, a member of the American Medical Association's legislative council, agreed that Congress must step in and regulate cigarette advertising. "We must stop the seduction of youth and minorities," he said.

At yesterday's meeting of the House Energy and Commerce subcommittee on transportation and hazardous materials, the model who starred in the ads for Winstons, another R.J. Reynolds brand, also urged Congress to ban tobacco ads from places young people might see them.

David Goerlitz, who starred in the action-packed ads for six years, testified, "I have had children tell me that they smoked Winstons so that they could be just like me. . . . For that I shall always feel guilty."

U.S. Accused of 'Censorship by Intimidation' in Pornography Cases

Robert F. Howe, March 1990

First Amendment specialists have accused the Justice Department of deliberately abusing obscenity laws to drive mail-order companies out of business for distributing adult films and publications that were never determined to be obscene.

The experts say the department's National Obscenity Enforcement Unit has practiced censorship by intimidation, using laws meant to restrict the distribution of individual products in selective communities to eliminate national distribution networks for a wide range of films and publications. One of the cases they cite goes to trial tomorrow in Alexandria.

In the first federal case of its kind in the Washington area, Karl Brussel and his Connecticut-based Pak Ventures Inc. were indicted in December on charges of mailing obscene videotapes to individuals in Northern Virginia. Brussel and his company also were charged with mailing the videos and related advertising brochures to addresses in the Eastern District of North Carolina and two federal districts of Alabama.

"The goal [of multiple indictments] is to use prosecutorial threats and actions to coerce distributors of these kinds of materials to self-censor a broader range of materials than the government could achieve by law," said Bruce Ennis, counsel for the American Library Association.

Ennis and other First Amendment experts said that rather than foot the bill for separate defenses in several jurisdictions, some distributors have pleaded guilty and agreed to stop the sale of all adult materials nationwide.

A guilty verdict at trial would penalize the distributor for selling only goods that were determined to be obscene and only in the jurisdiction where the prosecution took place.

The Brussel case is an offspring of Project PostPorn, a nationwide investigation geared specifically toward mail-order distributors of sexually oriented films and publications.

The investigation was launched by the Justice Department's National Obscenity Enforcement Unit, formed in 1966 by then-U.S.

Attorney General Edwin Meese III shortly after the Attorney General's Commission on Pornography delivered its final report.

PostPorn debuted in July 1988 when Brent D. Ward, then U.S. Attorney in Utah, announced indictments in eight states of 13 corporations and 20 individuals who used the mail to advertise and distribute allegedly obscene products. Since then, four more corporations and eight more individuals have been charged in the investigation.

Prosecutors said PostPorn grew out of thousands of complaints filed with the Postal Inspection Service by consumers who received unsolicited brochures for adult products. Officials in Utah, where there are no adult theaters and bookstores, received 400 to 500 related consumer complaints monthly in 1986, according to Assistant U.S. Attorney Richard N.W. Lambert.

Mary Spearing, a prosecutor with the obscenity team, said PostPorn has been "a great success," with most cases resolved by guilty pleas. Five cases, including Brussel's, are pending, and three trials resulted in guilty verdicts in Louisville, St. Paul, Minn., and Harrisburg, Pa.

As a result of the two-year project, "the number of complaints to postal inspectors has gone down dramatically," Spearing said.

What distinguishes obscenity cases from most others, and enables federal prosecutors to bring several indictments against the same company selling identical materials in several of the nation's 94 federal judicial districts, is the community-standard test.

Under a 1973 Supreme Court ruling, jurors in an obscenity case must first decide whether the material at issue is obscene. The three-part test requires that jurors determine whether it lacks social, artistic or scientific value; violates standards of existing state law; or, judging by contemporary community standards, appeals solely to prurient interests.

"You can commit the crime in 94 districts simultaneously," Spearing said. Bringing indictments against the defendants in several jurisdictions, she added, "was a deliberate statement" intended to create a "greater deterrent."

First Amendment specialists accuse prosecutors of bringing charges only in conservative communities, where they have a greater chance of empaneling a jury that will judge sexually oriented materials obscene.

"The technical term is 'forum shopping,'" said Herald Price Fahringer, general counsel to the First Amendment Lawyers Association. "They take you out into the conservative areas—the Bible Belt or somewhere—where they have the best chance."

Maxwell Lillienstein, counsel to the American Booksellers Association, said the prosecutors' choice of venue amounts to "a kind of entrapment." He added that his group worries that prosecutors may extend "this kind of censorship by intimidation to mainstream wholesalers and booksellers . . . who sell art books, sex education books, books like 'Joy of Sex'—some very big sellers, in fact."

Laurence E. Tribe, a professor at Harvard Law School, said prosecutors' time and money would be better spent safeguarding women and children who are victimized by producers of extreme pornographic films.

A federal judge in an early PostPorn case ruled that investigators were technically entitled to prosecute a distributor of adult films in any jurisdiction where the films were mailed and then judged obscene. However, U.S. District Judge Thomas Penfield Jackson in the District also found that "simultaneous criminal prosecutions of the same, individual for the same offense in four separate federal judicial districts . . . . cannot possibly be consistent with Due Process."

Jackson forbade the government to bring additional indictments against Avram Freedberg, the subject of charges in Utah and grand jury investigations in four other jurisdictions. Freedberg's company, Consumers Marketing Group Ltd., pleaded guilty before his first trial, agreeing to pay a $600,000 fine and stop all distribution of sexually oriented materials.

Martin Garbus, an attorney for Brussel, has also asked a federal judge to prevent the government from bringing new indictments against his client.

Garbus said prosecutors have wasted thousands of taxpayer dollars hounding Brussel over mild adult films. The 14 videos that will be considered by a jury this week are "not sadomasochistic, they're not kiddie porn, they're not bestiality," Garbus said. ". . . This is the stuff you can get in the video shops, that they show in hotel rooms."

Garbus, who helped defend comedian Lenny Bruce in obscenity trials three decades ago, accuses the prosecutors of crusading. "I've met these people," he said. "They think this is worse than cocaine . . . . It's like the last 30 years have not happened in this country."

If Brussel is convicted in this week's trial, in which he faces the first of four counts of mailing obscene material, he could receive a maximum sentence of five years in prison and a fine of $250,000. However, according to court papers, prosecutors have offered him an out: Plead guilty in Alexandria, serve three years in prison, pay $750,000 in fines, forfeit all business assets and close up shop nationwide.

Kennedy vs. Murdoch on Anti-Monopoly Rule

Eleanor Randolph, January 1988

Wicked Teddy Kennedy. There he was, sneaking around the nation's capital last month, putting one over on the Federal Communications Commission and sticking it to Rupert Murdoch.

Poor Rupert Murdoch. Because of Kennedy, he is probably going to have to sell either a newspaper or a television station in both Boston and New York.

A lot of people feel that this puts a real strain on Murdoch, whose global media empire stretches from Australia to Hong Kong to America to Europe and whose reported net income last year was a $500 million dollars, give or take $50 million.

One of the groups most upset about Kennedy's end-run around the FCC is the Freedom of Expression Foundation. The group had appealed to the FCC to lighten up on Murdoch and scrap the 14-year-old anti-monopoly rule that says you can't own a newspaper and a television station in the same city.

The foundation has its freedom to express these views, courtesy of contributions from a lot of media companies, including those that own the Washington Post, the New York Times and Fox Broadcasting Co. Fox Broadcasting is owned by Murdoch, who became an American citizen in 1985 so he could own television stations and establish what is so far a grade-B network.

Another person indignant about Kennedy's antics is New York Mayor Ed Koch, who said Kennedy's "sneak attack on the First Amendment" was evidence of a serious "character flaw." It was a liberal's revenge, the mayor avowed, against a media baron whose editors dutifully pursue Murdoch's conservative line.

When Mayor Koch was candidate Koch in 1977 and a longshot at that, Murdoch began promoting him in the New York Post, the paper Murdoch will have to sell by March 6 because of Kennedy. Koch also does a commentary for New York's Channel 5, the station that Murdoch can keep if he sells the Post.

But maybe that's a coincidence.

Murdoch has said through his New York public-relations firm that Kennedy's action was "cynical and mean-spirited." This comes from a man who has summarily ousted hundreds of employees, from

330

union members to top editors, to pursue a brand of colonial journalism that would have been the envy of Ferdinand and Isabella.

This also comes from a man who had lunch one winter day in 1980 with President Carter and then endorsed him two days later in the New York Post as the better of two top Democrats running in the New York presidential primary. The other Democrat was Ted Kennedy.

A week later, under pressure from a Carter appointee, the Export-Import Bank gave final approval to a low-interest, $290 million loan for an Australian airline partly owned by Murdoch.

Maybe that was also a coincidence.

What is so lovely about this battle between the media's Godzilla and the Senate's King Kong is that it's a good matchup. There are no amateurs, no political virgins.

The difference is that Kennedy's action, however sneaky, serves the public interest. Murdoch's outcry, no matter how cloaked in the royal robes of the First Amendment, basically serves his company's bottom line. In the name of the public's interest, Murdoch is talking about his own.

Sure, Kennedy tricked Murdoch, just as he tricked the White House, which apparently had no idea that President Reagan was agreeing to such a matter when he signed the omnibus federal spending bill a few weeks ago.

But the senior senator from Massachusetts has gotten away with it, at least so far, because a few key legislators felt that the FCC had launched a deregulation spree that had turned into a demolition campaign. Along with the dust and detritus, the agency last August tossed out the Fairness Doctrine that required television stations to air community issues occasionally instead of "I Love Lucy."

Kennedy and Sen. Ernest F. Hollings (D-S.C.) decided that if the FCC could surprise Congress, Congress could surprise the FCC. Washington is full of weapons for the artful in-fighter, and these two didn't learn their legislative footwork in ballet school.

They got other Democrats to agree that the FCC should stick to its old rules and not make another exception for Murdoch, who had already received two FCC waivers for the Boston and New York markets. Kennedy said, in effect, that everybody else has complied with the FCC cross-ownership requirement for 14 years, so it's your turn, Rupe.

In Boston, it's easy. Both properties make money and, if Murdoch sells the television station, as expected, he will make a lot more profit than if he sells the Boston Herald. The New York Post is the problem, and Murdoch has convinced a lot of people that if the paper folds and

1,000-plus employees are put out of work, they can pin the blame on Teddy.

Blaming Kennedy is easy, convenient and off the mark. If Murdoch kills the paper, it will be for one reason: he can make more money closing the New York Post than selling it.

Falwell vs. Hustler on the First Amendment

Eleanor Randolph, March 1988

When the Supreme Court ruled, 8 to 0, that Hustler magazine didn't have to pay the Rev. Jerry Falwell $200,000, people who poke fun at the famous for a living took a deeper breath of free air.

Here were the nation's institutionally straight-laced, and generally elder, jurists trying to decide between a preacher and a porn magazine. Justice Sandra Day O'Connor is as prim as the Queen Mum, and most of her colleagues have the look of men who would disapprove of a Betty Grable pin-up.

Yet, this court agreed that a Hustler drawing, which portrayed Falwell as a drunk having sex with his mother in an outhouse, fell under the protective cloak of the First Amendment. And if Falwell's feelings were hurt or even if the former Moral Majority leader broke out in a case of holier-than-thou roseola, he joins a long list of modern and historical figures who have suffered at the hands of those who use ink to draw blood.

The court soundly reaffirmed the basic human need and the established American right to mock public figures. Sometimes, like Mark Russell, we are clever about it. Sometimes, like Hustler publisher Larry Flynt, we aren't. In the Hustler-Falwell case, the satire was a slimy piece of work.

But who draws the line between what is good taste and what isn't? You? Your congressman? Your mother?

My mother couldn't stand cartoons that showed Richard M. Nixon with an afternoon shadow, which means under her law that nobody could show a Republican President who wasn't clean-shaven. She had no difficulty whatsoever with a depiction of President Jimmy Carter as a grasshopper.

Satire is always funnier when it is aimed at somebody who deserves it, that is, not me or anybody I like.

The key here is that Falwell, who has preached to a flock of television viewers, is a well-known public figure. In this historic decision, Chief Justice William H. Rehnquist, who seemed as an associate justice to question the basic case that underlies modern libel law, has now taken on the mantle of chief justice. This lofty opinion reaffirms the 24-year-old New York Times v. Sullivan decision that makes it especially tough for anybody famous to win a libel action.

Rehnquist, whose caricature in most recent cartoons shows his hair slicked down, looking like a man on a street corner selling stolen watches, wrote in the decision: "The sort of robust political debate encouraged by the First Amendment is bound to produce speech that is critical of those who hold public office or (who are) public figures . . . . Such criticism, inevitably, will not always be reasoned or moderate; public figures as well as public officials will be subject to 'vehement, caustic, and sometimes unpleasantly sharp attacks.'"

A few historical reminders are necessary. The opinion mentions George Washington appearing in political cartoons of the day as an ass. But that was when cartoonists were being civil.

Members of President Andrew Jackson's Cabinet appeared as rats in a famous cartoon of the day. The drawing was widely circulated after they resigned because the President was caught, ahem, "paying too much attention to" the wife of his secretary of war.

More than a century ago, Gilbert and Sullivan's buffoon in H.M.S. Pinafore was patterned on Disraeli's First Lord of the Admiralty. Disraeli told his associates that the show "made him feel 'quite sick.'"

Modern examples are even more graphic:

Upset about Nixon's campaign tactics in one of his comebacks in 1954, political cartoonist Herblock drew him climbing out of a sewer. More recently, after Vice President Bush declared he had won a television battle with CBS News anchor Dan Rather, Herblock showed Bush as a boxer, one hand raised in victory, the other hand serving as a fig leaf. Bush's shorts, labeled "Iran-contra connection," were around his ankles.

Paul Conrad of the Los Angeles Times has drawn Democratic candidate Gary Hart mooning the press corps. In another fairly notorious Conrad cartoon, California's very proper Republican governor, George Deukmejian, stands nude before an anonymous questioner. The Duke, as Deukmejian is called, is being charged with vetoing a strip-and-search bill.

Conrad once reportedly told former Times publisher Otis Chandler: "Your job is to build bridges. Mine is to burn them."

Lawyers for the Association of American Editorial Cartoonists and such satirists as Russell argued that editorial cartoons would have been jeopardized by a decision against Hustler because "satire's instrument is the direct, often crude and tasteless, ad hominem attack."

Falwell and his lawyers contended that a line of outrageousness exists and that Hustler crossed it. Ad hominem is one thing, but this is ad matrem. Larry Flynt went after the guy's mother.

The Supreme Court refused to draw the line in the lawbooks and agreed with Appeals Court Judge J. Harvie Wilkinson, who wrote what is perhaps the simplest and most eloquent explanation of our constitutionally protected freedom to ridicule public figures:

"No one is sued for expressing pleasing sentiments. Either the First-Amendment protects speech that makes someone uncomfortable, or it protects nothing."

Practicing Law in the Advertising Age

Ruth Marcus, June 1987

By today's standards, the ad seems staid, even timid. "Do you need a lawyer?" inquired Phoenix lawyers John Bates and Van O'Steen, promising "legal services at very reasonable fees."

The young lawyers' advertisement in the Arizona Republic for their legal clinic trumpeted no celebrity endorsements, no holiday-special discounts, but it drew the wrath of Arizona bar authorities. They accused the pair of violating a disciplinary rule, similar to that in force in almost every state, prohibiting lawyers from publicizing themselves through newspaper ads, radio or television announcements, or even display advertisements in the Yellow Pages.

That local disciplinary action ended up before the Supreme Court, in Bates v. State Bar of Arizona. In the view of many legal scholars, the decision handed down 10 years ago, on June 27, 1977, revolutionized the practice of law in this country more than any other Supreme Court decision in history.

Rejecting the warnings of the organized bar that freeing lawyers to compete in the "hustle of the marketplace" would "tarnish the dignified public image of the profession," the high court ruled 5 to 4 that lawyers have a constitutional right to advertise their services.

A decade later, advertising has become a way of life for many American lawyers. The practice of law has evolved into a more cutthroat, dollar-oriented business, a change due in large measure to the loosening of restrictions. And the debate outlined in the Bates case rages on.

Many lawyers are appalled at what they regard as the shameful spectacle of lawyers hawking their wares on billboards and matchbook covers. Retired chief justice Warren E. Burger has said he would "dig ditches" before resorting to advertising and bemoaned the marketing of legal services like "other commodities from mustard, cosmetics and laxatives to used cars."

Others—even some officials of the legal establishment, which battled vigorously against the Bates result—view advertising as a healthy unleashing of market forces that has cut the cost of basic legal services for many consumers, once befuddled about where to turn for legal help.

"I think it's been a good thing," said Thomas S. Johnson, an Illinois lawyer who chairs the American Bar Association Commission on Advertising. "It's opened the marketplace and has made lawyers more available to more people."

The changes wrought by Bates have touched almost every lawyer in America. Sole practitioners, finding their businesses squeezed by high-volume legal clinics with million-dollar television advertising budgets, may invest in a full-page spread in the Yellow Pages. Blue-chip law firms that once questioned whether it was unseemly for their lawyers to carry business cards now hire high-priced public relations consultants to develop marketing strategies and make sure their partners get good ink.

Bates, written by Justice Harry A. Blackmun, is "probably the single most important Supreme Court opinion affecting the structure of the practice of law and the delivery of legal services," said New York University legal ethics expert Stephen Gillers. "In a way it seems like longer [than 10 years since the decision] because we've seen so much legal advertising."

In 1978, the year after Bates, only 3 percent of lawyers polled by the American Bar Association Journal reported advertising. By 1983, the ranks of the advertisers had climbed to 13 percent; two years later, 24 percent of lawyers said they advertised.

"It's a lot more than I expected," said Johnson. "At the time the decision was handed down it was about as popular as venereal disease with the bar leadership."

Today, lawyers invest millions of dollars in the war for the hearts, minds and checkbooks of potential clients. In 1978, lawyers bought $900,000 worth of television time, according to figures compiled by the Television Bureau of Advertising. Last year, that figure reached nearly $47 million.

In a 1983 study of the effect of advertising on the cost of legal services, the Federal Trade Commission concluded that fees for legal services such as wills, bankruptcies, uncontested divorces and uncomplicated accident cases were 5 to 13 percent lower in the cities that had the fewest restrictions on advertising.

"As advertising increases in the legal service market, prices will decline" said the FTC, which surveyed 3,200 lawyers in 17 states.

Advertising "forced lawyers to become more efficient," said Gail Koff, a founding partner of Jacoby & Meyers, a 150-office legal chain that is one of the country's heaviest advertisers. "In midtown Manhattan an uncontested divorce cost $1,500 13 years ago," she said. "Our fee now is about $500."

Others, including the president of the American Bar Association, suggest that clients may get inferior service from lawyers who advertise. "The best value will be found in the nonadvertising group of lawyers," said ABA President Eugene C. Thomas, a Boise, Idaho, lawyer. "The better services are being provided by whose who are not advertising. That's the reason why the others are advertising."

"I couldn't disagree with him more," responded Koff, whose firm spent nearly $5 million on television advertising last year. "Your attorney out there who is not advertising is basically taking as clients whoever he can get to come through the door and doesn't have the specialization behind him, doesn't have the system and support services that a large organization can offer."

Indeed, a 1979 American Bar Foundation survey of 74 Los Angeles residents found that the 22 who went to Jacoby & Meyers were more satisfied with their lawyers' services than the 52 who sought help from traditional firms.

A fraction of the advertising has met opponents' worst fears, bordering in their view on the tasteless or straying far over that line.

In one commercial for divorce lawyers, shown on local television, a whirring chainsaw cuts the couple's couch in half, then buzzes ominously over the family dog. A Wisconsin lawyer's television spot features him rising from the water to the strains of "Swan Lake," festooned with jewelry, to offer, "If you're in over your head because of inflation . . " In the District, the bar's legal ethics committee ruled that Ashcraft & Gerells television commercial featuring Redskins running back John Riggins violated the bar's rules against testimonials. "Holiday special—give that spouse of yours something he or she has been wanting for a long time—a divorce," a Florida lawyer's ad urged.

"What kind of professional, or what can people think about professionals when they know . . . you're going to knock 10 percent off because it happens to be . . . a summer special?" Maryland State Bar Association President Vincent Ferretti Jr. asked at a hearing last year by the ABA Commission on Advertising.

Maryland District Court Judge Thomas E. Sisk Jr. told the same commission that Maryland lawyers "feel that some type of cheapness has pervaded the practice of law in Maryland, and they uniformly blame it on the distasteful advertising."

Advertising, he said, "has sucked the rural counties absolutely dry of personal injury cases" as clients turn to the city lawyers whose ads they see on television. Baltimore is one of the heaviest television legal advertising markets in the country.

Others assert, however, that the vast majority of legal advertising is quite respectable and dignified. "Every once in a while a schlocky ad appears and everybody gets upset, but that's rare," said Johnson, who heads the ABA advertising commission. "Ninety-five percent of it is dignified and there's been an enormous increase in the tolerance by other lawyers."

What once was shocking now seems acceptable. The American Bar Association's Standing Committee on Ethics permitted a lawyer to set up a tent at a state fair, complete with a sign outside that he would write wills on the spot.

"The bar would have reacted in horror years ago," said Georgetown University law Professor Samuel Dash, a committee member. "Today, we found that there was nothing really improper on that."

One state ethics panel passed on the ad of an attorney who billed himself as "The Lawyer Who Makes Housecalls." In Rhode Island, the state bar counterattacked with its own ads, warning potential clients not to choose lawyers simply because they advertise.

And enterprising lawyers have pushed the boundaries of Bates, entering such new advertising frontiers as "telemarketing," in which customers are called and asked if they want to join a prepaid legal services plan, a sort of legal version of health insurance, and direct-mail solicitation in which lawyers write, for example, to accident victims or their survivors to offer their services.

J. Anthony Clark, who has done work for Montgomery Ward's legal services plan, said he cringed when he discovered the group was telemarketing. "I said, 'There is no way you can do that. That is entirely unethical,'" he said. But after researching the issue, Clark said, he concluded that it would be permitted by the ethical rules in many states.

The elite firms of Wall Street and K Street may not have bought television ads, but they too have felt the impact of Bates. Many top law firms have hired public relations consultants who issue press releases heralding the firms' latest acquisition of big-name partners or urging reporters to call the firm's experts for quotes.

"Lawyers said, 'Well, I might not advertise in the conventional sense, but since it's permissible to do so I'm going to consider other ways to market my practice . . . that might be considered more dignified,'" Johnson said. "It is unlikely that would have happened if the Bates decision had not come down."

"The whole legal profession top to bottom has been forced to come into the 20th century," Koff said. "I think a great deal of that comes from the fact that lawyers have been allowed to advertise."

CHAPTER THIRTEEN

Media Ethics

The Media and the March

Eleanor Randolph, April 1989

Suppose you feel strongly about abortion rights. You marched with 300,000 people last Sunday. You work for a newspaper. Was that the wrong thing to do?

At several newspapers this week, editors and reporters have been at loggerheads over whether it was appropriate for journalists to participate in last Sunday's march here.

At The New York Times, the issue arose when Supreme Court reporter Linda Greenhouse told Washington bureau chief Howell Raines that she had marched in the abortion rights parade. The focus of the marchers was on the Supreme Court—in particular a hope that their numbers could persuade the court not to reverse its 1973 Roe v. Wade decision that granted a constitutional right to an abortion.

Raines said that his first reaction was that reporters must often wrestle with their own feelings to be objective and that "people's private expressions are their own business." Raines said later that he went back to Times guidelines on such questions and found that his view was not in line.

Times policy states: "The integrity of the Times requires that its staff members avoid employment or any other undertakings, obligations, relationships or investments that create or appear to create a conflict of interest with their professional work for The Times or otherwise compromises The Times' independence and reputation."

341

"As it turns out, it is also (Times Executive Editor) Max Frankel's strong feeling that this should not be allowed," Raines said of participation in the march. "Max's view is that, as an example, you cannot cover the White House and wear a campaign button."

Raines said that no one, including Greenhouse, would be punished for marching and that Greenhouse would continue to cover the court—even when the abortion issue is before it.

"We have full faith and confidence in her professionalism," Raines said. "It's part of our profession that we try to discipline our opinions, not that we're opinion-free."

After hearing that a number of Washington Post reporters and editors had participated, Washington Post Executive Editor Benjamin C. Bradlee and Managing Editor Leonard Downie Jr. sent out a strongly worded memo to the staff.

The memo said: "We once again remind members of the newsroom's professional staff that it is unprofessional for you (as opposed to your relatives) to take part in political or issue demonstrations, no matter on which side or how seemingly worthy the cause. It is the choice we make when we choose to work in this business and for this newspaper.

"In the case of those who forgot about this on Sunday, I expect each of you to recuse yourself from any future participation in coverage of the abortion issue," they said.

The memo stirred some criticism from a few members of the staff who felt that it limited their rights for personal participation in behalf of causes on their off hours.

"If you marched in a demonstration, you wouldn't then turn around and cover it," said Amanda Spake, an editor for The Washington Post Magazine. "But in terms of saying that we are not supposed to be involved in demonstrations, period, I don't understand that. Where do you draw the line? Contributions? Religious organizations?"

Boyce Rensberger, The Post's science editor, said he watched the parade with his son. He sent Downie a memo that said, in part: "I am puzzled about the principle behind your recent edict on participating in demonstrations. How can the Post permit reporters and editors to express their opinions on events in the news through Op-Ed pieces, news analyses and regular columns but prohibit the same people from expressing their opinions through the right of peaceable assembly?"

A number of editors at newsrooms in New York and Washington thought the answer had been settled 20 years ago when reporters were barred from demonstrations about subjects they covered—such as the Vietnam war.

In recent years, journalism codes have become stricter in many areas. Some editors refuse to belong to clubs or civic organizations for fear that there will be a conflict.

And most newspaper editors now ask their reporters to reveal any potential conflicts—such as a stock interest in a company that might be affected by a story.

"I'm not going to punish anybody who did go," Downie said of the march. But he added that among younger members of the staff it was time to focus on the policy and other ethical issues.

Raines agreed. "This became what I would call a clarifying situation," he said.

Plagiarism and News

Eleanor Randolph, March 1988

When Sen. Joseph R. Biden Jr. (D-Del.) quit the presidential campaign after he borrowed a British politician's speech, political speechwriters around the country cringed. A few, after making certain they weren't being quoted for the record, whispered that it could happen to anybody.

Much the same kind of thing has been happening in recent weeks to reporters watching two journalists become unemployed overnight. A veteran foreign correspondent of the Chicago Tribune and a longtime drama critic of the St. Paul (Minn.) Pioneer Press Dispatch were accused of plagiarism in the last month. Both resigned, to the embarrassment of their newspapers and the chagrin of their friends.

David Hawley, a drama critic for 9 1-2 years in St. Paul, wrote his last column a few weeks ago, apologizing to his readers for using part of a New York Times review published six years earlier. Hawley said his notes were "commingled" with part of The Times' review of the same play.

Ten-year veteran Jonathan Broder left the Tribune after a Chicago woman compared his article Feb. 22 on problems in the West Bank with an earlier column in the English-language Jerusalem Post. Broder's article and the Jerusalem Post's began with virtually the same sentence. For about the first 10 paragraphs, the language was so similar that it appeared as if the same piece of work had simply passed through two different editors. The most plausible reason given for this lapse was that covering the "pressure cooker of Israel" is one of the daily newspaper reporter's most difficult assignments.

In numerous phone calls to me in recent weeks, journalists have said it seems unfair to wipe out a man's career simply because he used someone else's words. The reality, unspoken by some and hinted by others, is that journalists borrow, adapt, use and occasionally even steal from each other like schoolboys. When somebody steps over the line, it surprises a lot of people that there is one.

A few British journalists in recent days said they were shocked that such a minor thing as putting your byline on someone else's copy is considered a firing offense in this country. Said one: "I'd be out of business if they did that to us." One of Broder's fellow American journalists, who also covered the Middle East from Jerusalem, gave the

Yankee cast to this argument: "Everybody rewrites the Jerusalem Post. That's how foreign correspondents work."

The key word, however, is "rewrites." Rewriting is what St. Petersburg Times chairman Eugene Patterson described as "low-level plagiarism" to a Los Angeles Times reporter a few years ago, and it happens every day at every news organization in America.

Most reporters don't do all of the work that appears under their name. As they write, someone often feeds them the reports on their subject matter by the wire services, such as Associated Press or United Press International or Knight-Ridder.

Some reporters may see a good quote in the AP story and call the person quoted to get it firsthand. Other reporters pick up the quote for their articles and say it came from the AP. Many just shove it in their stories, unchecked and unattributed.

Nobody complains at AP. Newspapers pay for use of the wire service, including everything it provides: facts and quotes, scoops and color. But what this does is create the "myth of exclusivity," as it's called by the ethics police in journalism schools and media think tanks.

These purists say "picking up the wires," as it's known, is like taking the first toke of marijuana that leads automatically to heroin. Many of us have been guilty of using wire copy, however, without going on to steal a column from the competition.

Still, plagiarism is more common than it should be, and part of the reason is that people who start borrowing liberally from an accepted source of background material get in the habit.

Roy Peter Clark, associate director of the Poynter Institute for Media Studies in St. Petersburg, says that, when he started reporting a story on "the unoriginal sin" of plagiarism a few years ago, he found examples at almost every news organization. "Once I started calling newspapers, I don't remember speaking to an editor who didn't give me a case," he said.

The easiest way to avoid plagiarism is to give credit. But the average journalist enjoys giving credit about as much as your local 7-11.

Here's the way it works: Say, the Arkansas Gazette has a scoop. The bigger papers then move into action, marshalling their best reporters to confirm information on it. If they confirm it, more than likely the story goes in the paper under the big time reporter's name. No mention of the Arkansas Gazette. If it can't be confirmed, the big guys give credit. Giving credit in this case has one advantage: If the Gazette turns out to be wrong, credit turns instantly into blame.

Occasionally, reporters are caught not doing their work and not attributing it to the person who did. Hawley and Broder remind us that, if somebody else writes it first, it's theirs. For people whose commodity is language, plagiarism is stealing, as much as taking someone else's tape recorder and selling it on the street.

Managing Confidential Sources

Eleanor Randolph, June 1988

Dan Cohen, a Republican politician in Minneapolis, called reporters from four different news organizations the week before the 1982 gubernatorial elections in Minnesota. He was offering what he thought was a good deal. What he got was a bad one.

In return for a promise that his name would never surface, he would pass along a document that he thought would make news. All four reporters agreed, and he handed them copies of a 12-year-old shoplifting charge for $6 worth of jewelry against the Democratic woman running for lieutenant governor.

Two news organizations, the Associated Press and television station WCCO in Minneapolis, used the story without Cohen's name. Over protests by reporters who made the agreement with Cohen, the editors at the two other news organizations—the St. Paul Pioneer Press & Dispatch and the Minneapolis Star Tribune—used the story and Cohen's name. They also explained that Cohen was a friend and associate of the Republican running for governor.

The shoplifting story disappeared in the firestorm over Cohen's dirty trick. The Democratic woman went on to win; Cohen went on to lose his job at a local advertising agency.

And Cohen's case—routinely referred to among reporters as the "burned source" case—is about to make journalism history.

Next month in a county courtroom in Minneapolis, Cohen's lawyer will argue that the two newspapers breached their contract with him. He's asking for damages in excess of $50,000. Lawyers for the newspapers are arguing that editors had a right to cancel any verbal contract their reporters made with Cohen because he was trying to manipulate the news on the eve of the election.

As Minneapolis Star Tribune executive editor Joel Kramer described the philosophical question recently, there are very few absolutes in journalism. (He wasn't speaking about this specific case, he said, and he wasn't the editor when it happened.)

"To me, an agreement of confidentiality to a source has a very high value in our business," he said. "But I can personally think of hypotheticals in which I would reverse that agreement of confidentiality." The hypothetical he used was that a source wanted

347

confidentiality to confess that he was about to commit a murder. In that case, Kramer said, he would call the police.

Fine, but what happens to the rest of us who, on occasion, promise we won't use somebody's name in far less extreme cases. Move over, used-car salesmen. Journalists are about to take your place on the public's believability scale.

Maybe we should issue a warning to future sources: "A deal's a deal, except when we decide it isn't."

Part of this is fallout from the famous Janet Cooke case, when a Washington Post reporter wouldn't reveal the name of a 8-year-old heroin addict who turned out to be a fabrication. After that, the rule in journalism has been that reporters have to tell their editors who their sources were.

It's a good rule, now that it has settled in. It allows an independent assessment of the value of the source and the worth of his information. But the idea was that this provided some internal protection against bad stories—not that an editor could veto a reporter's promise of confidentiality. The choice was to use the information or not use it.

Last year, Newsweek revealed that Lt. Col. Oliver North had been a source for many of its stories on the administration's foreign policies. The reason given for the revelation was that North had lied about those stories on Capitol Hill.

Journalists around the country howled at Newsweek for committing such a sin. Even some journalists at Newsweek quietly spread the word that they did not agree with their own company's decision. A deal is a deal, they explained, even if it's not a good deal.

This April, the New York Times mentioned in a story on fund-raising that Sen. Joseph R. Biden, Jr. (D-Del.) withdrew from the presidential race "after Dukakis aides leaked a videotape" showing that Biden had borrowed a major part of his speech from a British politician.

In the internal memo of the Times, an editor wrote that this slip was against Times policy. Even though a Dukakis aide later admitted he was the source, "we have never reported who made our information available (just as we have never said, for example, whether Daniel Ellsberg was our source for the Pentagon Papers). The flat assertion that the Biden disclosure came from the Dukakis staff makes us seem to be identifying a confidential source—not our practice."

Promising confidentiality to a source shouldn't be as routine as it is, and some news organizations have started telling reporters that they cannot make such a pact without approval by an editor. But once a reporter agrees to shield a source, his word should be enough. When the reporters in Minneapolis found out that they had been overruled, it is a wonder they didn't quit in protest.

Dan Cohen will be in court next month saying that when the newspapers published his name, his reputation was damaged. His wasn't the only one.

The Other Side of the Pen: Reporters in the News

Eleanor Randolph, June 1988

Probably the best way for a journalist to learn the facts of life about journalism is to be the subject of a story or even a small article in a small newspaper.

A newspaper story—any story—hits its subject like a cold shower. And sometimes, it's one of those experiences that are most educational when enjoyed firsthand.

The first time I read a story about myself (just a paragraph really), I could not breathe properly for five minutes. My first name was misspelled, and the salary increase I reportedly had received by going to a new job was double the real thing. Moreover, the reporter had not called to ask and had not noticed that my name, which appeared correctly over a news story almost every day, was spelled the hard way.

It was a good lesson; and most of the time I remember it. When I don't and someone calls up to say, "You misspelled my name," I don't argue with them anymore.

If you need evidence that journalists complain about almost anything written about them, a weekly publication called Roll Call that circulates most of its 16,000 copies on Capitol Hill learned that in Washington, at least, a lot of reporters can't even take a joke.

Roll Call ran pictures in its June 19 issue of 12 reporters with Capitol Hill credentials. Under it was a box labeled "The Press Test," asking readers to match pictures with names. The headline, which was clearly meant to be funny, said "Know Your Enemy."

James Glassman, publisher of Roll Call, said that in the next week he got a number of calls from reporters pictured on page 13 of his news magazine. "A lot of them were really upset," Glassman said. "I couldn't believe it."

Even more startling was that Mark Nelson, chairman of the standing committee of correspondents who cover the Hill, wrote Glassman an official letter of protest. "We were surprised that Roll Call was so short of advertisements the other week that it devoted an entire page to a cheap shot at reporters who you labeled 'the enemy.' Gosh, and we thought you were reporters, too," said Nelson, a reporter with the Dallas Times Herald.

In a new issue, Glassman rejoined, "We've decided to sponsor a Continuing Education course in Remedial Humor for journalists only." The newspaper will probably get a few calls complaining that reporters do have a sense of humor after all.

Journalists who cover the media can tell horror stories about what it's like to report on reporters. Andrew Radolf, a reporter for Editor & Publisher magazine, once said that when he wrote a tough column on a major newspaper chain, a representative of the company called his editor to complain that he was drunk when he wrote it. Since such an occurrence is not entirely unheard of in our trade, I asked him about it. Radolf said he seldom drinks at parties, much less at the office.

Such complaints might come from the county commissioner or the mother of a beauty queen who thought—wrongly—that the appearance of a reporter merely meant some well-deserved publicity. But it seems odd from a newspaper company where people should know better.

Journalists who find themselves on the other side of a reporter's notebook or a television camera often experience a kind of epiphany. An editor of the Atlanta Journal-Constitution complained recently that after years of giving interviews he can remember being quoted correctly only once.

George Crile, who used some fairly questionable methods in a CBS Reports documentary on retired General William C. Westmoreland, was stunned at the cluster of cameras that besieged him while Westmoreland's libel suit against CBS was still in court. Crile once told a group of print reporters: "I'm shocked at the way the media cover these things; they're like a bunch of hungry animals." Somebody replied quietly: "George, you have met the enemy and he's in our business."

A delicious piece of nasty writing isn't nearly so amusing when you know the target. Columnist and New Republic Editor Michael Kinsley, who has one of the sharpest pens in the business, thought a recent piece in Spy magazine about Eric Breindel, an editor of the New York Post, was "too cruel even for somebody who generally likes and approves of (and publishes) cruelty." Breindel, he explained, is a friend.

The New York Times puts out an internal "bulletin of second-guessing" called Winners & Sinners. It noted in this month's issue that, "When you buy a printing press, it comes with a mighty potential to cause pain. . . ." The Times editors criticized an article that gently mocked a woman who gave lectures about astrology and tarot.

Journalists forget that their cleverness is not always met with the same appreciative audience outside the building as in the company cafeteria. A good time to remember this is when they see their picture in Roll Call and find themselves joining the legions who complain about the media.

Public Topics and Private Lives

Eleanor Randolph, March 1989

When the Miami Herald lurked outside Gary Hart's Capitol Hill townhouse two years ago to see if a blond visitor spent the night, the press said the episode was a fluke.

Hart's sex life became an issue only because Hart made it an issue, we said.

Ken Bode, an NBC News correspondent, told me at the time: "Gary Hart is the sole point of interest (for us) on this because he was the one with the reputation."

Coverage of the John Tower affair makes it clear that Hart wasn't a one-night stand. Except for a few pompous columnists, most of whom live in New York or Washington, the media is composed of human beings. Like everybody else, we love stories about sex and power and cocaine and something that Tower called "beverage alcohol." We've simply had a hard time figuring how to label it news.

Because of Tower, a public servant's private life now is officially considered newsworthy.

Maybe it won't be news in the New York Times, at least not at first. But somebody will print it—Newsweek or Time maybe, the Boston Globe—and then it hits the news circuit.

In decades when it was taboo to publish stories on a politician's antics during his off-hours, politicians didn't bother dredging up personal stuff on their opponents. Now, with the media's encouragement, the political operatives have returned to their muckrakes.

Reports about Tower's drinking and womanizing were not the result of an investigative effort like Hart's downfall courtesy of the Miami Herald. One foray by the Washington Post and CBS News even backfired. Following up on a paragraph in the Wall Street Journal the day before, the two quoted a former Air Force sergeant as saying Tower had fondled a woman while touring a military base more than a decade earlier. Their source, it turned out, had a history of mental problems.

The damaging allegations came mostly from Tower's former Senate colleagues and his party's conservatives, who decided that he was a flawed candidate. Paul Weyrich, a spokesman for the "New Right," complained publicly about the drinking problem. And as conservative columnist Kevin Phillips told CBS News shortly after

Tower's defeat: "He's been a skirt-chaser and a cork-popper for 20 years, and (the Bush administration) knew it."

The media did its part, of course.

The Wall Street Journal's conservative editorial page, for example, said: "If the Senate is entitled to pass judgment on John Tower's personal history, then the public is also entitled to know salient facts about those who judge Mr. Tower."

Beside that editorial, the Journal reprinted an article from the Dec. 4, 1972, edition of the Atlanta Journal about an event that happened to Sen. Sam Nunn (D-Ga.) on Oct. 31, 1964. Nunn, 26 at the time, apparently went to a party and then had some trouble driving home. He hit a parked car and drove into a ditch. Surely, this means he dare not run for President.

Two days later, the conservative Washington Times did a story headlined, "Sex and Booze Turn Hill into a School for Scandal." It prattled about various members of Congress, including a senator allegedly having sex during lunch in a private dining room at a Capitol Hill restaurant, congressmen who have had affairs with assistants, homosexuals and more.

Several weeks ago, when Rep. Donald E. Lukens (R-Ohio) was indicted in Columbus for allegedly having sex with a minor, one of the major networks sent several staff members to investigate. Lukens, who is single, has said he was "set up" and pleaded not guilty.

"Here is a minority congressman, a man of very little consequence," said an outraged Norman Ornstein, a favorite quote merchant of the Washington media. "The fact that he might have had sex is an interesting little sidebar. But with only 22 minutes of evening news, to take any share of the resources for that story tells me something about a change in news judgment I don't want to hear."

Suppose politicians such as Lukens decide to fight back. Suppose they decide that the Wall Street Journal is right when it says, "The public is also entitled to know salient facts about those who judge." Does that include knowing "salient facts" about the network crews nosing into Lukens' background? Or the people who write editorials for the Journal?

Congressmen still angry about losing their pay raises and possibly their honoraria have begun privately expressing irritation at journalists who also receive whopping fees for speeches around the country, without much written about it in the media.

"If the press is too self-righteous, they may find themselves in trouble," Ornstein warns. "We may start to see pressure building to turn on the journalistic profession for its own hypocrisies."

Those of us who throw stones would do well to start building brick houses. Sure, we can say we don't want to be Secretary of Defense. Of course, we work for private companies. But what if John Tower calls a news conference to talk about drinking and carousing in the Washington press corps?

Under the new rules, it's news.

Crossing the Line: Re-creations as News

Eleanor Randolph, August 1989

William Hurt, the actor, recently appeared on television as the real William Hurt. He sat in a Manhattan courtroom defending himself against a woman who was not his wife but who nevertheless wanted support for their six-year-old child. She dabbed her eyes a little. Hurt hissed angrily at her attorney. It was good television.

More recently, Felix Bloch, the U.S. diplomat on paid leave and under investigation, was represented on "ABC World News Tonight" by an actor who was handing a briefcase to another actor. They were supposed to be passing secret data from the United States to the KGB. It was also good television.

But it all gets very confusing. When are the actors real news and when is the real news merely acting? All of television becomes more like that film commercial that has the four female swimmers standing by the pool. They all look like flesh and blood until the starter gun goes off, and three of them dive into the water. The fourth one can't dive, can't swim. She just stands there, a life-sized photograph, nothing more.

Old-timers, the people who want news to be news and entertainment to be entertainment, recognize that in the long run it doesn't pay to confuse the viewers, especially when you want them to believe you are telling the truth. Media critic Ben Bagdikian called ABC is reconstituted videotape of Bloch "pure poison."

Reuven Frank, former president of NBC News, called this tendency another part of "the gospel of 'do anything to get an audience.'" He added that, "Stations say they do it because cable does it. It's the dope pusher's argument: 'If we don't sell it to them, somebody else will.'"

Frank and Bagdikian are crying in television's creative wilderness. They are outshouted by programs like "Yesterday, Today and Tomorrow," NBC's latest venture into pop-news. The show (I am resisting the television industry's hope that news shows and quasi-news shows be called broadcasts) has promised that when they can't get the picture, they'll "simulate" it. That's a fancy way of saying they'll fake it.

Even at the "Tiffany network," CBS President Howard Stringer hasn't ruled out "re-creations" on some of the soft news shows. (The hard-news operators, including Dan Rather's executive producer, Tom Bettag, have threatened to throw their bodies in front of the camera if somebody in the marketing department tries to put actors on their evening news.)

After ABC News ran its "simulation" a few weeks ago, I got a call from Michael Linder, executive producer of "America's Most Wanted." This is the Fox Television show that has been doing Docu-Dragnet— adaptations of genuine crime stories done with the aid of actors and sets and plastic blood. If the television critics are appalled, the advertising salesmen have noticed that people put down their zappers to watch.

On hearing the outcry about ABC's venture into his area of expertise, Linder called to complain about the National Academy of Television Arts and Sciences. This is the group that gives Emmys—the nice golden trophies that television people present to each other the way newspaper people give each other Pulitzers and movie people give each other Oscars.

Linder said he had submitted his show for the News and Documentary Awards to be given out this September. The people in charge of these awards sniffed that his programs couldn't qualify; he had to enter in one of the entertainment categories.

James Cannon, president of the academy, said recently that the rules don't allow anything but "news and actual footage . . . . We have a clear-cut policy that we do not honor dramatization of news."

If ABC News submitted its big scoop on the Bloch case complete with its simulation, for example, Cannon says: "We would throw that out so fast you couldn't believe it. We're absolutely adamant about that."

Cannon does say that, for the academy, such rules are not carved in stone. He does not expect any of the guidelines for the Emmys to change soon, but Cannon also said the academy is "reacting to" the trend. The awards committee has started talking about news enhancement, as some reporters call it, trying to decide whether a little hamburger helper can be weighed as red meat.

Maybe it's time to remember all those people in Appalachia who thought those pictures of men stepping on the moon were just the latest installment of "Star Trek." They told interviewers that television was just a box with lights and dots that made pictures. It didn't give milk like a cow. It couldn't make toast.

In the cities, we felt sorry for those people: Poor uneducated rubes, we sniffed. Maybe they had it right all along.

Video Releases: Government Sponsored News on Local TV

Eleanor Randolph, June 1990

Several months ago, ABC News staged a video to illustrate a Soviet agent handing a suitcase to accused spy Felix Bloch. The news world, including media pontificators like me, went bananas.

This is fiction, we argued. People will begin to doubt the facts. They will stare at the screen and wonder what is real and what is reel.

Now, it turns out, we were pointing angrily at the networks while the worst abuses were happening at local television stations.

Burdened by the heavy cost of having a Washington bureau or even subscribing to a Washington news service, some stations are simply taking snippets of videotape from politicians and using them as part of their local news shows.

The Washington Journalism Review quoted Jim McLaughlin, an anchorman in Fort Myers, Fla., as saying that, "With Senate feeds and House feeds, we pretty much have it covered." McLaughlin hails from station WINK, which, as it turns out, is not a joke. WINK and about 21 other stations phoned by the Review said they generally have no problems using congressional footage as news.

Newspapers aren't exempt from this kind of thing, either. Some news releases make it into the papers with only one addition—a reporter's byline. But most journalists know that this is considered bad form. And most newspapers make certain that if an advocate on one side of the issue produces a release, the other side at least gets to comment on it. Pretty basic stuff, this.

Most television reporters are pretty good about balance as well. But, hey, these are hard times. Having a bureau in Washington is expensive. Subscribing to a video news service is expensive. And many local stations have expanded their evening news programs to a full hour. Something's got to fill the time, right?

Enter an army of videotechnicians who work on Capitol Hill feeding "sound bites" to hungry local news shows.

Stations are supposed to identify political footage with something called a "sponsorship ID." The Federal Communications Act says that if any "political broadcast matter" or any material involving "discussion of a controversial issue of public importance" is given "to a station as an inducement for broadcasting such matter," the viewers should know it.

Are these Video News Releases or VNRs, as they are called here, about political matters? What else. Are they about controversial issues of public importance? Of course. Are stations being given these videotapes by members of Congress as an inducement to broadcast? You betcha.

In fact, you and I and the rest of the nation's taxpayers are contributing a goodly amount of money (by our standards, not those of Congress) to make certain that these videotapes look like they came from the networks.

You and I send more camera crews to most committee hearings on Capitol Hill than all of the networks and television news organizations combined. These cameras assure that, if our representatives in Congress say something particularly self-serving or their opponents say anything particularly stupid, their words and gestures are registered forever on tape.

Every Wednesday in front of the Capitol, the nation's public servants can be seen lathered with pancake makeup, preaching into microphones on the subject of the day. Tourists passing by often think that this duet between the person holding the mike and the person speaking into it connotes the usual relationship between a reporter and a pol.

Wrong. The person asking the question is a member of the politician's staff. It adds a touch of reality, but only a touch.

"Congressman Smith, how do you feel about the agricultural-support bill that you have been working on so feverishly this session?"

"Senator Jones, what was in the resolution you brought to the floor today?"

Give me a break. More to the point, give the viewers a break.

At the Federal Communications Commission, one lawyer said that if viewers see what they think is promotional material masquerading as news, they can call in a complaint. The agency then calls the station for a response and, if the problem persists, the station may be reprimanded or forced to pay a fine.

Here's the address: Federal Communications Commission, 1919 H St. N.W., Washington D.C. 20554. Send complaints directly to the chairman, Alfred C. Sikes. He will be delighted to hear from you. It's his job.

Naming Rape Victims

Eleanor Randolph, May 1990

The big tough media here have a secret that most people would find surprising, even unthinkable: They have their limits. In particular, journalists here as in most other cities will not publish the name of a woman or man who has been raped.

Thus, the most famous rape victim in the country—a woman who was assaulted sexually and left for dead in Central Park a year ago—is seen on television here sprinting away from the cameras. The tabloids here refer to her as "The Jogger" and the New York Times simply calls her the woman or the victim.

Virtually every reporter in this city knows her name. Newsweek, in a recent story, did not reveal the woman's identity. But the magazine, like other publications, is printed where she works and where her family lives and where she was educated. For those who still can't figure it out, Newsweek also published the case number and noted that her name and other details are publicly available at Manhattan Supreme Court.

A newspaper for black readers, the Amsterdam News, did publish her name as an act of protest, because the alleged assailants were black and Hispanic. But the rest of the media here decided not to follow their lead. Such contortions seem odd for people who spend most of their time pushing to publish every important detail or embarrassing tidbit.

What makes it even more odd is that many of those pushing to have the names of rape victims published are the victims themselves. There is now a movement by some women to take the secrecy out of rape by getting victims treated in a more ordinary fashion.

If it seems crazy, here is their reasoning: By keeping their rape stories hush-hush, the media are contributing to the view that being a victim of rape is something to be ashamed of. "Protection" is a misguided paternalism of the male-dominated press, they suggest.

They are right, of course, in the abstract. It is also correct to say rape is not sex (still viewed primarily as a private matter). It is violence, which becomes the concern of the state.

But there is little understanding of rape beyond its victims and their families. Take the comment by Texas gubernatorial candidate Clayton Williams that rape is something a woman can't do anything about so she should "just lie back and enjoy it." Around the country, there are plenty of people like Clayton Williams (men mostly) who still confuse the pleasures of sex with the horrors of rape. But one place where there are fewer of them is Des Moines, Iowa.

Last year, the editor of the Des Moines Register (a woman) wrote a column explaining why the paper does not run the names of rape victims. Editor Geneva Overholser also called for rape victims to come forward, to reveal their names and to explain what this crime does to a woman and her family.

Nancy Ziegenmeyer agonized about Overholser's challenge and finally decided to shed the protections provided for her by the media. She told about how she felt when a man attacked her as she was studying papers in her car. She told about her agony, how she faced her children, her husband. The newspaper followed her through her court testimony and reported the conviction in January of her attacker.

In Des Moines, because of Nancy Ziegenmeyer, most people know that rape isn't a little romp in the backseat. Elsewhere, Ziegenmeyer has also become something of a heroine and a voice for women who have suffered alone. Without a computer muffling her voice, without a blur over her face, she tells her story on "Nightline" or "Donahue" or in Baltimore last week where she said: "Rape is nothing that you did. This is not your fault."

Does Nancy Ziegenmeyer's success mean rape victims should be treated the same as mugging victims, with their names logged into the crime reports? The answer is not yet.

Right now the ban on using victims names should be flexible. If a woman wants her name used and wants to talk about the attack, that's a good reason not to protect her. But if the woman—like the New York jogger—wants her name kept out of the news, it should stay out of the news.

Some critics suggest that there are lots of other people who would like to keep their names out of the news. Aren't these the people who beg editors to spare them the limelight and still end up squinting into the cluster of flashbulbs instead,?

Yes, it's an inconsistency. But naming rape victims in the hope of demystifying this crime could do exactly the reverse. Wanda Robinson, chief of Baltimore's sex offense unit, told the Baltimore Sun recently that she believes revealing victim names will make them more afraid to report the crime.

Until society recognizes that rape isn't sex, the media should continue being ultra-sensitive about these victims. Instead of telling

them that their names will not be used, the press should start asking
them if their names can be used.

Media Credibility

Eleanor Randolph, November 1989

For the last few decades, the scruffy American media have been cleaning up their act. Not everybody, of course. Geraldo Rivera's routine is about the same low-level sludge as it always was.

Conversely, for years newspapers such as the St. Petersburg (Fla.) Times have had a code of ethics so squeaky clean that it stands as an example for students of both journalism and religion.

The fat, red-nosed reporter who swipes a family photo for the morning paper and makes up the dead man's quotes and wears a suit that doubles as pajamas appears only in history books or speeches at newspaper retirement parties. Instead of bellying up to the local bar, journalists now settle into hardback chairs at college seminars where they sip Saratoga water while agonizing about what's wrong with the news business.

With such purification going on, a recent (Los Angeles) Times Mirror Corp. poll of public attitudes toward the media came as something of a surprise. The poll shows that fewer people believe what they read in daily newspapers and see on television than four years ago.

On the Times-Mirror "believability" score, daily newspapers dropped 19 percentage points. The networks did a little better: NBC lost two points, ABC five and CBS eight. CBS' Dan Rather lost 10 points on this scale, and ABC's Ted Koppel nine. Columnist George F. Will lost 15 points in believability since 1985 and Rivera 48 points.

Cable News Network, with a five-point gain, was the only one that did not slip in the believability scale.

Andrew Kohut, former president of the Gallup Organization which did these polls, said he and other analysts of the data believe that a very strange thing has happened. As the press started cleaning house, the public noticed the house was dirty.

This is not particularly good news for people like me who write critical pieces about the media. Already, there are those in the news business who suggest—some more bluntly than others—that media writers would have to crawl up the evolutionary scale to rank somewhere in the lizard family.

I disagree, of course. I think that the problems of the media deserve debate. Public debate. We discuss everybody else's problems publicly. It's only fair.

Nevertheless, I feel that the media can only be so pure.

For example, my friend Al Hunt, Washington bureau chief of the Wall Street Journal, recently ran into trouble with the ethics police. His case is one that will be a staple of journalism seminars for years.

Hunt and his wife Judy Woodruff, who appears on the MacNeil/Lehrer NewsHour, sponsored a dinner to raise money for children with spina bifida. They became involved in the fund-raising because they have a child with a mild case of this debilitating disease. Both feel that there are many children with severe cases and little money who need help.

But the hand-wringing began when Hunt called friends who work for companies such as Searle or CBS to ask them to buy a table for $10,000. At the Journal, which covers such businesses, some staff members were upset. Others were outraged.

On the night of the dinner, Hunt made another misstep, as he acknowledged to his staff later. C-SPAN planned to air the dinner live but could not do so until a late House session ended. C-SPAN employees were told that they would miss an hour of the dinner program because Rep. Bob Dornan (R-Calif.) planned to speak for an hour on the abortion issue.

Under a system known as "special orders," Dornan routinely talks for an hour on the House floor after the close of regular business. Because C-SPAN has agreed to air all House operations, this is a fairly easy way for Dornan and his colleagues to get an extra hour of prime-time cable coverage.

Hunt called the House that night to find out why C-SPAN cameras were still aimed at the House floor, and the operator put him through to Dornan. Hunt asked bow long the congressman planned to speak. When Dornan asked why, Hunt explained the situation. Hunt says he never asked Dornan to cut it short, but Dornan got the message anyway and yielded the limelight.

Since then, the Journal has been a hotbed of debate about whether a Washington journalist should lean on politicians and business leaders, even for a good cause.

Peter Kann, publisher of the Journal and a close friend of Hunt, called after I wrote a recent article in the Washington Post to say he thought Hunt's effort was "terrific. I applaud it in every sense. I think some of this ayatollah-ism in the press gets very unattractive."

The debate should prove comforting to the public. When today's journalists agonize about whether they are doing the right thing, they're far ahead of some of their seedy predecessors. Reporters, for example, no longer routinely pay for interviews. Most won't dress up like doctors or nurses to interview the wounded as they did after the sinking of the Titanic. Fewer journalists make up quotes and invent the people who said them.

Modern journalists are not saints. But they have something their forebears didn't: the germ, at the very least, of a conscience.

Bonfire of Inanities

Howard Kurtz, May 1990

Ten days ago, during the tense deliberations in the Bensonhurst racial-murder trial, the New York Post gave front-page display to some remarks by the Rev. Al Sharpton that could only be described as inflammatory.

"If the jurors come back with less than murder . . . you are lighting a match to the end of a powder keg and telling us to burn the town down," the rotund reverend declared.

Several weeks before that, however, the New York media paid scant attention to another bit of news involving this Brooklyn preacher-without-a-congregation. A former aide, testifying at Sharpton's fraud and grand larceny trial, said that Sharpton had paid young blacks $5 apiece to attend his rallies. Asked why the payments were made, the witness, Kevin Watkins, said: "Because Rev. Sharpton had no followers."

At a time when tabloids and television have been conveying the impression that the nation's largest city is a simmering stewpot of racial hatred, it is worth pondering why we in the news business give such prominence to professional provocateurs like Reverend Al. Fortunately, there was no immediate outbreak of violence following Friday's acquittal on one of the two white defendants accused of murdering a black teenager in Bensonhurst last summer. But to an unsettling degree, we distort the larger picture by training our blinding spotlight on an assortment of kooks, crazies and crackpots whose mission is to divide and polarize.

This is not to say that the messenger is to blame for reporting bad news, or that those outside the political mainstream should simply be ignored, whatever their grievances. It is simply a plea for greater restraint before turning over the media megaphone to self-appointed agitators who speak for no one but a tiny band of extremists. At the very least, we ought to constantly remind readers and viewers that these folks are a fringe element, rather than magnifying their presence in the interest of heightened drama.

When New York Mayor David Dinkins made a televised appeal for racial harmony 10 days ago, he drew the loudest applause from assembled dignitaries by calling on the media to do their part. Dinkins has taken to scolding the press for giving extremists a soapbox.

367

"The dialogue is dominated by those who can shout the loudest and spew the most venom," he said. "They're good copy, no doubt. They're quotable, of course. But quoting them often sheds more heat than light. It is incumbent upon those in the media to seek out and cover those whose views may be less confrontational—even if we're not as loud, even if we don't speak in perfect sound bites." The truth is that while New York Newsday's cover was proclaiming a "City on the Edge" (with a burning match set against the Manhattan skyline), 95 percent of New Yorkers—black, white, Hispanic, Asian—were riding the subways, tending to their jobs, taking their kids to the playground and otherwise going about their business. If they were on edge, it was largely because the media kept warning them (by quoting people like Sharpton) that riots might be imminent. The alleged triggerman, Joseph Fama, was convicted of murder Thursday.

Sharpton, for his part, insisted Friday that he has played "a positive role" by demanding racial justice and said Dinkins should "stop blaming the movement that got success here . . . . Dinkins says the media shouldn't cover his critics. I think any politician would wish that. What have I done against him, other than take him off the front page?"

Another black activist who has been much in the news here is Robert (Sonny) Carson, a convicted kidnapper who led a violent protest march after the Bensonhurst killing and later announced that he is "anti-white." For four months, most of the city was unaware that Carson was leading a small group of blacks in a racially charged boycott of two Korean grocery stores in Flatbush. The protests began after a minor altercation between a black woman and one of the merchants.

Then a strange thing happened. The New York Post began covering the boycott and openly criticizing the rest of the press for ignoring it. Slowly, the remaining tabloids, followed by other news organizations, descended on Church Avenue. Then the television crews showed up, giving Carson and his band an audience of millions. Suddenly Dinkins was being denounced for failing to end the boycott. But the minicams never pulled back far enough to show that there were only a few dozen chanting protestors, or that some blacks in the neighborhood thought the boycott was unfair.

As columnist Pete Hamill put it, "Most blacks who are brave enough to speak about . . . diversity, to express doubt or skepticism about the brainless oratory of the haters, are subject to the contempt of the race-racketeers. They are dismissed as Uncle Toms. They are called Oreos." Sharpton and attorneys Alton Maddox Jr. and C. Vernon Mason have achieved their prominence by attaching themselves to victims of racial crimes, as they did after the 1986 killing in Howard Beach. The trio took center stage during the 1988 furor over Tawana Brawley, the black teenager from Dutchess County who told a shaky story about being abducted and raped by a group of white men.

Day after day, the media covered their wild charges. Sharpton & Co. accused an upstate prosecutor and a policeman who committed suicide of participating in the attack. They cried cover-up while refusing to allow Brawley to testify. Sharpton called the state attorney general a racist and likened him to Hitler. Sharpton charged that Brawley had been assaulted by a cult, with links to the Irish Republican Army, run out of the Dutchess County sheriff's office. Reporters began to openly question whether such increasingly bizarre accusations were news, even while scribbling in their pads.

"I'm not sure we haven't made the reputations of Maddox, Mason and Sharpton by giving them publicity," Frank Devine, then editor of the New York Post, said at the time. "I've certainly thought about just not covering one of their press conferences, and I don't think there's an editor in town who hasn't thought about it." But in that overheated atmosphere, no one dared be the first to ignore a new charge.

Once a grand jury found that Brawley's story had been a hoax, one might have expected the trio to be viewed as discredited. But Sharpton says, "I don't see how a guy's a charlatan one time and a saint the next. I don't take back anything I said with Brawley. I still believe her."

Maddox and Mason are now fighting disbarment proceedings over their conduct in the case. Sharpton, who was once an FBI informant, was indicted last year on charges that the charitable organization he heads is a phantom group designed to provide him with cash and boost his other career as a record and concert promoter.

But I have yet to read a news story that begins: "The indicted Rev. Al Sharpton, who pays people to appear at his demonstrations and once publicized the false claims of Tawana Brawley, said today . . . ." During the Brawley saga, reporters at least had the excuse that they had to quote Sharpton because they had no access to the family. But since Yusuf Hawkins was killed in Bensonhurst by a white mob last August, his angry and articulate father, Moses Stewart, has been constantly available to talk about his son's death. Sharpton has become a mere sideshow, but the media still insist on treating him as the main event.

Last year, after a white jogger was raped and brutally beaten in Central Park, allegedly by a group of Harlem youths, Maddox said: "I have not seen any evidence of a rape . . . . What are we going to do, take some white person's word?" As Sharpton's lawyer, Maddox denounced prosecutors at the fraud trial as "evil."

Mason responded to Dinkins's racial-harmony speech by calling the mayor "a traitor . . . . He is a lover of white people and the system. And last night he bashed black people. He ain't got no African left in him. He's got too many yarmulkes on his head." Not long ago, the North Jersey Herald & News of Passaic, N.J., took a small but revolutionary step. Its editorial board announced that the paper would no longer publish most comments by Sharpton, calling him "a reverend of racism and a minister of hate."

It would obviously be wrong for newspaper and television executives to jointly ban anyone from access to the media, no matter how distasteful their views. Nor is it our job to play down the racial tensions that all too obviously exist in cities like New York. But it might do wonders if we exercised a bit more caution about where we trust our microphones.